THE
PAKISTAN
CAULDRON

THE
PAKISTAN
CAULDRON

Conspiracy,
Assassination
&
Instability

James P. Farwell

Foreword by Joseph D. Duffey

Potomac Books
Washington, D.C.

Library of Congress Cataloging-in-Publication Data
Farwell, James P.
  The Pakistan cauldron : conspiracy, assassination & instability / James P. Farwell ; foreword by Joseph D. Duffey.—1st ed.
      p. cm.
  Includes bibliographical references and index.
  ISBN 978-1-59797-982-5 (hardcover : acid-free paper)
  ISBN 978-1-59797-983-2 (electronic edition)
  1. Communication in politics—Pakistan. 2. Political leadership—Pakistan. 3. Khan, A. Q. (Abdul Qadeer), 1936–. 4. Bhutto, Benazir, 1953–2007. 5. Musharraf, Pervez. 6. Pakistan—Politics and government—1988– I. Title.
  JA85.2.P3F37 2011
  954.9105—dc22

                                                            2011014001

Printed in the United States of America on acid-free paper that meets the American National Standards Institute Z39-48 Standard.

Potomac Books
22841 Quicksilver Drive
Dulles, Virginia 20166

First Edition

10 9 8 7 6 5 4 3 2 1

For Dan Devlin

Pakistan

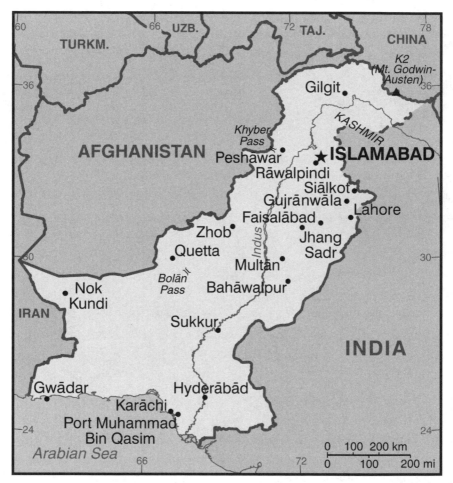

CIA World Factbook 2011

Contents

CONTENTS

Foreword

A senior U.S. diplomat was asked recently, "How are we doing in Pakistan?" He replied, "It's a very complicated issue. . . . It's not how 'we' are doing at all. . . . The question is, 'How is Pakistan doing?'"[1] In a recent article, Deepak Chopra and Salman Ahmad wrote that "Pakistan is a war zone but its battle is far more cultural than military."[2] The fact is, Pakistan's fortunes are central to stability in Central and Southwest Asia. How it addresses its tough challenges affects the war in Afghanistan, the battle to discredit and marginalize violent extremism, and U.S. national security. For those who seek a greater understanding of what makes Pakistani politics tick, this book is required reading.

James Farwell has advised the Department of Defense and Unified Combatant Commands (COCOMs), such as the U.S. Special Operations Command and the U.S. Strategic Command, for nearly a decade. His background, understanding, and gift for narrative based on carefully researched and documented sources yield important and relevant insights. Farwell carries no ideological candle. He avoids "selling" a point of view as to decisions of any White House administration. His focus is on history and today's Pakistani leaders. He writes as an informed analyst and historian with the expertise of a veteran information strategist and internationally respected political consultant. *The Pakistan Cauldron* spells out what we know and should understand about Pakistani politics based on public sources as well as a significant number of interviews—some on the record, others confidential with insider and knowl-edgeable sources.

Farwell's style is fluent and a pleasure to read. He helps us understand brutal decades of political rivalries, tribal emotions, a troubled search for na-tional identity, and the blatant corruption that today hamstring many of the prominent leaders of Pakistan and have put a nuclear-armed country at risk for the future. This book is full of concrete lessons that should prompt Washing-ton decision makers to ask hard questions about what drives Pakistani politics; its culture of paranoia, betrayal, and assassination; its political traps; and how to avoid self-deception while defining what is plausible as we seek to forge a viable partnership in combating Al Qaeda and the Taliban.

Farwell offers fascinating new perspectives on Pakistani political and mili-tary leaders by examining how they have employed strategic communication—in deeds and words—to influence attitudes and opinions. The sharp-edged portrait that emerges is of a dysfunctional political culture and government. Americans are always on the lookout for reliable friends. But Farwell cautions that in the chaotic world of politics, alliances and friendships are transactional. Countries have their own agendas. And they pursue them ruthlessly.

Pakistani leaders are tough-minded nationalists. This mind-set has been a key to their survival and it shapes their worldview. They tend to be both highly skilled and highly manipulative. They know how to exploit the relationship with the United States to secure financial and military assistance as well as politi-cal support. They have shown a gift for storytelling in soft-soaping skeptical American lawmakers to keep the aid spigots open. Lies have been no impedi-ment as they have locked arms with North Korea and China in developing nuclear weapons, stolen precious secrets, trafficked in nuclear technology, en-gaged our enemies behind our backs, diverted foreign aid meant for schools to a military machine, or sought U.S. support for the nation's policies with respect to India, whose power Pakistan both respects and mortally fears.

Why does the United States tolerate Pakistani double-dealing? The an-swer is that, for better or for worse, a stable Pakistan—and a secure nuclear arsenal—is critical to the stability of Central Asia. During the Cold War, that held true as Washington mobilized allies to fight communism. Pakistan then played a central role in defeating the Russians in Afghanistan and forcing their departure, which some believe accelerated the collapse of the Soviet Union. However, the victory came at a price. The problem with creating a dependency is that it is hard to restrain. Once the last Soviet tank departed Afghanistan, we left Pakistan to its own devices, precipitating a deep bitterness rooted in the perception that we had cut adrift a staunch ally at a time when it needed our sustained assistance. Ever since, Pakistan has had no scruples about pursuing interests that it recognized conflicted with those of the United States.

A majority of Pakistanis have eagerly embraced this duplicity. Today, serious questions persist as to whether Pakistan is helping or sabotaging U.S. efforts in Afghanistan. As Farwell points out, Pakistan worries that American efforts are promoting an Afghan government that serves the interests of India while undercutting Pakistan's security and which aids rival ethnic groups like the Tajiks at the expense of Pashtuns, with whom the nation identifies. Those policies are unacceptable to Pakistan, and we have to recognize and deal with this reality. It's an insight that inevitably should color how we approach achieving success in Afghanistan. He understands that this attitude stems from a historical view as well as the sad fact that Pakistani leaders allow paranoia to color feelings about the United States and to shape its dealings with our nation.

In dissecting Pakistani politics, the book focuses primarily on three colorful figures—A. Q. Khan, former prime minister Benazir Bhutto, and former president Pervez Musharraf—and how they affected Pakistan's political dynamics. As Farwell observes, however, although the players may have changed, in key respects the game remains the same and understandable: Pakistan first.

The nuclear scientist A. Q. Khan helped to develop the Pakistani nuclear program. Many believe that he acted as a Lone Ranger, freelancing on the open market as a nuclear trafficker. This book's contention that Khan acted at all times with the government's knowledge and approval underscores the ruthlessness with which Pakistani leaders have, with the exception of Benazir Bhutto, consistently played games with the United States. How Musharraf dealt with Khan and shut him down presents an object lesson in hard-boiled politics. *The Pakistan Cauldron* concisely dissects Musharraf's strategy and tactics, which aimed to shield Pakistan from criticism, continue the flow of U.S. aid, and protect the nuclear program. It presents a convincing case study in how, at their best, Pakistani politicians adroitly use strategic communication to achieve critical political goals.

Benazir Bhutto promised to lift the veil from the Pakistan nuclear program. It's not clear what she might actually have done, had that opportunity come. Still, her pledge to do so may have been a motivating factor in her assassination. The book examines Benazir's political history from the standpoint of how she and her adversaries in the military employed strategic communication to advance their own agendas. It is a fascinating portrait of powerful players locked in an edgy conflict for control of a nation.

In Farwell's view, Benazir Bhutto's historical importance, and the true tragedy of her assassination, was that it deprived the world of a powerful voice for a tolerant form of Islam. His examination of how she approached her return to power in 2007, and how an isolated Musharraf made mistake after mistake as he tried to counter her strategy, illustrates the pitfalls of a nation whose politics are dominated by the military and a need to keep Washington happy, instead of by the welfare of its citizens.

Pakistan suffers still from the wound of Benazir's murder. When you examine how Pakistan Peoples Party president Asif Ali Zardari, his opposition Pakistan Muslim League–N leader Nawaz Sharif, and the military and intelligence services operate—manifested in their strategic communication (a term that includes actions as well as words)—one sees the volatility of Pakistan and why serious doubts persist as to its future stability.

Too often these days a book is recommended as "timely." But in this case, that term correctly describes Farwell's incisive analysis. He understands political and strategic communication. He knows politics. He is totally in command of his brief. Highly respected among those with whom he's worked in national security circles, Farwell evaluates with great skill and understanding the politics of a nation whose problems will challenge us for years to come. That prospect makes this valuable work even more relevant and important.

> —Joseph D. Duffey, who has served as assistant secretary of state for education and cultural affairs, director of the U.S. Information Agency, chairman of the National Endowment for the Humanities, chancellor of the University of Massachusetts at Amherst, and president of American University

Acknowledgments

Any book of this nature depends upon the generosity and counsel from colleagues whose critical comments and suggestions provide focus and objectivity. Their support was critical. Whatever success this book enjoys owes much to all of them.

My great and close friend, Dan Devlin, whose untimely passing was a tragic loss, encouraged me to write the book and blessed it with his wholehearted support and insights. A distinguished American, Joseph Duffey offered a generous and gracious foreword for which I am deeply grateful. My editor, Jim Wade, did splendid work, as he always does. Marvin Weinbaum of the Middle East Institute was a wonder, reviewing the manuscript several times and offering keen observations and invaluable counsel. Maj. Gen. David Scott (Ret.), Mark Siegel, Col. Stephen Padgett, Stan Schrager, Ron Faucheux, Sir Richard Dearlove, and Al Bynum provided essential critical insights and suggestions that helped structure the book and ensure accuracy and clear writing. Gretchen Peters, Douglas Farah, Scott Sullivan, Zahid Hussain, Ron Moreau, Peter Galbraith, Tony Clifton, Ayesha Jalal, Sophia Meunier, Jerry Renne, Paul Huxhold, Joe Gaylord, Nasim Ashraf, Arnaud de Borchgrave, Christina Lamb, Bill Bryant, Teddy Tzavellas, Shuja Nawaz, Julian Wheatley, Chris Stewart, Trita Parsi, Ahmed Rashid, Maajid Nawaz, Walter Isaacson, and a wide circle of other key individuals who for different reasons could speak only off the record provided personal support, generously allowed me to interview them, and offered exceptional counsel and insight that clarified critical issues.

There is no way to properly express the depth of my appreciation and gratitude to my editors at Potomac Books, Hilary Claggett and Julie Gutin. They are world-class editors. And their graciousness, wisdom, and on-point comments and efforts made this a much better book.

My literary agent, Henry Morrison, has stood by me over the course of other literary projects for many years, and he merits my special gratitude. My wife, Gay, has been unstinting in her patience and support.

All of these individuals merit my deepest and most humble appreciation.

Since shortly after 9/11, I've had the honor to work with an extraordinary group of individuals in the Department of Defense. They are talented, hardworking, patriotic, and a credit to our country. But while I've served as an independent consultant to the department—my work is neither political nor partisan—all of the views expressed in this book are my own. None represent or should be ascribed to the U.S. government or to any of its departments or agencies.

Introduction

It seems odd that a fellow like nuclear scientist A. Q. Khan could stand Dwight Eisenhower's concept of Atoms for Peace on its head and turn Pakistan into a nightmare for those whose dreams are haunted by mushroom clouds. Status is an elusive quality. An international pariah, Khan was placed upon a pedestal at home by his fellow citizens. He inspired pride and imparted energy to those in search of a secure identity.

Like her audacious father, Zulfiqar Ali Bhutto, former prime minister Benazir Bhutto (referred to throughout this book as Benazir, as she was popularly known) towered above other politicians.[1] Dazzling, feudal, obsessive, idealistic, and charismatic, she inspired a legion of supporters and critics. She was fiercely nationalistic and ambitious. The hopes that she stirred among some Pakistanis posed an existential threat to figures within her country's military-intelligence establishment.

Both of these colorful individuals confronted Pervez Musharraf with grave challenges. Former president Musharraf's chief strategic goals in dealing with Khan's nuclear trafficking and the assassination of Benazir were to sustain his government's credibility and to ensure his political survival.

This book reviews the careers of all three principals in this story, but it is not a collective biography. What the key players did—and why and how—offers critical insights into Pakistan's secretive, paranoid, dysfunctional government and politics. The lessons remain critical today. The players may have changed, but to a remarkable degree the game remains the same. As the United States works in an uneasy relationship with Pakistan in fighting violent extremism, it's helpful to understand how Pakistan's politicians, including its highly political military and intelligence establishments, have seen themselves and how they operate. This book seeks to do so by focusing upon how well or poorly they have applied principles of strategic communication. Senator Lloyd Bentsen once said that politics is a contact sport. Pakistanis employ that rule with unconstrained vigor.

Musharraf's and Benazir's champions and critics divide fiercely on their performance as political leaders. This book describes the conflicting views about them, but judgments on Benazir's overall record in government as prime minister and Musharraf's as president are for history to make.

More relevant here are the perceptions they engendered and the way these perceptions influenced how the key players viewed one another, their actions, and their communication strategies. Musharraf was an individual. His behavior may be particular to Pakistan, but his mind-set and attitude were forged and nurtured by the culture of a military that, as in many nations, neither respects nor trusts its own civilian population. Musharraf receives more emphasis, because as president, he faced crises as he sought to gain legitimacy in office while jousting with the judiciary, confronting violent extremism, and dealing with Benazir.

Twice the military had ousted Benazir from her post as prime minister. Her critics contend that neither of her tenures was marked by greatness. But during her first term (1988–1990), a deeply hostile military-intelligence establishment hampered her every move, plotted her murder, and as she began to ask hard questions about Pakistan's nuclear program, ousted her. While her champions point to a host of accomplishments during her second term (1993–1996), her critics allege gross corruption, incompetence, arrogance, and hypocrisy.

Titling her first book *Daughter of Destiny* was no accident. It revealed how she saw herself. She was courageous to a fault. Her eloquence and formidable intellect are indisputable. Indeed, her death may have caused the greatest loss by silencing a uniquely powerful voice for a tolerant interpretation of

Islam. But she was a human being, not a goddess. Politicians who become imbued with a sense of manifest destiny tread a precarious path. The cheers from the crowd are seductive. They blind tribunes to the concept that no human being is invincible. Besides, events have a way of sweeping up political ambition. In her final weeks, Benazir faced tough choices, relentless foes, and a government that failed to see that its own fortunes were inextricably tied to hers. She was a potential game changer. That possibility mortified and galvanized her adversaries.

Different challenges beset Musharraf. An accomplished, patriotic soldier and by his own lights an idealist, he was impossibly cross-pressured. Striking the right balance among competing political interests would have challenged the most formidable political leader, and he was a creature of the military, not politics. By 2007, he found himself increasingly isolated. While he was brilliant in handling Khan, his cavalier treatment of the judiciary backfired. Ebullient and supremely self-confident, Benazir presented him with unwelcome complications. In that explosive political environment, the two ambitious leaders opened negotiations to share power by forging a coalition that served the interests of both but that neither desired or intended to respect. Musharraf's critics darkly suspect that he may bear more responsibility than is commonly understood for Benazir's assassination.

Pakistani politics are devious, complicated, and nuanced. In a place where contriving conspiracy theories is a national sport, politicians are always suspects for possible betrayal. Alliances are expedient. Trust is a rare quality. Many believe one would have difficulty spotting an honest political leader with even the brightest light from Diogenes's lantern. The experiences of Khan and Benazir well illustrate these lessons, and they offer new ones for the future as we seek to better understand the nuances of Pakistani politics.

Benazir Bhutto famously said that in Pakistan, there is always a story behind the story. It was an understatement.

THE ORGANIZATION OF THIS BOOK
Part 1 examines A. Q. Khan's activity and Musharraf's well-executed plan to secure his silence and protect Pakistan's nuclear secrets. U.S. objectives are ir-

relevant here. Musharraf's communications strategy and tactics were played out for Pakistani interests, not ours. Khan's enterprise spawned a host of conspiracy theories. These notions provide insight into the often bizarre dynamics of Pakistan's political mind-set. Many seem lurid, except in the context of Pakistani politics.

Part 2 reviews the careers of Benazir and Musharraf and the events surrounding her assassination, and lays out guiding principles, seen from an autocrat's perspective, for strategic communication. It assesses how these worked and illustrates what can happen when a government is run by leaders whose key constituencies are the military and leaders in a foreign capital rather than the voters at the ballot box. It describes the conflicting views expressed about them, their strategies and tactics as they progressed through their careers, and the hard-nosed conflict between the two that competing ambitions ignited.

Part 3 examines how Musharraf responded to Benazir's assassination and describes the inept strategic communication that his team employed to maintain the government's credibility in the aftermath. It assesses the possible complicity of key players in that assassination.

Part 4 examines how events are unfolding in Pakistan today. President Asif Ali Zardari is not a strong or natural political leader. Yet he has proven steadfast in opposing violent extremism as Pakistan confronts new challenges from the Taliban and Al Qaeda at home and through entanglement with its neighbor, Afghanistan. The current military leadership under Lt. Gen. Ashfaq Parvez Kayani has challenged violent extremism more vigorously than their predecessors did, although at this writing, Kayani has bristled at what he views as overreaching by the United States inside his country. Kayani has also displayed sophistication in messaging. Still, the government's approach to political communication remains conventional. While battlefield success may be achieved, Pakistan has yet, as counter-radicalization expert Maajid Nawaz has ably pointed out, to forge an effective strategy to counter extremist ideologies that spur militancy. When the United States took out Osama bin Laden on May 1, 2011, U.S. sources indicated Americans acted without providing prior notification to Pakistan, although the Inter-Services Intelligence (ISI) sources have told the Pakistani newspapers that in fact they actively cooperated in the operation. The attack on bin Laden has complicated Pakistan's already difficult relationship with America and the West. The emotional response and anger, conspiracy theories, and sense of betrayal are outgrowths of a political culture that has developed over decades. Dealing with Pakistan in the post–bin Laden era requires a clear grasp of political dynamics that have shaped it.

WHY STRATEGIC COMMUNICATION IS RELEVANT

Strategic communication offers an ideal lens through which to examine the dynamics of Pakistani politics. What is strategic communication? The Pentagon saddles itself with cumbersome definitions that focus on process rather than the art. Political leaders are more direct. The art of strategic communication is the use of words, actions, images, and symbols to mold or shape the attitudes and opinions of target audiences to influence behavior and advance interests, policies, and objectives. What politicians do not do—giving rise to strategic ambivalence—can matter as much as their actions.

It's helpful to bear in mind that politicians and military leaders may think of strategic communication somewhat differently. The Pentagon employs strategic communication in its sophisticated notion of "operational design" as an integral part of operational planning. In this approach, strategic communication "attempts to understand the ways different audiences understand or frame the meaning of military, diplomatic or other influencing actions."[2] It plays a key role in a formalized process of critical and creative thinking to address complex, ill-structured situations. It supports the battle command as it finds actionable problems and solutions. The notion recognizes that kinetic solutions—that is, military force—is only one element of power. Broadly, operational design recognizes the need to understand culture, to be adaptable, and to root inquiry and learning based upon observing differences. This time-honored approach is followed in politics and political campaigns.

For the military, design and planning work together. Planning is a formalized approach the military uses to influence events before they occur to achieve a defined end state that reflects a commander's intent.[3] The notion recognizes what politicians have long known: Nothing in politics is settled. The achievement of one objective merely sets the stage for what follows. The director of the School for Advanced Military Studies, Col. Stefan Banach, phrases it this way: "Design provides an approach for how to generate change from an existing undesirable situation to one that is better."[4]

Hopefully this book will help policymakers and action officers ask hard questions about Pakistan. What drives Pakistani politics? How do Pakistan's political leaders view their challenges? How does that view shape the way they think and respond, and what can we expect? How does their culture of paranoia play into things? How do we deal with their ingrained fears that behind every corner lurks political betrayal or assassination? What are the political traps to avoid? How do Pakistani leaders perceive their interests, and why do they differ from those that Washington may see? Why is it hard to establish what Washington considers stronger bonds of trust? How do we avoid our own self-deception and, while defining what is plausible, forge a viable partnership in combating Al Qaeda and the Taliban? The answers to these questions are influenced by how—as well as how well or badly—Pakistan's leaders have applied the principles of strategic communication.

As we look to other crises and events, perhaps in other places, what lessons for the future can be drawn from the way the political players in this semi-authoritarian state operate? Understanding what its political leaders say and do to advance their agendas offers instructive lessons for the road ahead as we work with Pakistan and other nations to discredit, marginalize, and defeat violent extremism and to advance our vital national security interests.

PART I.
MUZZLING THE SCIENTIST

A. Q. Khan's activity epitomizes the paranoid nature of Pakistani politics and its fascination with conspiracy theory. Khan gave new meaning to the concept of entrepreneurial spirit. With an ego larger than the subcontinent and the promotional skills of P. T. Barnum, he was a thief for his country. Whether he acted for himself, for Pakistan, or at different times for either or both is disputed. His actions offer a fine case study for examining how President Pervez Musharraf was at the top of his form in applying the principles of strategic communication to protect what he saw as Pakistan's best interests.

Chapter 1

THE CURIOUS CASE
OF A. Q. KHAN

Watching Richard Lester's film *A Hard Day's Night* about the Beatles or footage of fans mobbing Michael Jackson conveys a sense of the popularity that nuclear scientist A. Q. Khan achieved with Pakistanis. For helping Pakistan acquire nuclear weapons Khan became a national hero and an international pariah.

A. Q. Khan's story has been well told elsewhere by outstanding journalists and scholars, including Douglas Frantz, Catherine Collins, Adrian Levy, Catherine Scott-Clark, Michael Laufer, Gordon Corera, William Langewiesche, Steve Weissman, Herbert Krosney, Thomas C. Reed, Owen Bennett Jones, Danny B. Stillman, and the International Institute for Strategic Studies.[1] Relevant here is the use by Pakistan and notably President Pervez Musharraf of strategic communication to deceive the United States and others about its program and then to silence Khan once his actions became politically too costly.

Pakistan's relentless quest to acquire nuclear weapons, a jewel in its defense crown, is the story of a nation driven by its insecurity and its perceived threat from India. Pakistani identity and the leadership's perception of security are linked to the program. This single topic reveals much about the secretive, paranoid nature of the Pakistani government. Having chosen to acquire nuclear weapons, it let nothing stand in the way. Its strategic communication with the United States, on whom it has keenly depended for aid, has been measured, duplicitous, and calibrated to providing a stream of misleading information and outright lies. Its disingenuous behavior offers an object lesson in dealing with other states: The Pakistanis' own interests come first, and their use of strategic communication reflects that reality.

The process of partition with India in 1947 had been bitter and left lasting tensions whose imprint is felt still today. Dr. Ayesha Jalal has written a fine history that describes the politics of Mohammed Ali Jinnah, Jawaharlal Nehru, and Lord Mountbatten and the acrimony that arose as Pakistan was created.[2] Nehru's Congress Party wanted power and acted ruthlessly to exclude Jinnah and his Muslim allies from sharing it, an attitude that made partition inevitable. Since Pakistan's founding, the army has used anxiety over India as an excuse to meddle and control Pakistani politics.

On May 18, 1974, India detonated a nuclear bomb under the Thar Desert. India's action reverberated in Pakistan. Military leaders clamored for Pakistan to acquire its own capability. Pakistani prime minister Zulfiqar Ali Bhutto was resolved that his country would attain the bomb. He had already famously declared in 1965: "If India builds the bomb, we will eat grass or leaves, even go hungry, but we will get one of our own. We have no other choice."[3] By 1972, his messianic complex was in full flower.

On January 20, 1972, he convened a secret meeting of scientists on the lawn of a colonial-era mansion in Multan. The event had the air of a revival meeting. His face flushed, he whipped the crowd into frenzy. Bhutto's press secretary Khalid Hasan described the scene to the BBC: "He said: *We are going to have a bomb*, like, *we're going to have a party*. And he said: *Can you give it to me?* So they started shouting like school children. They said: *Oh yes, yes, you can have it, you can have it.*"[4] The scientists promised Bhutto one in five years. Impatient, Bhutto demanded that they do it in three.

Into this picture stepped A. Q. Khan, a metallurgist working in the Netherlands with a Dutch company called URENCO. A Dutch-British-German consortium, URENCO was building centrifuges to enrich uranium for peaceful nuclear power. India's 1971 defeat in the Bangladesh war had turned Khan into a fervent nationalist. Khan volunteered to help Bhutto by stealing top-secret information on nuclear materials and technology from URENCO. He proved to be an excellent spy and thief.

Pakistan's attitude is important and shades its current perspectives. Bhutto told fellow Muslim leaders around the world that if the United States, England, France, China, Russia, and Israel were entitled to the bomb, why shouldn't a Muslim nation have one? He touted the concept of an "Islamic bomb" everywhere, although his goal was to secure one for Pakistan. Bhutto grasped clearly that Western nations would take a dim view of an Islamic nation developing or gaining nuclear weapons. He and fellow Muslims despised the United States for what they considered its grotesque hypocrisy, which they blamed on unfair bias and prejudice. Refusing to cede to the United States any moral high ground, Pakistan felt no scruples about saying or doing whatever it took to develop its own nuclear weapons program.

That issue was a sensitive one, because while Pakistan wanted U.S. financial assistance, the United States opposed Pakistan acquiring nuclear weapons. Secretary of State Henry Kissinger threatened to make an example of Bhutto, should he proceed. The defiant Bhutto stood his ground, as did his successor, Muhammad Zia ul-Haq, who seized power in a July 1977 coup. After the Soviets invaded Afghanistan in 1979, the United States wanted Pakistan's cooperation in cutting the communists to their knees and expelling them from the country. The Afghan war cross-pressured American policy. The United States could not have it both ways and relented on the nuclear program. The Pakistanis took full advantage of the relaxed pressure to proceed.

At the center of one aspect of the program stood A. Q. Khan. Whether Khan merits his favorite moniker as the father of Pakistan's nuclear bomb is disputed. His nemesis, Munir Ahmed Khan, headed the Pakistan Atomic Energy Commission (PAEC) from 1972 until 1991.[5] Munir always contended that while A. Q. Khan certainly led in developing the centrifuge technology to create the highly enriched uranium needed to make a nuclear bomb, he also claimed credit for the real work done by the PAEC. There was no love lost between the two men.

There are two ways to produce a nuclear bomb. One entails "developing fissile material through uranium enrichment. The other involves reprocessing spent fuel from a nuclear power reactor to make a plutonium bomb."[6] Khan focused on enrichment, while Munir's team focused on reprocessing. In 1981

Ronald Reagan became president. Reagan continued Jimmy Carter's policy of benign neglect of Pakistan's program. The collapse of the Soviet Union ranked among Reagan's top three goals, along with cutting taxes and reducing the size of the U.S. government.

But Reagan laid down conditions on American aid. The United States would look the other way providing that Pakistan (1) did not actually manufacture a nuclear weapon, (2) did not transfer nuclear technology to a third party, and (3) kept the program secret.[7] Zia cheerfully assented to this charade, even as Washington was showing off to Pakistani foreign minister Sahabzada Yaqub Khan a scale model of the nuclear bomb his nation was constructing.[8]

Congress was less forgiving. In 1985 Senator Larry Pressler had passed an amendment to the Foreign Aid Act that required yearly certification from the White House that Pakistan did not possess a "nuclear explosive device," whatever that meant.[9] The amendment was specific to Pakistan and conditioned the continuance of aid upon the certification. The language used deliberately loose terms and afforded plenty of leeway. Pakistan played its role with aplomb, assuring Washington envoys that it was not building a bomb. Although Zia ran a ruthlessly repressive regime at home, lacked popular legitimacy, and had radicalized Pakistan, the Pakistanis noted that his actions counted for nothing in Washington. Unwilling to alienate Zia, though, the Reagan administration circumvented the law by asserting that Pakistan had not stockpiled sufficient materials to build a bomb.[10]

Defeating communism came first. By focusing solely on that goal, the parties learned another lesson: Informed decisions in complex political situations carry long-term consequences. That the U.S. government allowed Pakistan to act deceptively about its nuclear program also taught the Pakistanis that such games work. That realization affected attitudes in the Pakistani military-intelligence establishment, which innately linked the United States and Israel to anti-Islamic sentiments and viewed U.S. policy as biased toward India. It accentuated its tendency to deal duplicitously.

In March 1983, Pakistan successfully conducted a "cold test" of a warhead, triggering a nuclear implosion device without using fissionable material. In this instance, the PAEC, not A. Q. Khan, was the lead player. Pakistan's program moved forward. Progress was kept carefully concealed. Playing a key role, China helped design a trigger mechanism, centrifuges, and vacuum systems, and provided rocket propellant, fissionable material, and maraging steel.

Although more than a decade would pass before Pakistan detonated a nuclear bomb, it had materials to spare. By now, Khan had built up a global network of suppliers who sold "dual-use" items. These goods had one utility that passed legal, commercial standards in exporting countries and one that, because they could be used to form a nuclear weapon, did not. Khan had proven industrious in recruiting and mobilizing vendors across the globe for whom profit trumped other considerations. The nuclear program was expensive. Lacking financial reserves, Pakistan needed money to fund it.

Happily, in Zia's finance minister, Ghulam Ishaq Khan, Pakistan had a resourceful official. Between 1973 and 1988, he controlled the nuclear project's finances. Here was another lesson the Pakistanis drew: Pakistan could redirect aid money without prompting U.S. objections. Khan diverted it to help fund the nuclear program.[11] Billions in military aid had flowed to help fight the Soviets. The bounty included $800 million worth of dual-use equipment. Investigative reporters William Burrows and Robert Windrem report:

> None of it, including $250 million worth of advanced computers, had so much as been reviewed by the Pentagon's Defense Trade Security Administration to see whether it was too sensitive to export. The particularly sensitive equipment included high-capacity computers, some of which could have been used for refining a bomb design, plus millions more in oscilloscopes, zirconium, pressure-measuring equipment, laser systems, neutron generator systems, and telemetry systems for missiles. Congressional investigators came to believe that tens of millions of dollars' worth of the equipment was diverted to the nuclear program.[12]

The practice did not end there. The fact is—and the sources are credible, although for obvious reasons they decline to be identified—subsequent U.S. aid was diverted to fund Pakistan's purchase of centrifuges and to enrich uranium. That U.S. tax dollars funded the nuclear program was extraordinary. One can understand why Senator John Kerry and Senator Dick Lugar's 2010 aid package for Pakistan sought to establish oversight and auditing procedures aimed at controlling the use of our tax dollars, although Pakistanis saw the senators' behavior as heavy-handed and resented it. Meanwhile, not only was Pakistan lying about what it was up to, but it was taking its show on the road. A. Q. Khan aggressively sought opportunities to traffic in nuclear materials. Estimates of his activity vary. The International Institute for Strategic Studies concluded that more than thirty companies and middlemen sold nuclear-related goods to Pakistan.[13] Frantz and Collins report that fifty-one companies, organizations, and fronts were used as false "end-user" recipients for nuclear-related material.[14] The network was solid enough to function even after Khan was removed from Khan Research Laboratories (KRL) in 2001.[15] As European vendors came under close scrutiny, Khan shifted his base of operations to Malaysia and Dubai. Khan or Pakistan engaged with Iran, the Democratic People's Republic of Korea (DPRK, or North Korea), Libya, Iraq, Syria, Saudi Arabia, and China. The nature of these dealings varied.

Papers that came to light in March 2010 indicated that Pakistan provided Iran bomb-related drawings, parts for centrifuges, and lists of suppliers. There appear to have been contacts between the Iranian military in Iran and the Pakistanis, and Khan dealt with the Iranians directly, probably under instructions from, the *Washington Post* reported, "senior elements of Pakistan's military if not by its political leaders."[16] An eleven-page narrative Khan prepared in 2004 expressed doubts about Iran's ability to master nuclear technology but that Iran had promised financial aid in a deal "worth almost $10 billion."[17]

Khan got nowhere with Iraq or Syria. There were substantial contacts with the Saudis, but what arrangements were concluded is unclear.[18] Journalist A. J. Venter has raised the possibility that Saudi Arabia has an arrangement with Pakistan to provide nuclear support should Iran develop a nuclear bomb.[19] Former Central Intelligence Agency (CIA) analyst Michael Scheuer, a provocative writer who excites both high praise and sharp criticism, seems to think Saudi Arabia may have nuclear weapons.[20] It does seem plausible that Saudi Arabia may have worked out a security arrangement with Pakistan. Still, concluding that Saudi Arabia has nuclear weapons is a stretch. Acquiring such weapons could impel Iran to move rapidly to acquire them as well, a result the Saudis want to avoid. It could trigger a nuclear arms race in the region, another consequence that the Saudis seem averse to, and would unfavorably complicate their relations with the United States.

Pakistan wound up acting as a proxy for China, especially in dealing with North Korea.[21] Khan helped facilitate that relationship. He negotiated a turn-key deal with Libya for advanced centrifuges said to be worth $100 million,[22] although some have suggested the true value would have been $500 million to $1 billion.[23] Who else Khan engaged in nuclear deals remains undisclosed. It does appear there was an additional party. Pakistani officials have denied knowledge of what Khan was up to. They deny authorizing him to transfer nuclear technology to any third party.[24]

INDIA SHUFFLES THE DECK

On May 11, 1998, India conducted a hot test of its bomb in the Pokhran Desert in Rajasthan, the same location used in 1974 for its first nuclear test. The test, which involved five blasts, caught Washington and Islamabad flat-footed. When President Bill Clinton protested, India's prime minister, Atal Bihari Vajpayee, responded by threatening additional action that would halt Pakistan's meddling in Kashmir.[25] Fearful that nuclear war could break out, Washington pleaded with Prime Minister Benazir Bhutto's successor, Nawaz Sharif, not to conduct a hot test of Pakistan's own bomb.[26] President Bill Clinton dispatched Strobe Talbott to extract from Nawaz a commitment to refrain from doing so. Nawaz gave him the commitment, but he was lying. Pakistan proceeded with the tests.[27] On May 28, 1998, in the heart of the Ras Koh Mountains, Pakistan conducted the first hot test of its bombs. A. Q. Khan and his deputies were present, but as observers. To avoid disputes between the KRL and the PAEC, a scientific officer who had designed the trigger, Muhammad Arshad, was given the honor of pressing the button. The test was a success, and Pakistan's possession of a nuclear bomb became irrevocably public.[28]

Khan rushed to seize all credit. Cardboard cutouts of his face were hung from street lamps and Pakistanis danced in the streets. Khan stoked the media fires. His behavior placed the government in a difficult position. Pakistan needed U.S. assistance. As Washington stepped up pressure, the Inter-Services Intelligence (ISI) investigated Khan's finances in 1998–1999. The outcome led to a reduction of some of his autonomy to travel and negotiate deals.[29]

On May 8, 1999, Chief of Army Staff (COAS) Pervez Musharraf launched an attack on Indian positions in Kashmir.[30] Pakistan's forces suffered a humiliating military defeat. Nawaz's assent to or ignorance of Musharraf's plan is disputed. It opened an irreparable fissure between them. In July, at Musharraf's behest, a frightened Nawaz flew to Washington and pleaded for Clinton's help in negotiating a cease-fire with India so that Musharraf could withdraw his troops.[31]

Pakistan pulled back and the Kargil War was resolved, but the residue left a poisonous political environment. Fingers pointed as the key players pinned the blame on rivals. An angry Nawaz tried to fire Musharraf but was outmaneuvered. In October 1999, Musharraf seized control. He appointed three jihadist lieutenant generals—Jamshed Gulzar Kiyani, Mohammed Aziz, and Muzaffar Usmani—to senior posts and Lt. Gen. Mahmood Ahmed to head the ISI. Musharraf stayed on as COAS while naming himself president.[32]

CONFRONTING KHAN

Musharraf realized that A. Q. Khan was a problem. Khan's undisciplined behavior had compromised the security of Pakistan's nuclear technology.[33] After 9/11, President George W. Bush told Musharraf, "You are with us or against us."[34] Musharraf decided to move against Khan and pledged his support to Bush. But Khan's immense personal popularity among the Pakistanis and his protection by powerful allies required caution.

Musharraf's problem involved sensitive issues of strategic communication and political challenges on multiple fronts. First and foremost came protecting Pakistan's nuclear program. The nuclear weapons were a defense against India. The program employed 6,500 scientists and 45,000 other workers.[35] No Pakistani leader could afford to lose those jobs. He also needed to keep U.S. aid flowing. The aid, which amounted to more than $11 billion since 9/11, was vital to Pakistan's stability.[36]

Musharraf also had to worry about the army. Despite official denials, the military's participation or complicity in international nuclear trafficking was a fact.[37] Pakistani military and intelligence ties with violent extremist groups made the issue especially sensitive.[38] Musharraf worried about a coup. Violent Islamists, whose numbers included members of the military and intelligence services, grew hostile after Musharraf drew closer to Washington.[39]

He recognized that any action he took had to avoid destabilizing the government. Khan's popularity and powerful allies made that a real concern. The Pakistanis celebrated Khan. His success aroused nationalistic pride. Many Pakistanis shared Zulfiqar Ali Bhutto's view that Western criticism of its nuclear program was hypocritical, and Musharraf wanted to sustain the global procurement network that supplied the nuclear program.

There is no moral judgment here. Musharraf did not flinch from dissembling with the United States about what he was doing or why. He admired America, but he was the president of Pakistan. He liked to quote Winston Churchill. Usually, he did so awkwardly. But he understood Churchill's dictum that nations have interests, not friends. Pakistan's came ahead of America's. Americans want to think of Pakistan as a "strategic ally." Pakistanis view the relationship as transactional.

Chapter 2

REMOVING KHAN
FROM PLAY

Musharraf's handling of A. Q. Khan is a case study in strategic communication. The president developed a bold plan to neutralize Khan and restrain him from causing problems, such as the disclosure of support by Pakistan's military for Khan's nuclear trafficking. Musharraf showed verve, strength, energy, and imagination. Khan's ego made him a loose cannon. He had to be isolated. Musharraf executed a superb plan for doing so.

In 2000 Musharraf summoned A. Q. Khan and informed the scientist that he was under surveillance. Musharraf wanted to be sure that Khan understood that he meant serious business and that Khan's celebrity would give him no pass. Musharraf also expressed concerns about financial improprieties at Khan Research Laboratories.[1] In 2001 Khan was gently relieved of his position, forced to retire with honors from Khan Research Laboratories, and "promoted" to the position of scientific adviser to Musharraf.[2]

Musharraf moved to distance the government from Khan. Khan was reeling but continued to run his network. He filled import orders, arranged for exports to Iran and North Korea, and pursued a deal to sell Libya the turnkey uranium enrichment weapons program. Musharraf understood, however, that Pakistan could no longer maintain the veil of secrecy. Besides, Washington was demanding action. The United States had tracked Khan for many years, dating from his stint with URENCO, and had intervened at critical times on his behalf.[3] It was aware that Pakistan had forged a nuclear pact with Iran in 1987, when A. Q. Khan, Buhary Seyed Abu Tahir, and his uncle Farouq met Iranian scientists and Gen. Mohammed Eslami of Iran's Islamic Revolutionary Guard in Dubai and sold them at least $3 million worth of obsolete P-1 centrifuge machines—paid for in cash.[4]

Journalists Catherine Collins and Douglas Frantz contend that in 1975 the "CIA could have stopped Khan before he had even begun to help Pakistan build its nuclear arsenal."[5] Their journalism is excellent, but that assessment may not be entirely correct. A. Q. Khan worked on the approach that used centrifuges to highly enrich uranium. But Munir Khan and his team pursued a parallel approach that was based on plutonium. Interdicting A. Q. Khan would not have stopped Munir Khan from developing a weapon. The arrest would have stopped his proliferation activities. But Khan was acting with the military's knowledge and consent, and German intelligence contends that proliferation continued after Khan was put under house detention. Arresting him in 1975 might have put a stop—or least the brakes—on proliferation, but that is not certain.

Musharraf handled the controversy over Khan's trafficking with North Korea by denying that Pakistan was doing business with Pyongyang and by assuring audiences that any such activity had ended with Benazir Bhutto's ouster in 1998.[6] Musharraf was lying.[7] Washington was incredulous. Still, Musharraf stuck to his guns. It was hard-nosed strategic communication. There was no way to explain away the obvious. Nor was there any question that the Pakistanis found the relationship with North Korea desirable. The premise of Musharraf's effort to deflect Washington's scrutiny might have been rooted in the old joke: Who are you going to believe, your lying eyes or me?

Washington knew the truth. A 2002 analysis sent to President George W. Bush had concluded that North Korea had been enriching uranium in "significant quantities" and faulted Pakistan for selling it centrifuges and data to build and test a uranium-fueled nuclear weapon.[8] Actually, Pakistan had shared nuclear technology with North Korea since 1997, when Nawaz was prime minister. Although Benazir Bhutto later tried to distance herself from this trafficking, she had dealt personally with the North Koreans and bartered high-speed centrifuges and blueprints for the production of nuclear weapons in exchange for short- and intermediate-range ballistic missiles.[9] Musharraf maintained that Pakistan was not supplying the North Koreans with nuclear technology or material. From his viewpoint, given that neither he nor his military seems to have had any real desire to shut down the program of nuclear trafficking, his twist of the facts made sense.

A second prong of Musharraf's strategy fell into line with the familiar gambit that had served Pakistan well in dealing with the Americans. He told Washington what it wanted to hear, even when the United States kept up the pressure to shut down Khan. In September 2001 a U.S. government report had exposed publicly the Khan-brokered Libyan nuclear program deal.[10] In March 2003 the United States imposed sanctions on KRL but consciously avoided punishing Pakistan. In June 2003 the International Atomic Energy Agency (IAEA) revealed the existence of secret centrifuges in Iran in which traces of highly enriched uranium were found. In August 2003 Iran acknowledged that it had obtained foreign assistance for its program. All eyes turned toward Pakistan. In December 2003 Libya accepted the arrival of IAEA inspectors and answered questions about its deal with Pakistan.

Following in his predecessors' footsteps, George W. Bush had turned somewhat of a blind eye to Pakistan's acquisition of nuclear weapons. The U.S. government had recruited Pakistan as an ally during the Soviet-Afghan war in the 1980s. After 9/11, Pakistan was reenlisted as a partner in fighting Al Qaeda. Musharraf extracted a stiff price in foreign aid for helping, but he grasped that Washington's tolerance of the nuclear program was limited. His strategy balanced pleas of ignorance with commitments for action.

Musharraf was on his game with Washington. Indeed, he proved better at keeping his politics together with Americans than with Pakistanis. Bush liked the general, but when it came to nuclear proliferation he was resolute. In a face-to-face meeting with Musharraf in New York during September 2003, Bush demanded that Pakistan cease proliferating. The next day, a U.S. government official had laid out drawings of Pakistan's P-1 centrifuge and other evidence that proved Khan's activity.[11] Professing ignorance but recognizing that times had changed, Musharraf promised to deal with the problem.

In placating Washington, Musharraf knew that silencing Khan was a priority. He exercised tight message discipline in executing his information strategy. The core elements of his scheme were to blame Khan for anything controversial, cast the Pakistani government as innocent (and, if necessary, as having been duped by a celebrity), and above all, characterize Khan as a free-lance entrepreneur who colluded with a small group of scientists for his own personal gain at Pakistan's expense.[12]

Like any political leader, Musharraf had flaws. As chief of army staff, his decision to invade Kashmir had proved to be ill judged. The events of 9/11 and assassination attempts on his life changed his attitude toward violent extremists. Still, he had supported activity by Islamic extremist groups to conduct the insurgency in Kashmir. He had a history of double-dealing the United States. He was not a natural politician. But Musharraf's antenna was alert. His strategic communication to neutralize Khan and protect Pakistan was excellent. Khan was thoroughly scapegoated: He wanted the fame, and Musharraf made certain the scientist also got the blame.

Smoothing over relationships with the Americans was one challenge. Musharraf had his own politics to square away. His strategic situation was sensitive. The talk about stopping proliferation and reining in Khan alienated Pakistan's militant Islamists. This faction included members of the military and intelligence community who saw the militants as helpful. As 2003 drew to a close, some of them decided to kill him.

On December 14, 2003, a bomb attack targeted his convoy as it crossed a bridge near X Corps headquarters (HQ) in Rawalpindi. A mobile phone call detonated more than 550 pounds of explosives. Musharraf survived thanks to a signal jammer system in his bulletproof car.[13] Air force officers allied with Islamic extremist Maulana Masood Azhar—once a Musharraf protégé—were implicated in the failed attempt. Azhar was angry that Musharraf had cozied up to the Americans and was dumping Khan.[14] The would-be assassins struck again on December 25, when suicide bombers rammed a van into the presidential convoy.[15] Musharraf's driver instinctively slammed on the brakes, but with sharp instincts, Musharraf ordered the man to speed ahead. His savvy, gut call saved his life.

The first assassination attempt hardened Musharraf's resolve.[16] He realized he was going to have to take action, if for no other reason than to preserve his own safety. One day later, the Inter-Services Intelligence raided Khan's house on Hillside Road. It caused an instant media sensation. Reporters demanded to know whether Khan was running a private nuclear bazaar and whether he was under arrest. In a sign of how shaken by events Musharraf must have been, the government waited seven days to issue a statement.

But his strategic communication strategy was solid. The official line was that the government was merely debriefing Khan. Foreign Ministry spokesman Masood Khan insisted that Khan was "not under arrest, he is not under detention, he is under no restriction."[17] Musharraf focused on key objectives: silence the scientist while minimizing controversy.

A disgruntled A. Q. Khan would strike back at the government several times, most notably in September 2009, while Asif Ali Zardari was president, with the publication of Simon Henderson's story in the *Sunday Times* of London. Concerned about his safety, Khan had taken measures to protect himself and his family. His daughter Dina had slipped out of Pakistan with a stack of documents meant to provide an insurance policy. Should he die or disappear, she was directed to release them to Simon Henderson.[18] The letter offered a vivid picture of the mental state of a frightened, shocked, and bitter Khan. Henderson reported:

> Just four pages long, it is an extraordinary letter, the contents of which have never been revealed before. Dated December 10, 2003, and addressed to Henny, Khan's Dutch wife, it is handwritten, in apparent haste. It starts simply: "Darling, if the government plays any mischief with me take a tough stand." In numbered paragraphs, it outlines Pakistan's nuclear co-operation with China, Iran and North Korea, and also mentions Libya. It ends: "They might try to get rid of me to cover up all the things they got done by me. . . ."
>
> Years earlier, Khan had been warned about the Pakistan army by Li Chew, the senior minister who ran China's nuclear-weapons programme. Visiting Kahuta, Chew had said: "As long as they need the bomb, they will lick your balls. As soon as you have delivered the bomb, they will kick your balls." In the letter to his wife, Khan

rephrased things: "The bastards first used us and are now playing dirty games with us."[19]

The core of Musharraf's campaign was damage control. Insisting that Pakistan would never proliferate, he took pains to separate Khan and KRL from Pakistan and the institution of the military.[20] A detention order under the 1952 Security Act of Pakistan was issued, allowing ISI to hold detainees for up to three months.[21] When a freewheeling ego with a penchant for embarrassing enterprise like Khan is detained, it's important to find out what he did, who he talked to, and the details of his operation. Musharraf had Khan interrogated daily. Whatever its prior complicity, evidently the government lacked confidence that it had an accurate or complete picture of Khan's activities. The interrogations produced fuller—and probably complete—details.[22]

All of this drilling unsettled Khan. He slipped a note to his son asking:

Why is no one talking about the retired and serving generals who sanctioned the nuclear deals, such as Mirza Aslam Beg, who actively promoted sales to Iran when he was chief of army staff in 1990, and General Jehangir Karamat, Musharraf's ambassador to Washington, who negotiated a missiles-for-enrichment technology exchange with North Korea.[23]

The answer, of course, was that exposing military activities in trafficking was inconvenient.

Khan was not the sole target of Musharraf's campaign of influence. Authorities seized and interrogated KRL scientists and staff. A close Khan associate, Dr. Mohammed Farooq, was publicly linked to an investigation for selling off nuclear technology. On January 17, 2004, ISI picked up five more KRL employees, including Brig. Sajawal Khan Malik, who had worked for Khan since 1976, and Maj. Islam ul-Haq, his principal staff officer. Each family was told a different story. Maj. Gen. Shaukat Sultan, the public relations chief for the intelligence services, coolly insisted that nobody had been arrested. As the Foreign Ministry did, he characterized the process as simply a debriefing. Almost immediately government lawyers accused Sajawal of trafficking in nuclear plans, materials, and technology.

The ISI's action angered the families of KRL employees. The son of General Sajawal issued a sharp rejoinder: "Our fathers had for years gone about their daily jobs in the full belief that they were doing their country's bidding." He insisted that KRL had engaged only in country-to-country activity and wondered why Pakistan's government was accusing the employees of personal greed and treachery.[24]

A son of Brigadier Sajawal, Dr. Muhammad Shafiq ur-Rehman, heatedly denied that that Khan had trafficked without government sanction:

> Kahuta was a closely guarded establishment with tight rules and regulations, ringed by the Pak military and by legions of intelligence agents, from multiple bureaus, the road to it protected by anti-aircraft positions, jets, and soldiers. How did the scientists get around all of these tiers of security? Suggestions that anyone could wander in and steal a canister of UF6 or even highly enriched uranium, perhaps also a warhead design, without being noticed were absurd. Given that transfers were made using military C-130's, how did these transport aircraft fly in and out in large numbers, and regularly, without the military and its chief knowing?[25]

Asim Farooq, the son of Dr. Mohammed Farooq—the former head of KRL's foreign procurement—added: "My father was not a spy or a thief or a profiteer. He's a scientist who did what his country asked him to do. We have been told by the ISI to keep quiet, and only if we do, will my father eventually be freed."[26]

Musharraf let them rattle on. Wisely avoiding engaging them in political cross fire that would have confused the picture, he maintained message discipline. The government drove its message, picturing Khan as an independent operator while denying that the Pakistani government trafficked in nuclear materials. It played like a scene out of the film *Casablanca*: The government was shocked—*shocked*—at what Khan and his network had been up to.

Musharraf moved to butter up the world media. He maintained strong message discipline. On January 23, 2004, at Davos, he denied to CNN correspondent Christiane Amanpour that the head of the army had approved any nuclear transfers to Iran. Blaming Iran for misinformation, he declared ominously that Pakistan had investigated and found evidence that "violators" and "enemies of the state" had sold nuclear secrets abroad for "personal financial gain. . . . This I know, there is no official of the state or government involved at all. These are individuals. . . . There is no such evidence that any government or military personally was involved in this at all." Asked how something so secret could have been transferred without the government's knowledge, he replied smoothly:

> This is very much a possibility. Our nuclear program was totally covert in the past. A lot of authority and autonomy had to be given to individuals and scientific organizations to move forward and if some of the irresponsible got involved and misused capabilities, that is really a pity and that is what happened. So now that it is overt, there is total custodial control and checks and balances introduced. It is not a possibility any more. . . .
>
> Now that someone accused them, we started investigating them. It is not a question of changing stance . . . it is just that names have been revealed and we have information and we have investigated and we are coming to certain conclusions now.

In case anyone missed the point that this case was about the greed of private individuals and not a rogue state, he stressed that "some individuals were involved for personal financial gain." Musharraf sounded like an outraged cop at the scene of a drug bust:

> But let the world not imagine that it is Pakistan alone which has done that. There is an underworld which is getting uncovered. An underworld of individuals and maybe some organizations and factories involved in the manufacture of refined items. It is a whole

list of underworld elements involved. I would like to say there are European countries and individuals involved so let it not be said that there were only Pakistanis involved.

Amanpour was skeptical when Musharraf implied that concerns were overblown, suggesting that only ideas or paper were taken out of Pakistan, not materials. She countered, "You say even a bolt of a rifle cannot go missing without the highest levels of command knowing about it. So how can nuclear technology transfer take place without the highest levels of government or military command knowing about it?"

Musharraf replied:

Nuclear technology is in computers, on paper and in the minds of people. The other thing I said earlier is that individuals who are responsible for developing things themselves are involved and there was a covert plan or covert development going on. This possibility did exist in the past, but now they do not, certainly.[27]

Adrian Levy and Catherine Scott-Clark were no less incredulous of Musharraf's claims:

He seemed to have forgotten the 5832 centrifuges, each the size of a washing machine, ordered by Pakistan from Tradefin, that were still sitting in containers in an industrial park north of Johannesburg. Or the 5 containers seized by MI6 in Taranto; the Libyan WMD program; 40 missing canisters of highly enriched uranium, the largest of which was supposed to be the size of a small car.[28]

Meanwhile, Musharraf delivered more hammer blows in the media that isolated Khan. On January 26, 2004, he publicly declared that Khan was to blame for what had happened and ordered him placed under house arrest. One wonders how much of that posturing was done for Western consumption, because other spokesmen busied themselves with softening the blow for Pakistanis by characterizing the action as simple house detention.

Still, the government wanted everybody to feel that Pakistan's leadership was faultless in this imbroglio. Lt. Gen. Khalid Kidwai, head of the Strategic Plans Division, conducted a presentation for the Pakistani press. He unveiled a twelve-page confession from Khan in which he admitted to providing Iran, Libya, and North Korea with technical assistance and components. Conceding to "oversight and intelligence failure"—familiar rhetoric that made whatever the government had done guilty of merely a bureaucratic snafu—Kidwai claimed that Khan accumulated millions of dollars through trafficking,[29] although no one has exactly identified where Khan stashed this trove. No foreign members of the press were invited to his event.

Major General Sultan weighed in, assuring everyone that "General Pervez Musharraf neither authorized such transfers nor was involved in any way with such [nuclear trafficking] deeds, even before he was president."[30]

Such was the government's public posture. In private, Musharraf took a different tack and personally apologized to Khan, pumping him up with the declaration: "You are still my hero." It's not entirely clear what Khan thought of all this maneuvering, but he could hardly have felt reassured when, on February 4, 2004, the National Command Authority met to agree on the wording of a formal apology that Khan was to deliver on television. Afterward, Khan was handed his marching orders: He was going to deliver a public apology. Moreover, Washington had insisted that Khan deliver the apology in English. Khan agreed—as if he had much choice—but, his back up, he refused to use a teleprompter. Instead, he read his prepared statement from notes. Taking no chances with this loose cannon, Musharraf made sure the speech was broadcast with a time delay, in case Khan deviated from the carefully prepared text.[31]

Khan appeared before the cameras and broadcast his statement:

My dear ladies and gentlemen, *Assalam-o-Alaikum* [peace be upon you]. It is with the deepest sense of sorrow, anguish, and regret that I have chosen to appear before you in order to atone for some of the anguish and pain that have been suffered with the people of Pakistan on account of the extremely unfortunate events of the last two months. I am aware of the vital criticality of Pakistan's nuclear program to our national security and the national pride and emotion which it generates in your hearts. I am also conscious that any untoward event, incident, or threat to this national security draws the greatest concern in the nation's psyche. It is in this context that the recent international events and their fallout on Pakistan have traumatized the nation. I have much to answer for it.

The recent investigation was ordered by the government of Pakistan consequent to the disturbing disclosures and evidence by some countries to international agencies relating to alleged proliferation activities by certain Pakistanis and foreigners over the last two decades.

The investigation has established that many of the reported activities did occur, and that these were inevitably initiated at my behest. In my interviews with the concerned government officials, I was confronted with the evidence and findings, and I have voluntarily admitted that much of it is true and accurate.

My dear brothers and sisters, I have chosen to appear before you to offer my deepest regrets and unqualified apologies to a traumatized nation. I am aware of the high esteem, love, and affection in which you have held me for my services to national security, and I am grateful for all the awards and honors that have been bestowed upon me. However, it pains me to realize in retrospect that my entire lifetime achievements of providing foolproof national security to my nation could have been placed in serious jeopardy on account of my activities, which were based in good faith, but on errors of judgment related to unauthorized proliferation activities.

I wish to place on record that those of my subordinates who have accepted their role in the affair were acting in good faith like me on my instructions.

I also wish to clarify that there was never ever any kind of authorization for these activities by the government.

I take full responsibility for my actions, and seek your pardon.

I give an assurance, my dear brothers and sisters, such activities will never take place in the future.

I also appeal to all citizens of Pakistan, in the supreme national interest, to refrain from any further speculations and not to politicize this extremely sensitive issue of national security.

May Allah keep Pakistan safe and secure. *Pakistan Paindah Baad* [Long Live Pakistan].[32]

Washington responded warmly to this act of contrition, although the whole thing felt like Kabuki. Ostensibly pleased, President Bush gushed: "A. Q. Khan confessed his crimes and his top associates are out of business."[33] Not to be outdone, Secretary of State Colin Powell crowed: "The biggest proliferator is now gone and so we don't have to worry about proliferation from A. Q. Khan or his network." He exonerated Pakistan's government of involvement in the scandal.[34] National Security Adviser Condoleezza Rice brimmed: "A. Q. Khan, in a sense, has been brought to justice because he is out of the business that he loved most."[35] One almost got the impression that Musharraf half expected Bush to award him the Presidential Medal of Freedom.

But anyone who believed that Pakistan intended to prosecute Khan was sadly mistaken. The day after Khan's confession, Musharraf pardoned the metallurgist. Clearly unsurprised by this turn—CIA director George Tenet had previously placed Khan in the same pantheon as Osama bin Laden—the U.S. government supported the pardon as an internal Pakistani matter.[36]

Khan's televised confession touched off a firestorm of speculation.[37] Some figured that Musharraf simply wanted to avoid having Pakistan declared a rogue state. Musharraf's aides laughed after they read Bush's speech. One was quoted as cheerfully proclaiming: "We were back in the old relationship, you know the one, where we do as we please and they do as they please."[38]

Less amused were the Swiss. Bush's response infuriated Swiss authorities. Swiss officials had asked the Bush administration four times for documents related to Khan's black market activities that were needed to convict three Swiss men—Urs Tinner[39]; his brother, Marco; and their father, Friedrich Tinner—who had been accused of helping Khan set up a secret Malaysian factory to make components for gas centrifuges. The U.S. government refused despite a post-9/11 contract between Switzerland and the United States to cooperate on criminal cases.[40] U.S. weapons expert David Albright opined that no one should have been surprised,[41] as the three Swiss had been cooperating with the U.S. government.[42] The Swiss could only nod. In their 2011 book *Fallout*, Catherine Collins and Douglas Frantz examined the role played by the Tinner family in working for the CIA and the agency's operation to penetrate Khan's network and retard efforts by Iran and Libya to obtain nuclear arms.[43]

At Georgetown University on February 5, 2004, Tenet had boasted about how the CIA had penetrated Khan's network:

> What did intelligence have to do with this? First, we discovered the extent of Khan's hidden network. We tagged the proliferators. We detected the network stretching from Pakistan to Europe to the Middle East to Asia offering its wares to countries like North Korea and Iran. Working with our British colleagues we pieced together the picture of the network, revealing its subsidiaries, scientists, front companies, agents, finances, and manufacturing plants on three continents. Our spies penetrated the network through a series of daring operations over several years.[44]

Time magazine elaborated, quoting Tenet pronouncing: "We were inside his residence, inside his facilities, inside his rooms. . . . We were everywhere these people were."[45]

Adding up the score, Musharraf found good reason to smile. His campaign had come off as flawlessly as these efforts ever do in the messy world of politics. Nine KRL scientists and key staffers had been arrested and placed in limbo in a well-guarded cantonment. Khan and his private network had been busted. Khan was also isolated, with his phone line severed, newspaper deliveries halted, and access to television denied. The government considered the case closed. No further detentions were needed or sought. No one was prosecuted. No intelligence was shared. Musharraf had pledged to give the United States unlimited access to Khan through ISI interrogators but later reneged. By May 2006, Tasnin Aslam, a Foreign Ministry spokeswoman, stated that the matter was closed. Musharraf's campaign of influence netted an important bonus.

With Khan out of the way, the government could continue nuclear trafficking. In 2006, with Khan still under house arrest, analyst John Wilson of the Institute of Peace and Conflict Studies reported that the network was functioning as before:

> He could not have succeeded in setting up any network without State support which, in Pakistan, means the Army, and an entire chain of traders, amenable politicians and bureaucrats spread throughout the Western world. It is now well-known that AQ Khan had set up his liaison men, contacts and agents in the US, UK, erstwhile W. Germany, France, the Netherlands and other European countries, West Asia and Malaysia. Several shell companies were floated to help the network in smuggling nuclear materials and technology. There have been no attempts to dismantle these links in the global nuclear black market chain.[46]

In the Byzantine world of Pakistani politics, it was business as usual. The hapless IAEA director Mohamed ElBaradei dismissed Khan's revelations as "just the tip of the iceberg" about illegal trafficking.[47] Curiously, the director seemed unperturbed, stating that the emerging picture suggested that only individuals had engaged in illicit trafficking, not governments. Why would he have come to that conclusion?

Musharraf's actions provide a good example of how effective strategic communication serves the interests of a political figure. Even under the administration of Asif Ali Zardari, the government of Pakistan has tried to keep the lid on. While some curbs have been lifted on Khan's de facto house arrest, the Lahore High Court in March 2010 banned Khan from talking about nuclear weapons technology and ordered him to inform security agencies before leaving his house.[48] As of this writing, in 2011, Khan is allowed to travel outside of his home only with a military escort and his passport has been lifted.

Chapter 3

CONSPIRACY LAND

The controversy over A. Q. Khan illustrates the paranoid, conspiratorial nature of Pakistani politics and the government's ability to apply principles of strategic communication to get what it wants. Khan has never been released and remains under close government supervision. The decision to shunt him aside has given full flower to Pakistan's culture of conspiracy. Journalist Gordon Thomas theorized that Khan could be on a Mossad hit list.[1] A *Daily Times* editorial worried that the Taliban would kidnap him for a hefty ransom, hence the government was keeping him under heavy security his for his own good.[2] The state's public posture toward detaining him has varied. In August 2009, Khan challenged the restrictions. The Lahore High Court lifted the restrictions,[3] then promptly reinstated them.[4]

Khan's daughter Dina has complained bitterly about his house detention. Permission to visit him is often denied.[5] Complains the disgruntled nuclear scientist: "Police are still standing outside my residence. . . . They are still asking people questions. I am not aware of any softening in the security cover."[6]

WHY DOES KHAN WORRY THE PAKISTAN GOVERNMENT TODAY?
Khan's forced retirement and detention—with a limited ability to move around under military escort—have spurred speculation. That is Pakistani politics. Khan's ostensible release in February 2009 occurred after Benazir's husband,

Asif Ali Zardari, became president. One can see why Musharraf wanted to muzzle Khan. But why did Zardari? Or was Zardari merely holding Khan accountable for his behavior? Under his late wife's leadership, the Pakistan Peoples Party (PPP) argued for disclosure, not secrecy. Zardari has maintained restrictions, confronting the challenge of protecting his own position while pacifying the powerful conservative lobby in Pakistan, which is demanding that Khan get greater freedom.[7]

Competing theories have emerged to explain who's doing what to whom and why. Each offers a window into a political culture that breeds conspiracy theory. They are theories, nothing more, but illustrate the sometimes odd mindset that many consider endemic to Pakistani politics.

> ## THEORY 1
> Although A. Q. Khan's freedom is restricted, relaxing his isolation discharged a promise made to a national hero while bolstering the credibility of Zardari and a military that had grown unpopular.

People live vicariously through celebrity heroes. Pakistanis experienced A. Q. Khan's success and his glory as their own. Detaining Khan and forcing him out of power were politically risky. Musharraf's strategy aimed to defuse that political bomb and did so by indicating the government would relax its restraint on him.[8] Musharraf and Zardari felt the same pressure. Each leader capitalized on popular sentiment to strengthen his own position.[9]

Both presidents sought to answer critics who felt Pakistan was growing too close to the United States. Many Pakistani Islamists loathe the United States for the same reasons that Osama bin Laden set forth in his fatwa of August 23, 1996.[10] Bin Laden excoriated the United States for occupying Islamic lands; stealing the Muslims' oil; dictating to its rulers while protecting tyrants; humiliating Muslims; terrorizing neighbors; supporting Israel, Russia, and China against Muslims; using bases in the Arabian Peninsula to fight the neighboring peoples; killing more than a million Muslims; and sowing division among Islamic states.

Many Pakistanis believe that U.S. drone attacks have abused Pakistan's sovereignty. Many also resent U.S. pressure to fight fellow Pakistanis or Muslims. Pakistanis feel that after the Soviets' 1989 withdrawal from Afghanistan, the United States deserted its longtime ally. They resent what they perceive as a strong bias toward India.

In that light, action by Musharraf and later Zardari to leverage their dealings with Khan and neutralize popular hostility at home to their leadership makes sense.

THEORY 2
Relaxing restrictions on Kahn was part of an implicit understanding between Pakistan and the United States.

According to this theory, Washington had penetrated Khan's network, knew what Khan had done, and believed it could exert control over Pakistan's next moves. Thus it did not object to easing restrictions on Khan. Conversely, under this theory, Musharraf believed that assurances to Washington that Khan was out of action protected its nuclear program, kept $1.5 billion in annual U.S. assistance flowing, and arguably has allowed Pakistan to continue nuclear trafficking.

What do these theories reveal about Pakistan's strategic thinking?

MUSHARRAF'S PERSPECTIVE
Several factors may have influenced Musharraf's strategy for handling Khan. All demonstrate duplicity in dealing with Washington.

1. Protecting Pakistan's nuclear program and trafficking required him to crack down on Khan and his operation. Such action would reassure Washington. The Khan network's proliferation activities posed a threat to continued U.S. assistance and led to pressure from the International Atomic Energy Agency. Pakistan could not afford any imposition of sanctions for nuclear trafficking.

2. Prosecuting Khan would have been futile. Lax export laws made a viable legal case difficult. The political blowback would have extracted an unwelcome toll on Musharraf or Zardari.

3. Khan's daughter Dina had fled to London with documentation that exposed Pakistan's program and proliferation. In September 2009 sections were published, but as Khan was ostensibly released, the Pakistani government hoped to keep them quiet.

4. Khan's role may have been less pivotal than he claimed. His most important contribution was the development of centrifuge technology. Munir Khan says the Pakistan Atomic Energy Commission achieved other key steps and that Khan took credit for others' work. If Munir Khan is correct, removing A. Q. Khan did not impair Pakistan's program. Musharraf's assurance that Pakistan had put Khan's network out of business would be technically true while leaving Pakistan other venues through which to traffic.

5. In July 2011 A. Q. Khan released documents that alleged North Korea had paid $3 million to senior officers in the Pakistani military to obtain secret nuclear technology. Pakistani officials have challenged the authenticity of a letter from a North Korean official. There's no evidence that Musharraf was part of that scheme. Still, one may reasonably presume that elements of the military agreed with Musharraf's decision to isolate Khan or encouraged him to do so. If Khan's assertion is true, that would furnish a good reason why certain of Musharraf's colleagues would have agreed with his action or, at the least, not objected to it.[11]

THE U.S. PERSPECTIVE

Several theories have circulated as to a possible understanding that the U.S. government may have reached with Pakistan over how to handle Khan. Some argue that President George W. Bush believed that in sidelining Khan, Pakistan did halt nuclear trafficking. In this view, Pakistan made a full or reasonably full, if confidential, disclosure to the United States as to what Khan and Pakistan had done and what it was doing. Administration critics contend that such trust was misplaced, given credible intelligence that revealed Pakistan's true attitude toward Khan and nuclear proliferation. Enlisting Pakistan against Al Qaeda, meanwhile, outweighed other considerations. Hence, while expressing concern over Khan's release, the United States let it pass. Robert Oakley, a former ambassador to Pakistan, told the Associated Press soon after Khan's confession, "The most important thing is to get as much information possible as to where the links [to accomplices] were . . . we have to make sure it doesn't happen again."[12]

ISSUES THESE THEORIES PRESENT

These conflicting perspectives regarding A. Q. Khan's program have fueled speculation over various issues.

> ### ISSUE 1
> Did American leaders trust Musharraf's assurances that for three years he had suspected Khan was sharing nuclear technology with other countries but lacked convincing proof?[13] Did they believe that Pakistan would stop trafficking in nuclear technology?

The George W. Bush administration debated how to handle Musharraf.[14] Officials feared damaging their uneasy alliance with Musharraf. Although in 2003, the United States sanctioned Khan Research Laboratories, pointedly, no sanctions were leveled against Pakistan itself, as if the separation between the two was meaningful. Still, the White House had to wonder how far Musharraf could be trusted. Even after Khan was forced into retirement in 2001 and subjected to increasing constraints, he kept operating. In 2002, a Pakistani C-130 was tracked carrying North Korean missiles that could carry nuclear warheads.[15] Only in 2004 did Khan issue his public confession and apology, which he later recanted.

One U.S. official acknowledged that the issue came down to whether KRL, or Khan, was proliferating on its own or with the knowledge of the Pakistani leadership.[16] President Bush trusted Musharraf. Famously, in June 2001, Bush had declared that he had looked Russia's Vladimir Putin in the eye and "was able to get a sense of his soul."[17] He applied this same approach to Musharraf.

One day after Musharraf unilaterally abrogated Pakistan's Constitution in 2002 and arrogated to himself the power to dissolve Parliament and appoint the military chiefs and Supreme Court justices, Bush declared: "We believe, and judging from many of his statements, that President Musharraf wants to develop strong democratic institutions." He stated that Musharraf "was still tight with us in the war against terror" and proclaimed, "I appreciate his strong support."[18] Their relationship was marked by tensions, but Bush tended to operate on his personal instincts. That approached played to Musharraf's advantage in allaying Bush's concerns.[19] Even in 2008, when Musharraf's domestic support was crumbling, Bush emphasized his support.[20]

Once Khan was detained, Bush and National Security Adviser Condoleezza Rice issued supportive statements. Secretary Colin Powell reported on Musharraf's assurances: "He said, 'Four hundred percent assurance that there is no such interchange [with North Korea] taking place now.'"[21]

Although Powell is a smooth operator who is naturally gifted at calming troubled waters, others continued to question the administration's judgment. Did the Bush administration choose to ignore a deeper reality about nuclear trafficking in the interest of strengthening an alliance with Pakistan to fight violent extremism? Why did the White House believe Pakistan would stop trafficking? Why would it have, given real concerns about North Korea's nuclear program and its illicit activities in pursuit of weapons of mass destruction (WMD)? Did it know more than we have been led to believe?

U.S. leaders understood that Musharraf faced a sensitive task in balancing his support for Washington in fighting Al Qaeda (his views on the Taliban were more complicated) and his efforts to keep his internal politics together. Yet, as journalist Gordon Corera observes, Musharraf "chose his words very carefully, a lesson they had learned from dealing with him over a range of issues, not just A.Q. Khan."[21] Politics in Pakistan can be deceptive. Musharraf had a generally pro-Western outlook, but he viewed issues from Pakistan's perspective. As Pakistan's president, he recognized that the national interests of Pakistan did not necessarily converge with those of the United States.

Did the White House understand, as Adrian Levy and Catherine Scott-Clark assert, that Musharraf's assurances were a canard?[23] Was Washington aware of a 2006 German Federal Intelligence Service (Bundesnachrichtendienst, or BND) fifty-five-page "early warning" intelligence assessment? Pooling knowledge from German, British, French, and Belgian spies, the report detailed Pakistani–North Korean proliferation activity.[24] As it was provided to IAEA board members, presumably Washington also had access to it. The report damns Pakistan and raises serious questions as to what U.S. policymakers were thinking.

The BND report concluded that even though Khan was under house arrest and several of his European collaborators had been arrested in Germany, Switzerland, and South Africa, Pakistan had continued its proliferation business, almost from the moment that Khan made his televised confession. The report states: "Since the beginning of 2004 extensive procurement efforts for the Pakistani nuclear sector have been registered."[25] It described a nuclear black market that traded on surplus goods that Pakistan possessed. It stated that the KRL remained a central institution in the Pakistani nuclear program, served by an array of front companies that are past masters at disguising the real end users for the components and equipment they purchase in Western Europe.

BND sources told Levy and Scott-Clark that even after Khan was out of business, the Pakistani–North Korean relationship "was also still very much alive." The authors quote the BND report as finding that "the export of arms equipment is currently noted to be North Korea's most important source of income" with Pakistan among its key clients, as well as Egypt, Iran, and Syria.[26]

The BND is an authoritative source. Its report ought to inspire curiosity. Its conclusions reflected the attitudes of Musharraf aides, who did little to conceal their contempt for U.S. objections against Pakistan's nuclear trafficking. Given what Washington must have known, another question surfaces. Would Washington have stood by unless it believed that everything in Pakistan's program was traceable and controlled? For example, when Khan's deals with Libya, Iran, and other countries were examined, it turned out that hundreds of millions of dollars worth of equipment apparently destined for Libya had vanished from a shipping point in Dubai without explanation. There's been much speculation where that equipment went. Would the United States not have insisted on obtaining answers from Khan—even if through Pakistan's government?

What adds a sharp edge to this inquiry is that Pakistan's good faith as an ally in fighting militant extremism has been highly questionable,[27] although in 2010, the Pakistanis took steps to crack down on the Taliban in some parts of the country.[28] More broadly, one must ask whether Washington had—and for that matter, has —a realistic strategy for dealing with Pakistan, informed by a real understanding of growing hostility there to U.S. policies and actions.

Questions abound. Why has the United States refrained from acting more aggressively to restrain Pakistan's dealings with North Korea? What has it done to address proliferation by China? Although some argue that China ceased to supply Pakistan with nuclear technology in the late 1990s, plausibly China continues to use Pakistan as a proxy for nuclear proliferation.[29] U.S. policy has consistently treated North Korea as a pariah state that poses a threat to American and regional security. An important U.S. goal has been preventing, deterring, and interdicting North Korea's illicit activity.[30] What are the hidden truths?

From those queries flow new ones. Did Washington not know that while lambasting Khan publicly, in private Musharraf was reassuring the scientist? Journalists knew, so one must presume Washington did as well. Did not Musharraf's behavior tip off the United States that the Pakistani president might be double-dealing?

Even though in theory Khan was out of business, hundreds of thousands of the components that he had amassed vanished. Let's return to the vanished equipment. More than $500 million of dual-use engineering equipment, much of it from Germany, had been shipped to the Sudan between 1998 and 2001. Though destined for Libya, Libya did not receive it. By 2006, another unknown Pakistani entity had seized control of the equipment and redirected it. Shipping containers—one filled with centrifuge components and a ton of high-strength aluminum, the other with precision tools—were also rerouted. Of seven sets of rotors for centrifuges that left Pakistan in 2000 and arrived in Dubai, only two reached Tripoli.[31] Did that discrepancy not trigger alarms in Washington? What did Washington think had happened to them? The disappearance of this equipment was no secret. Libya made a full disclosure of what it had purchased and received.

Although it's possible that this equipment went to Iran, no evidence confirms that conclusion and Iran's relationship with Pakistan at that time was less than cozy. Could the United States have been a party to seizing the equipment? Could it have had it sent to a friendly third party? Could it have been a covert action to alter the parts originally destined for Libya as part of an operation to funnel defective materials or components to Iran in order to retard its program? Could such an arrangement be part of the understanding reached with Musharraf? No one has supplied answers.

The current U.S. administration's posture over Khan's detention is more understandable. Pakistan confronts a crisis in fighting the Taliban, while cooperating with U.S. forces in fighting Al Qaeda (whose links with both the Afghan and Pakistani Taliban have become entwined) and attempting to stabilize itself. President Barack Obama has worked to strengthen America's relationship with Pakistan. It has been a rocky road. When U.S. forces took out Osama bin Laden in 2011, Pakistan received no prior notification of an assault that took place inside its borders, angering Pakistan. Heating up new controversy over Khan would not improve matters.

> ISSUE 2
>
> Was Khan's relaxed detention part of a strategy aimed at ensuring his silence to cover up Pakistan's nuclear trafficking?

In this scenario, Khan may have acted solely for his own profit, or, as some contend, perhaps he played different roles in different transactions. Collins and Frantz contend that Khan became wealthy by siphoning off from Kahuta and sales to Iran.[32] It is quite likely that Pakistani military or intelligence officials profited from his trafficking, and officials may have been keen to cover up that relationship.

> ISSUE 3
>
> Is it possible that Pakistan relaxed restrictions on Khan in full concert and cooperation with the United States, in a scenario that Khan is a U.S. intelligence asset?

The idea that Khan might have consciously acted as a U.S. intelligence asset is preposterous. On the other hand, Collins and Frantz make a convincing case that the CIA had penetrated Khan's operation thoroughly and had manipulated it for U.S. purposes in order to retard Iran's nuclear program. In short: Khan was not an asset, but apparently his network was turned into one through the involvement of the Tinner family.[33]

When the ISI initially questioned Khan, allegedly he told it everything. Despite the fact that the ISI never gave U.S. interrogators access to Khan, does the well-documented intelligence partnership between the U.S. and Pakistani services following 9/11 mean that the United States was briefed on everything that Khan provided to other countries? When Khan enjoyed relaxed restrictions, what was the quid pro quo? What did Khan provide to the Pakistani government in return?

Finally, the U.S. reaction to Khan's release is interesting. At first it was shrill, prompting lawmakers like Representative Jane Harman to propose legislation tying U.S. aid to gaining access to Khan. As time passed, the hue and cry died down, and Ambassador Richard Holbrooke quashed any notion that the United States would fight to have Khan interrogated. Contrary to statements that the ISI did not grant the United States personal contact with Khan, did it secretly gain access to Khan, with the understanding that Khan could then be released? Did the CIA merely reengage with its long-term intelligence asset one last time, ensuring that it had all the information it needed from Khan before agreeing to his release?

PART II.
A WOMAN OF COURAGE

Benazir Bhutto and Pervez Musharraf had storied careers. In both cases, their successes and failures depended on the strategic communication each employed. She was a master of the art. As a man of the military, he employed its principles well in handling the army. Although he dealt adroitly with A. Q. Khan, overall after becoming president, the dynamics changed and eventually overwhelmed Musharraf's ability to survive politically. His fortunes declined as he miscalculated in dealing with the Pakistan judiciary, violent Islamists, and Benazir.

Chapter 4

THE MYSTERIOUS
ENCOUNTER

December 27, 2007, began early for Benazir Bhutto. Around 2:00 a.m., Lt. Gen. Nadeem Taj paid her a surprise visit at Zardari House in Islamabad.[1] The Director General of Inter-Services Intelligence, one of the country's three intelligence agencies, brought startling news: Taj advised her against appearing at a campaign rally at a Rawalpindi park scheduled for later that day. Apparently he was, as the United Nations Commission that investigated her assassination put it, "concerned about a possible terrorist attack against her and urged her to limit her public exposure and to keep a low profile at the campaign event at Liaquat National Bagh (Liaquat Bagh)."[2]

The Pakistani daily newspaper, *The News*, reported: "One source privy to the discussions claimed the spy chief categorically told Ms. Bhutto not to go to Liaquat Bagh to address the rally. He said credible information had been received that there would be an assassination attempt on her life during the public meeting." According to the report, "'Benazir was caught in two minds for some moments but Rehman Malik forcefully refused to take that advice. He (Rehman Malik) told the gentleman: Benazir cannot sit in confinement. She is a leader and she has to address tomorrow's rally because that is very important,' the source said. And then the intelligence boss left."[3]

Taj was perhaps the last person she might have expected to bear cautionary news for her safety. He was hardly a welcome visitor. She was wary of the ISI. Her concern was built upon a lifetime of well-justified hostility to the organization. Years before, a previous ISI chief, Hamid Gul, had allegedly plotted to assassinate her.[4] When that effort fizzled, his behind-the-scenes scheming had helped secure her dismissal as prime minister. More bitter was the unfair cruelty Gen. Zia ul-Haq had meted out to her beloved father, Zulfiqar Ali Bhutto, Pakistan's first elected prime minister.[5] Even today, he remains the most popular politician the nation has produced. Bhutto's supposedly loyal chief of army staff, Zia, had ousted him in a surprise coup for which the ISI had deviously set the stage.

The ISI had framed Zulfiqar Ali Bhutto on trumped-up charges of murder. A kangaroo court had found him guilty and sentenced him to hang. The appeal was a fixed game. *Newsweek* reporter Tony Clifton, who covered both Benazir and Zulfiqar Ali Bhutto, observed that Zulfiqar had tragically failed to grasp the fact that his life—and not merely his political position—stood in peril at the hands of the well-manipulated men in judicial robes. He did not see through the charade. At the end of each day during the trial, he would join reporters, laughing and joking, and treated the affair as political theater. That Zia had jailed him seemed an inconvenience, not an omen. In the West, an indictment ruins political reputations. In those days in Pakistan, jail time was viewed by many as a badge of honor.[6]

Only too late did the prime minister realize that the legal formalities were a cloak donned to provide a sheen of legitimacy for judicial murder. The court proceedings were a travesty. Zia viewed Bhutto as a mortal enemy, a secular politician hostile to his deeply felt fundamentalist Islamic values. All too often in Pakistani politics, inconvenient adversaries are not merely shoved off the political scene but silenced—permanently. Zia was a man with an agenda. His true aim was to establish Pakistan as a bastion for his very strict interpretation of Sunni Islam. Zia's coup marked a historic departure from the nation's more tolerant, pluralistic political culture that its founders Mohammed Ali Jinnah, Allama Iqbal, and the Pakistan Muslim League had envisioned. A committed democrat who was determined to make her voice felt, Benazir had opted for a life in politics and resolved to return to Pakistan to pick up her father's fallen standard and reclaim his populist legacy. It was a bold ambition and Pakistan's politics were dangerous and unpredictable. Her return to this volatile environment helped frame the context for her encounter with Taj.

BENAZIR RETURNS

Benazir Bhutto came back to Pakistan on October 18, 2007. Her flight from Dubai had taken two hours. Packed with members of the press and Pakistan Peoples Party supporters, the plane's cabin erupted with cheers and clapping that drowned out the sound of the engines as the wheels touched down at Karachi's Jinnah International Airport.[7] The PPP had worked hard to get out a large crowd to welcome her. She deplaned wearing a *shalwar kameez* (tunic and baggy trousers) in emerald green and white, Pakistan's national colors. As her foot touched the tarmac, tears welled in her eyes, and she raised her hands in prayer.[8] Sticking close to her were her chief of security, Rehman Malik, and PPP chairman Amin Fahim. A mob of media and officials were gathered on the tarmac. The excitement was gripping. Overwhelmed with joy and emotion, tens of thousands of people broke through police barricades at the terminal, hoping for a glimpse of the daughter of Zulfiqar Ali Bhutto.

"*Jeay* Bhutto!" they cried. "Long live Bhutto!"

A tearful Benazir exclaimed that being home felt like a miracle.[9] She stepped into a converted container truck, from which bulletproof screens around the top had been removed, and embarked through crowds that packed both sides of the road upon a slow-moving, ten-mile journey to the tomb of Mohammed Ali Jinnah, where she would pay homage. There had been talk of taking a helicopter, but she had dismissed that suggestion. Crowds drain politicians or bring them alive. Benazir drew energy from the people. An Eastern fatalist, her safety did not worry her.

"Neither she nor her father were devout Muslims, but when you grow up in an Islamic society, the words you hear most are 'Insha'Allah'—'If God wills it,'" says Tony Clifton. Though he had not accompanied Benazir Bhutto or Fahim on the 2007 trip, he knew both of them well. "Both were optimists. Both probably believed that Allah would will them long and powerful lives, so be happy and don't worry." Certainly that was the note Benazir struck that evening. The atmosphere was festive. PPP tricolor flags and banners lined the streets. She liked sticking close to the people. They chanted slogans and cheered.

She was taking an enormous risk. No one questioned her physical courage. By her returning to Pakistan, her allies worried that she was endangering her life. Indeed she had confided to friends in Washington shortly before heading home that she did not expect to survive. Musharraf and his allies disliked Benazir. They were hostile to sharing power with this strong-willed, unpredictable rival in a new government. Among those upset by her return, the Muttahida Quami (United National) Movement (MQM) was especially notorious. In May, its members had murdered lawyers opposed to Musharraf's cavalier suspension of judges. The MQM had burned five lawyers alive in their chambers, blocked medical treatment of their victims, and killed the ambulance drivers who came to treat them. It had been a massacre.[10]

Happily, at least this day, the MQM held itself in check. Still, dire rumors persisted. Benazir had powerful enemies. There were death threats. Authorities took these seriously and, hoping to keep her safe, deployed twenty thousand officers for security, in addition to the security that her Pakistan Peoples Party had provided. Huge crowds jammed the streets, slowing her journey from the airport, which took hours. Better than anyone else, Benazir described the scene in vivid detail.[11] She saw crowds packed ten and twelve people deep in a line stretching as far as the eye could see. The mood was joyous. Music pulsated from boom boxes, blasting the traditional anthems of thirty years of PPP campaigns, interspersed with the latest Pakistani rock music. Supporters, she said, danced around the vehicles, throwing rose petals and cheering "my return and the return of democracy. People were hanging on from trees and from telephone and electricity poles, attempting to catch a glimpse of me."[12] Everywhere there was a sea of black, red, and green flags in the colors of her party.

A double cordon of security protected her vehicle. The government provided some members of her security force. Others included unarmed former police and military men considered loyal to the PPP. Perhaps inevitably, their fears proved justified. Her enemies struck as the convoy reached a darkened stretch in the road, where the lights had gone out or had been turned off. A suicide attacker detonated a powerful blast with high explosives. It wounded 500 and killed 139 people, including 70 security men. Luckily, at the time, Benazir had taken a breather from crowd pleasing and was sitting inside the truck. She was shaken but survived.

THE TAJ ADMONITION

Fast-forward to December and the meeting with Lt. Gen. Nadeem Taj. Controversy swirls as to what Taj told her. Only Benazir, Taj, and her security counselor, Rehman Malik, were present. What he told Benazir remains undisclosed. What he knew is undisclosed. Pakistan's intelligence network is a labyrinth. It includes parties with different agendas. Knowing that a plot may be afoot and being able to stop it are two different things. Perhaps, unable to stop the assassination attempt, he was attempting to dissuade Benazir from attending a rally that might take her life. Skeptics wonder why Taj would go out of his way to protect a politician he was politically opposed to. But politics is a game of interests. Four confluent rationales reflect his interest in giving Benazir a warning.

First, Taj perhaps recognized that preserving her safety served the interests of ISI and President Musharraf. Taj's visit came amid especially sharp differences that had emerged between Benazir and Musharraf. In January their two political parties would face off against each other in scheduled parliamentary elections. Originally, they had discussed sharing power. But any trust between them had ruptured after October 18. Musharraf proved unresponsive to investigating the Karachi bombing and proceeded within days to declare a state of emergency and suspended the Constitution. A furious Benazir deeply suspected that the government had been involved in the Karachi assassination attempt. From that point on, tensions between the Musharraf and Benazir camps continued to heighten.

Musharraf was calculating. He did not want to share power with Benazir and he believed she could be politically neutralized. Benazir and her supporters were (and remain) scathing in their appraisal of his failure to do more—much more—to assure her safety. The gulf on this issue between the two camps was extraordinarily wide. He perceived the situation differently. He believed he had gone beyond the call of duty to protect her. In that equation, from his perspective, her safety mattered. Were assassins to kill her, they would kill his own political fortunes. Violent extremists would have appreciated that outcome.

After 9/11, Musharraf had begun cooperating more closely with the United States in battling Al Qaeda. That alienated violent Islamists. Their anger had prompted eighteen attempts upon his life. Assassinating Benazir would be a double play. It would eliminate two irritants from the political scene. In this scenario, Taj and Musharraf sought to avoid that outcome.

Taj was Musharraf's close ally and a trusted counselor. Three years earlier, it was Taj who had initiated talks to break an anti-Musharraf alliance between Benazir and Nawaz Sharif. The leader of the Pakistan Muslim League—now the PML-N Party—Nawaz had served twice as prime minister. Nawaz was the one leader besides Benazir strong enough to threaten Musharraf in the coming elections. Musharraf had seized power in 1999 through a coup that had ousted Nawaz. Musharraf disliked Benazir, but Nawaz was anathema. In any event, Musharraf's political survival required him to divide his opposition. Assassination would unite it.

Second, Musharraf and Taj believed they could outmaneuver Benazir. By nature, the president brimmed with confidence. He was a military man and a commando, not a career politician. He was deft in dealing with the army and Washington, but not so much in dealing with his own public. His 2007 campaign strategy to keep the presidency was clumsy. An avoidable battle with the judiciary and Pakistan's very activist legal community had backfired, depleting his standing with voters. Still, the jaunty career soldier was easy to underestimate.

Benazir and Musharraf were fiercely competitive. At different times, each bested the other. She had complained about him as a dictator. Her efforts, which set the stage for her 2007 return, were effective in casting doubts upon his credibility. Still, in their final negotiations to share power, he had seized the advantage. He had secured from her a commitment to refrain from opposing his bid for a new five-year term. In return, Benazir had received no political guarantees. Pragmatically, she maintained that she was flexible as to what position she might occupy in a new government. She coveted the job of prime minister, an office that, if regained, she would hold for the third time. For that to happen, a two-thirds majority in the next National Assembly would have to approve a constitutional amendment lifting a two-term limit. Benazir believed she would obtain the needed votes.

After all, the PPP was likely to sweep the coming national elections, providing they were open and fair. People had wearied of military rule and Musharraf was growing more isolated and tight-fisted. The demand for change was in the air. Politically, the PPP dominated the streets. It was hungry for power and in Benazir it had an able, ambitious leader who rallied the party. Still, this was Pakistan. Fears abounded that the vote would be rigged. Already the PPP had amassed substantial evidence to show that the ISI was planning to do just that. She would win a fair election. But PPP supporters worried whether there would be one.[13]

Third, Taj and Musharraf believed that the military had the power to block major political changes. The army was and remains the pivotal player in Pakistan politics. They reckoned that any political leader would be forced to reach an accommodation with that powerful body.[14] Securing a third term as prime minister would not make that political reality moot. Insiders who know Pakistan's army and how it viewed Benazir insist that it was willing to work with her. Her problems lay more with the intelligence establishment. From Musharraf's perspective, no opposition leader was preferable, but if they had to deal with one, better to deal with Benazir than Nawaz. Unlike Nawaz, at least she had not tried to kill him.

Finally, Taj and Musharraf apparently believed that they could leverage potential legal issues to force Benazir to an accommodation. Unresolved criminal charges hanging over her head had sullied her reputation while she was in exile. A legal mechanism was required to ensure that she could contest new elections unburdened by fear of prosecution. Musharraf solved that problem by passing the National Reconciliation Ordinance (NRO), a law that gave Benazir and her husband legal immunity.[15] He also cleared the way for them to keep more than $1 billion in a Swiss account that her critics claimed had been illegally looted from Pakistan's treasury while she had served as prime minister between 1993 and 1996.[16] In raising that issue, one notes that she and her husband, Asif Ali Zardari, had always fiercely denied such charges, dismissing them as political smears, and insisting that all of their activity had been legal under Pakistan law.

Dubbed by wags the "National Robbers Ordinance," the constitutionality of the National Reconciliation Ordinance was hotly disputed.[17] Musharraf knew that and banked on the idea that maintaining its validity required continued government support. Even then, there was the judiciary, which Musharraf's high-handed tactics proved unable to control. Indeed, in October 2009 the Supreme Court put the NRO on hold, requiring parliamentary ratification within three months.[18] By mid-November, it became buried for good as the government withdrew it from consideration.[19] Taj and Musharraf had anticipated that might happen and saw it as a political weapon.

In short, Musharraf's political interests mandated keeping Benazir alive. Why Taj or Musharraf failed to act more aggressively to protect her is sharply disputed and has inspired deep bitterness. Perhaps they lacked sufficient details that might have deterred her from attending the rally. In any event, she turned aside Taj's warning. From her perspective, death threats were hardly novel. They had inundated her campaign. She must have asked herself: Was this one genuine? How could she be certain? The breakdown between Musharraf and Benazir worked against her. She did not believe Musharraf cared about her safety. After Karachi, she worried that he might be its greatest threat. She and her team believed that the government invoked the specter of death threats as a tactic to keep opposition politicians away from voters. A red flag raised by the ISI chief merited attention. Yet absent hard evidence, Benazir refused to be cowed. She had faced the public repeatedly. She would do so again. She did worry about her safety. But she would not allow threats to cut off her contact with voters.

Taj's warning went unheeded. This is a book about strategic communication, but it uses this concept to examine a culture of conspiracy and assassination. The scenario presented here seems highly plausible. But others are possible. Here is one, and it is merely a hypothesis: what if Taj anticipated that Benazir would reject his advice? Was the meeting a setup intended to ensure her attendance at the Liaquat Bagh? That seems unlikely, but ISI skeptics would answer that it was capable of any deception.

A WOMAN OF COURAGE

By nature a fatalist, Benazir confronted death courageously. Besides, isolation from voters mortified her. It could undo her. She had been gone from Pakistan for a decade. Her last tenure as prime minister had proven frustrating.

Although she lacked parliamentary votes to effect reforms that she had wanted to push and confronted hostility from the military-intelligence establishment, critics had charged she left the economy in a shambles.

Pervez Musharraf, Nawaz Sharif, Swiss investigators, and other critics had labeled her a thief. Plus, her power-sharing talks with Musharraf had provoked outrage among Pakistanis. Polling revealed that many believed that she was out for herself, not the country. She had fences to mend.

Benazir was also on to Musharraf's game. She had devised a savvy plan of her own for strategic communication rooted in public exposure and in putting pressure on Washington—which, on this issue, had clout with Musharraf—to force free and fair elections. It was a smart gambit. The PPP believed it had incriminating evidence about Musharraf's government, especially the ISI. Ironically, Benazir had friends within the intelligence services who fed her the information detailing an ISI scheme to rig the elections scheduled for January 8.

Who knows whether the ISI would have gotten away with a scheme to rig the 2008 elections. Important here is that Musharraf believed his side would prevail. That confidence argues against the suggestion that he intended she suffer harm. It strengthens the conclusion that Taj did try to warn her away from danger. But the truth remains obscured. In late September Benazir had delivered a speech sponsored by the Middle East Institute in the caucus room of the Russell Building at the U.S. Senate. Her appearance was conscious strategic communication. Mark Siegel notes: "We had hoped that by generating press attention and congressional focus, Musharraf would hesitate to cause her harm upon her return to Pakistan."

It was a tough speech. She made clear her intent to crack down on ISI abuse. Her words provoked an angry response. Almost immediately, Musharraf called Benazir. He had thought she was returning to Pakistan after the scheduled January 2008 elections. He lit into her plans to return sooner. He made clear that her safety rested in his hands. "The conversation left her shaken," recalls Siegel. "It was a very threatening phone call." It registered on both Benazir and her team grave concerns that Musharraf would act ruthlessly to block her return to power. Benazir clearly believed that Musharraf was complicit in plots against her life.[20] Though mindful of security concerns, she attended a rally that afternoon at Liaquat Bagh, a famous park on Muree Road in Rawalpindi. Ironically, it was named for Pakistan's first prime minister, Liaquat Ali Khan, after his assassination there in 1951. The park was renowned as a gathering place for political speeches. Later the government would claim that security forces had flooded the area to provide protection. Photographs and video disclose nothing of the sort. Clearly it did not exist as she concluded her speech and was escorted swiftly into her Toyota Land Cruiser.

The vehicle drove up to the gates. Just outside, it encountered an unexpected crowd waving signs and chanting pro-Benazir slogans. No one is certain who the people were. Not one to duck her fans, she poked her head through the vehicle's sunroof and greeted the crowd. She waved and chanted the familiar slogan, "Long Live Bhutto." Whether by a bullet or a bomb blast, moments later, she was dead.

Chapter 5

A LIFE ROOTED IN BLOOD AND TURMOIL

B enazir opens her autobiography with this declaration: "I didn't choose this life; it chose me."[1] She was, Mary Anne Weaver observed,

> an Eastern fatalist by birth, Western liberal by conviction, and a people-power revolutionary—who has carefully modeled herself on Evita Perón and Corazon Aquino—through sheer necessity. She is an expensively educated product of the West who has ruled a male-dominated Islamic society of the East. She is a democrat who appeals to feudal loyalties.[2]

In a letter he wrote from his death cell, her father, Zulfiqar Ali Bhutto, reminded her of a story as she was growing up and offered his own cogent insight into his daughter's character:

> In the winter of 1957, when you were four years old, we were sitting on the terrace of 'Al-Murtaza.' It was a fine morning. I had a double-barrel gun in my hand. One barrel was 22 and the other 480. Without a thought, I shot a wild parrot.
>
> When the parrot fell to the ground near the terrace you cried your eyes out. You had it buried in your presence. You cried and cried. You refused to have your meals. A dead parrot in the winter of

1957 in Larkana made a little girl weep in sorrow. Twenty-one years later, that little girl has grown into a young lady with nerves of steel to valorously confront the terror of the longest night of tyranny. Truly you have proved beyond doubt that the blood of warriors runs in your veins.[3]

Years later, the story had retained its formidable impact. She described it to the Academy of Achievement in London as among her most vital inspirations. "For me," she stated, "human life is very, very sacred."[4] She was full of life. Her friends found her wit and vitality infectious. She dazzled. Politically, she had a rare star quality.

Her enemies had a different take on Benazir. Some refused to take her seriously because she was a woman. Those who did take her seriously regarded her as smart, gifted, dangerously unpredictable, pompous, and corrupt. Voters find politics largely about hope and fear. For politicians, it is also about paranoia. They fear what they cannot control. She temporized, but she was not easily controlled.

Benazir's death reshaped the political dynamics in Pakistan. It eliminated the one player who might have led a popular upheaval that could have effected real change.[5] Deciphering the evidence that surrounds her murder and Musharraf's campaign for political survival requires us to understand why she was killed and who stood to gain. Confluent questions help frame the investigation:

- Who was the real person behind the persona of Benazir Bhutto?
- How did the tragic experience of seeing her father, Zulfiqar Ali Bhutto, manipulated, set up, double-crossed, and hanged shape her attitudes?
- How did Zia ul-Haq's harsh treatment change her and harden her hostility to Pakistan's military-intelligence establishment?
- How did her marriage to Asif Ali Zardari, whom she married after interviewing a number of prospects, shape her politics? How did the criminal investigations and indictments against them, and Zardari's imprisonment for years, affect her worldview?
- How did military hostility affect her attitudes?

- Did she pose an existential threat to powerful military-intelligence or political interests in Pakistan and elsewhere?
- What evidence supports or refutes her suspicions about the complicity of individuals she believed were plotting her assassination?
- What campaign of influence did Musharraf mount to protect his position? How well did it succeed?
- How did Benazir's own superb skills at strategic communication set the stage for her return and lay a foundation for success?

A DAUGHTER DESTINED FOR POLITICS

Benazir Bhutto was born into a storied dynasty.[6] Her family comprised wealthy landowners in Larkana, in Sindh Province. From an early age she enjoyed privilege and luxury.[7] Her mother was an Iranian Shiite. The rest of the family was Sunni.[8] Her childhood was spent on a ten thousand–acre estate, where highly affluent and elite families "live in walled compounds, ringed by rifle sights; where landlords are often brutal and peasants are serfs; where women are in *purdah* and men enjoy their whiskey and their pheasant shoots."[9]

Later the family moved to Karachi. Zulfiqar was determined to raise his children in a way that made them feel at ease in a modern world.[10] She had an English governess and learned table manners, netball, and cricket. She dressed in clothes bought from Saks Fifth Avenue. She attended school at the Convent of Jesus and Mary, run by Irish Catholic nuns, where Mother Eugene taught her students "to reach for the moon, and the lodestar. . . . It was all about reaching out."[11]

The name Benazir was apt. It means "unique, without comparison." Her family and friends called her Pinkie.[12] Her father inspired her keen interest in politics. When she was six years old, he read her tales about Napoleon. Two years later, she met Zhou En-Lai. She was ten when her father awoke her in the middle of the night to tell her that John F. Kennedy (JFK) had been assassinated.[13]

At sixteen, she entered Radcliffe. She considered that period the "most profound influence in my formative years."[14] It was a time of turmoil and change in America. Students were out in force protesting against the war in Vietnam. She revered Robert F. Kennedy and Dr. Martin Luther King, Jr., who, she recalled years later, had made her feel that "if you didn't like something, you could do something about it."[15] She thought herself an idealist: "My generation grew up in saving the world. . . . I discovered that life was more than my homework and my tuitions and my tutorial. Life was about the larger issues where we could all play a role."[16]

As with many Pakistanis, the nation's humiliating defeat in the 1971 war with India transformed her into a fiery nationalist. It was an exciting time. Her father traveled often to the States. Through him, she engaged with powerful figures on the world stage. She met then U.S. ambassador to the United Nations George H. W. Bush, who handed her his card and told her: "Call me if you ever need anything." Eighteen years later, at the White House, she asked for sixty F-16s.[17]

She attended and loved Oxford in the mid-1970s. She was a star. She drove a yellow sports car, presided over the scene like a princess, and became the first Asian elected as president of the Oxford Union Debating Society. Quinn Peeper, a student at University College while she attended Lady Margaret Hall, described her as "a force of nature. She was very one-to-one. She'd look you in the eye and make you feel you were the most important person in the world."[18]

Walter Isaacson knew her as a friend at both Harvard and Oxford. An insightful student of human behavior, he remembered her intensity and how "she locked onto your eyes and pushed her ideas with a real fervor. She was very high energy, but also very earnest." He confirms the impressiveness of her election, noting that "she saw that as adding to Pakistan's prestige and helping the cause of both her father and her country."[19]

The Oxford Union was seen as a training ground for future politicians. The post of its president was highly sought after. Unless one attended Oxford or Cambridge, one might not fully appreciate the unique importance of Benazir's achievement. For years, winning that "glittering prize" had led to an invitation to stand for Parliament. She was drawn to the art of debate. "The power of oratory," she wrote, "had always been a great force on the Asian subcontinent, where so many were illiterate. Millions had been swayed by the words of Mahatma Gandhi, Jawaharlal Nehru, Mohammed Ali Jinnah, and, indeed, my father. Storytelling, poetry, and oratory were part of our tradition."[20]

She would hone this skill and put it to fine use then and in the years ahead. No fan of Richard Nixon, as Watergate inflamed Washington, she reminded an audience at the Oxford Union of the story—a pure invention by an early biographer—of George Washington's cutting down a cherry tree, then being unable to lie and deny responsibility for doing so. "Well," she said, "Americans began with a president who couldn't tell a lie and now they have one who can't tell the truth."[21]

As she had at Radcliffe, she capitalized on her father's fame and power to network with figures like Margaret Thatcher. In a pithy commentary published in the *Observer*, the historian William Dalrymple, who knew her well, superbly expressed what others who knew her have said about the ease with which this attractive cosmopolitan woman crossed cultures:

"London is like a second home for me," she once told me. "I know London well. I know where the theatres are, I know where the shops are, I know where the hairdressers are. I love to browse through Harrods and WH Smith in Sloane Square. I know all my favourite ice cream parlours. I used to particularly love going to the one at Marble Arch: Baskin Robbins. Sometimes, I used to drive all the way up from Oxford just for an ice cream and then drive back again. That was my idea of sin."[22]

Dalrymple noted acutely, "It was difficult to imagine any of her neighbouring heads of state, even India's earnest Sikh economist, Manmohan Singh, talking like this." He also reports the surprising information that while fluent in English, her first language, she spoke Urdu "like a well-groomed foreigner, fluently but ungrammatically. Her Sindhi was even worse; apart from a few imperatives, she was completely at sea." One can see why her key enemies in Pakistan had difficulty empathizing with her and saw her as trouble.

A privileged and affluent upbringing often inspires a sense of entitlement. Dalyrmple keenly observes that "the sophisticated gloss and the feudal grit" distinguished her political style.[23] She was smart, tough, and almost as ambitious as her father was.

Chapter 6

THE POPULIST ARISTOCRAT

Zulfiqar Ali Bhutto (ZAB) was a mesmerizing populist and a powerful intellectual. He was the first Pakistani graduate of the University of California–Berkeley, where he had developed an interest in socialism. He went on to study at Christ Church, Oxford, a fitting choice for a Pakistani aristocrat. Returning home, he entered politics and served as foreign minister to President Ayub Khan. Khan had seized power in 1958, jettisoned the Constitution, declared martial law, and installed himself as the martial law administrator. Martial law was lifted in 1962 and a new Constitution enacted. It was a flawed effort, as it guaranteed that the less populous West Pakistan enjoyed the same number of seats in Parliament that East Pakistan did, under a "parity principle."

Khan's fortunes declined after Pakistan suffered humiliation in 1965 clashes with India over Kashmir. In June 1966 Bhutto resigned. Politicians may pledge eternal friendship, but in politics eternity can be brief. In October 1966, Bhutto founded the Pakistan Peoples Party, a Sindh Province–based populist party, and set out to wrest power away from Khan. Popular discontent in 1968 and 1969 forced Ayub Khan to step aside. Chief of Army Staff Gen. Yahya Khan became president, set aside the Constitution, and declared a new martial law.

The strategic situation was tricky. The military disdained the civilian leadership, but the Pakistanis had had their fill of the generals. Bhutto exploited their discontent. With that peculiar conceit that often afflicts those from privileged backgrounds who envision themselves in the role of national savior, he presented himself as the tribune of the common people. He played this role with consummate skill.

But politics is also a game of mobilizing political bases, and Pakistan was divided between east and west. The challenge of unifying a nation with its two parts separated by a thousand miles was perhaps insuperable, and ethnic differences ensured bitter rivalry. The Pashtun-Punjabi-Mohair-dominated west controlled the lion's share of Pakistan's resources. The army officers were mainly Punjabi, and their key military bases were located in the west. Punjabis looked down their noses at the Bengalis. East Pakistan's population naturally resented its status as second-class citizens. In the wake of the Kashmir fiasco, Ayub Khan faced a rising tide of political opposition.

Mujibur Rahman's Awami League, the dominant party in East Pakistan, joined Bhutto and the PPP in moving to sideline Yahya Khan. Worn down, Khan announced that he would not run in the 1970 presidential election. Better known for his affinity with alcohol than political dexterity, Khan pledged to serve only until a new government was elected.

For the elections, Yahya Khan abolished the parity principle. As strategic communication, his move sent a strong signal about fair play, and the elections were considered free, fair, and open. But his decision had fateful consequences. Having a larger population, inevitably East Pakistan could lay claim to a greater number of seats in the new Parliament, especially as geographic bases dictated how voters cast their ballots.

The December 1970 elections proved a debacle for the military rulers. The election was hugely polarized. Rahman played to his base in the east, while Bhutto played to his in the west. They produced a political deadlock twisted by competing political ambitions. In Bengal, the Awami League ran the tables, winning 162 seats out of a possible 164. In the west, Bhutto's slogan *Roti, Kapra, Makan* (Bread, Clothing, Shelter) struck a responsive chord. The PPP trumped its competition there, garnering about 39 percent of the vote. It carried two of the four western provinces, snagging 81 seats out of 138. Punjab and Sindh formed the PPP's political base. Neither party won seats in the base of the other.

Bhutto's victory was a testament to his energy and charisma. He over-came fierce opposition, backed by the intelligence services, from well-funded Islamists who attacked Bhutto for his un-Islamic lifestyle and smeared him by alleging that his mother was a Hindu.[1] The results surprised the military, which was poorly attuned to the shifting currents of democratic politics. It had anticipated a divided and dysfunctional Parliament, thus setting up Yahya Khan as the power broker among "monkeys dividing the spoils (*bandar bat*)."[2] Instead, they wound up with two influential political opponents, who were unfriendly rivals but united against a military dictatorship.

Flush with victory, Rahman demanded the post of prime minister. In Parliament, East Pakistan's larger population would give his party a majority of the seats. Bhutto felt that he was entitled to be prime minister. No fan of Bhutto's, Pervez Musharraf wrote that, mad for power, the PPP leader acidly pledged to break the legs of any newly elected member of Parliament from the West who dared to attend a National Assembly meeting in Dhaka, capital of East Pakistan.[3] Khan was prepared to accede, but Rahman, the Awami League leader, foiled his opportunity by making onerous demands for autonomy in East Pakistan and more economic resources than the military was prepared to grant.[4]

As negotiations ensued, Bhutto realized that Khan could be manipulated and did so masterfully. Funny, smart, charming, and hopelessly ruthless, Bhut-to stoked the fires of parochialism. Critics say he stirred emotions, chanting the slogan *Idar Hum, Udhar Tum* (Here it's us, there it's you).[5] Others deny that he did so,[6] but opponents tagged him with the slogan and in politics perception becomes reality. Rahman proved ZAB's unwitting accomplice. He showed no comprehension of strategic communication as a national leader. He behaved arrogantly. He made no effort to position himself as a national leader. He failed to provide a unifying national voice, a talent that most leaders who compete for power in democracies strive to achieve. Instead, Rahman set the stage for an inevitable national breakup.

The dove of peace had no home in this harsh landscape. Perhaps all along Rahman was looking for an excuse to proclaim secession but, hell-bent on pursuing his own agenda, Bhutto fearlessly stirred the pot. A stronger, wiser

Khan might have averted the coming political train wreck. Had Rahman become prime minister, the two parts of Pakistan might have remained unified. Instead, fiercely competing egos caused the talks to break down. Pushed to the wall, on March 25, 1971, Yahya Khan outlawed the Awami League and detained Rahman. East Pakistanis were outraged. Events spiraled out of control. Any deal would have been difficult to cut. Pashtun mind-sets were steeped with racism. The military and intelligence services viewed the Bengalis as closer to Hindus, a view that almost by definition rendered them disloyal.[7] Ever since Pakistan's chaotic founding, charges of Bengali collusion with India had been a familiar refrain in West Pakistani politics.[8] Nothing could break the deadlock between east and west. By March 1971, Khan's patience was exhausted. Egged on by Bhutto, he launched an invasion against the Bengalis.

Bhutto's enthusiasm for Khan's move was deeply cynical. Khan foresaw that it would prove a fiasco, destroy his credibility, and force him to step aside. Pakistan's ruling clique had blundered badly in misjudging the elections and then going to war. Nor had they any concept of what message their actions would communicate.[9] The Pakistan Army's behavior was a disgrace. It used its machine guns liberally, setting the Bengalis back on their heels. The fighting left one million dead and displaced four million more. The Hindus of East Pakistan suffered badly amid this mayhem.

Khan's army outraged Indian prime minister Indira Gandhi. She was the wrong adversary to tangle with. On December 3, 1971, she angrily dispatched her army across the East Bengal border. The Indians made short work of the cocky Pakistanis.[10] Two weeks later, seated at a table at the Ramma race course, a humiliated Pakistani Lt. Gen. "Tiger" Niazi signed the instrument of surrender, while satisfied Indian victors stood over him glowering.[11] The new state of Bangladesh was born, midwifed by Pakistani political ineptitude and what Musharraf later characterized as operational incompetence.[12]

There was scant evidence that the military had learned much from its political imbecility. The blame for its defeat was swiftly pinned upon others. Such insularity in Pakistan's military is typical and has profoundly impaired its ability to embrace democratic processes. The defeat cast into high relief the military's arrogance, providing a window into the dynamics of Pakistani politics. The military did not come to terms with its responsibility because it felt no need to do so. The same attitude would color Musharraf's behavior after Benazir's assassination. Although in 2011 threats from the Taliban and heightened tensions with the United States over drone attacks and other differences have caused the military to seek a more united front with the civilian government, the army remains a power unto itself.

For four decades, Pakistan's defeat has cast a shadow over its politics and deepened its sense of insecurity. The war cost Khan his job. He had wanted to tough it out, but junior military officers and civil servants refused to support him. Khan reluctantly stepped aside, paving the way for Bhutto.[13] Rahman might have been chosen to lead, but his vow to make Pakistan secular had alienated the officers. By contrast, they warmed to the creed of Bhutto's PPP was "Islam, socialism, and democracy," and the fact that its founding documents had referred to jihad against India.[14] Bhutto seemed the safer bet. He received the nod to take office as prime minister.

Talented politicians often excel as masters of deceit. Bhutto's worst victim was himself. His behavior influenced Musharraf's view of Bhutto's family. Denouncing Bhutto as "despotic" and presiding over a "dictatorial, suppressive rule," Musharraf wrote:

> An autocrat at heart, Bhutto got a kick out of being head of a martial law regime. . . . During his time the press was suppressed more than ever before or since. Many editors and journalists were arrested for dissent, and newspapers and journals were closed down. Political opponents were arrested on spurious charges; some were incarcerated in a notorious gulag-like prison called the Dalai Camp and some were even murdered mysteriously.[15]

Obsessed with his own agenda, Bhutto misread the army's deep hostility toward him and failed to grasp the emerging influence of religious parties like Jamaat-e-Islami (JI). The JI was poisonous and set out immediately to discredit Bhutto. The defeat in the Bangladesh war had spawned a raft of conspiracy theories. As JI members saw it, the loss in Bangladesh was the handiwork of shadowy forces that had sold out their country.

Their opportunity presented itself soon enough. Bhutto supported making Bangladesh an independent nation. His opponents seized upon that stance to mount a campaign called *Bangladesh Na-manzoor* (Bangladesh is unacceptable). It was effective strategic communication, made more so because Bhutto failed to see how destructive it became. Islamist students spread rumors on campuses and in mosques. They darkly charged that Bhutto was deliberately creating division within an Islamic nation and faulted him for deviously goading the military into a war that he believed would fail in order to seize absolute power.[16] Like much political propaganda, it drew strength from half-truths, calling out Bhutto for his cynical cheerleading as Pakistanis marched off to war. Naturally, in this twisted tale the army escaped all blame for its failure. Crucially, while the JI campaign gained limited traction, it helped forge a fateful alliance with the military.

Videos uploaded to the website YouTube offer an uncensored visual record of Pakistan's recent history. There is ample footage of Bhutto, and it is striking. He is kinetic. He is equally at ease attired in expensive suits strutting about foreign capitals and in the *awami* (people's) shirt and Jinnah cap haranguing working people. Bhutto had the gift of eloquence and could whip up the crowd. A celebrity, he cut a dashing figure in the media. He inspired pride in ordinary Pakistanis.

Unfortunately, he failed to deliver at home. The PPP victory had been based on a platform that promised land redistribution, universal education, and an end to the economic power of the twenty-two families who controlled 70 percent of the country's industrial capital, 80 percent of banking, and 90 of the insurance industry.[17] Making good on his heady promises was a steep mountain to climb. Benazir has offered a spirited defense of her father's record,[18] but most observers consider her father's record as prime minister a failure. Turning away from the free market, his socialist policies reversed economic growth, falling from 6 percent to 4 percent, and drove out foreign investment capital.[19] He generated sizzle. But behind its facade, his PPP was viewed as a motley crew of racketeers, lawyers, and feudalists that prospered. Bhutto's populism was a posture, not a blueprint for action. Stephen Cohen records that while at first voters were relieved as power passed from the "wine-soaked generals and bloodthirsty colonels,"[20] on second look, the voters weren't so sure they liked what they saw. A new Constitution invested Bhutto with complete executive power, and he grabbed for every inch of it. He grew increasingly oblivious to a growing disenchantment among everyday Pakistanis. He did recognize that his radical ersatz-socialist ideology would annoy the conservative military, and with good reason, he feared a coup. But like many politicians who believe they are smarter than anyone else, he left himself open to a sucker punch.

He fell for a whopper when selecting his top military commanders. He looked for pliable sycophants. Unfortunately, unless you really know the players, that effort can prove treacherous. In Pakistan, the Chief of Army Staff holds the pivotal position. Lt. Gen. Ghulam Jilani Khan, the head of Inter-Services Intelligence, talked up Lt. Gen. Muhammad Zia ul-Haq. Benazir described him as a "short, nervous, ineffectual-looking man whose pomaded hair was parted in the middle and lacquered to his head. He looked more like an English cartoon villain than an inspiring model for the leader of the Pakistan Army. And he seemed so obsequious."[21] Less attuned to current realities, her father bought Khan's pitch and promoted Zia over more senior officers into the COAS slot.[22] This mistake would cost him his life.

A radical Islamist, Zia was obsessed with propagating Islam. Zealously, he urged all ranks of the army to offer prayers, which were preferably led by commanders. He directed that training programs include religious instruction. Prayer halls were organized in all army units.[23] A sectarian army was sharpened into a spear-carrier for Islam. This transformation left a lasting mark and sharpened the military's hostility toward the more secular Benazir Bhutto when she later emerged as a national leader. Benazir's gender and feminism were viewed as a threat to conservative Islamic culture.

There is irony in Zulfiqar Ali Bhutto's opportunism. Supreme in his self-belief, he thought he could play the Islamic card. Ayub Khan had created a precedent for using religion to thwart opponents. On his watch, Pakistan was renamed an Islamic republic, although his interpretation of Islam leaned toward moderation compared to what followed under Zia.[24] Bhutto cynically fostered radical Islam in a culture where, previously, religion "was, largely, confined to an individual's private realm."[25] Forgotten was Mohammed Ali Jinnah's vision of a progressive, secular nation.[26] Bhutto established a Council of Islamic Ideology, declared the minority sect of Ahmadis non-Muslims, and appointed the nation's first minister for religious affairs. He ordered that copies of the Quran be placed in first-class hotels. He decreed that there must be different school curricula for Shiites and Sunnis. Impoverished imams received new government support.[27]

Newsweek's Tony Clifton was bemused by the metamorphosis. "Bhutto had always been pretty secular," he says. "Strict Muslims don't drink, but the way you got to know Bhutto was by kicking back and having a few whiskeys with him at the end of the day. And suddenly, overnight, he was banning the stuff."[28]

No less telling was how Bhutto comported himself while hosting an Islamic Summit Conference at Lahore in February 1974. The attendees included the major players in Bhutto's world: King Faisal of Saudi Arabia, President Anwar Sadat of Egypt, Col. Muammar Qaddafi of Libya (protected, as usual, by a female security team), and Palestinian warhorse (or, take your pick, notorious terrorist) Yasser Arafat. They gathered for three days and elected Bhutto the chairman of the Islamic Conference. The election garnered headlines but little support among the true believers at home, who knew better. During prayers at the mosque, Tony Clifton, who was present, noticed how Bhutto "didn't quite have the religious ritual down. Bhutto was always a split second behind, watching out the corner of his eye, taking his cues from the others." Bhutto attempted to prove that he was a devout Muslim, but the Islamists were not convinced.

Far too late, Bhutto discovered that the Islamists and conservative military leaders were pulling the same wagon. Army leaders also loathed Bhutto's left-wing secularism and distrusted him as subversive to their interests. Their concern was well justified when Bhutto created a Federal Security Force, a praetorian guard led by former general Akbar Khan, in 1972.[29] It was not a good move. Bhutto merely infuriated the military high command without weakening it.[30] He also appointed a War Inquiry Commission in late December 1971 to investigate the Bangladesh war fiasco. To no one's surprise, the report—clearly intended to undercut the army's credibility—found the army guilty of committing widespread atrocities. The report also recommended "moral reform" to address the "lust for wine and women, and greed for lands and houses" of senior officers.[31] Bhutto had set out to disgrace the army. Their response was to get rid of him.

Shrewdly, the military recognized that while Bhutto had gained power through an election, elections could be his Achilles' heel. They contrived a clever scheme that was coldly executed and, as is often the case in Pakistan, involved the Directorate for Inter-Services Intelligence. In October 1976, the ISI submitted a disingenuous fifty-three-page position paper that offered up a case for holding early elections and establishing a renewed mandate for Pakistan's most esteemed leader. Titled "General Elections," its blatant flattery painted a fraudulent "can't lose" pro-Bhutto scenario:

We cannot hope to explore all the revolutionary changes, reforms and achievements of the present government under the leadership of Mr. Bhutto in this brief paper; suffice it to say, his leadership proved to be a breadth [sic] of fresh air in the acrid and suffocating political atmosphere, a dawn of hope in the dark days of economic chaos, a shot in the arm for the revival of the spirit of [the] Pakistan movement. He has given back the "soul" to the people and gave them direction to follow in the new constitution.[32]

The premise in this political con game portrayed Bhutto as a powerhouse who had achieved dizzying heights in popularity, while his sleazy opponents lay scattered and in disarray. Vulnerable to flattery, Bhutto took the bait. He even let ISI select Election Day. It was like allowing an opposing general to choose the battlefield. The ISI picked a date for National Assembly elections that suited its purpose, at Bhutto's expense, on March 7, 1977. Elections for provincial assemblies were scheduled for three days later.

Bhutto never cottoned on to the well-conceived trap until it was too late. Far from rolling over as the ISI had assured Bhutto they would, the religious parties pulled out all the stops. The Islamists rejected Bhutto's candidacy and his party out of hand. Off his game, Bhutto did little to further his cause as a populist by running on such slogans as "Undisputed Leader," "Supreme Leader," and "Great Leader." It felt as though he had mistaken Pakistan for North Korea.

The ISI agents were pros. They only partly rigged the election. Opposition candidates from religious parties within the opposition Pakistan National Alliance (PNA)—especially the Jamaat-e-Islami—were abducted to prevent them from qualifying. Apparently few votes were affected, but the tactic provoked protests and cast doubt on the legitimacy of the election. Bhutto, meanwhile, watched grimly in the company of the U.S. ambassador as the initial returns filtered in.

Here was another lesson in politics. Strongmen who decide that democracy is for lesser mortals often show an inability to read vote patterns. On Election Day, the most paranoid politicos are the ones tipped as the heavy favorites. The bell rings, the polls open, and it seems like every hour the same question pours in: How is the vote going? Political consultants enjoy offering the same mischievous response: Turnout is low in our areas. It drives candidates nuts.

The smart pols know to take a breath and wait for the picture to become clear. The early returns can be as reliable as a favorite in a horse race. And so it went for Bhutto. Initial counts indicated the PPP had taken a shellacking, but actually, his party had won decisively. In signing off on the ISI rigging scheme, he had inadvertently slipped a noose around his neck. The tragedy was Bhutto would have won any honest count.

The damage was irreparable. The religious parties cried foul and challenged the outcome. Here emerged another lesson: The candidate, having boxed himself in, had no place to turn and had to give some ground. Politics, as Rab Butler rightly said, is about the art of the possible. But Bhutto had no intention of sharing power, much less surrendering it. One misjudgment led to another. As protests erupted, he ordered the army to shoot the protestors. The soldiers refused.[33] Gleefully closing the trap, Zia and the ISI advised the opposition not to trust Bhutto.[34]

Political deadlock paralyzed the country and provided a pretext for the army to make its move. On July 5, 1977, Zia launched Operation Fairplay.[35] He ordered Bhutto's arrest. In a fine display of on-target strategic communication, Zia advised the Pakistanis that he was merely acting in the name of preserving election integrity.[36] It was a canard, as the coup had been long planned. The whole thing came off without a hitch. Zia called for new elections in ninety days. As with his military colleagues, elections ranked at the bottom of his true agenda. Zia had less interest in a civilian government than most people in uniform did. His pro-democracy posture was chicanery.

Bhutto's credibility had depended on popular support. The ISI's dirty tricks transformed his image from superstar to unprincipled hack. By discrediting Bhutto's legitimacy, Zia and the ISI could justify his ouster. They may not have heard the term "strategic communication," but they applied its principles. While the military paraded under the banner of integrity, other Bhutto opponents did their part. They provided third-party validation for change by leaking stories to the newspapers, which ran them with lurid headlines like "Bhutto tried to kill me!" and "Bhutto kidnapped me." From his prison cell, a stoic Bhutto managed to keep his sense of humor. He told a reporter who wondered how he was passing the time, "I'm reading a lot of Napoleon to learn how he kept his generals in line when I couldn't control mine."[37]

Benazir had entered the picture just prior to the coup. Arriving home from Oxford, she had planned to join her father's team as an adviser. Instead, she bore bitter witness to the perfidy. The ISI's behavior imprinted itself upon Benazir for a lifetime. As prime minister, she would try in vain to curtail the meddling of the military and intelligence service agencies. Each side recognized in the other a mortal enemy.

Washington might have propped up Bhutto against Zia, but Bhutto was deemed unreliable after rebuffing Henry Kissinger's plea to refrain from developing nuclear weapons. Bhutto's ouster pleased Washington.[38] Many Pakistanis believe that Kissinger, an avid student of Prince Klemens von Metternich, orchestrated Zia's takeover.[39] That's extremely dubious, although the rumor fed Pakistan's culture of conspiracy theory. Still, Benazir learned a valuable lesson: In Pakistani politics, enlisting American support was a smart move.

Zia was candid about his desire to support the spread and purification of Islam. He projected himself as its champion.[40] He had no use or tolerance for secularists. As Dr. Ayesha Jalal astutely observes,

Zia's ascent marked a major shift in the role of Islam in Pakistani politics. Prior leaders thought of Pakistan as Islamic, but their sense of Islam was more in line with Mohammad Ali Jinnah's view of an enlightened, moderate form of it. Zulfiqar Ali Bhutto had invoked Islam in his own strategic communication to bolster his political credibility, but his embrace was cynical. At heart, Bhutto was a secularist, an intellectual who devoured new ideas, and a leader for a modern world. Under Zia, Saudi influence crept in and the Salafists began to make themselves felt. Zia survived in power as long as he did because he championed Sunni Islam against threats posed by the rising influence of Shiites in the wake of Iran's 1979 revolution and the Soviet takeover of Afghanistan.[41]

Topping his agenda was getting rid of the troublesome Bhutto. Bhutto was indicted for conspiracy to murder Ahmed Raza Kasuri, a former PPP member who had joined the opposition.[42] Most journalists describe the charges as trumped up, but Kasuri himself has insisted that they were based on fact.[43] From prison, Bhutto wrote an impassioned memoir refuting the accusation.[44] But the deck was stacked. Five handpicked judges in the Lahore High Court, wearing black robes and white wigs, sat beneath a red satin tasseled canopy and heard the case.[45] The proceedings were a legal travesty. Presided over by acting chief justice Maulvi Mushtag, a Zia crony, the court predictably returned a guilty verdict and sentenced Bhutto to the rope. The Supreme Court rejected his appeal on a narrow 4–3 vote.[46]

Was Zia's action purely a Pakistani decision? In his memoir, Brig. Gen. Syed A. I. Tirmazi claims that

the US was fully involved in exploiting the situation [stirring up the political opposition in the country] and aiding the Opposition Political parties and ultimately getting him [Zulfiqar Ali Bhutto] removed and ensuring that he is hanged. It is generally believed that the U.S. wanted ZAB to be removed from the political scene of Pakistan mainly on two accounts. First, for the nuclear policy that he framed and tried relentlessly [to] pursue and secondly, from apprehensions that ZAB was influencing the minds and policies of a number of Islamic and Third World countries. He posed a serious challenge to the US interests in the region. "Tally-ho. Kill Zulfiqar Ali Bhutto," yelled the self-proclaimed policeman of the world.[47]

In an illustration of Pakistani paranoia run amok, Tirmazi cites a secret memo purloined from the U.S. Embassy, declaring: "It was a telegraphic message from Washington. When decoded, it contained directions for the local US offices to ensure that ZAB was hanged."[48] Tirmazi was a director of the ISI and served as its chief of staff, which makes him a well-informed insider. In his account, neither the ISI chief nor Zia denied the contents when the message was presented to them, and no one in Pakistan's government, then or now, has commented on it. That Washington might have given instructions or advice to execute Bhutto is potentially explosive, if the charge is credible.

Tirmazi's allegation is ridiculous. It would have trouble making it into a spy thriller. Whatever Kissinger's views on Bhutto—or whatever encouragement he may have given the military to oust him—by the time the PPP leader was tried and hanged, the U.S. administration had completely changed. Jimmy Carter had become president, Cyrus Vance was secretary of state, and Stansfield Turner was the director of the Central Intelligence Agency. It is inconceivable that any of these men would have issued or countenanced the issuance of such an instruction. In Pakistan, the army makes the political decisions on life and death, and the decision maker was Zia. There seems little doubt that Zia wanted Bhutto killed or that he was responsible for Bhutto's execution.

When evaluating Zia's actions and his disposition of Bhutto's fate, it is important to recognize how they illustrate the tendency of Pakistani political players to take outlandish theories seriously. They also employ the principles of strategic communication and disseminate conspiracy theories to justify their actions. The dynamic persists in Pakistani politics.

In the meantime, Bhutto's fate was sealed. People demonstrated and protested against the scheduled execution, shouting "Bhutto *ko reha karo* (free Bhutto)!" Taking no chances, Zia declared martial law. Detained in a police facility, Bhutto was allowed occasional visits from Benazir and her mother, Nusrat. At his request, her brother, Mir Murtaza, then an Oxford student, remained in England to organize international protests. Zia was besieged with foreign appeals for clemency. He turned a deaf ear to all of them.

On April 4, 1979, dressed in rumpled clothing, a frail Bhutto was unceremoniously dumped into a litter, carried to a wooden scaffold, had a hood placed over his head, and was hanged.[49] It was another moment that would be etched in Benazir's memory. Zia would remark later that his biggest mistake was failing to hang Benazir.[50]

Chapter 7

THE YEARS HARDEN HOSTILITIES

After her husband's execution, Begum Nusrat Bhutto had been slated to serve as her husband's political heir, but she preferred that her older daughter, Benazir, occupy this role. As Nusrat was already chairperson of the Pakistan Peoples Party, the party made Benazir cochair. Bhutto's two sons, Mir Murtaza and Shah Nawaz, fled into hiding in Afghanistan. Nusrat spent four years in and out of prison or under house arrest and then went into exile in France.[1]

Zia oriented Pakistani politics toward a very strict interpretation of Sunni Islam. Thousands of madrassas were set up and served as recruiting centers to fight for jihad in Afghanistan. The rights of non-Muslims were severely restricted. Devout military officers were favored in promotions. While Musharraf advanced during Zia's rule, he later harshly criticized the dictator. He blasted Zia's regime for the use of lashing, pointing out: "I noticed that only the poor were given this punishment—those who were involved in petty crimes. The rich and the influential involved in large-scale crime and corruption managed to avoid this particular form of justice."[2] Musharraf was critical of Zia's hypocrisy, noting that Zia outlawed music while apparently "in private he personally enjoyed good semi classical music."[3] Musharraf's observations, published in 2006, provide an insight into how he viewed his own narrative about himself as president.

One precious political asset eluded Zia, legitimacy. The downside anytime the military stages a coup somewhere is that while guns can trump votes in seizing power, gaining real authority requires legitimacy, recognition by a populace that those with power are properly entitled to exercise it. Dictators scheme to convince the people that they are always doing the right thing. They argue that despite appearances, they are true democrats at heart and earnestly hope to restore democracy, only now is not the right time. It is an awkward dance that usually is settled at the end of a gun barrel.

But dictators keep trying. For that reason, even these politicians don't *think* in terms of strategic communication. They engage in it. Zia was no exception. He was going to do as he pleased, but he wanted the people to agree that he was the right leader. Certain that voters would see the light in 1984, Zia held a referendum to consolidate and legitimize his rule. Zia's faction won more than 95 percent of the votes, less than what Joseph Stalin used to garner in the Soviet Union but still a decent majority. What makes these election exercises amusing is how dictators try to outwit everyone by asking for a vote on a point from which they can extrapolate a desired message. Zia wisely avoided asking voters what they thought of him. Instead, the referendum asked voters if they supported Islam as the ideology of Pakistan.

As Fatima Mullick and Mehrunnisa Yusuf of the Quilliam Foundation observed in an extremely insightful assessment of Pakistan,

> An affirmative answer was assumed to mean endorsement of the regime. Consequently, all parties except the Jamaat-i-Islami were de-legitimized and scores were arrested and tortured. The press was heavily censored and journalists publicly flogged, the incipient women's movement was attacked, assaulted and arrested, educational syllabi were "Islamized" to endorse Jihadism, laws were introduced to make adultery a crime against the state, stoning to death was prescribed as a punishment, and the testimony of women was reduced to half the value of men.[4]

Zia's rule meant rough times for Benazir. In March 1981 she was arrested and imprisoned several times, apparently on suspicion that she had participated with her brother Mir in the hijacking of a Pakistan International Airlines plane. She suffered through house detention, then imprisonment in Karachi Central Jail and the Sukkur jail.[5] She would particularly remember the five months she spent in solitary confinement during 1981 in the Sukkur jail, where interior temperatures reached more than 120 degrees. Her health suffered. She received no medical care.[6] Her friend, ambassador Peter Galbraith, then working with the U.S. Senate Foreign Relations Committee, persuaded the committee to intervene, and pressure from Washington secured her release.[7] Galbraith's efforts saved her life.

The unsavory details of Benazir's time in prison illuminate why, in 2007, some military and intelligence leaders were fearful of payback should she regain power. Libby Hughes's biography of Benazir recounts:

Benazir was flown out of Karachi to Sukkur jail, far away in the Thar Desert. Here, her cell seemed more like a cage, with barred doors on two sides and barred windows on four sides. At night, there was no electricity, and she shivered as the cold winds swept across the desert and whipped through the open bars of her cell. Without blankets or warm clothing, the cold bothered her, making it hard to sleep on the rope cot.[8]

It was a difficult time. Her health was at risk:

Within her jail cell, Benazir was suffering from a different kind of torture. The daytime heat in May soared to 120 [degrees Fahrenheit]. . . . The hot desert dust swirled into her cell, crusting her face. Her skin cracked and peeled, and unsightly blisters appeared on her face. Without the proper diet, her hair began to fall out in clumps, too.[9]

As to her jailors, they "began suggesting suicide as a way to end her physical suffering. They told her that her party leaders were deserting her."[10]

Mary Anne Weaver adds: "From time to time, one or another of her guards would leave a bottle of poison in her cell. If General Zia had a purpose in mind in subjecting her to all this, it was apparently to break her and to humiliate the Bhutto family."[11] In 1993, Benazir's memory of the nightmare remained vivid: "Even now, though so many years have passed, I shudder when I think of it. . . . It was like being buried alive in a grave. You live, yet you don't live. The days turn into months. You grow older, but there's no measure—nothing is a landmark."[12] She has described her most harrowing moment:

> The day that a jail official told me—falsely—that I was to be tried inside the jail, by a special military tribunal, and sentenced to death. I was stunned—I couldn't believe that they'd do it, though one side of me said that they would. A few hours later, someone left a bottle of poison inside my cell.[13]

Her father's murder, Zia's persecution of Shias, and his ruthless efforts to break her spirit and destroy her family left a lasting mark, but Benazir was a woman of immense personal strength. Undaunted, after her release she decided to establish herself as a national leader. To proceed, however, she needed a husband. Pakistani culture would not countenance a single woman leading a political movement. Although opposed in principle to arranged marriages, she opted for one. It was, she explained, "the price in personal choice I had to pay for the political path my life had taken. My high profile in Pakistan precluded the possibility of my meeting a man in the normal course of events, getting to know him, and then getting married."[14]

Astonishing her friends, she chose a playboy named Asif Ali Zardari, best known for polo and a fast lifestyle. She described him admiringly in her autobiography as "the heir to the chiefdom of the one hundred thousand-strong Zardari tribe."[15] Zardari is personally well liked by his friends and many journalists who have covered him, but he has drawn controversy. Writing in the *New York Times*, John Burns presented a different view: "[B]y the Bhuttos' standards, Zardari's family was of modest means, with limited holdings and a rundown movie theater in Karachi. Zardari's only experience of higher education was a stint at a commercial college in London."[16]

Her future security adviser and current Pakistani interior minister Rehman Malik played middleman in the marital negotiations, which took place in

London. After their first meeting, Zardari sent her roses, mangoes, and candy. Although rumors abounded that her cosmopolitan sophistication had made finding her a match with a proper Muslim somewhat challenging, those who knew her well say that despite tensions that arose later, she was besotted with him. One journalist and close friend to Benazir, who would speak only off the record, observed: "She was very apprehensive about marrying him. It was a political move. But then she fell in love with him. It was remarkable."

Within seven days, she agreed to become engaged. He gave her a heart-shaped ring of sapphires and diamonds. In 1987 they married.[17] Amid the thicket of accusations to follow and throughout his many years behind bars, she stood up for him staunchly. For political reasons, she needed a husband. But people change and politics is corrosive. The process can turn normal people into caricatures of themselves. The Benazir who served as prime minister was a different woman than the student who lit up Radcliffe and Oxford. Reflecting on the accusations of corruption that would afflict her second term, the same journalist concluded that Benazir became "a woman brought low by her man."

Benazir would always contest the accusations, but there is no avoiding the fact that many who knew her well, deeply admired her, and counted themselves as her friends remained deeply skeptical about Zardari and his influence upon Benazir.

Chapter 8

PRIME MINISTER AT THIRTY-FIVE

On August 14, 1988, Zia ul-Haq died in a mysterious plane crash after visiting a firing range at Tamewali, near Bahawalpur. There he had watched troops in a U.S. M1 Abrams tank miss all ten of their targets. The fatalities in the crash included U.S. ambassador Arnold Raphel and Brig. Gen. Herbert Wassom. Power devolved to two Zia confederates—Inter-Services Intelligence chief Gen. Hamid Gul and Chief of Army Staff Gen. Mirza Aslam Beg—who were committed Islamists. The two radicals controlled Pakistani security policy. A third player was the nation's seventy-three-year-old president, Gen. Ghulam Ishaq Khan. A major player, Khan's office wielded constitutional authority to appoint and dismiss prime ministers.

The cause of the crash remains a mystery. Relevant to Pakistani political thinking, some Pakistanis perceive it was a U.S. conspiracy. As evidence, they point to the fact that the Federal Bureau of Investigation (FBI) was ordered to stand down from conducting a detailed investigation or to demand autopsies (although Pakistan didn't, either). Pakistani Brig. Mohammad Yousaf has argued that these U.S. actions led to a cover-up. Aside from dampening the investigation, in his view the U.S. government's appointment of Robert Oakley as the new U.S. ambassador was revealing, since "he could be relied upon to sit on the lid of the can."[1] Others suspect that an ally of the Bhutto family or the Soviet security service (the KGB) or elements of the Pakistani military might have been responsible for the crash. Yousaf dismisses these ideas as implausible and insists that the death of the two Americans was unintentional.[2]

Yousaf's book mainly presents an interesting analysis of the war against the Soviets. But its accusatory opening chapter on Zia's death underscores Pakistani political paranoia. The United States has been and remains a favorite target for such thinking. His cynicism is common. While events in Afghanistan and Pakistan today present current challenges in dealing with Pakistanis, the tensions are long-standing.

Zia had previously scheduled elections. Gul reluctantly concluded that a semblance of civilian government was necessary and announced that the elections would be held. In a devious move, Zia had set Election Day in November to neutralize Benazir's ability to campaign. His sources had informed him that Benazir was expecting a baby, and Christina Lamb recounts that Zia had anticipated Benazir would be unable to campaign. "But for once she had out-witted him. Knowing his spies would obtain her medical records, she had managed to have them swapped and [she] was actually due in September."[3]

Nothing was quite what it seemed. The generals thought democracy was fine as long as they could pick the election winner in advance. Their game plan was to manipulate the polls, not rig them. That kept things tidy, which Gul and Beg thought desirable. The military funded and controlled a coalition of religious parties under the banner of the Islami Jamhoori Ittehad (IJI), or "Islamic Democratic Alliance." Its members included the Jamaat-e-Islami and its leader, Qazi Hussain Ahmed. When the Islamist balked, Gul forced Ahmed to back his chosen candidate by threatening to withhold the government's support as partners in Afghanistan and future jihad operations.[4]

Against them stood the thirty-five-year-old Benazir Bhutto. Returning to Pakistan, she was welcomed home with a spontaneous outpouring of grassroots support. Her chief causes were restoring democracy and social justice. The Pakistan Peoples Party was the underdog, and its members knew that they confronted a formidable machine that would say or do anything to win. Their forecast proved accurate. Although General Beg had personally promised Benazir that elections would be free and fair,[5] he and Gul disenfranchised a fifth of traditional PPP voters—namely, impoverished farmers and working-class citizens in towns and cities—by turning away from the polls all voters who lacked a national identification card.[6] This action deprived 20 percent of registered voters their right to vote, and these mainly poor farmers and urban workers were core constituencies of the PPP.[7]

The IJI distorted the issues and launched a no-holds-barred personal smear campaign. Ambassador Husain Haqqani wrote that

> Gul and his deputy, Brigadier Imtiaz Ahmed [Billa], tried to rile Islamists with inflammatory statements such as: "The ISI has intelligence that Benazir Bhutto has promised the Americans a rollback of our nuclear program. She will prevent a mujahedeen victory in Afghanistan and stop plans for jihad in Kashmir in its tracks."[8]

Gul's presenting the IJI as the guardians of Pakistan's nuclear program sent a powerful message, which highlights reservations that would arise in 2007, when Benazir announced that she was disposed to make A. Q. Khan available to the International Atomic Energy Agency for interrogation and would hold parliamentary hearings about the nuclear program. Pakistan's nuclear program was as sensitive an issue then as now.

Fatwas circulated that denounced the concept of having a woman as prime minister. Leaflets appeared featuring doctored photographs of Benazir dancing in a Paris nightclub. Candidates were advised to brand her a security risk. Posters labeled Benazir and her mother "Gangsters in Bangles" and superimposed their heads on figures of women in swimsuits who were riding bicycles. They dredged up a photograph of her mother dancing with President Gerald Ford and spread more rumors that Benazir would be a U.S. puppet.[9]

Benazir's close friend and counselor, Mark Siegel, is a sophisticated political strategist and a former executive director of the U.S. Democratic National Committee. The skullduggery of Gul and company astonished even this seasoned veteran. He recalls:

> You know how we sometimes say your opponents will do *anything* to win? They gave new meaning to that concept. Four weeks before the election, the Nawaz Sharif coalition, ISI and their PR [public relations] flacks met. They realized that the smear campaign against

Benazir was not working. That's when they concocted the strategy of discrediting her by attacking her husband, Asif Ali Zardari. They decided to label him "Mr. Ten Percent." That's where the moniker came from. It was mud, but it stuck. A month before the election, a month before he could even be Mr. One Percent, they had painted him as corrupt. They also hatched a scheme to call her best friend in the States the "Executive Director of the Hindu Zionist Lobby in America." They were something else.[10]

Charges of dirty tricks did not faze the military. It was a political campaign, but "campaign," after all, is a term of war. Keeping a straight face, General Beg would subsequently insist: "It was one of Pakistan's fairest ever elections. Not one man was killed."[11]

As Election Day rolled around, the anti-Benazir team was missing just one thing: votes. The PPP won a popular majority of the votes. Ambassador Galbraith recalls the victory as one of the great triumphs of democracy. (A distinguished diplomat, in 2009, his refusal to countenance election fraud in Afghanistan's presidential election exposed the willful incompetence of the United Nations.) Galbraith makes the point that in taking on Zia's cronies and Pakistan's ruthless military and intelligence apparatus, Benazir not only demonstrated unique courage, but in winning, she also made it triumphantly clear that Pakistan's people wanted a democratic form of government. He says,

It was an extraordinary thing. I was with her on the greatest day of her life: November 16, 1988, the day she won as Prime Minister. That was the cap of an eleven-year struggle from the moment her father was arrested through the nightmare of the trial and his execution and her own imprisonment. In 1981, the Reagan Administration prohibited the U.S. embassy in Islamabad from even contacting the Bhutto family. This was the cold war. Washington thought she was a leftist and anti-American. They under-estimated her. She charmed people. She persuaded them that she understood American concerns. She talked with a candor that people found amazing. It had an impact and she made a difference. By the time that she won in 1988, the Reagan administration told the military they had to have her.[12]

Galbraith declares:

People could make their voices heard. She led Pakistan to a historic victory that showed what was possible. She was the embodiment of hope. Her great achievement was the restoration of democracy. It was an achievement she had *twice*, in 1988 and 2007. In both cases it was the culmination of a long struggle and in 2007, one she paid for with her life.[13]

The game, however, was not over. Pakistan had a parliamentary system whose prime minister was selected by Parliament, not by a direct vote of the people. The PPP had secured only 92 of 215 seats in the lower house. This number was substantially more than any other party had won, but it represented only a plurality. Once again, deadlock gripped Pakistani politics. Gul and Beg struggled to cobble together a coalition government led by the religious parties. Benazir tried to see President Khan, but Khan stonewalled. His game was to afford Gul and Beg every opportunity to fix the results. Their inability to pull it off reveals how weak their position had become.

Benazir caught a lucky break when U.S. Secretary of State George Shultz had appointed Oakley as the new U.S. ambassador to Pakistan. Although, as Mark Siegel remarked, "seven years earlier she couldn't even get an appointment with him," suddenly Washington was whistling a new pro-democracy tune.[14] No stranger to tight corners, Oakley understood the state of play in Pakistan. He bided his time. When two weeks had elapsed without the formation of a government, Oakley pounced. He made a formal call on President Khan and suggested politely—but with steel in his voice—that it would be a good idea to designate Benazir Bhutto as prime minister. Khan acceded.

Gul and Beg were infuriated but stymied. Oakley's intervention undercut their ability to block a PPP government. They quickly changed their tactics and maneuvered to limit her power. The inexperienced Benazir was understandably nervous. For her first meeting with these generals, she insisted that Oakley accompany her. A breakthrough was achieved. The generals agreed to let her take office, on three conditions: leave the army alone, avoid meddling in Afghan affairs, and don't interfere with the nuclear weapons program.[15] At Oakley's insistence, she retained the current foreign minister, who was perceived as close to the United States. On December 2, 1988, she was sworn in. Once again, U.S. backing counted with Pakistan's military.

The military did not accept defeat gracefully. The day she set foot in the prime minister's suite of offices, she found them completely stripped. The president had appropriated all of the official files. Her riposte was ingenious. She gathered up her close staff, and they flew to Downing Street for a crash course on how to run a prime minister's office.

It was a tough time for Benazir. Despite a pledge of cooperation from the military, tensions were manifest. Phone calls were misdirected and files went missing. The ISI blackmailed her servants and compelled them to inform on Bhutto and her associates.[16] Her tenure proved deeply frustrating. Her status as a rookie showed. Husain Haqqani points out that not only was this post her first experience in government but also many PPP members with government experience had been co-opted by the military, leaving "only inexperienced radicals or idealists to serve at her side."[17] A hostile military and sniping Islamists, who questioned her faith, didn't help.[18] Several religious edicts were issued, declaring "that a woman could not be head of government in an Islamic country." Qazi Hussain Ahmed chimed in, denouncing her as decadent and Western.[19]

Assessing Benazir's career after her assassination, Christina Lamb, a fervent admirer, observed that aside from dealing with a hostile military-intelligence establishment, Bhutto had to contend with her own troublesome supporters. Many of them focused on making money rather than lifting up their nation. That situation substantially contributed to limiting her achievements:

> After years of dictatorship, everyone expected jobs and patronage from those now in power. Her followers regarded her as Queen

Bountiful. Everywhere she went she was mobbed by supporters waving petitions demanding jobs as recompense for their sacrifices during martial law. Under 11½ years of dictatorship an awful lot of people had suffered for the PPP. With the treasury coffers empty, she could satisfy few of them.

As I reported at the time: "Bhutto already has the biggest cabinet in Pakistan's history and an entire battalion of advisers, known locally as the 'Under19 team' or 'Incompetence Incorporated.'"

This is not patronage politics, however. In the new government's terminology it is people's politics. When ministers ignore their government work to spend all day arranging jobs for their voters and licences for their patrons, this is not corruption or nepotism it is people's government. Using the same ploy, they have renamed many of the country's schools as people's schools, and thus claim to have created thousands of new schools.[20]

Benazir was playing against tough adversaries who wanted to get rid of her, not deal with her. Misjudgments—such as failing to court Khan, who might have proven more amicable—hurt.[21] Some fault her for failing to appoint able advisers. Lamb, then covering her for the *Financial Times,* believes that she had such strong popular support that she could have achieved far more than she did. Other skeptics feel that rather than capitalize on her moral authority to provide progressive leadership, she defensively shrouded herself in a chador, prayed at the tombs of saints, and got nothing done while a cloud of corruption began to hover over her inner circle.

Siegel, who bore witness to Benazir's challenges, acknowledges that she made her share of mistakes. But, Siegel contends, her achievements were impressive:

She set up women's development banks. She joked that the banks were for women, run by women—but, always tolerant, they would take men's money. She set up police stations manned by women, because she knew that women would talk only to women. She was the first person to appoint women to the judiciary. Pakistani women had been banned from competing in Olympic sports. She changed that. She was from rural Sindh. She thought beyond the urban salon chatterbox base of the intelligentsia. She knew that women lacked choice and nutrition. She put together a cadre of 100,000 women health workers and they spread out from village to village teaching about maternal health and child nutrition and birth control. She built 46,000 primary and secondary schools. She electrified most of the villages in rural Pakistan.[22]

Among the most frequent criticisms lodged against Benazir was her failure to repeal the draconian *Zina* (fornication) ordinance that degraded women.[23] Siegel acknowledges Benazir left this task undone. "The issue was close to her heart," he says. "But it couldn't be done. Not by her, not at that time. She lacked the support. Tackling that issue would have brought down her government without eliminating that law. You do what you can." Ironically, Musharraf got this job done, repealing the Zina law in July 2006.[24]

Her opponents worked overtime to destroy her. Although Husain Haqqani suggests that Jamaat-e-Islami and Qazi Hussain Ahmed led the IJI election alliance,[25] the power player was Nawaz Sharif, who would have become prime minister had the IJI prevailed in the election. Nawaz was an industrialist whom Zia ul-Haq had appointed chief minister of Punjab. Tariq Ali writes that this longtime political rival and foe of Benazir's, along with his brother, netted more than $3 billion from politics in a nation enveloped by corruption "like a sheet of water."[26]

Backed by the military, Nawaz busied himself by stirring up violence in the Sindh on the pretext of demanding provincial autonomy.[27] As head of the government in Pakistan's largest province, he wasted no time encouraging the religious parties to question her philosophy, while playing to anti-Sindh prejudices among the Punjabis.[28]

Gul and Beg also labored ceaselessly to create trouble. They had imagination and knew what they were doing. People think gangsters are always stupid. Actually they can be extremely clever. Gul and Beg understood strategic communication. In a devious gambit they ignited a firestorm over Salman Rushdie's *The Satanic Verses*, whipping up clerics into a frenzy. The clerics chanted slogans denouncing the "Crusader-Zionist conspiracy."[29] The controversy went global and forced Rushdie to secure bodyguards. In Tehran, Ayatollah Ruhollah Khomeini blasted the United States over the matter.

At home, Benazir faced other mounting roadblocks. In Islamabad, the ISI-backed Islamists attacked the U.S. Information Agency (USIA) building and denounced Benazir as too pro-American. She further alienated the military when she refused to lend credibility to General Beg's obvious lie about whether Pakistan had broken a promise to the United States to limit uranium enrichment while Zia ul-Haq was president.

Determined to fight back, Benazir tried to block Hamid Gul from succeeding Beg upon his retirement, set for 1991. They outmaneuvered her. Allegedly, in revenge, Gul plotted to have her assassinated. According to one account, he recruited Osama bin Laden for the job. Reportedly, bin Laden was amenable, providing the generals guaranteed Nawaz succeeded her.[30] In May 1989, she discovered the plot, fired Gul as ISI chief, and replaced him with Lt. Gen. Shamsur Rehman Kallue, a PPP ally. Unwilling to back down, Beg countermanded her instruction. Throughout her tenure, the military privately conducted its own foreign policy and came within a whisker of provoking a new war with India. Only U.S. intervention averted that one. Benazir was prime minister, but the military declined to disclose or discuss with her its plans or actions. Their secrecy imposed a major constraint on her ability to govern.

That was notably true of Pakistan's nuclear program as well. In 1987, A. Q. Khan had blown the cover off of it, bragging to an Indian journalist that Pakistan had the bomb. In Benazir Bhutto's mind, apparently that revelation provided no confirmation of how developed the nuclear program was. Though curious, she could obtain little information. She was allowed to visit Kahuta, where she received an overview of the weapons' development, but access to secrets was denied. Quoting Gen. Feroz Khan, Douglas Frantz and Catherine Collins state: "She was in the picture of what was going on with the bomb, but only to an extent."[31] A report prepared for Secretary of Defense Dick Cheney concluded as well that she lacked influence over the program.[32]

Benazir resolved to find out the truth, a decision that may have brought matters with a hostile military to a head. She was hoping to persuade Washington to sell Pakistan sixty F-16s. The hitch was that the aircraft was capable of carrying a nuclear warhead. As noted earlier, in 1985, Congress had passed an amendment to the Foreign Aid Act sponsored by Senator Larry Pressler that prohibited the U.S. government from providing foreign aid to Pakistan unless the president could stipulate that Pakistan did not possess a nuclear explosive device. In one of history's ironic twists, Peter Galbraith, then working for the Senate Foreign Relations Committee, had written the language of the original amendment, which Senators Alan Cranston and John Glenn had sponsored. Senator Larry Pressler kept Galbraith's language but watered down some of his conditions.[33] In a second irony, the amendment was a pro-Pakistan action, although years later, in a losing bid for reelection, Pressler drew large financial support from the Indian-American community, which had thought he had been tough on Pakistan. Anxious for Pakistani support against the Soviets in Afghanistan, meanwhile, the Ronald Reagan administration did not accept the tougher version.

On June 5, 1989, CIA director William Webster held a meeting with Benazir Bhutto at Blair House. There he showed her a scale model of the Chinese model that A. Q. Khan was using for Pakistan's nuclear device and explained that the Americans knew its dimensions and could monitor the enrichment level that Pakistan's centrifuges produced. Surprised, Benazir asked for specific guidance as to how Pakistan could avoid Pressler Amendment sanctions. She was told that as long as the enriched uranium remained in a gaseous form and no core was created, there would be no "nuclear explosive device." Developing a metallized core, however, would cross the line. She pledged to keep that from occurring.[34] President George H. W. Bush told her the following day that her commitment was sufficient to enable him to certify that Pakistan did not violate the Pressler Amendment.

Although Benazir had made her commitment, the Pakistani military had its own agenda. It pressed forward with the development of its nuclear program. In 1990, Peter Galbraith and Mark Siegel took back channels and reported to Benazir that gaseous uranium had been metallized and a core created. The line had been crossed. Consequently, the Bush administration would not certify on September 30 of that year that Pakistan did not possess a nuclear explosive device; thus all aid would cease. Siegel remarked, "Benazir was shocked and argued that it couldn't be true, that it contradicted her specific instructions." A few days after Galbraith and Siegel left for Washington, Benazir confronted the military, which confessed to conducting the conversion from gas to metal.[35] In fact, Pakistani scientists had converted highly enriched uranium gas into 275 pounds of bomb-grade heavy metal and had machined it into perfect spheres that constituted the cores of atomic bombs. There was enough to make six to eight bombs.[36]

Angry at her meddling, the military decided to oust Bhutto. They worried about how Washington might react, but U.S. attention was diverted by the looming conflict with Iraq over Kuwait. They grabbed the opening. On August 6, 1990, while the world focused on Saddam Hussein's invasion of Kuwait, President Khan fired her as prime minister.[37] His action left her extremely bitter toward the military and intelligence services, which she felt should have leveled with her about its actions in moving ahead with the nuclear program. It would be one more reason that many of these figures opposed her return in 2007.

New elections were called for October 24. This time the generals got their act together and backed Nawaz. Gul and the ISI managed Nawaz's campaign, which spread new rumors that Benazir was a security risk to the protection of nuclear secrets and had pro-India proclivities.[38] Benazir adviser Mark Siegel was her Washington representative and speechwriter. He had advised her during the previous election and had helped press Congress to demand that Pakistan recognize her victory so that she could take office as prime minister. During her term as prime minister, his closeness to Bhutto had become well publicized. It was not helpful with Pakistan voters. The religious parties ridiculed him as "Benazir's Jew," while lambasting her as fronting a U.S.-Zionist conspiracy.[39] The tactics were underhanded, but Benazir and Siegel maintained their sense of humor. Her opponents' dirty tricks would not stop her.

Vote rigging hamstrung the new elections. Benazir's opponents went for broke. Their strategy worked. They held the PPP to eighteen seats. Nawaz became the new prime minister. The bombastic Pakistan Muslim League leader spent more of his first term in backroom plotting than in problem solving. But his period in office was beset by crises. Matters came to a head when Ramzi Yousef attempted to blow up the World Trade Center in February 1993. Yousef was a Pakistani and an ISI trainee. The U.S. government pressured Nawaz to shut down ISI-backed militant training camps and to crack down on the ISI. Nawaz tried, but the ISI simply shifted the camps from Pakistan to eastern Afghanistan.

An impatient President Khan accused Nawaz of incompetence, nepotism, and corruption. Nawaz fired Khan. Khan fired Nawaz. The deadlock was broken only when the new COAS, Gen. Wahid Kakar, who had taken office in January 1993, forced both to step aside.

New elections in October 1993 replayed the previous contest. This time, the PPP prevailed. Prime Minister Benazir Bhutto had learned more about politics, but far less than she imagined. Despite her vigorous denials, critics argued that her idealism had slipped away and that, obsessed with her prior dismissal, she behaved arrogantly and disdained liberal politics.

Since the president retained the power to dismiss the prime minister, she chose carefully, selecting an apparent PPP ally, Farooq Leghari, for the post. She handed him the foreign affairs portfolio in exchange for his commitment never to exercise his constitutional power to remove her from office. Her new director general for military operations was Pervez Musharraf. He got right to work, setting up or forging links to jihadi groups:[40]

Jamaat-e-Islami (JI, Islamic Party), which he helped to provide fighters for Kashmir[41]

Ulema Islam (Assembly of Islamic Clergy), which funneled students into military training

Markaz Dawa al Irshad (MDI, Center for Preaching and Guidance), which built a university campus near Lahore with $1 million in financial support reportedly from bin Laden. Its military wing, Lashkar-e-Taiba (LeT, Army of the Pure), was renamed Jamat ul Dawa (Group of the Call to Islam). Under Musharraf's patronage, it became Pakistan's largest jihadi organization, and it maintains 2,200 offices nationwide and some two dozen camps from which to launch fighters.[42] A secretive organization that conceals the real identities of its key officials, its recruits have high-quality weapons and state-of-the-art technology.[43]

Ahmed Rashid reports that Bhutto, anxious to curry favor with a still hostile military, supported Musharraf's embrace of the Taliban. Somewhat disingenuously, she would later plead naïveté.[44] Rashid says that she supported the Taliban's formation in 1996.[45] At the time, the ISI was still working closely with former mujahideen leader Gulbuddin Hekmatyar, who Gen. Stanley McChrystal would later identify as a key Taliban leader in 2010.[46] Although Benazir forged ties to elements within the ISI, the relationship remained uneasy. As Tony Clifton wrote, "In fact, during her reigns fundamentalism and the Taliban prospered."[47]

In the land of political conspiracies, there were plenty afoot. Benazir discovered that the ISI had created a slush fund that had been used to oppose her in the 1990 elections. In September 1995, she also discovered that Maj. Gen. Zahir ul-Islam Abbasi, director general of the infantry corps at the Pakistan Army High Command, was plotting a new coup to overthrow her, although eventually they got her out after Leghari dismissed her.

How does one assess her second term as prime minister? Her strategic communication was poor. She left office haunted by charges of corruption and incompetence. Prosecutors hounded her husband. She rejected advice from a close and savvy senior counsel to deal with the criticisms instead of ignoring them. In his words, Benazir's unwillingness to confront corruption charges caused unnecessary grief for both herself and the country:

> The charges presented Benazir with her own problem in strategic communication. The key question was not whether her or husband's actions would pass muster in another country. It was whether what either did violated Pakistani law. Her point was, they broke no laws. I said to her: come clean with the facts, lay everything out, let people see and make their own judgments. That approach would

have strengthened her position considerably. Her failure to do that was unfortunate.[48]

Years later, as she prepared to return in 2007, polling showed that while Benazir was the most popular political leader, doubts persisted as to whether she was putting herself or Pakistan first. These attitudes show that inadequate strategic communication can have a lasting effect.

On her policies and her performance as an executive, her supporters and opponents divide sharply. Critics contend that in Washington and London, she spoke eloquently about reform, democracy, and equality for women but did little to put her ideas into practice at home. In Islamabad, they say, she was egotistical and ineffective. *New York Times* reporter John Burns wrote that

> when she took office as prime minister again, after a victory in 1993, Bhutto struck many of her friends as a changed person, obsessed with her dismissal in 1990, high-handed to the point of arrogance, and contemptuous of the liberal principles she had placed at the center of her politics in the 1980s. "She no longer made the distinction between the Bhuttos and Pakistan," said Hussain Haqqani, Bhutto's former press secretary. "In her mind, she was Pakistan, so she could do as she pleased."[49]

Burns reported that during this period, Karachi street wars scared off foreign investors. Inflation climbed to 20 percent. Perhaps 70 percent of its 130 million people were illiterate. Millions lacked proper shelter, schools, hospitals, or safe drinking water. Benazir spent much of her time negotiating loans to stave off default on more than $62 billion in public debt.[50]

In her previous terms, in Tony Clifton's words,

> Benazir talked a good game about everything from improving education of women, raising the incomes of the rural poor, land reform, stamping out corruption and limiting the power of the Mullahs, to grandiose schemes like running gas and oil pipelines from Central

Asian Islamic republics like Afghanistan, Kazakhstan and Uzbekistan through to refineries and loading jetties on the warm coasts of southern Pakistan.[51]

She never realized any of these aims.

Critics focused much of their fire on her husband for allegedly corrupt practices. While a verdict on the guilt or innocence of Benazir or Zardari falls outside the scope of this book, the existence of these allegations, the controversy they generated, and their political impact matter. They affected the military's perspective of Benazir as prime minister and the Pakistanis' attitudes toward her when she returned in 2007. Musharraf believed she was corrupt and that belief affected his perspective. Certainly the allegations concerned her. As noted earlier, she viewed passage of the National Reconciliation Ordinance, which insulated her from criminal prosecution, as essential so that she could return home and contest the 2008 elections.

Later, Zardari and Benazir strenuously denied all allegations of corruption. She wrote,

Despite years of political harassment and subsequent witch-hunts by successive Pakistani dictators in a bid to destroy my reputation both within Pakistan and abroad, not a single charge filed against my husband or myself was proven in a court of law. Yet as one charge was dismissed, another was filed. As bail was granted in one court, it was denied in another. My husband and I ultimately came to spend more time and energy defending ourselves against contrived charges in courts all over the country than we could spend fighting to re-establish democracy in our homeland. But that was clearly the point of the exercise. We were being pressured to quit politics, or be eliminated through judicial manipulation so that the only force left to form a national government would be the military establishment.[52]

It's apparent that Nawaz Sharif worked tirelessly to discredit her. He did not hesitate to have her prosecuted in an effort to disable her politically. The

Bhuttos' 1999 conviction by the Lahore High Court for corruption was over-turned in 2003 precisely because politics had rigged the result.

Husain Haqqani supports Benazir's contention that political corruption has been a familiar tool in Pakistani politics used to discredit the opposition. In 1988, he was aligned with Nawaz. Haqqani declares:

> As in several other third world countries, corruption and nepotism are endemic in Pakistan. The civil service and military officers enjoy vast amounts of perquisites and privileges and are not above corruption. Politicians, because they are out of power (and occasionally in prison) for long periods of time and are insecure about their tenures in office, tend to line their pockets with money from graft and kickbacks. There is no excuse for corruption, and many officials in Pakistan—whether political appointees or permanent employees of the state—remain incorruptible and are recognized in society for their honesty. It must be said, however, that as part of its justification for its own intervention in politics, Pakistan's military has made a concerted effort since the 1950s to paint politicians and political activists as corrupt. In the period of partial civilian rule beginning in 1988, corruption charges were frequently bandied about, making it easier to get rid of politicians who did not otherwise see eye to eye with the security establishment.[53]

A competing view about the financial dealings of Benazir and her husband portrays a more ominous picture. The widely held perception of their corruption damaged their credibility. Zardari's moniker Mr. Ten Percent may have stemmed from the ISI's election smear in 1988. But his critics believe it was well merited. Benazir Bhutto's own brother Murtaza dubbed him "Asif Baba and the 40 Thieves."[54] Imprudently, Benazir had appointed Zardari her investment minister. Reporting solely to her, he had been responsible for all domestic and international investment offers to Pakistan.[55]

Allegations that Zardari enriched Benazir and himself through government kickbacks surfaced at home and abroad.[56] The press exposed their acquisition of a new, twenty-room mansion, with two farm lodgings and staff accommodation, in Surrey, England, on 350 acres, dubbed Surrey Palace.[57] At first, they denied owning the property. Finally in 2004 Zardari admitted that it was his.[58] His delaying tactics in English courts included claims that he was mentally ill.[59] The case was finally dropped in 2008, but the contradictions in what they asserted, their efforts to postpone the legal proceedings, and Zardari's plea for a delay on account of mental illness raise grave questions as to what really transpired.[60]

New York Times reporter Burns conducted a major investigation into their financial dealings. He disclosed that "in 1995, a leading French military contractor, Dassault Aviation, had agreed to pay Mr. Zardari and a Pakistani partner a $200 million commission for a $4 billion jet fighter deal." Reportedly, the deal foundered only when Benazir was washed out of office. In a second deal, "a leading Swiss company hired to curb customs fraud in Pakistan was paid millions of dollars between 1994 and 1996 to offshore companies controlled by Zardari" and by Nusrat Bhutto. In a third deal, for $10 million, a gold bullion dealer in the Middle East received a monopoly importing the gold that sustained Pakistan's jewelry industry.[61]

Other allegations included the claim that over eight months in 1994 and 1995, Zardari spent $660,000 in jewelry, including $246,000 at Cartier and Bulgari in Beverly Hills "in barely a month."[62] Neither husband nor wife cared to explain how they had that kind of cash handy.

In 2003, a Geneva magistrate found them guilty of money laundering. The verdict was reversed, but the Swiss have talked about a retrial. In 2005, Paul Volcker led an Independent Inquiry Commission into illegal payments to Saddam Hussein's regime arising out of the oil-for-food scandal. Questions emerged as to Benazir Bhutto's involvement in Petroline FZC, which allegedly had traded $144 million of Iraqi oil and made illegal payments of $2 million.[63]

Journalist Lamb considered the financial dealings of Benazir and Zardari a blemish that created huge political problems for the prime minister:

Most of the army's unease about what they referred to derisorily as the "democratic experiment" came from the growing perception that Pakistan had never had such a corrupt government. The central figure was Benazir's husband, Asif, who went from being known as Mr. Ten Percent to Mr. Thirty Percent. As the Financial Times correspondent, I often met foreign businessmen who told me that they were being openly asked for kickbacks to secure government contracts.

"They're about as subtle as a train wreck," said one. When I tried to bring this up with Benazir, her eyes narrowed angrily.[64]

As Benazir Bhutto pointed out, they faced charges at home and abroad. Zardari spent eight years (1996–2004) behind bars as a result of criminal charges at home, until Pakistan's Supreme Court released him on bail.[65]

Complicating matters, during her second term as prime minister, her political life was marked by more personal tragedy. In September 2006, her brother Murtaza was killed in a bizarre shoot-out at a police roadblock on a dark, empty street near his Karachi home. Zardari critics alleged that he had wanted Murtaza out of the way for leading a breakaway faction of the PPP. There was bad blood between the two men, complicated by a family dispute over land.[66]

Though warm and charming socially, some contend that as a public official, she was suspicious of everyone, including her husband. To avoid unnecessary surprises, reportedly she had their phones tapped. One might have supposed that would provoke howls of protest but, as one highly respected journalist notes, she had a temper that intimidated even her most senior advisers.[67] Perhaps it was not surprising that no one challenged her conviction that nothing could, or would, stop her when she wanted to return to Pakistan in 2007.

Her supporters tell a markedly different story about her performance as prime minister, casting her as a valiant leader doing a remarkable job under extremely demanding circumstances. Siegel points to her historic achievement in eradicating polio in Pakistan:

She didn't just do it, she did it in a way that demonstrated fortitude and political skill. She cared passionately about health-care issues for women. She knew people might be afraid. So she made an appearance on national television and administered her own daughter, Aseefa, the first dose of vaccine. She did that with a national audience watching, in front of a thousand women with their babies on the lawn of the Prime Minister's residence. Other women followed suit. Within two years, polio was eliminated from the nation.

Siegel also defends her record in improving the economy:

She was that rarest of people, a true idealist who believed in what she was doing. She quadrupled foreign investment and built power-generating plants all over the country. Her enemies can say what they want about Pakistan's economy, but it was her work that got the World Bank to designate the nation as one of the ten emerging markets in the world. She became, as JFK once said about himself, an idealist without illusions. But over and over again, she put her life on the line for her ideals.[67]

Still, in Pakistan's polarized political environment, there was no way to halt the mounting fusillades of criticism. Her adversaries had the louder voice. On November 5, 1996, President Leghari sacked her and placed Benazir and her husband under house arrest.[69] Murtaza's murder apparently prompted Leghari's action. Benazir's insinuation that it was Leghari who bore responsibility for her brother's death infuriated the president. She later apologized.[70] In 1998, she fled Pakistan and went into exile in Dubai.

Relevant to unraveling Benazir's assassination is what her second term revealed about the person she had become. She finessed questions about her brother's murder. Her enemies took note: She was as tough as nails. Islamists disliked and distrusted her as a woman. They believed that she and Zardari had abused the government out of greed. No one was certain where she would take a stand when she entered a political brawl, which made her unpredictable. Keeping your enemies off balance can be a great strength, but in places like Pakistan it can provoke extreme action.

Amid the sharply conflicting views over her record as prime minister, the military-intelligence establishment remained, as it always had, hostile to the Bhuttos and the PPP. There seemed no reason to doubt that whatever her public posture, she would behave vindictively toward them. They viewed any alliance that enabled her to regain power as unacceptable.

Musharraf considered the tenures of Benazir and Nawaz as prime minister the "dreadful decade of democracy." He felt the experience offered

> quite a few lessons in the high politics of Pakistan. The pattern in my country has been repetitive: elected officials have been vulnerable to corruption and create conditions that lead to an army takeover, while those in opposition and many from other walks of life, particularly the intelligentsia, frequently appeal to the army to take power or change the government.[71]

Musharraf, however, is on all sides of the issue. He castigated both the failure of democracy in Pakistan and martial law under army rule. He drew three key lessons from army rule:

> First, whenever the army gets involved with martial law, it gets distracted from its vital military duties. Military training and operational readiness suffer. Second, when we superimpose martial law and place the military over the civilian government, the latter ceases functioning. When martial law is later lifted, the civilian functionaries remain ineffective. Their growth is stunted. Last, I learned that whatever the law, civil or military, the poor are always victims of oppression. The rich and powerful generally remain above the law.[72]

The ambiguity troubled Musharraf during his presidency. He never did resolve it, either substantively or in his strategic communication.

Chapter 9

MUSHARRAF BATTLES
TO SURVIVE

Nawaz Sharif rebounded as prime minister in 1997 after his party, the Pakistan Muslim League–Nawaz, routed the Pakistan Peoples Party. Tariq Ali contends that, far from cleaning up the government, the Nawaz Sharif family used the opportunity to amass an even greater fortune at the public trough than Bhuttos' critics claimed Benazir and Zardari had done. Indeed, it was an achievement of epic magnitude.[1] While failing to pay his own property taxes, he energetically put the finances of Benazir and her husband under a fiscal microscope. Hoping to finish them politically, his investigators elevated Zardari's reputation from "Mr. Ten Percent"[2] to "Mr. Thirty Percent."[3]

Nawaz promoted Pervez Musharraf over more senior officers to become the chief of army staff. Their lances crossed when Pakistan launched the Kargil War in 1999, and COAS Musharraf and Nawaz blamed each other after total war nearly broke out with India. Musharraf has always denied that Pakistan initiated the offensive or that it was a defeat. He has insisted that Pakistan preempted "India's planned offensive" and actually helped set matters "in the direction of finding a solution to Kashmir."[4]

Others recall the situation as far more precarious. Apparently at Musharraf's suggestion, Nawaz flew to Washington and asked President Bill Clinton to mediate a resolution with India. Perhaps fearful of a nuclear exchange that could obliterate his country, the prime minister even took his entire family with him. Clinton obliged, but he forced Pakistan to pull back troops from the Kashmir territory that it had seized.[5]

Afterward, there was no end to the finger pointing. Focusing on his own strategic communication, Nawaz had articles planted in newspapers blaming the Pakistan Army for Kargil. He even placed a full-page ad in an American newspaper that Musharraf felt maligned the army and created a "divide between it and the government."[6]

The general officer corps was furious with Nawaz and joined a long line of skeptics. It judged Nawaz a poor leader and looked around for a plausible rationale for a coup. Nawaz sensed trouble brewing and turned again to Washington. His key play was offering to help kill bin Laden by allowing U.S. Special Forces to train a Pakistani commando unit that would infiltrate Afghanistan and stage a hit. Nawaz had learned from the Bhuttos' experience. Lacking the power to control the Pakistani generals himself, he hoped that perhaps Washington could ensure restraint. He mounted his own campaign of influence aimed at investing the United States in his government's survival.[7] While not a bad idea, his strategy was not especially deft for holding the military at bay.

Nawaz saw Musharraf as a threat. He made his move as Musharraf traveled to Sri Lanka for its army's fiftieth anniversary celebration. As Musharraf's plane took off, Nawaz signed papers that retired him and appointed Lt. Gen. Ziauddin Butt the new COAS. Nawaz played hardball. He ordered air traffic controllers to deny Musharraf's plane—commercial flight PK 805, which bore two hundred passengers, including Gen. Nadeem Taj—permission to land at Karachi on his return. From the cockpit, Musharraf radioed forces loyal to him and talked to the control tower, cautioning the craft only had a few minutes of fuel left. Air traffic controllers ordered the plane to divert to Nawabshah in Sindh Province, where Nawaz had sent his own jet and security team to seize Musharraf.[8]

Musharraf was lucky. Nawaz's strategy backfired as key military allies got wind of what was happening and rallied. *Newsweek* reporter Zahid Hussain wrote a vivid account of what transpired,[9] which Musharraf's own memoir affirms:

> Lt.-General Mahmood Ahmed, the corps commander at Rawalpindi, and Lt.-General Mohammed Aziz, Chief of General Staff,

were playing tennis when they heard about Sharif's decision. The two generals rushed to the General Headquarters to mobilize their forces for the counter coup. The situation was delicately balanced. Loyalties were not clearly defined. Entrenched in the PM House, General Ziauddin was issuing orders and making new appointments. He was desperately trying to garner the support of the commanders. He sacked both General Aziz and General Mahmood. But it was too late. Brigadier Satti's 111 Brigade had already moved to seal the PM House. There was utter confusion in the country as the state-controlled Pakistan Television went off the air.[10]

Later, on the ground, Musharraf was filmed wearing combat fatigues, smoking a cigarette, and armed with a pistol.[11] Musharraf later discounted the image as atypical of himself. At 10:15 that evening, Pakistan TV announced the dismissal of Nawaz Sharif's government. Early the next morning, Musharraf addressed the nation and, assuming the role of "reluctant coup maker," declared to his countrymen: "I wish to inform you that the armed forces have moved in as a last resort to prevent any further de-stabilization."[12]

Musharraf's actions and words were an excellent use of strategic communication. He rallied the people with a cause and seized the moral high ground. Nawaz provided a perfect scapegoat. Had the prime minister's plot succeeded, innocent lives would have been lost. Musharraf optimistically called upon citizens to look to the future. His instincts were on target. His message resonated. He represented stability, dignity, and integrity. A Pew Global Attitudes Project survey in 2002 showed that by a margin of 76 percent to 16 percent, respondents thought Musharraf had a positive impact on Pakistan.[13] Although conducted two years after the coup, it indicated how well Musharraf managed his strategic communication when he first seized power.

After the coup, the military reclaimed center stage. Nawaz was lucky to escape with his life. Fortunately, he enjoyed close ties to Saudi Arabia. Although convicted of hijacking, he avoided prison through an agreement that exiled him to the Kingdom for ten years.[14]

Musharraf was at the helm of power. He went to great lengths to avoid declaring martial law, which he says he did against the counsel of close army colleagues, including Lt. Gen. Mohammed Aziz and Lt. Gen. Mahmood Ahmed, as well as the corps commanders.[15] Instead, Pakistan would remain a constitutional state with a "transition government."

In his mind, that meant keeping the Constitution operational, "except for a few clauses."[16] Musharraf's loaded language led to significant political problems down the road. In May 2000, the Supreme Court supported Musharraf's actions with two conditions. Elections had to be held in three years and no structural conditions in the Constitution could be introduced. In his memoir, Musharraf quotes Abraham Lincoln to vindicate what he termed his decisions "not to abrogate the constitution and not to impose martial law."[17] Musharraf's autobiography was written for a Western audience, but one gathers that he sincerely believed his words.

The events of 9/11 scrambled Pakistani politics further. Musharraf says Deputy Secretary of State Richard Armitage admonished that the United States would bomb Pakistan "back to the stone age" unless it cooperated in fighting terrorism.[18] Musharraf used the situation to strengthen his ties with Washington and, confronted with a demand to help fight Al Qaeda, his position at home. Warned by Musharraf aides that U.S. criticism of the 2002 referendum to reform the constitution would "undermine his position in the army and make it more difficult to help Washington, Bush administration officials refrained from commenting on the controversy."[19] The strategy worked pretty well. Musharraf's approval rating in opinion polls—which, one should note, were somewhat biased toward urban areas[20]—remained high until 2007, although he never quite established a firm political legitimacy.

Musharraf's first salvo against the judicial branch of Pakistan's government was fired at the Supreme Court in March 2007 when he ousted Iftikhar Chaudhry. An avoidable blunder in strategic communication and politics, his action ignited a firestorm of protests from lawyers. Two years earlier, Musharraf had appointed Iftikhar Chaudhry to the position of chief justice. Chaudhry proved to be a strong advocate for human rights and due process. Accounts vary as to what prompted Musharraf's battle with the judiciary. The conventional wisdom was that Musharraf feared that Chaudhry would obstruct his attempt to win a new term as president. The Constitution prohibited the president from also serving as the COAS. It restricted former military officers from running for pubic office for a period of two years after leaving the service. And it denied anyone from running for a third term as president.

Cogent observers discount that analysis. They contend that Musharraf's political problems could have been finessed. Besides, Musharraf recognized eventually that the trade-off for a new term would be to surrender his position as COAS. Noted scholar and Pakistani analyst Shuja Nawaz believes that Prime Minister Shaukat Aziz may have set off Musharraf by complaining that the court was interfering with civil service promotions.[21] Journalist Ahmed Rashid believes Musharraf became worried by Supreme Court rulings against police abuse and torture, forced marriages, discrimination against women, and high-rise developments that threatened the environment. Owen Bennett Jones also points out that in 2006, the court had blocked a deal to privatize Pakistan Steel Mills that would have enriched government cronies. Above all, however, controversy erupted when the courageous Chaudhry demanded the release of hundreds of "missing" people from Baluchistan and the Sindh Province.[22]

In September 2007 Musharraf amended the Constitution, seizing sweeping powers, setting a date in October for new parliamentary elections, and establishing himself as president. Igniting further controversy, he retained his post as COAS, despite having promised to relinquish it.[23] In the October election, pro-Musharraf parties won the most seats, but Islamic candidates fared better than expected. The parliamentary opposition forced an agreement that gave Musharraf the powers he sought and extended his term until 2007. In exchange, Musharraf promised to step down as COAS by the end of 2005 and to allow Parliament to serve out its five-year term. In late 2004, however, Parliament passed a bill that allowed Musharraf to remain as COAS through the end of his term.[24]

Musharraf's failure to grasp the political blowback from his insistence on holding both jobs illustrated his finite understanding of how his long-term survival required savvy strategic communication. Understandably he wanted to keep his army post, for the COAS is the power center. Politically, there was no way that power grab was going to hold. He made no serious effort to lay out a credible rationale that justified his position. Instead, he muscled his way into extensions in both jobs at the cost of political legitimacy. The move was a huge mistake and he paid for it dearly.

Newsweek journalist Ron Moreau recounts,

> A key problem was that Musharraf didn't have confidence in the political system or in his ability as a politician to keep the power he would give up by leaving the COAS post. Musharraf's biggest problem, and that of most Pakistani military men, is that he both hates and distrusts politicians. He always had to tilt the playing field to his advantage. He wasn't adept at putting together political coalitions. Had he done so, he might well have kept his job and made the politics work.[25]

Offering a similar view, *Newsweek*'s Zahid Hussain remarks, "Musharraf was a typical army person and that was the reason for his downfall. He could not read the minds of the people. He always thought he could control the situation. He misjudged the political situation badly. It came back to haunt him."[26] Shuja Nawaz also points out that Musharraf simply did not trust democracy, with all its "noise and confusion." He "felt strongly that whenever he left office, particularly once he shed his military rank, the country would revert to its Hobbesian state of political anarchy and would need to begin anew the passage to democratic norms."[27]

The Pakistani people saw Musharraf's efforts differently. The military had ruled the nation for half of its existence, and the people wanted to decide the future for themselves. While Musharraf seems sincerely to have seen himself as the "liberal autocrat," he was head of state in a nation that wanted to rid itself of autocrats, not embed them.

Chapter 10

CUTTING THE CARDS

Musharraf's deteriorating political position worried Washington. The United States had pressured him to give up his military position and become a civilian head of state.[1] He had proclaimed himself a "liberal autocrat," but no one was convinced. In the West, he advocated for an Islam of "enlightened moderation" and promoted democracy.[2] In Pakistan, his stubborn insistence on holding both the chief of army staff and presidential slots fueled resentment. He needed to shore up his position.

The United States was committed to Musharraf. President George W. Bush, for whom rapport with foreign leaders mattered a good deal,[3] liked the Pakistani general. The American military felt comfortable with him. Vice President Dick Cheney apparently believed he was America's best bet in South Asia. Musharraf is an easy target for criticism, but he needs to be judged in the context of Pakistan's Byzantine political environment. Only two constituencies really mattered to him—the Pakistan Army and Washington. But his situation was more complicated and nuanced. While he enjoyed military support in many quarters, it was elements of the military and intelligence establishment that almost certainly tried to assassinate him.[4] After 2007 popular discontent escalated sharply as he grew more isolated and out of touch.

Pakistani military expert Shuja Nawaz describes Musharraf as a "sharp and intelligent officer who impressed most of his superiors and had a rich military career, as an artillery commander, staff officer, and then commander of troops."[5] In his own mind Musharraf was a staunch patriot who devoutly believed that given three more years in office he could have set Pakistan on an even keel.[6] He revered Turkish leader Kemal Atatürk, but he was no Atatürk. Many raised sharp voices against him. Shaheen Sehbai acidly observed that he "was an insecure officer, thrown up by his faithful friends. Basically he was a tin pot dictator who was soon to fall into the trappings of palace intrigues to keep him in power at any cost: political, moral, social, religious, national, disintegration."[7]

Musharraf's military background shaped his mind-set. He was not a gifted politician. The Pakistani military meddled in politics and was highly political. Still, a military commander leading a nation as a president is a different matter. He was an autocrat, not a democrat, but his power was not absolute. He operated under wide political, cultural, and institutional constraints.

Musharraf had to stage a delicate balancing act that would have challenged any politician. Competing interests cross-pressured him. The country needed foreign assistance. On that count, Musharraf delivered. After 9/11, Washington cut checks for billions of dollars in exchange for Pakistan's cooperation in battling Al Qaeda. Yet the aid won him few points with the fundamentalist religious parties. Worse, the anti-Islamists never accepted that Musharraf was serious about fighting extremism, although he did support rounding up foreigners tied into Al Qaeda.[8]

Even that commitment raised doubts. Vali Nasr judged that it was democracy, not violent extremism, that most worried the president: "Pakistan's contribution to fighting Al Qaeda is open to question; the Taliban hiding in Pakistan are terrorizing southern Afghanistan; and in Pakistan, there is now more violence, extremism, and instability than when Musharraf took over in 1999."[9] It didn't help that key political allies in the North-West Frontier Province (NWFP)— recently renamed Khyber Pakhtunkhwa—and Baluchistan included religious parties whose views hardly represented the "enlightened moderation" that Musharraf spoke up for in London and Washington. Benazir skeptically groused that "under General Musharraf's regime, the defeated and demoralized Taliban have regrouped and reasserted themselves and now pose a serious threat to the takeover of Pakistan."[10] Pakistani journalist Amir Mir concluded in 2006: "The top military leadership, despite claiming to pursue a liberal political agenda, continues to rely on Islamic fundamentalists as political allies."[11]

Dealing with violent extremism created deep fissures at home. Most Pakistanis worried about the growth of religious extremism and disliked the Taliban, although the problem grew into a major domestic crisis only after 2005. Yet people deeply resented U.S. pressure as an infringement upon their sovereignty and an affront to their pride. Joining George Bush as an ally would have raised hackles. What many saw in Musharraf was a willing accomplice to a foreign power. That stance smelled of betrayal and fed the culture of conspiracy theories. Being too friendly with Washington was a risky business. Two attempts on Musharraf's life in December 2003, carried out by those who viewed him as cozying up too closely with Washington, nearly succeeded.[12]

It is vital to understand the changing mind-set of the Pakistanis toward Al Qaeda, the Taliban, and religious extremism. Many are very hostile to extremists. The International Republican Institute (IRI) reported that as of July 2009, 90 percent of Pakistani respondents considered religious extremism, and 86 percent the "Taliban and Al-Qaeda operating in Pakistan," as a "serious problem in Pakistan."[13] Emmy Award–nominated journalist Gretchen Peters points out that Pakistanis increasingly label the Taliban as gangsters. Indeed, the Taliban have kidnapped hundreds of Pakistanis or extorted money from their families, especially in the North-West Frontier Province. Attitudes have hardened considerably in 2009 amid bloody Taliban attacks launched against the Pakistan Army's general headquarters in Rawalpindi as well as shops or marketplaces in major cities such as Peshawar, Dera Ghazi Khan, and Lahore; the Islamic University in Peshawar; and other targets.

The indiscriminate murders of military personnel and civilians have shaken people up and threatened national stability. Extremists have taken a toll on the country, one that many believe is unappreciated by the outside world. Husain Haqqani has chided U.S. critics, declaring that Pakistan had "lost more lives to terrorism than any other country in the world" and that people "did not recognize the sacrifices rendered by Pakistan."[14]

Musharraf did cooperate with the United States in fighting Al Qaeda, whose members included Arabs, Chechens, Uzbeks, and other non-Pakistanis. He had, Shuja Nawaz reports, no love or affinity for the Taliban or their methods of operation. He was by nature a liberal, Western-oriented individual. He found Taliban methods anathema. But realpolitik dictated his policy. He did what any Pakistani leader would do: work to ensure a Kabul government that was, at a minimum, neutral towards Pakistan and preferably favorable, but under no circumstances favorable to India.[15]

Musharraf avoided targeting Afghan Taliban leaders who refrained from attacking the Pakistani military. Things changed, Shuja Nawaz says, mainly when, at the behest of the United States, Pakistan sent troops into the Federally Administered Tribal Areas (FATA). Many Pakistanis hold the United States responsible for the consequences that have followed.

Ahmed Rashid concurs, adding:

Musharraf was very decisive in dealing with domestic issues, but he acted against the Taliban only under acute pressure from the Americans. The army has never gone against the Afghan Taliban. He was badly advised and misjudged the situation after 2001. He was under the mistaken impression that foreigners drove problems with the Taliban and that one could draw a distinction between the Afghan and Pakistani Taliban. For one thing, the ISI [Inter-Services Intelligence] had no intention of splitting the Taliban and any moderates [in the Taliban] had been betrayed to Mullah Omar. When the Afghan Taliban fled to Pakistan after the Americans invaded Afghanistan, they radicalized the Pakistani Taliban. Until the two failed assassination attempts in December 2003, Musharraf's attitude was to let sleeping dogs lie. Leave the Pakistan Taliban alone and they would leave the government alone. Instead, after 2004, they grew into an increasingly serious threat and challenged the government. Musharraf should have gone after the Taliban immediately while integrating the Pashtuns into the state structure.[16]

In his book *Descent into Chaos*, Rashid had elaborated on the challenge that the government needed to meet:

In reality, what has kept the people marginalized has been the lack of political choices or freedoms. Meaningful development could only follow a change in the political status of FATA, more political freedom for its people, and FATA's entry into the Pakistani mainstream—all of which the army refused to contemplate. Instead, Al Qaeda and the Taliban were carrying out political changes by renaming the region the "Islamic Emirate of Waziristan" and implementing their brutal code of behavior.[17]

He added:

The growth of Taliban sympathies in FATA was also a direct result of gravely misguided policies by [U.S. Secretary of Defense Donald] Rumsfeld and the Pentagon, which treated FATA as a war zone and never insisted that Musharraf offer real political solutions to the people. At the same time, Rumsfeld forced the U.S. military to become captive to Islamabad's whims and fancies. There was no U.S. political strategy for dealing with the army's support to the Taliban or with the real problems of FATA. Pakistan asked for weapons and helicopters, diverting the real issue of its lack of political will to a supposed lack of weapons capability.[18]

The policy that Musharraf, the army, and the ISI developed to maintain influence among the Taliban and Afghan Pashtuns had two tracks—"protecting the Taliban while handing over Al Qaeda Arabs and other non-Afghans to the United States."[19]

One factor that apparently did not influence Musharraf's views about the Taliban was India, although India was and remains a central Pakistani concern. Warning a group of congressmen on Capitol Hill that India is the big elephant in the room, Ambassador Haqqani declared in late 2009 that "Pakistan is wary of the Indo-US relation, which is robust and multifaceted," and advised that the key to winning Pakistan's trust is to "treat Pakistan at par" with its neighbor.[20]

Some, like the counterterrorism expert Michael Scheuer, have argued that:

> minus the U.S. and its allies, Musharraf would [have been] able to fully support the Taliban and its allies, destroy Karzai's government, and re-establish Pashtun rule in Afghanistan. This process would yield a Pakistan-friendly, insular Islamist government in Kabul, the chance of gradually quieting the fierce anti-Islamabad discontent in the Pashtun tribal areas, and the recreation [sic] of a balance of power between Pakistan and India.[21]

Shuja Nawaz discounts India from Musharraf's Taliban equation. He points out that controlling Afghanistan to provide

> strategic depth is a defunct concept put forth by Generals Hamid Gul and Mirza Aslam Beg. Upon their retirement, the military did not favor, support or consider it, and for good reason. It was impractical. The notion that an attack by India would enable Pakistani forces to escape into Afghanistan would serve no purpose. It made no sense. Why would the Indians pursue you? Any conflict would be over if they took Lahore or the cities along the border. That would be the end of Pakistan.[22]

Still, the fear that India could establish a beachhead in Afghanistan from which to undermine Pakistan remains a deep, continuing Pakistani concern. U.S. support for Afghan political figures whom many Pakistanis consider close to India has clearly affected how the Pakistanis view the Taliban and Pakistan's posture toward Hamid Karzai's government.

Americans rightly have zero tolerance for violent extremism and terrorism. Pakistanis dislike being victims of violence as much as Americans do. But understanding the motives behind Musharraf's actions, as well as those of his Pakistani colleagues and the influential political figures with whom he had to contend, requires comprehending what they believed was vital to protecting their nation's security.

In this context, Musharraf went as far as he probably felt was politically possible in Pakistan's political environment. He was an assertive president but did not wield absolute power. Musharraf's warm relationship with the Bush administration left Benazir isolated for eight years in a political desert. Although the United Kingdom was encouraging engagement between Musharraf and Benazir in 2004 and 2005,[23] no one at the State Department would meet or even talk with her except for the Pakistan desk officer, who had no power. Engagement between Musharraf and Benazir and their teams had commenced with five meetings in 2005 and 2006, but nothing concrete was produced.[24]

Attitudes shifted in 2007 as Musharraf's stumbles at home hobbled him politically. State decided to reengage with Benazir about a possible return to Pakistan. "Prodded by the Brits," Benazir's counselor Mark Siegel, who was personally involved in the negotiations, says, "in 2007, State finally engaged with us and directly with Benazir through the Assistant Secretary of State for South Asia Richard Boucher. We had been offering a framework for the restoration of democracy in Pakistan, with free and fair elections. The plan would restore the 1973 Constitution. Musharraf could remain as president and head of state, but the position would be more of a figurehead. Functionally, the post would carry no power, similar to the Westminster model."[25]

A series of high-level meetings ensued. Boucher visited with Benazir several times. Secretary of State Condoleezza Rice spoke to her twice. Zalmay Khalilzad, a loyal Bush adviser who had served as ambassador to Afghanistan and became U.S. ambassador to the United Nations, was trusted by all parties and helped bring the Bush administration and Benazir together. Benazir's team worried that what motivated Rice and the White House to deal with them had less to do with promoting democracy in Pakistan than preserving Musharraf's position. The United Nations Commission that investigated the assassination echoes their view. It concluded: "Both governments gave priority to ensuring a continued leadership role for General Musharraf, as they believed this was vital for the ongoing war against terror, while at the same time they believed the effort could be strengthened with a credible civilian partner heading the government."[26]

Hoping to break the logjam, Benazir and Musharraf met face-to-face in Abu Dhabi in January and again in July 2007. She wrote that these discussions were cordial but elusive.[27] New discussions between the sides took place in Dubai and Islamabad during August and September 2007 as the parties searched for common ground. Benazir had different priorities. She wanted a guaranteed election process that eliminated the ban on more than two terms as prime minister. Musharraf wanted a guaranteed outcome that kept power in his hands. The United Nations Commission reported that Benazir's "most pressing concern was the creation of a legal mechanism to eliminate old criminal corruption charges against her and her husband; for General Musharraf, the most immediate issue was ensuring PPP support for his re-election as President."[28]

Security was an absolute priority for Benazir's team. They pushed hard and firmly believed they had received a commitment. "Washington promised us," Siegel emphasizes, "that they would guarantee her safety." No point arouses him to greater anger and frustration. "They never lived up to their promises to press Musharraf."[29] Clearly, it was in Washington's interest to take every step possible to protect Benazir.

There seems little doubt Musharraf failed to comprehend how badly his political position was eroding at home. Even so, the prospect of Benazir returning prior to the elections—scheduled for January 2008[30]—made him uneasy. He was insistent that she wait. She refused to agree. In *Reconciliation* she stated that "it was decided" that she would be in Pakistan by December 31, 2007. Musharraf apparently took that to signify an agreement that she would delay her return until after the elections.[31] She had always intended to return in the fall. The PPP Executive Committee selected the October 18 date and announced it publicly.

It seems clear that the Bush team trusted Musharraf far more than Benazir and was not interested in any outcome that undermined him. The White House sided with Musharraf, preferring that she delay until after the elections. Says Siegel: "They did it directly and through Congressman Tom Lantos, who was Chairman of the House International Relations Committee. She stood her ground. We were also deeply worried about her safety. We demanded that President Bush, Vice President Cheney, or Secretary Rice personally call Musharraf and make clear that they would hold him *personally* responsible for Benazir's safety. Would you believe they refused? The stand-up guy in Washington proved to be Joe Biden, then serving as Chairman of the Senate Foreign Relations Committee. He delivered the message bluntly. Unfortunately, Musharraf wasn't much interested in Biden's views." Siegel remains convinced that had the White House made the call to Musharraf, Benazir would be alive today.[32]

While he may have underestimated the damage sustained by his cavalier treatment of the judiciary and anything-goes pursuit of a new term for president, Musharraf understood the need to freshen up his image. He could not ignore the signals from Washington that favored partnership with a civilian leader. Pickings were slim. Benazir's reappearance on the horizon was timely. The alternative was the conniving Nawaz. There was no way Musharraf was cutting any deal with him. There was no forgetting that his 1999 coup, which ousted Nawaz, came after the Sindh politician hatched a scheme that would have resulted in his plane crash. It was Benazir or nothing. Deputy Secretary of State John Negroponte delivered the message that the U.S. would stand by him, but he needed a democratic facade on the government and Benazir was "the right choice for that face," recalled Bruce Riedel, a former U.S. National Security Council staff member.[33]

Bhutto had a ready answer to objections over her past performance. She laid the blame on obstruction by the ISI, the military, and the nuclear establishment. Her friend, former ambassador Peter Galbraith, backed her up: "Without controlling those, she couldn't pursue peace with India, go after extremists, or transfer funds from the military to social programs. Cohabitation with Musharraf made sense because he had control over the three institutions that she never did. This was the one way to accomplish something and create a moderate center."[34]

There were stark differences in the aspirations of the key players. The Bush team hoped for fusion and dreamed of two pro-Western leaders marching forward together under the banner of democracy and antiterrorism. Obviously the outcome of the January 2008 parliamentary elections would influence what happened. In one scenario, a Pakistan Muslim League–Qaid (PML-Q) victory would result in Chaudhry Pervez Elahi becoming prime minister. Other options for sharing power were discussed. But it was all very fluid. No power-sharing agreement was actually finalized. Musharraf and Benazir approached matters from a different angle. He had branded her a thief. She had labeled him a dictator. Neither contemplated an exchange of olive branches. They were a lion and lioness, circling each other, deciding whether to share or fight. This was raw, calculating politics.

Chapter 11

THE RED MOSQUE

Before negotiations with Benazir were concluded, a new crisis confronted Musharraf that compounded his problems. Aggressive protests by Pakistan's lawyers over Chief Justice Chaudhry's ouster had unleashed furious public opposition.[1] In July 2007 violent clashes broke out at the Red Mosque (Lal Masjid) in Islamabad that led to a seven-day standoff and a bloody assault by commandos that left more than a hundred people dead and many more wounded.

Under the supervision of radical cleric Abdul Rashid Ghazi, militants occupied the mosque and used it as a transit station.[2] Located near the Inter-Service Intelligence headquarters and built like a fort, the mosque complex included schools, a woman's seminary, and a library. Its first imam was Maulana Muhammad Abdullah Shaheed, who had been close to Zia. Assassinated in 1998, his sons, Ghazi and Maulana Abdul Aziz, took control; made it a center for Islamists; and called for the overthrow and even assassination of Musharraf. They engaged in constant conflict with authorities. Both brothers had contacts with Osama bin Laden.[3]

For months, the mosque's students had taken to the streets and protested the sale of movies in video shops. They seized a brothel owner. On July 3, students stole radio sets and weapons from Pakistan Rangers. Other students attacked the Ministry of Environment building and set it on fire. Clashes continued until midnight.[4]

Although Ghazi denied it, the militants holed up in the mosque were well-armed members of Islamist groups including Jaish-e-Mohammad (JeM), which had been charged with assassination attempts on Musharraf and an attack on India's Parliament.[5] It appears that more than a thousand people crowded inside the mosque complex. Tensions mounted to a boiling point after militants kidnapped policemen and seven Chinese workers who were accused of running a brothel.[6] A sharia court was declared.

A standoff ensued between July 3 and July 11. Musharraf cut the complex's electricity, sending temperatures soaring, and heavily armed rangers surrounded the complex.[7] A curfew was imposed and people were warned that violators might be shot on sight, although authorities relaxed it for two hours each day so that provisions could be delivered to those inside.[8] The siege was punctuated by the exchange of automatic gunfire. Photojournalist Javed Khan and a ranger were killed. Others were wounded. A black flag depicting two crossed swords and a verse of the Quran was visible on the mosque's rooftop.[9] Forces inside were observed with 3mm rifles, Kalashnikovs, .222 rifles, hand grenades, petrol bombs, tear gas shells, and light weapons. The militants used loudspeakers to broadcast threats that any government action would prompt retaliatory suicide attacks.[10]

National Assembly members from religious groups tried to mediate a resolution, but failed.[11] The government offered the militants 5,000 rupees and a free education. Many surrendered during the first couple of days.[12]

At first, hoping to avoid violence, Musharraf had vacillated. Eventually it became too much. The actions of Ghazi and his followers embarrassed Musharraf. Fed up, he threw down the gauntlet and accused Ghazi of surrounding himself with suicide bombers. At a midnight press conference, Deputy Interior Minister Zafar Waraich warned those inside to surrender: "We ask them to lay down their arms. But if anyone comes out with weapons, he will be answered with bullets."[13] Deadlines were set, then extended. After the fourth deadline, Aziz was captured as he tried to escape while dressed in a burka. Authorities claimed that more than a thousand male students and four hundred girls of the madrassa surrendered.[14]

Many expected a nonviolent resolution, as the government had successfully negotiated previous peace agreements with the Taliban. The government's message was plain: no tolerance for violent extremists but amnesty for those who left the mosque voluntarily. Ghazi had access to the media and indicated a willingness to negotiate. "He read the terms and conditions of his surrender to the TV stations," journalist Nicholas Schmidle said.[15] Ghazi and Aziz both commented to the media. Ghazi denounced what he termed a government "smear campaign" and promised that they would lay down their arms if security forces agreed not to fire on them and did not arrest them. Posturing himself as a humanitarian, Abdul Aziz urged students to surrender or flee: "I have told them not to sacrifice their lives for me."

Officials questioned Ghazi's sincerity and rejected the conditional offer to surrender.[16] Deputy Information Minister Tariq Azim Khan declared that Ghazi "should surrender himself. If there are cases against him, let the court decide."[17]

On July 6, Musharraf's plane had been fired upon as he left Baluchistan.[18] That day, thoroughly annoyed, Musharraf issued a final ultimatum to the militants that they ignored. At 1:00 a.m. on July 7, members of the elite Special Services Group, Pakistan Rangers, and the antiterrorism squad of the Punjab police attacked under cover of darkness.[19] The operation continued for several days amid fierce fighting. The militants used machine guns, rocket launchers, and Molotov cocktails. More than a hundred people were killed in room-to-room fighting. Ghazi reportedly died after being wounded in the leg and asking to surrender as troops flushed out militants.[20]

Musharraf made no apologies. Intelligence officials reported finding letters from Al Qaeda leader Ayman al-Zawahiri written to Ghazi and Aziz. Officials blamed foreign fighters for the breakdown in negotiations.[21] Extremists responded with a series of suicide attacks. Concerned about "Talibanization," Musharraf declared in a national televised address that Pakistan faced a war of "moderates versus extremists."[22] Vowing war against militants, he declared:

> We have been up against our own people . . . they had strayed from
> the right path and become susceptible to terrorism. What do we as
> a nation want? What kind of Islam do these people represent? In the
> garb of Islamic teaching they have been training for terrorism . . .

they prepared the madrassa as a fortress for war and housed other terrorists there. I will not allow any madrassa to be used for extremism.[23]

THE POLITICAL IMPACT

Musharraf failed to identify or mobilize influential people and coalitions to rally public support. There was no "social network mobilization." He denounced terrorism. His team issued tough statements denouncing violent extremism. Yet their rhetoric remained general. Musharraf did not establish clear objectives. He did not invoke concrete examples of how terrorist violence hurt every Pakistani or drive his message in a way that evoked emotional resonance. Violent extremists had struck brutal blows. Innocent people had been murdered. There was an air of unease.

What Musharraf needed to do was make a clear case as to why Pakistan could not afford to allow Ghazi and his militant supporters to get away with acting like gangsters. The government did strive for a peaceful resolution. But it did a poor job of communicating that point. Enticements motivated many militants inside the mosque to surrender peacefully. Still, when the crunch came, strategic communication failed to persuade the Pakistani people that enough had been done to avoid injury or death to innocent civilians.

Musharraf needed to stand tough. But he had to consider better how a broader audience might perceive his words and actions. Only after the incident did he tie Ghazi and his brother to Al Qaeda and to foreigners. That was a missed opportunity. He talked about "moderates versus terrorists." He did not talk in terms of "us versus them" and he failed to define "them" as foreigners, until it was too late. Then he did so too tepidly. This crisis might have offered a cause around which to rally all political parties. Later, as Chief of the Army Staff, Ashfaq Kayani understood that political reality. In 2009 he bluntly told Pakistan's political leadership, "It's us or them." The strategy was right and it worked for Kayani. It would have been a good one for Musharraf to follow.

The media hurt more than it helped. Freedom of the press is vital to democracy, but in a crisis like the Red Mosque conflict, it cuts both ways. Strategic communication needs to factor in that dynamic. The game is not to silence opponents. It's to win the argument. Although generally supportive after the event, the media, especially television, had provided a platform to Ghazi. Adept at making his views heard during the conflict, Ghazi's on-target strategic communication denounced what he claimed was the government's excessive force against civilians who were ready to compromise. The government may have correctly judged Ghazi as disingenuous, but his statements deepened the public's doubts about Musharraf. Tony Schwartz's famous dictum that emotions are best aroused when information or feelings that people already have are channeled to one side of a debate held true. Media reports left an impression that Ghazi had been killed when he could have been taken captive.

Strategically, Musharraf was poorly positioned to deal with the Red Mosque conflict. He failed to grasp that or develop a cohesive information strategy. In the aftermath, suspicions about Musharraf's sincerity worsened. For many, the government had seemed too ready to employ lethal force where more peaceful means might have worked. One problem, as Dr. Marvin Weinbaum keenly observed, was that the ISI and the government had allowed the militants, most from the Pashtun areas, to establish themselves in the mosque. "The authorities," he concluded, "waited far too long to act. Just why is hard to fathom since it was well known that the militants had brought in a large number of arms."[24]

Sadly, having blundered in dealing with the lawyers and the judiciary, Musharraf's tactics in taking down the Red Mosque reflected a more measured approach. They were reasoned and well justified. Ghazi and his militants had broken laws, disrupted the peace, and committed murder. Musharraf accorded them every opportunity to lay down their arms.

All of this controversy came as the Pakistanis hoped to see a peaceful resolution to problems with the Taliban. Many blamed the United States for the tensions. Many felt that American intervention next door—followed by what they viewed as an ill-advised refusal to deal with the Taliban—had sent the Afghan Taliban fleeing into their country, giving rise to unrest and violence that were largely absent prior to 2005. Although in 2010 the political environment shifted to favor a tougher stand against the Taliban, in 2007, the military-intelligence establishment believed that Pakistan was paying the price for a U.S. problem, and that while fighting the Taliban served U.S. interests, the opposite held true for Pakistan. Ultimately, many people bought into the idea that excessive force had been used against Ghazi's group at the mosque. That conclusion seems absurd to those with zero tolerance for violent extremists, but it wound up being what many Pakistanis carried away from the crisis.

Reaction in the Pakistani media was mixed. *The News* wondered why action hadn't been taken earlier. *Dawn* and the *Pakistan Observer* supported Musharraf. *The Islam* thought the crisis could have been resolved peacefully.

Historian Ayesha Jalal, who was in Pakistan when this pivotal event took place, feels that the Red Mosque crisis represented a new turning point against Musharraf:

> At first, he was criticized for not doing enough to contain the crisis. People on his team had links to individuals inside the mosque. They were in direct communication. More than a political crisis, this was a major media event. Indeed, one cannot ignore the role that Pakistani media has played in dealing with Islamic discourse. The reporting has often irresponsibly inflamed emotions. Musharraf's own strategic communication was deeply flawed. He temporized, and his ambiguity and failure to provide strong leadership or a clear message about the behavior of people inside the mosque deepened the crisis and led to many deaths. The clash with the judiciary had hurt him politically. His mishandling of this crisis accelerated his slide in public opinion.[25]

Dr. Jalal is correct. The judicial crisis that began in March had compounded Musharraf's challenge. In March 2007 and beyond, Musharraf's cavalier use of violence to quell the lawyers' protests against the suspension of judges cost him politically. So had his strong-arm tactics to muzzle the media, especially television, about the issue. He had offered no credible rationale for his disagreements with the judiciary. The judicial crisis was alive in July 2007. The two crises drained his credibility. No one was calling Musharraf a liberal autocrat. His military background had not prepared him to meet these political challenges, which a more natural politician might have finessed. Polling confirmed the Pakistanis' rising hostility against the military's dominance in politics. These attitudes and opinions helped shaped the political environment when the Red Mosque crisis exploded.

Where did this predicament leave Musharraf as the situation increasingly mandated a deal with Benazir? Viewed in tandem, the research from the International Republican Institute and the Pew Global Attitudes Project was revealing.[26] In September 2006, IRI polling found that Musharraf had a strong approval rating of 63 percent compared to only 14 percent who disapproved. The greater than four-to-one approval ratio is powerful for any incumbent, especially a president who had held office as long as Musharraf had. There were, however, warning signs that should have caused Musharraf to think about his strategic communication. His political party, PML-Q, was showing poorly in responses to a question on whether it had performed well enough to merit reelection, with 37 percent saying yes and 35 percent saying no. Incumbents who score less than 50 percent on this question generally face difficulty winning the next election.

By March 2007, as conflict with the judiciary broke out, IRI polling showed that Musharraf's approval rating had already dropped to 54.2 percent, with the percentage of those not approving nearly doubling to 26 percent. An April–May 2007 poll by Pew showed about the same number, with Musharraf getting a 56 percent positive rating. The latter was good news for Musharraf. His positive rating was still greater than 50 percent, even though 72 percent did not support his decision to suspend the chief justice and 80 percent agreed the chief justice should be reinstated. But doubts were creeping in. Fissures in his support were showing. He needed to act.

By June, the attrition was serious. His approval had dropped sharply to 34 percent, while disapproval had climbed to 49 percent. By September, his approval had collapsed to 21 percent, with disapproval at 62 percent. An IRI poll released in July, prior to the attack on the mosque, showed that the issue raised concerns among 71 percent of respondents. That finding should not have necessarily hurt Musharraf. Attitudes were running against the Islamists. People worried about their running a self-proclaimed sharia court, their moral policing of shops, their provocative speeches, their possession of weapons, and their kidnapping of officers. Interior Ministry spokesman Brig. Javed Iqbal Cheema declared: "The government is very much determined to crack down on extremists and flush them out."[27] There was opportunity, but Musharraf failed to exploit it. His credibility diminished.

By September, after the government's forces had attacked the Red Mosque and more than a hundred people died, 62 percent of respondents said that the army should not have any role in the government. They felt that way even though, at the time, 74 percent thought religious extremism was a serious problem.

The handing of the Red Mosque crisis offers lessons. Al Qaeda and the Taliban are quick on the uptake. They understand strategic communication. While launching attacks on civilians to create fear and to deprive authorities of legitimacy, they know their violence breeds hostility. Their rulebook does not include fair play. They don't flinch from taking lives and then blaming the United States or its allies for the deaths. In October 2009 the Taliban set off a car bomb in Peshawar that tore through a bustling marketplace and killed women and children.[28] In December, two blasts devastated the busy Moon Market in Lahore.[29] Al Qaeda and the Taliban disowned responsibility for these attacks and blamed "the U.S. and its agents across the world."[30] In March 2010 Jamaat-e-Islami leader Amir Syed Munawar Hasan blamed Blackwater (now renamed Xe Services LLC) "for all terror attacks in Pakistan under the supervision of Interior Minister Rehman Malik."[31] Similarly ruthless tactics are evident next door in Afghanistan, where Taliban propaganda constantly blames the Afghan government or U.S. forces for extremist violence.[32]

Anti–violent extremist information strategy needs to anticipate these challenges. It needs to devise a compelling, credible narrative, and themes and messages that bolster the credibility of moderates while discrediting and marginalizing violent extremists. Musharraf forged a working relationship with the United States to deal with Al Qaeda, but he failed to forge or execute an information strategy that would have strengthened him politically or made his country more security in fighting violent extremism.

Chapter 12

BHUTTO AND MUSHARRAF
REACH AN AGREEMENT

Musharraf did have a narrative about fighting for Pakistan, stopping violent extremists, and working for economic stability. But it was not compelling and it was falling on deaf ears. He played for time as he negotiated with Benazir Bhutto. He made no bones about his distrust of both Benazir and Nawaz Sharif. He has written:

> Former prime ministers Nawaz Sharif and Benazir Bhutto, who had twice been tried, been tested, and failed had to be denied a third chance. They had misgoverned the nation. Furthermore, they would never allow their parties to develop a democratic tradition, as was clear from the fact that neither Benazir Bhutto's party nor Nawaz Sharif's had held internal elections. In fact, Benazir became her party's "chairperson for life" in the tradition of the old African dictators![1]

Musharraf's moralizing missed the critical point. Politics abhors formulas. But here's one precept you can bank on: Politics does make strange bedfellows. Benazir and Musharraf needed each other. In July 2007, the Pakistan Peoples Party had decided at its Central Executive Committee meeting in London that Benazir's leadership was critical to winning the January elections. It was decided that she would return to Pakistan in September. Concerns about security were raised. Benazir was concerned about security, but she still believed the military was somewhat exaggerating the specter of death threats as an excuse to keep her away.[2] An unhappy Musharraf viewed her early return as a breach of their agreement. It infuriated him and eroded what little trust existed between the two. There are different views as to her perspective. The United Nations Commission of Inquiry's report asserts that Musharraf's angry response to news that she would return early stunned her.[3] Some journalists who covered Benazir believe that while no agreement may have been reached with Musharraf as to the timing of her return, she changed her plans to capitalize on an emerging political opportunity.

In any event, Musharraf declared, "We struck a deal."[4] The terms were simple. Musharraf would engineer an amnesty that would lift all criminal charges against Benazir and Zardari, unfreeze a billion dollars in a Swiss bank, and allow her to come home and lead the PPP in the new parliamentary elections. He supported lifting the two-term limit for prime ministers, although that required a constitutional amendment. Musharraf refused to give up his authority to dismiss her from her post, but that issue didn't seem to faze her. Any effort to oust her would endanger Musharraf's standing in Washington. He could not afford that risk and she sensibly doubted Musharraf would take it. Besides, she could deal with that issue if she regained power and doubtless would have, given her belief that the office of the presidency needed to be reformed along the lines of the 1973 Constitution. On her side, the PPP agreed not to oppose Musharraf's bid to run for a third term as president in September 2007.[5] Benazir insisted on only two conditions. First, Washington had to guarantee that Musharraf would respect free and fair elections. Mark Siegel reports that gaining this concession was her chief political goal:

> The thing that she wanted . . . the bottom line . . . was a free and fair election that she could compete in. That's all she wanted from Musharraf because she was absolutely convinced that the PPP could sweep all provinces. The PPP had a strong ground operation in all four of them. She understood the strength of her base. She understood how unhappy the middle class young people had become with the Musharraf regime. She thought that she could put together

a strong coalition. She had run for Prime Minister twice before and had returned after a long exile in 1986 and understood the nature of the ground game and how to dominate the media in 2007. Pakistan has a rabidly free media and she knew how to play all of them.[6]

Her strategy was predicated upon the PPP's winning sufficient seats in Parliament to repeal the constitutional prohibition against serving a third term, which Musharraf had inserted primarily to block Benazir's resurgence. Siegel is convinced—and he is probably correct—that she would have won an overwhelming victory in the January 2008 elections.

Second, Benazir insisted that Musharraf give up his post as chief of army staff prior to the election.[7] Although he later reneged, Musharraf promised to resign as COAS before November 15, 2007, and to take the oath of office as a civilian if he won a new term.[8] On October 4, 2007, a national reconciliation accord was reached and an ordinance promulgated.[9] The National Reconciliation Ordinance (NRO) provided an amnesty for politicians who served in Pakistan from 1988 to 1999, thus clearing Benazir and Zardari of corruption charges. The amnesty covered members of the Pakistan Muslim League–Nawaz but did not abrogate Nawaz Sharif's agreement to remain in exile.[10] Far from being greeted as a vindication of justice, the NRO unleashed a storm of public protest as a shameful backroom deal to whitewash corruption.[11]

The Musharraf-Benazir accord provoked its own groundswell of protest. Her supporters felt that she was selling out and worried that Musharraf planned to snooker her. She was receiving amnesty but was left otherwise empty-handed. Many concluded that her lust for power had trumped her judgment. The International Republican Institute's September 2007 polling showed that by a margin of 47 percent to 27 percent, the Pakistanis believed she was promoting her own interests and not democracy.[12] By 49 percent to 35 percent, respondents opposed the deal she had cut with Musharraf. After the October 18, 2007, Karachi bombing, opposition to the deal skyrocketed to 61 percent.[13] She gamely defended the strategy, insisting that joining the military-led government would be good for the country's "democratic, constitutional and development interests."[14]

Benazir was on top of her strategic communication. A first-rate politician, she understood what messages she needed to get across. She had promised to reform the military and intelligence services, bring effective democracy, help stabilize the situation in Afghanistan, put the welfare of the people first, and bust up the drug cartels that funded terrorism. She had written about it in a *Wall Street Journal* editorial in June.[15] In August, she resolutely advised the Council on Foreign Relations:

> Military dictatorship, first in the '80's and now again, under General Musharraf, has fueled the forces of extremism, and military dictatorship puts into place a government that is unaccountable, that is unrepresentative, undemocratic, and disconnected from the aspirations of the people who make up Pakistan. Moreover, military dictatorship is born from the power of the gun, so it undermines the concept of the rule of law and gives birth to a culture of might, a culture of weapons, violence and intolerance.[16]

She demanded that the United States condition its aid to Pakistan upon restoration of democracy and free, fair, and impartial elections. She gave no quarter to the Pakistani military and intelligence services for their links to violent extremists and their habit of demonizing political parties: "[T]he real choice that the world also faces today is the choice between dictatorship and democracy, and in the choice that we make between dictatorship and democracy lies the outcome of the battle between extremism and moderation in Pakistan."[17]

Benazir also singled out the U.S. government's support for that military:

> The West's close association with a military dictatorship, in my humble view, is alienating Pakistan's people and is playing into the hands of those hardliners who blame the West for the ills of the region. And it need not be this way. A people inspired by democracy, human rights and economic opportunity will turn their back decisively against extremism. . . . I plan to return this year to Pakistan

to lead a democratic movement for the restoration of democracy. I seek to lead a democratic Pakistan that is free from the yoke of military dictatorship and that will cease to be a haven, the very petri dish of international terrorism.[18]

Heralding a new day, she cited Ukraine's Orange Revolution—a popular movement that united Ukranians against a Russian-backed autocrat—as one strategy to rid Pakistan of its military dictatorship. One might dismiss that rhetoric as a ploy to impress a Western elite. But she did not limit her trumpet call to Western venues in Washington or London. In a 2004 interview with the *Asia Times*, she denounced Musharraf as a false opponent of extremism. "It is a fact that the Musharraf regime was the biggest supporter of the Taliban, who harbored Al-Qaeda," she commented acidly. "It is dictatorship that leads to the rise of extremist groups."[19] She repeated her themes over and over again. Her comments after returning to Pakistan in October 2007 were no less defiant.

Newsweek's Ron Moreau admired her resolution but thought her message created problems for her:

She was determined to go on long marches and hold large rallies to put pressure on Musharraf. She just wanted to become a player again. She was a very smart, popular, and powerful figure.

She came across the last year of her life as incredibly pro-American and parroting every American line, whether it was about India, militancy, the Taliban—it was totally in opposition to what the national security establishment wanted. She was too much Washington's girl. She was a very intelligent, smart woman, but politically she was foolish in allowing herself to become defined as so close to America.[20]

MUSHARRAF SOLDIERS ON

While Benazir was reaching out to those in power in Washington, Musharraf pressed on at home. He campaigned to keep his job while attempting to defuse the controversy over dual office holding.

- On September 28, 2007, the Supreme Court removed obstacles to Musharraf's reelection bid, allowing him to stand for elections in October. The Pakistan Muslim League–Qaid government passed a constitutional amendment in the National Assembly that allowed him to keep his two jobs as COAS and president.

- On October 2, he named Lt. Gen. Ashfaq Kayani as the vice chief of the army, effective October 8. Kayani became COAS on November 28, when Musharraf finally resigned that post. Kayani will continue in that position until 2013.[21]

- On October 5, the Supreme Court ruled that the presidential election could take place as scheduled but issued a mandate to withhold official results until after the court ruled on legal challenges. While few observers predicted the court would void the result, the ruling left Musharraf in political limbo. He refused to stand down as COAS until his reelection was judicially confirmed.[22]

- On October 6, he won provisional reelection. He captured 98 percent of the votes cast by Pakistan's 1,170-member Electoral College. The college included the Senate, the National Assembly, and the four provincial assemblies of the Sindh, the Punjab, Baluchistan, and what was then called the North-West Frontier Province.

- About 57 percent of the total possible vote from all of the national and provincial legislatures went to Musharraf. Yet two-fifths of the body had abstained (members of the Benazir-led PPP) or resigned in protest (mostly members of the Islamic Coalition Party).

- Musharraf's abuse of the judiciary was the bomb that had exploded in his face. His insistence on standing for reelection while still serving as COAS weakened him further. Opposition parties called the move unconstitutional and petitioned the Supreme Court to block it.[23]

- On November 24, the Pakistan Election Commission confirmed his reelection as president.

Chapter 13

KARACHI

Benazir Bhutto had landed in Karachi on October 18, 2007. She traveled in a caravan from the Jinnah International Airport to Jinnah's mausoleum. Her return was triumphant. Amid the huge crowds, as noted in chapter 4, it took her convoy nine hours to cover a distance of 5.6 miles. At one point, it took longer than three hours to move half a mile.[1] There was a carnival atmosphere, but this circus was taking place in a dangerous venue. As the sky darkened, she noticed that as her caravan approached street corners, streetlights began to dim and then go off. There was "a clear pattern" to this occurrence,[2] so much so that the actions seemed deliberate. A supporter, Senator Rukhsana Zuberi, went to the power station and tried to get the lights switched on. They stayed off, Benazir heard later, to keep her from getting so much publicity on television.[3] More critically, jammers designed to block cell phone signals that could detonate a bomb remotely ceased to function properly.

Lights were off as Benazir's vehicle crossed a bridge near the Karsaz neighborhood. The darkened scene erupted in total chaos as suicide attackers struck. Fortunately, she was inside her vehicle and protected by a large security cocoon comprising two cordons. The inner cordon consisted of security guards engaged by the Pakistan Peoples Party, the outer cordon of Sindh police and plainclothes security from the Intelligence Bureau (IB). The attackers penetrated the outer but not the inner cordon.[4]

Two police vehicles bore the brunt of the blasts, which destroyed three police vans and killed 20 policemen. At least 139 people were killed, mostly security personnel, and 500 were wounded.[5] Benazir reported that the explosion killed 50 PPP security guards.[6] The suicide bomber attack was the worst in Pakistani history.[7] Seated inside her vehicle, Benazir escaped injury and was escorted promptly to her residence, Bilawal House.

People were quick to assign blame for the attack. Naturally, the identity of the culprits and those who dispatched them depended on who was making the accusation. From Dubai, Zardari told the ARY television channel: "I blame the government for these blasts. It is the work of the intelligence agencies."[8] He offered no basis for that accusation. In Islamabad, Interior Ministry spokesman General Cheema pronounced it the "handiwork of militants who have been creating acts of terrorism in the country."[9] Deputy Information Minister Tariq Azeem pointed out that militant leader Baitullah Mehsud had made a prior threat.[10] Reuters, however, reported that Mehsud had denied any involvement.[11] PPP spokesman Farhatullah Babar took the same position as Mehsud. Later, Babar reported that following the failed October suicide attack against her in Karachi, Mehsud had sent two separate messages to Benazir that stressed his innocence.[12] Musharraf condemned the attacks and called Benazir to promise that he would launch an independent investigation. He pledged that it would be completed as soon as possible.[13]

As usual, it was Benazir who offered the broader perspective. "It was an attack on democracy and it was an attack on the very unity and integrity of Pakistan," she told a press conference, wearing a black armband in memory of the victims. She pledged to defy the Al Qaeda "cowards." She blasted the government for ignoring her forecast that bomb squads aimed to kill her. In her view, Musharraf could have taken steps to ensure her protection. The event shattered any trust between them.

Perhaps the explosives provided the most ominous evidence. Karachi police, who believed there were two attackers, said that between twelve and fifteen kilos of high-grade RDX explosive or C4 plastic explosive and ball bearings had been used.[14] Both are associated with security forces. Indian counterterrorism expert Bahukutumbi Raman commented:

> This, if confirmed, would indicate the presence of accomplices in the security forces. This would also indicate that this could not have

been a lone-wolf operation by an angry individual not belonging to any organisation. Only an organisation, with contacts and financial resources, would have been able to get such a large quantity of the explosive.[15]

The astute Raman raises a related question. While the high number of deaths among security personnel may have resulted from a bomber's penetration of the outer cordon, did the fact that the blast took place within the inner cordon suggest the bomber was one of the security people?[16]

Benazir Bhutto demanded an inquiry and filed a First Information Report (FIR) to trigger an investigation that, not surprisingly, went nowhere.[17] She also revealed that she had sent a letter to Musharraf naming "three individuals and more" who should be investigated should she be assassinated (the information came from phone intercepts by the United Arab Emirates).[18] The three included:

- Hamid Gul, the former Inter-Services Intelligence chief who is reportedly still associated with the ISI as head of its ultra-secret *S* section, which conducts covert operations
- Brig. Gen. Ejaz Shah (Ret.), the director of IB
- Chaudhry Pervez Elahi, the PML-Q Chief Minister of Punjab and one of Musharraf's closet political allies

Others she suspected included:

- Arbab Ghulam Rahim, the Sindh chief minister and rival political leader of the Pakistan Muslim League–Qaid, whom Zulfiqar Ali Mira, a Sindh PPP leader, quoted as stating a day before the attack that "Benazir's caravan will end at midnight"[19]
- Hassan Waseem Afzal, the former deputy chairman of the National Accountability Bureau

Benazir blasted Musharraf for barring her from using private cars or vehicles equipped with tinted windows and police mobile outriders that could provide cover for her vehicle, and for failing to provide jammers to counter remote-controlled bombs. How such measures might have prevented the Karachi attack, in which her vehicle crept along slowly in a large crowd, is unclear. Presumably she was looking ahead to a future event, where such measures could save her life. It was a reasonable view. Signal jammers had saved Musharraf from assassination in December 2003. It's puzzling why the government neither provided them nor allowed her to obtain them privately.

Mark Siegel reports that the government had also denied visas for Blackwater Security as well as the London-based ArmorGroup, two firms with a great deal of experience in protecting diplomats and VIPs. Pulitzer Prize–winning journalist Ron Suskind alleges that Benazir herself made the decision not to use Blackwater, concerned about being connected to the controversial firm or making any suggestion that only Americans could protect her.[20] Siegel goes out of his way to set the record straight: "Suskind is not accurate about Blackwater. She wanted them.[21] She wanted jammers that worked. The government declined to provide them. There was no excuse for their refusal."[22]

Benazir's team searched high and low for jammers that would work. Peter Galbraith reports that she was finally reduced to asking Iraqi president Jalal Talabani to provide them along with an operator. "It reflected the desperation of her situation," he says. "That she had to turn to the President of Iraq for protection against IED's is almost too absurd. To me, a central question is why didn't the government provide her with the security she needed? She felt they ought to be providing security. She was very upset that they weren't."[23]

Musharraf's failure to cooperate more closely with Benazir on security and assure her safety was a major political misstep. It was both foolish executive leadership and inept strategic communication. It produced calamity for both. The intelligence the United Arab Emirates had provided Benazir included not only names but cell phone numbers of highly placed individuals close to Musharraf who were believed to be plotting her assassination. Although the information was given to Musharraf, for reasons never explained, neither Musharraf nor his government acted on it.

Still, the coin has two sides. Serious death threats had surrounded Benazir when she arrived. They persisted until her assassination. They rightly worried Benazir and those around her. In Karachi, thousands of supporters had been waiting for her, and there was no way she would avoid immersing herself in them. Christina Lamb was the only correspondent with her on the caravan bus to Mohammed Ali Jinnah's tomb. "This is why I came back," Benazir told her, as the caravan wound it way through the streets jammed with cheering supporters. "Look at the crowds, the women, the children who have come from all over. These are the real people of Pakistan, not the extremists."[24] Benazir refused her security people's entreaties to cower behind a bulletproof shield affixed to her vehicle. She understood the risks. Foolish or fearless—or both— she remained determined. "I put my faith in God and I trust in the people of Pakistan," she told Lamb,[25] who considered Benazir "the most courageous woman I ever met."[26]

Reaching out to supporters is one thing, but it does not absolve a politician from taking commonsense precautions once a clear and present danger manifests itself. The media heavily covered the caravan. There would have been no problem making a powerful case to a national audience that, if for no other reason than to protect the safety of those around Benazir, death threats had necessitated a change of plan. Such an announcement would have preserved her well-merited reputation for courage, shown concern for her supporters, and scored points against the government.

One reporter who interviewed Musharraf after the event quotes the president as stating that he had phoned Benazir and advised her to avoid public rallies and appearances. Musharraf has claimed that he had warned Benazir against exposing herself to crowds because going out in an explosive political environment would put her life at risk. Apparently, she felt he was trying to keep her from campaigning and rejected the advice.

Siegel was always concerned for Benazir's safety. Well before the attack in Karachi, he had recognized the dangers and the intensity of people's animosity to Benazir. A sophisticated political strategist, Siegel advised her that she could mount a winning campaign without exposing herself to unnecessary danger. As her great friend and champion, Siegel understandably gives her the strong benefit of the doubt. He raises a valid point that it's unfair to blame the victim. She felt compelled to immerse herself in crowds of supporters Benazir wrote that she felt protected when she reached out and physically touched the masses of Pakistanis who supported her.

SHOULD BENAZIR HAVE TAKEN THE RISKS?

However a charismatic figure she may have been, after the Karachi attack Benazir bears a responsibility for the risks she took. The attack made clear that she was targeted. Her fatalism is no excuse. Politics changes people, even the best of them. The process can transform well-grounded sensibility into irrational behavior. Politicians become self-involved. Benazir was no exception, especially in energizing her base. Though fearless, she had an almost messianic sense of her role in Pakistan. Her message was that what she stood for was greater than herself and that history is greater than any single individual. Her return in 1988 had lit beacons of hope. In relighting those hopes in 2007, she owed her supporters a duty to avoid placing herself at unnecessary risk.

She dismissed Siegel's wise counsel, telling him "we don't do things that way here." Political consultants cringe when they hear a candidate make such statements. It is a common excuse, echoed from small-town America to foreign capitals. It's nonsense and marks the path to often-avoidable trouble or disaster. Benazir's tragedy was partly the result of her failure to heed Siegel's on-point counsel about campaigns. There may not have been a risk-free way to gain power in Pakistan, but she could have minimized the danger.

And then there is the matter of the safety of those around her. Benazir inspired intense loyalty, a tribute to her charisma. But each public appearance put close friends and supporters, as well as herself, in harm's way. Journalist Bronwen Maddox noted:

> Much of the coverage of her assassination has been reverential and she is rightly credited with enormous courage: she knew the risks but faced them anyway. Even at the start of her political career, she had gone almost straight from Harvard to a decade of solitary confinement, house arrest and exile.
>
> But that bravery came with, it seemed to me, casualness about the risk to those near to her. I travelled with her on her aircraft on

her return to Karachi in October and was repelled by her assumption that her devoted supporters should be subject to the same risks as her. "Everyone there knew he might die, but came for the sake of democracy," she said after the failed assassination attempt that killed 140 others. In that airy phrase, she was disingenuous about the motives of the crowd of hundreds of thousands, many extremely poor. Most had been bussed in from rural villages and Karachi slums by local party bigwigs, who were rewarded for the turnout.

The morning after the blast, in the hospital, widows, daughters and sisters tried to identify their relatives among the half-corpses. The women said that they were terrified about who would support their families.[27]

Tony Clifton summarized Benazir's mind-set this way:

She loved the crowds. She didn't like physical contact with them, although she loved the concept of it. Once we passed by women standing at the side of a road, just a mile or so from the opulent Bhutto family estate in Larkana, in the Sindh. Everyone one of them would have voted for her, although they were barefoot, in rags, but as we swept past in Benazir's motorcade, she ignored their waves and cheers and talked about how something had to be done to lift their lives. But she'd had years to do that, and had never lifted a finger.

Yet she believed it. What she could never bring herself to believe was that anyone would actually take a shot at her. Mere threats were one thing. But she acted in the certainty of belief that the crowds—*her people*—loved her, and somehow that and fate would see her through safely.[28]

Benazir was hardly the only populist leader who assumed the rules of political reality somehow did not apply to herself. Indira Gandhi made the same mistake shortly before her assassination and ignored explicit warnings to change her Sikh security team. She could not believe any member would turn on her. They shot her dead in 1984. President of Bangladesh Mujibur Rahman told Tony Clifton during a formal interview a month before his assassination in 1975 that worries about his safety were overblown. "My people love me," he declared.

Winston Churchill once said that "nothing in life is so exhilarating as to be shot at without result." The problem is, your enemies don't always miss. Indeed, just to make sure, in addition to bullets, they use bombs.

Chapter 14

THE STATE OF
EMERGENCY

A looming Supreme Court decision likely to nullify his election as president and the legality of holding down the posts of president and of the chief of army staff galvanized Musharraf. On November 3, 2007, dressed in a black *sherwani* (coatlike garment), he delivered a national television address. He deplored rising Islamic extremism. Then, citing Abraham Lincoln's suspension of habeas corpus without the assent of Congress as a precedent, he suspended Pakistan's Constitution and replaced it with a Provisional Constitutional Order.[1] Two years later, he claimed the action had been taken after consulting the nine corps commanders, the director general of the Inter-Services Intelligence, the prime minister, cabinet members, and governors.[2] His remarks annoyed his former comrades. They quickly contradicted him or declined comment.[3] Had Musharraf actually gained such support from fellow officers, you can bet he would have said so at the time.

Musharraf is not a rousing orator, and he would have done well to countenance his own advice against declaring a state of emergency. Technically, he did not announce martial law, although the media often referred to it that way, and the Constitution remained in place. His strategic communication was a mess.

Reporters watching the performance wondered, as Gretchen Peters remarked, whether Musharraf had strayed into the twilight zone.[4] Having concluded part of his speech in English for the chattering classes, he switched to Urdu to reach a larger Pakistani audience. Peters recounts that Mohammed

Hanif summed up the moment perfectly: "It was immediately clear to me that he had fallen into that aging dictator's familiar trap. He had written his own speech."[5]

Winston Churchill, Ronald Reagan, and Barack Obama have been renowned for writing or actively providing input into their riveting speeches, but on this make-or-break occasion, Musharraf did himself more harm than good. Hanif concludes that Musharraf

> talked, well, gibberish; the kind of stuff that only journalists and think-tank-*wallahs* would take seriously . . . for the forty minutes that General Musharraf spoke in Urdu, he didn't use one proper sentence. . . . And when he said, "Extremists have gone very extreme," it suddenly occurred to me why his speech pattern seemed so familiar. He was that uncle you get stranded with at a family gathering when everybody else has gone to sleep but there is still some whisky left in the bottle. And uncle thinks he is about to say something very profound—if only you would pour him one last one.[6]

Acting more as a generalissimo than as a president, by this time Musharraf had *twice* sacked Chief Justice Chaudhry, who had been restored to the bench in July,[7] and sequestered the jurist inside the Supreme Court along with ten fellow judges.[8] Musharraf denounced the judges for their corruption, abuse, and failure to help fight terrorists and extremists.[9] Paramilitary Pakistani Rangers surrounded the court building while troops stormed TV and radio stations. An enemies list was compiled of journalists and political opponents the government wanted detained.

If Musharraf expected to be hailed as the hero of the hour, he was sadly mistaken. *Dawn* called it "Gen. Musharraf's second coup," while the *Daily Times* bluntly informed readers that Musharraf had instituted "martial law."[10] Lawyers took to the streets by the thousands. The government responded harshly. Police beat them with long wooden canes.[11] Up to five hundred opposition activists, including cricket-star-turned-politician Imran Khan and chairman of the independent Human Rights Commission of Pakistan Asma Jehangir, were rounded up.[12] Members of the Pakistan Peoples Party and the Pakistan Muslim League–Nawaz protested, and thousands were arrested. Skeptics jeered at Musharraf's commitment to fighting terrorists. He was seen instead as a man battling for his job security, not a safer, more secure nation.[13] Seven of the seventeen judges rejected Musharraf's declaration of a national emergency,[14] the duration of which was left open-ended.[15]

Pakistanis refused to knuckle under Musharraf. The independent television network Geo TV set up secret transmission sites and broadcast from Dubai. Despite Pakistan's high illiteracy rate, its citizens included 17 million Internet users and 70 million mobile phone users who used their cellular technology as a "poor man's Internet."[16]

While Musharraf's strategic communication floundered, Benazir stayed on message. Returning to Karachi from Dubai, she demanded that Musharraf lift the emergency restrictions and hold elections. Her defiance startled Musharraf. Some have questioned whether she had a coherent plan for regaining power, but she was in touch with the majority of the public's opinions and had sound instincts. She had understood that Musharraf was in political trouble. That was why she returned before the elections. She had the right strategy: capitalize on public sentiment and generate unstoppable momentum.

The Karachi assassination attempt against her increased her determination. She shifted tactics. It was time to instill more fire in her cause. Zahid Hussain recounts: "Things changed dramatically after Musharraf declared the State of Emergency. Until then, she had focused her fire primarily upon Musharraf's allies and to rally her party behind her. Now she put Musharraf himself in her sights."[17]

At a packed press conference at her modest party headquarters in Islamabad, she gave Musharraf a deadline of November 15, the end of his current presidential term, to restore the Constitution, resign from the army, lift the media bans, and firmly set January 15 as the date for free and fair elections. If he refused, she would lead a 220-mile "long march" from Lahore to Islamabad. Leaving little doubt that she planned to lead a popular upheaval, Benazir charged that "an organized minority had seized control of the levers of the state," including government and intelligence officials with connections to extremists. The declaration of emergency had shattered her cooperation with Musharraf and broken their bond of trust.[18]

Alarmed, Musharraf slapped her under house arrest and forbade her to go outside and address the local and international media standing watch at the barricades. Police padlocked the gate and declared her home a "sub-jail." They also sealed the entire neighborhood.[19] The mass and highly effective demonstrations mounted by Pakistan's lawyers had demonstrated that marches could create substantial mischief. A charismatic politician like Benazir could send his government into a tailspin. Besides, she was giving him no quarter. "It's time for him to go," she advised Reuters by phone. "He must quit as President."[20] Lighting the fuse on yet another bomb, she charged that Musharraf and his forces were planning to rig the January elections. Still, like any good politician, she carefully kept the door open to talks should Musharraf lift the emergency.[21]

Musharraf found himself boxed. Capitulating to popular and international pressure, on December 15 he lifted the state of emergency. He tried to put a positive face on a political debacle and congratulated himself for saving Pakistan and for stopping "the wave of terrorism and militancy."[22] It was big talk with little effect. The stage was set for Benazir's tragic final act.

Chapter 15

LIAQUAT BAGH

Wearing a white *dupatta* (scarf) that covered her head and shoulders, a purple tunic, and a *haar* (garland) of red and white around her neck, Benazir Bhutto finished addressing the enthusiastic crowd at Liaquat Bagh. Getty Images photographer John Moore estimated its size at five thousand to eight thousand supporters.[1] McClatchy reporter Saeed Shah thought there were three thousand to four thousand people present.[2] Benazir had gone ahead with her plans despite Inter-Services Intelligence chief Lt. Gen. Nadeem Taj's warning.

In post-assassination interviews, Musharraf insisted that he also had "told her to be careful."[3] He declared,

> I warned her, because I got [an] intelligence report. . . . Indeed, there was a threat. I knew it. And not only me. But some certain friends of ours from the Gulf sent a special messenger to me,[4] indicating that there were certainly some groups, terrorists groups, who supposedly have come to Karachi, and they would do an attack on her. And I told her. I told her personally. . . . I told her, I'm warning you that there is a threat in Rawalpindi [at Liaquat Bagh] . . . I told her, "You must not go."

He pointed out that the first time she wanted to address a rally there, she was not allowed to go. She created, he remarked, "such a hue and cry that she is being restricted, of political activities being restricted. It had a lot of negative fallout on me."[5]

Gretchen Peters says Musharraf has a point, to some extent:

> In some ways, you have to feel for the guy. The streets were dangerous for her. She knew that. But since Musharraf had no idea how important it was to manage public opinion, his technique for keeping her safe was putting her under house arrest before planned political rallies. He said he had intelligence claiming she would be attacked, but he effectively mitigated the idea that he was her protector by putting razor wire and armed men around her house to prevent her from leaving. The major story would always be—and she would spin it this way—he was the military dictator who was locking up a great voice for Pakistani democracy.[6]

Given that his intelligence chief had sensed trouble and made a special effort to warn Benazir, Musharraf should have made a more forceful effort to dissuade her from attending the rally and delivering a very clear, blunt warning that attending would put her life at risk. He should have taken special precautions to secure the area.

It did not help that Benazir's security adviser, Rehman Malik, apparently dismissed the warning, although reports on what he said, when, and to whom, are inconsistent.[7] Security concerns had persisted at the planning lunch prior to the rally.[8] Yet, as she arrived at the Liaquat Bagh, many noticed the absence of police security.[9] Standing on the stage, Benazir herself voiced her apprehensions about the building and the area adjoining the park. No one acted to strengthen her security.[10]

The United Nations Commission of Inquiry focused on the security arrangements—more accurately, how neither the government nor the Pakistan Peoples Party arranged for adequate ones. It found that the Ministry of Interior, the ISI, and Military Intelligence (MI) had regularly reported warnings of death threats to her. Significant threats arose just before her return in October, in "early to mid-November, and from mid-to-late December."[11] Intelligence tip-offs were also communicated by Saudi Arabia and the United Arab Emirates. It also confirmed Lt. Gen. Nadeem Taj's warning.[12]

The government's approach to following up on this information and was incredibly sloppy, given the political stakes. Interior Secretary Syed Kamal Shah would later describe the federal government's role as advisory. He palmed off the responsibility for policing and security in Pakistan's federal system to provincial authorities. That evasion was a canard. Punjab home secretary Khusro Pervez characterized such federal advisories as "instructions." Punjab inspector general of police Ahmed Nasim echoes Pervez's interpretation.[13]

The exuses don't wash. Former prime ministers Shaukat Aziz and Chaudhry Shujaat Hussain had previously received very VIP-level security on direction from the federal government. For unexplained reasons, such security was not provided to Benazir. It bears stressing: Actions or the failure to act constitute strategic communication. The government's failure sent a clear signal to insiders and helped erode Musharraf's credibility after the assassination. The UN Commission characterized the government's shirking of its official and moral responsibility as "inexcusable."[14] It was also politically stupid.

Benazir's liaison with the government was through Senior Superintendent of Police Maj. Imtiaz Hussain (Ret.). She had known him from her second tenure as prime minister and trusted him. She did not trust three other candidates put forward by the ISI. Imtiaz received scant support from the government, which turned down or ignored his requests for beefed-up security, jammers, bulletproof vehicles, and trained police personnel to escort the former prime minister's entourage. He also advised her about her own responsibilities and cautioned her not to expose herself by standing through her armored car's escape hatch to wave to crowds. She did not respond warmly to that advice.[15]

The bottom line in this circus was that Musharraf failed to ensure a comprehensive security plan to protect his rival. His inaction forced her to rely on the PPP for security. The PPP had been able to recruit and mobilize about 5,000 enthusiastic volunteers who were organized into the Jaan Nisaar Benazir (JNB), a term that in Urdu means "those willing to give their lives for Benazir." About 2,000 of them had worn uniforms and formed a human chain around

Benazir's vehicle in Karachi, where their presence had saved her life. About 250 to 300 JNB had also traveled with her in the Sindh. None were at Liaquat Bagh.[16]

Liaquat Bagh is located in Rawalpindi, which houses the Pakistan Army Headquarters. The district police prepared a written plan that envisaged providing an elite force unit for Benazir's security by forming a "box" around her vehicle. That aspect of the plan was not carried out. The security plan detailed two security cordons—an inner one that secured the park and an outer one that secured the area surrounding it, including the exit. The plan called for the deployment of 1,371 police officers, of constables on rooftops around the park, and of three walk-through gates equipped with metal detectors at the park's entrance. The special branch closed the park and swept it for explosives on the morning of December 27.[17]

The police proved more interested in crowd control than in protecting Benazir. They initially frisked individuals entering the park but abandoned their posts early on.[18] Despite government claims that 1,300 or more security personnel (which would have been 20 to 25 percent of those present during the rally) had flooded the park, there is no evidence to support the assertion that this occurred. Nor was there evidence that constables carrying automatic rifles and binoculars were stationed on buildings around the park.[19] Benazir had only the thin protection of her own small team of fourteen bodyguards, wearing their usual white T-shirts emblazoned with "Willing to Die for Benazir."[20] Security was so lax, recalled security officer Chaudhry Aslam, that the police ignored a young boy who was wandering in the area and holding a pistol.[21]

After Benazir gave her speech, her bodyguards ushered her into the backseat of a Toyota Land Cruiser outfitted as an armored vehicle.[22] The car motored slowly to the gates. From the park, her vehicle was supposed to turn left toward Gawalmandi, but police blocked the road from the left side, forcing her vehicle to turn right.[23] A crowd of individuals waving Benazir banners and shouting party slogans was waiting. Blocked from moving forward, the Toyota came to a halt.[24] Who was in the crowd that prevented her from leaving is not clear.[25]

Video footage broadcast by the BBC's Channel 4 shows uniformed police standing about, doing nothing to hold back the crowd.[26] She was an easy target. Tauqir Zia, a retired general who sat in a car ahead of Bhutto, declared afterward: "But I would ask where was the security? How did they allow people to come so close to her?"[27] Witness Ghulam Murtaza's account parallels that of the BBC. He was standing ten to fifteen feet away from where the Land Cruiser was trapped. Instead of pushing the crowd back, police merely watched.[28]

As the crowd chanted party slogans, Benazir popped her head out of the roof.[29] She handed over a portable microphone to Safdar Abbasi and asked him to shout, "Jeay Bhutto!" She then joined in shouting the slogans while waving.[30] PPP chairman Amin Fahim was in the vehicle with her. He recalled: "No one asked her to stand, she wanted to wave at the crowd as she was very happy that day, that's why she came out of the sun roof."[31]

Amid the crowd, a clean-shaven young man wearing a white shirt, a sleeveless dark waistcoat, and rimless dark sunglasses, edged his way closer to the Toyota. Witnesses described him as having a "normal" haircut and being between twenty-two and twenty-five years of age.[32] His appearance was described as "reminiscent of plainclothes intelligence officials," although members of Al Qaeda and other militants wear Western clothing for disguise.[33] Party workers tried to stop the man as he drew a gun.[34] A BBC Channel 4 video captured the moment vividly. A highly focused assassin can be seen firing three rapid shots from a pistol in less than two seconds.[35] The UN Commission's report also describes three shots. A different video that was broadcast on YouTube projects the sound of four shots.[36] There follows almost instantly a blast from high explosives. Reports said the explosive weighed four to five kilograms and was wrapped with hundreds of pullets and ball bearings.[37] The blast killed the assailant and twenty-eight people. At least a hundred were wounded.[38] Benazir was rushed to Rawalpindi General Hospital, two miles distant, where an attending medical team pronounced her dead.

Inefficient—consciously or not—in providing Benazir's security at the park, the government was a model of efficiency in cleaning up the crime scene immediately. Rawalpindi police chief Saud Aziz received a phone call from a "close associate" of Musharraf's to clean up the crime scene right away. The fire department used hoses to wash down the area. Caretaker interior minister Lt. Gen. Hamid Nawaz (Ret.), who assured the press that 1,300 security people had been on duty at the park to protect Benazir, said that Aziz had informed him that after "securing important evidence," Aziz had hosed down the crime scene because vultures and crows were gathering around the spot. *The News* reported that eyewitnesses said that no vultures or crows were there at the time because it was already dark at 6:30 in the evening.[39]

The government's behavior recalls Benazir's adage that in Pakistan, there is always a story behind the story.

Chapter 16

"BUSHARRAF"
OF PAKISTAN

Benazir's assassination plunged Musharraf into a deep hole. Benazir had written an e-mail stating he would bear responsibility should she be assassinated. The letter shocked him. It presented a challenge that would trouble any politician. Yet, as with other 2007 political crises, Musharraf's response showed limited political dexterity.

What kind of executive was Musharraf? Former Inter-Services Intelligence chief Lt. Gen. Hamid Gul disliked Musharraf's cooperation with America but admired the president's energy, unconventional thinking, and willingness to roll the dice. Still, Gul considered him "imaginative without being realistic."[1] Lt. Gen. Talat Masood (Ret.) judged: "Musharraf was a good officer when he had no political ambitions. But he has not grown into a national leader. His whole mind is oriented militarily."[2] Ahmed Rashid thought him "very isolated," noting that "he's got a small group of advisers who don't contradict his views. He is a former commando who doesn't have much political savvy."[3]

Akbar Ahmed, an Islamic studies professor at American University and a former Pakistani envoy to Britain, believes that by 2007 Musharraf had started to think that he was a messiah: "People around him are now talking about God's destiny for Musharraf. When God enters the picture, politicians ignore the needs of mere mortals. . . . He's the man who would be king. He's hypnotized himself. It's the psychology of power. Who is going to tell him the truth?"[4] Musharraf's behavior bore out the impressions of all these observers.

Musharraf's father was a diplomat. His mother was an educated Muslim woman who worked for the International Labour Organization.[5] The second of three brothers, their son graduated from Saint Patrick's School in Karachi and studied mathematics at Forman Christian College in Lahore. Graduating eleventh in his class from the Pakistan Military Academy, the short, stocky, would-be president began his career as a lieutenant in an artillery regiment.[6] In the 1965 skirmishes with India, which inflicted heavy casualties, he drew praise for sticking to his post under shellfire and was awarded the Imtiazi Sanad for gallantry.[7] From Khem Karan, he wrote his first letter to his mother, "proudly saying that I was writing from India."[8] During the 1971 Bengali war, he led a company as a commando in the Special Service Group Commando Battalion. He gained a reputation as a "risk taker and inspiring leader" in battle,[9] but, in his words, he "broke down and wept" when Pakistan surrendered.[10] As a protégé of Zia ul-Haq's, he climbed the ranks, receiving his first star in 1988 and his second in 1991. In 1995, he assumed command of the elite I Corps.[11]

Prime Minister Nawaz Sharif named him chief of army staff, after first extracting the traditional assurance that tended to precede coups or dismissals of civilian governments to "remain apolitical."[12] It was not to be. Tensions escalated amid criticism of Nawaz's weak performance. Nawaz tried to smooth things over by naming him chairman of the Joint Chiefs of Staff committee. It improved nothing.

Musharraf took seriously his self-anointed titles of "liberal autocrat" and "reluctant coup maker." He reveled in his initial image of benevolent leader. Owen Bennett Jones believes that he "wanted a modern, liberal, prosperous, tolerant Pakistan."[13] Musharraf never possessed the powers of a dictator. Nor did he seek them. Musharraf presented himself as a reformer and promised to take Pakistan on a liberal course.[14] On seizing power, he had set forth a seven-point agenda that included cracking down on extremism and secularism. He was proud of his record in allowing a free press and boasted of it.

But reporters still encountered plenty of trouble. The ISI harassed journalist Christina Lamb, who says that Pakistani journalists were routinely subject to harsher treatment.[15] Apparently, Carlotta Gall was assaulted in her hotel in Quetta, Baluchistan, after making inquiries that made the government uncomfortable.[16]

His record as president was mixed. He repealed the Zina ordinance, but he backtracked on repealing the blasphemy law, a Zia concoction that jailed anyone merely accused of defiling the image of the Prophet Mohammed or of desecrating the Quran. He battled Al Qaeda but stepped up support for Kashmiri militants. He banned militant groups like Lashkar-e-Taiba, which simply chose another name and kept operating.

After 9/11, he did a lot of foot shuffling, but even providing limited help to Washington exposed him to assassination attempts. It bears stressing: Musharraf had limited power to make real reforms or to take on Pakistani extremists.

In 2009 Musharraf defended his cooperation with Washington, arguing that U.S. forces could have entered Pakistan and seized its nuclear assets. He said it was even possible "that the US and India could have jointly attacked the country."[17] Such claims were nonsense. Happily, he and Bush hit it off and grew close enough to earn the Pakistani a new sobriquet, "Busharraf."[18] The friendship warmed relations with Washington but created political problems at home. Whether they viewed the United States as an imperialist crusader bent on imposing its will upon a Muslim nation and controlling its nuclear arms or a puppet master for Pakistan's president, Pakistani resentment against America grew deeper and deeper.

Staying in power too long leads to isolation. Politicians lose touch with what the people are really thinking. In 2007, Musharraf had been president for eight years. Critics argue that he was surrounded by too many yes-men. His actions bear out that view.

FROM FLAG OFFICER TO PRESIDENT

Musharraf was eclectic in the elements used to define his narratives. The fact is, even able military officers find making the transition to civilian politics difficult. You can see it plainly when their strategic communication misfires.

In battling terrorism, Musharraf stood on both sides of the equation. At heart, especially after the assassination attempts on him, he wanted to crack down on extremism, a feeling that intensified as time passed. But for much of his tenure as president, his attitude seemed to be that while knocking out Al Qaeda made sense, and he worked closely with the United States to do so, somewhat to the ire of the ISI, controlling the Taliban suited Pakistani interests. His rhetoric, though, still inveighed against terrorism.

Reworking Winston Churchill, he warned that political injustice, poverty, and illiteracy were fueling religious fundamentalism and terrorism: "A new iron curtain seems to be falling. This iron curtain somehow is dividing the Muslim world on one side and the West on the other side."[19] He might have done better had he recalled a different observation from Churchill: "It is always dangerous for soldiers, sailors, or armies to play at politics."[20]

Career military officers are trained to wage war, not to become political leaders. Graduates of West Point receive a bachelor of science degree, not a bachelor of arts. One distinguished British air commodore has pointed out that many outstanding flag officers lack the oratorical ability to motivate a crowd. Few officers, no matter how gifted within a military setting, do well in elective politics. It's no accident that Kemal Ataturk, Dwight Eisenhower, and Charles de Gaulle stand apart as military leaders who became great heads of democracies.[21] Politics is an art that requires a wholly distinct set of skills from those honed in the military.

Most of his colleagues thought Musharraf was tactically sound, although his record as a military strategist was imperfect. The 1999 Kargil fiasco in Kashmir had been his brainstorm.[22] Musharraf's abrupt shift in the nation's strategic course to side with the United States after 9/11 revealed a similar lack of strategic planning and poor strategic communication inside and outside the Pakistani power structure. He made that decision in league with a few generals without consulting political leaders. He delayed for days before informing his cabinet.[23] The shift alienated radical Islamists, such as ISI chief Lt. Gen. Mahmood Ahmed, whom he replaced with the anti-Taliban officer Lt. Gen. Ehsan ul-Haq.

Musharraf kept his cool publicly after Bhutto's assassination. He knew that he had to project strength and calm. He had to absolve the government and its military and intelligence services of criminal culpability in the face of popular suspicion. There were two aspects to this problem. First, he needed to show that he was in control. Second, as the military was his strongest base, it had to be secured.

Fortunately, Lt. Gen. Kayani and the army stood behind him. Whether Musharraf devised a specific strategic plan for dealing with the aftermath of Benazir's assassination or simply muddled through, confident he would survive, is unclear. His efforts to influence public opinion were executed primarily through newspapers and broadcast media. He chose an effective channel, as Pakistan boasts a lively print and electronic media; yet he failed to comprehend that political communication today exists in an integrated vertical media space that entails molding opinions and attitudes from the grassroots upward through civil society organizations, political groups, the military-intelligence establishment, influentials, and the media. Skeptics argue that he had a limited ability to mobilize support, but there's little evidence that he seriously tried. Leaders can move opinion only if they conduct a campaign of influence properly.

In politics, the chickens always come home to roost. Hoping to manipulate the media, Musharraf put out a narrative that built upon his disingenuous embrace of democracy and that stressed his commitment to combating extremism and terrorism. He did a poor job of mobilizing his political allies and building coalitions that could provide third-party validation for his position and drive his message. Still, except for exaggerating Benazir's security at Liaquat Bagh—his team's post-assassination language was surprisingly consistent and disciplined. The police and lesser officials dropped the ball several times, but in this arena, their fumbles didn't count.

Politicians generally fall into one of two categories. The more gifted ones have peripheral vision. They take in what goes on around them, digest the situation, anticipate the land mines to avoid them, and capitalize on opportunity. Only a few measure up. Most operate like racehorses with blinders: focused on themselves, unable to see what is going on around them. Musharraf fell into the second category. Years ago, a poster in train stations depicted Julius Caesar on the steps of the Forum, his expression smug and self-satisfied. Unseen from behind, a gaggle of senators approached him with unsheathed blades. The caption read: "Did you ever wish you were better informed?" The unwitting Caesar encapsulated Musharraf.

In responding to Benazir's assassination, Musharraf and his team constructed a narrative around four confluent messages: Pakistan itself was the true victim of Benazir's assassination; violent extremists and terrorists were to blame; like Benazir, his government was fighting extremists while promoting democracy; and the evil perpetrators would be brought to justice.

He also excused his failure to protect Benazir by pleading ignorance of the security arrangements and arguing, incredulously, that the security apparatus reported to his prime minister, and therefore he bore no responsibility for them. Who was Musharraf kidding? Benazir herself had put him on notice about threats. It's clear from Taj's visit to her that the government was well aware that her life was under constant threat. Musharraf's close relationship with Taj renders implausible his claim of ignorance.

What could Musharraf have done? Realistically, his situation was nearly untenable. Almost certainly, her death killed his own political fortunes. A politician in that situation needs to swing for the fences. The possible tactics this book describes may seem cynical, but they are seen from an autocrat's viewpoint. This book argues at one level that Benazir's death was an irretrievable, tragic loss for Pakistan, the world, and her family. But at another, it is about strategic communication and how it can affect political fortunes, not morality.

The lessons from how well or poorly Musharraf applied the principles of strategic communication are not only applicable to Pakistan. They may apply in dealing with other authoritarian or semi-authoritarian regimes.

The analysis in chapter 17 presents thirty key precepts and tactics that surfaced in Musharraf's campaign. It reveals a kind of "government playbook," as viewed from his perspective, and then assesses how they all played out.

PART III.
DEALING WITH
THE ASSASSINATION

This section examines the campaign of influence that President Pervez Musharraf employed to limit the political damage caused by the assassination. It looks at how his team applied the principles of strategic communication, the aftermath of the tragedy, and the evidence as to possible suspects.

Chapter 17

THE CAMPAIGN
OF INFLUENCE

Benazir's assassination unleashed a tidal wave of anger. People felt bitter. While Musharraf had not liked Benazir, her death shocked him and his associates, and it showed. They froze. Poorly advised and isolated, Musharraf retreated into denial while his underlings put out conflicting stories. Realistically, his political fortunes had sustained a mortal wound, but his strategic communication worsened the situation and eliminated any chance he could recover politically. Politics is more fluid than it may appear. At a minimum, he might have gained more leverage in dealing with the aftermath of the assassination and political outcomes can be decided at the margins.

Journalists as well as Benazir's team believed that the Inter-Services Intelligence and Musharraf's Pakistan Muslim League–Qaid had intended to rig the elections.[1] Her assassination rendered that manipulation impractical as Chief of Army Staff Ashfaq Kayani pledged free and fair elections and made good on his commitment.

Musharraf failed to grasp his best opportunity to mobilize the nation behind him as a national leader, as President George W. Bush had done in the days following 9/11. He acknowledged that Benazir had been a nationally important leader. But he neither perceived her as a political figure who would unite the nation nor believed he needed a strategy for rallying the nation.

He felt that the Pakistan Army opposed her. He believed that Nawaz Sharif's Pakistan Muslim League–Nawaz Party despised her. Yet he had misread her political prospects and the political terrain. Journalists who covered the February 2008 elections agree that Musharraf seemed surprised when his party was soundly trounced at the polls. He had dismissed credible polling data provided him, putting his faith instead in data presented by sycophantic aides that suggested he was in good shape with the voters.

Hassan Abbas has suggested the assassination in August 2001 of Musharraf's chief of staff, Lt. Gen. Ghulam Ahmed Khan, deprived him of

> the most respected of Musharraf's generals and his greatest asset.
> . . . Apart from Generals Amjad and Mushtag, he was the only one
> who had the moral courage to dissent with the boss. . . . His death,
> which many believe was a conspiracy, was ominous for Pakistan.
> With his demise, Musharraf increasingly lost touch with reality and
> became a willing prisoner in a web of flattery.[2]

There's no question that Musharraf had enclosed himself in a small circle full of admirers and bereft of naysayers. It happens when politicians become too self-important. Henry Kissinger best summarizes the syndrome: "Those who say flattery doesn't work have never had it practiced on them."

The following key precepts defined what Musharraf needed for effective strategic communication after the assassination.

> **1.** Develop a narrative that defines a credible rationale which explains what you are doing and why. Define the stakes. Draw a clearcut distinction between what you and your adversaries stand for in a way that undercuts their credibility while bolstering your own.

Musharraf's campaign was methodical in getting out a message. Initially, key associates took the lead in speaking out. For a few days, he held his silence. Why he did that is unclear. This strategy made him seem remote and out of touch. First his team wheeled out Interior Ministry spokesman Brig. Gen. Javed Cheema, Prime Minister Muhammad Soomro, and Interior Minister Hamid Nawaz. These men stumbled in their assertions as to the cause of death and the security planned or provided at the park.

When Musharraf finally surfaced, the story became too much about himself instead of Pakistan as he fended off calls to resign.[3] Pakistan Peoples Party supporters had erupted in anger. Hoping to calm emotions, he declared a three-day period of mourning. He tried to identify himself with Benazir's goals of promoting democracy and fighting terrorism:

> Pakistan and the nation faces [*sic*] the greatest threat from these terrorists. I, on this tragic incident, want to express my resolve, and also seek solidarity from the nation, their cooperation, also to stand by me, that we will not rest with peace, until we eliminate these terrorists, and root them out. Because it is vital for the survival of our nation and for its development as these are a major impediment in our progress.[4]

The words were not credible. He had talked an antiterrorist line for eight years. He had gotten unimpressive results outside of rounding up Al Qaeda operatives. He needed to lay out a concrete action plan that Pakistanis believed was credible *and* that they would support. Pakistanis worried about religious extremism, but few wished to work with the United States in countering it. Polling by the International Republican Institute showed that 89 percent opposed cooperation with the United States, although 64 percent of respondents supported the Pakistan Army fighting extremists in the North-West Frontier Province and the Federally Administered Tribal Areas.

Musharraf's primary strategic goal should have been to *deflect the blame from himself*. He failed to drive a narrative or messages that could achieve it. He simply did not grasp that the assassination had blown apart his credibility. Already, the PPP suspected that he or members of his team were actively complicit in the assassination. Benazir had complained vigorously that Musharraf was out to get her.[5] As one skeptic put it, even if he didn't pull the trigger, Musharraf was cast in the role of Henry II who asked, rhetorically, "Will no one rid me of this turbulent priest?" Of course, Benazir had named plenty of other suspects, but for now it was Musharraf who held the spotlight.

How grave was his situation? An IRI poll taken January 19–29, 2008, showed that 62 percent of Pakistanis believed that the government, not Al

Qaeda, was responsible for Benazir's death. Only 13 percent blamed Al Qaeda. What made that finding worse was that 65 percent believed that the Taliban and Al Qaeda posed a serious problem, and a whopping 73 percent believed that religious extremism was a serious problem. Further, Musharraf's job approval had collapsed: 72 percent negative and 15 percent positive, versus only 26 percent negative and 54 percent positive less than a year earlier. Fully 75 percent believed Musharraf should have resigned.[6] People were never going to idolize him, but he had to work and neutralize the criticism that he or members of his team were involved.

Musharraf did understand the need to find a scapegoat. That was a smart play, but he fumbled badly. His first move was to order a crackdown on hooliganism under the Anti-Terrorism Act. That decision changed the discourse away from finding the murder culprits to asking why Musharraf was exploiting the assassination as an excuse to suppress political protests.[7] The tactic cross-pressured his message that he stood for democracy and against violent extremism.

Interior Ministry spokesman General Cheema was more on message. He spoke out prematurely about Benazir's cause of death. But he struck the right note in branding the assassination as "an act of terrorism"—not as an ordinary criminal case—and naming concrete suspects. He declared, "Al Qaeda and their facilitators, Baitullah, [and] Fazlullah are targeting the Army and the state institutions to destabilize the country."[8] The cabinet showed message discipline, echoing Cheema's statement and pledging "to fight the scourge of militancy and terrorism in all its forms and manifestations and to wipe out terrorists."[9]

Cheema drove the message by fingering a ringleader for the conspiracy— Baitullah Mehsud, the militant leader of Tehrik-i-Taliban-Pakistan (TTP).[10] Mehsud was highly visible. People knew who he was. He also seemed a plausible suspect. Pakistan's elite Special Investigation Group had found that of the twenty-six suicide attacks in 2007 where a head was recovered, the vast majority of the bombers were boys ages sixteen to twenty from the Mehsud tribe of Waziristan. Whether that analysis had been completed by December 28 is unclear. Although it did not do so, Pakistani intelligence, which apparently maintained ties to him, could have provided strong evidence to bolster this narrative.[11]

Linking Mehsud to the assassination offered Musharraf a good opportunity to move beyond general rhetoric to hammering a specific target as a terrorist. Indeed, as Mehsud had ties to Al Qaeda,[12] Musharraf could have blasted Mehsud for links to *foreign terrorist conspiracy* and set up an "us versus them" dichotomy. Pakistanis dislike violent foreign intruders. Blaming Al Qaeda—a terror organization led by foreigners—also had the convenience, at least as to the triggermen, of plausible truth.

Benazir had grasped the power of that idea. Her speeches had branded Pakistan's terrorist enemies as *foreigners*. Musharraf should have forcibly picked up that message and driven it. On this score, at least, he had credibility. He had delivered on his commitment to fight foreign Al Qaeda terrorists: Arabs, Uzbeks, Chechens, and other followers of Al Qaeda. In 2007 the military had tread softly as to the Taliban, but along with ISI it had detained more than five hundred Al Qaeda operatives. In Pakistan, Al Qaeda was a bogeyman. An anti–Al Qaeda message would have resonated.

Above all, Musharraf should have treated Mehsud as a criminal, not a political figure. Mehsud had been infamous for buying children as young as age eleven for suicide bombings and selling them to other groups for a profit of $6,000 to $12,000.[13] Musharraf could have appealed to parents to protect their children from false promises and a life of pain, suffering, and inevitable death. He could have presented graphic details from suicide attacks that had murdered innocent Pakistanis and used the concrete imagery to drive a dramatic narrative about the threat that violent extremists posed. He squandered that opportunity.

Once Mehsud and antiterrorism took center stage in his narrative, Musharraf needed to make Mehsud a poster child for what Pakistanis hated. Musharraf could not reclaim his popularity. He needed to try and blunt criticism by refocusing it against this different target. He could have framed a campaign that portrayed Meshud as a threat to the hopes and desires of all Pakistanis. Perhaps he intended to. But the attacks on Mehsud were clumsy. They increased doubts about the government more than hostility to Mehsud.

While scapegoating Al Qaeda, Musharraf also needed to show contrition and humility. He needed to acknowledge his opponents had a point about his high-handed approach to governing. He needed to show respect and call for common ground. On October 10, 2009, Musharraf seemed to accept the point somewhat, issuing an apology for sacking judges of the superior courts: "I think I committed mistakes which should not have been done at all. . . . Now, after seeing the incidents following his [the chief justice's] dismissal from office I realize I shouldn't have done that. Probably I won't commit such mistakes in the future."[14]

Good move, but two and a half years late. Mere rhetoric was not going to rescue his fortunes. Benazir had identified people she feared had planned to kill her. Musharraf needed to do *everything possible* to protect her, and then *communicate that he had done so.* Had assassins succeeded anyway, he needed to communicate that he had an action plan to find the would-be assassins and conduct a genuine, transparent investigation. Instead, the government took no real steps to launch an in-depth investigation into Benazir's assassination to hold culprits accountable.

He needed to make a credible, unequivocal pledge for free and open elections, as COAS Kayani did. Skeptics who believe Muslims dislike effective democracy are naive. Mark Siegel remarks that nothing was more important to Benazir and the PPP. What her team doubted was the government's good faith in allowing them. Benazir's team had a smart strategy to thwart vote rigging: public exposure. It assembled a 146-page report that detailed evidence of a government plan to rig the January 2008 elections. The report was compiled with help from friendly sources within the ISI.[15] Benazir planned to provide it to Congressman Patrick Kennedy, Senator Arlen Specter, and the press.[16] She was also going to deliver to Specter and Kennedy an explosive second report alleging that since 2001, the ISI had been diverting U.S. aid money intended to fight militants for a covert election operation.[17] Benazir's death did end the government's ability to rig the coming elections. Pakistanis were not going to tolerate more fraud at the polls.

Why did Musharraf hold back in calling for free elections? Apparently it defied his instincts. Isolating himself in Rawalpindi or Islamabad, he did not mount a campaign to reach out, Zahid Hussain has suggested, because "he simply did not think he needed one. He expected to win the 2008 elections and keep power."[18] His party's defeat in the elections, which took place in February after a month's delay, surprised him.

Meanwhile, Musharraf defended the military and intelligence services from blame. One would expect him to, but his coy defense of the ISI was too cute by half when he stated: "The ISI is doing exactly what the government wants it to do."[19] He failed as well to effectively address the controversy that erupted when CNN correspondent Wolf Blitzer broadcast an e-mail from Benazir, indicating it was to be released only if she were killed. In it, Benazir declared that if anything happened to her,

> [In] addition to the names in my letter of October 16th, I wld [sic] hold Musharraf responsible. I have been made to feel insecure by his minions and there is no way what is happening in terms of stopping me from taking private cars or using tinted windows or giving jammers or four police mobiles to cover all sides cld [sic] happen without him.[20]

Musharraf should have responded directly to this serious accusation. Instead he replied through a spokesman, who dismissed the e-mail. "It's a ridiculous statement which doesn't deserve a comment," Maj. Gen. Rashid Qureshi scoffed. "I don't want to dignify it by offering any comment on it."[21]

Obviously, what Musharraf should have done in the fall was to allow Benazir to bring in her own security team (e.g., Blackwater or ArmourGroup) as she had requested, and provide it strong support. He had refused. Having blundered on that issue, his strategic communication after the assassination should have *immediately* provided persuasive evidence that he and his team had amply warned Benazir about the danger of going to the park—as well as prior dangers—and argued she had ignored the cautions. He needed to drive the message that politicians should heed warnings.

The problem, as Gretchen Peters observes, is "that was asking him to embrace a standard of public relations for which he was never trained." Indeed, she notes, it is important to recognize that "the Pakistan military is extremely bad in managing the messages that come out about them." It is a lesson that remains unlearned, except for Kayani, who is well advised and has proven adept at it. A major general heads the Inter-Services Public Relations. Those military men who hold the leadership post usually have no training or background in public relations or in managing the media.

One issue that did concern Musharraf was U.S. support. He moved swiftly to protect his credibility on that front. Meeting U.S. Secretary of State Condoleezza Rice in Davos at the World Economic Forum in late January 2008, he stressed his commitment to fighting terrorism and extremism, and to restoration of democracy. Tactfully, no one mentioned that he had been the one to suspend democracy in Pakistan. They finessed his autocracy in their official statement by spotlighting "Pakistan's pivotal role in the global war on terror."[22]

In other messages to the nation, Musharraf and Soomro stressed the need to end the violent unrest that broke out after the assassination, ensure law and order,[23] and curb antistate conspiracy theories. They also appealed for brotherhood and unity while affirming the sanctity of the Holy Quran.[24] That overture was a good message but, as with other messages, remained undeveloped and undriven.

What was Musharraf's attitude? He refused to accept responsibility. In an interview with Fareed Zakaria for *Newsweek* published January 12, 2008, Musharraf focused on the assassination itself. He argued that Benazir had been targeted before and had been warned not to go to Liaquat Bagh. "And I told her," he declared. "I told her personally . . . that there is a threat in Rawalpindi, where she decided to go and address a gathering in Liaqat [*sic*] Bagh."[25]

Another well-respected reporter who covered Musharraf closely recounts an interview with him:

He was particularly cross when she got killed. He said she refused to be realistic about the risks, especially when it came to rallies. The highest risk moment is when you leave a rally. That's when an attack is most likely to strike. Musharraf said he felt fine entering a rally because everybody is checked. "During the time I'm speaking," he said, "I feel fine. When you really have to worry is when you leave. You can be dangerously exposed. When I'm done, I get out there as fast as I can."

The journalist notes, "Security checked people as they entered the park. Then they lost interest. That was typical for Pakistan. Her attackers were clever. They stayed outside the park gates and waited. That was, incidentally, a definite step-up in tactics for suicide attacks."[26]

Prime Minister Soomro promised that justice would be done. He ordered a judicial inquiry to be headed by a High Court Judge appointed in consultation with Benazir Bhutto's family and the PPP leadership. He warned "saboteurs and antistate elements" against exploiting the situation.[27] Soomro noted that the government of Punjab had also ordered an investigation that would be conducted under the supervision of the additional inspector general of the Punjab police.[28] Soomro was well respected and brought some credibility. His promise to launch an investigation was the correct move. Unfortunately, the government failed to carry through on this promise in a meaningful way.

SCOTLAND YARD VERSUS THE UNITED NATIONS

After the assassination, the PPP issued demands to call in the United Nations to assist the investigation. Musharraf instead summoned Scotland Yard, which has had a history of investigating assassinations in Pakistan. Left open were questions as to why he objected to the United Nations conducting an inquiry. He made a tactical error in providing oblique explanations. His response undercut the perception that he was committed to a serious investigation, especially once it emerged that the British investigation would be limited to the actual cause of death and not the circumstances surrounding it. Indeed, Musharraf was unnecessarily tentative about the PPP's demand. First he said that the government "may" investigate those whom Benazir named as suspects in her October letter to Musharraf. Later he said that an investigation assisted by Scotland Yard was already in progress and that people "should await the results of the investigation."[29] For someone who was strongly convinced he had done no wrong, those statements raised doubts about credibility.

Predictably, PPP members rejected a Pakistani investigation. They felt sure that Musharraf would produce a whitewash.[30] PPP leaders pointed out that the government had not investigated the Karachi attempt, and they foresaw no realistic possibility of securing a "transparent" one under President Musharraf now. Ironically, while PPP leaders dismissed a Scotland Yard probe of the assassination in favor of a United Nations–led effort,[31] Bhutto's husband, Zardari, was initially supportive of Musharraf's plan.[32] But once Scotland Yard released a report in 2008 that was inconsistent with what PPP eyewitnesses had described, the PPP stepped up its demands to bring in the UN.[33] In 2009 the secretary-general of the United Nations appointed a three-member commission of inquiry to determine the facts and circumstances of the assassination.[34]

Only days after Benazir's death, then-senator Hillary Clinton had given the PPP her support and had called for an independent, international probe.[35] The future secretary of state rebuked Musharraf: "I don't think the Pakistani government at this time under President Musharraf has any credibility at all. They have disbanded an independent judiciary, they oppressed a free press."[36] Her speaking out resonated well with the PPP, which finally got a UN commission to investigate after Asif Ali Zardari became president in September 2008. The commission's report was curiously limited in scope and assigned no guilt for any culprits.

After the assassination, the Pakistan Bar Council promptly demanded that deposed Supreme Court chief justice Iftikhar Chaudhry lead a judicial inquiry into Benazir's death.[37] Given the controversy over its relations with the judiciary, the government should have addressed the council's resolution forcefully either by agreeing to a probe or providing clear, convincing reasons why calling in an outside third party made more sense. Failing to do so was another strategic fumble.

Where was the military on this issue? It stood with Musharraf. Whatever his flaws as a civilian political leader, Musharraf knew military politics. Shuja Nawaz has pointed out that he put more than a thousand officers "into senior positions in the civil administration, academia, foreign service and even civil service training institutions."[38] They provided a base of support. He notes that

Lt. Gen. Ashfaq Kayani, upon taking over as COAS, both banned officers from meeting with any politician except with his express consent and ordered several hundred of Musharraf's officers who were in civilian posts to return to the army or retire.[39]

The Punjab government, meanwhile, offered a reward of 5 million rupees for anyone providing information about those who killed Bhutto.[40]

> **2.** Keep message discipline. Among the few universal precepts in political communication is *repetition* equals *penetration* equals *impact*.

Musharraf claimed that at Liaquat Bagh, a thousand police and sharpshooters were stationed to protect Benazir, a figure inflated to thirteen hundred men by his interior minister, Gen. Hamid Nawaz.[41] Opinions vary as to the accuracy of those numbers. Benazir supporters scoff at that assertion. Perhaps such security was on hand when Benazir entered the park, but it was virtually invisible as she made her departure. Interior Ministry spokesman Cheema released different stories about the cause of Benazir's death. But, on balance, Musharraf and key officials such as Soomro demonstrated reasonable message discipline.

The PPP also maintained strong message discipline in calling for an international investigation led by the United Nations. That appeal shored up the party's claim that it was the champion of open government while raising further doubts about Musharraf.

> **3.** Get ahead of the story by getting out your narrative first. It shows you are on top of the facts. Avoid the trap of key officials contradicting themselves.

The Pakistani Information Ministry moved quickly to identify Benazir's cause of death, but its story changed. On Friday morning, December 28, it said that her death had been caused by a wound to the neck.[42] Those who contend that a bullet hit her in the neck also argue that the bullet traveled to her head and exited out of the right side. That assertion might account for how shots fired by the shooter, who is seen in video footage standing behind Benazir and to her left, might have struck her.

By that evening, though, the official line had changed. Dripping with sweat, Javed Cheema began shouting with skeptical reporters when he denied the existence of any shrapnel or bullet wounds. Now he insisted that she had hit her head against the lever of her vehicle's "sunroof" while trying to duck:

> The suicide bomber was on the left side of the vehicle. When she was waving, three shots were fired. But none hit her. Then there was a blast as the suicide bomber exploded himself. With that pressure of the shockwave, Benazir Bhutto fell down and tried to tug down into the vehicle. When she was tugging down and was thrown by the force of that shockwave of the explosion, unfortunately one of the levers on the left side of the sunroof hit her on her right side which caused a fracture of the skull and that caused her death.[43]

Britain's Channel 4 broadcast a report that included photographs of the sunroof lever, but they showed no trace of blood.[44] The visual evidence did not support Cheema's latest story. Cheema then changed his explanation for the third time. That Saturday morning, the government cited a medical report that said shrapnel in Benazir's head had caused her death.[45] Later, Cheema offered a fourth version. Citing the same medical report, he claimed that Benazir had died as a result of a skull fracture sustained either when she fell against the lever of the sunroof after the explosion or when she ducked.[46]

On Tuesday, Prime Minister Soomro apologized for Cheema's statement. After trying in vain to defend the spokesman before skeptical newspaper editors, he advised them to ignore Cheema. Soomro offered no explanation as to Benazir's cause of death.[47]

No proof has emerged, but former ISI director Lt. Gen. Hamid Gul has suggested that she was indeed killed by a bullet fired by a marksman some distance from her vehicle. Gul may well know more than he reveals.

4. Invoke "democracy," "freedom," and "fairness" often as your core values. Denounce "terrorism" and "extremism." That's a crowd pleaser in Washington and keeps the aid dollars flowing. If complaints about repression grow too heated, explain that freedom and due process are suspended only as necessary to preserve democracy.

Musharraf and his team invoked "freedom," "democracy," "free and fair elections," "equal participation of all parties," "law and order," and the need to "combat terrorism and extremism" at every turn. It was a good play, although PPP critics greeted their statements as hypocrisy. Years before, the communists had discovered the power of claiming to support "democracy" in appealing to popular support. Not accidentally is North Korea officially called the Democratic People's Republic of Korea. East Germany's official name was the German Democratic Republic, and South Yemen—a Marxist state before its leaders threw in their lot to form the current Republic of Yemen—used to be the People's Democratic Republic of Yemen.

Muslims vary in their responses to whether they embrace the notion of "democracy." In Pakistan, 50 percent of respondents in a 2006 Pew survey responded that democracy could work well there.[48] Pakistanis desire democracy, but they want effective democracy. Even granting that it didn't poll the Federally Administered Tribal Areas and one other small area, the International Republican Institute's data strongly bears out that conclusion. Asked to choose between a stable and prosperous Pakistan ruled by a military dictatorship or a democratic government that led to an unstable and insecure Pakistan, by a margin of 77 percent to 20 percent, respondents picked democracy.[49]

One lesson in strategic communication when dealing with other countries is that we should distinguish between what Pakistanis expect from their own leaders and how they view American behavior. They perceive the United States as hypocritical in its support of authoritarian regimes around the world and overly intrusive in their own internal affairs. In 2011 drone attacks launched by Americans against targets inside Pakistan stoked intense fires of resentment. In Pakistan, discontent sharpened over Washington's muted response as Musharraf sacked judges, declared an emergency, and suspended the Constitution. The judiciary later found all of his actions to be illegal.

In 2007 the Pew Global Attitudes Project survey found that many Muslims disliked American ideas about democracy. Pew evaluated their response as a reflection of the way they feel that "the U.S. has implemented its pro-democracy agenda and America's democratic values."[50] In Pakistan, the Pew 2007 data found that 68 percent of respondents held an unfavorable view of the United States compared to only 15 percent who viewed it favorably. Subsequent IRI polling in 2009 puts Pakistanis' favorable attitudes toward the United States at 2 percent. For those seeking good news, the data revealed one plus side: In the same poll, the United States fared better than Iran, which had a favorability rating of only 1 percent.[51]

The polling data reveals a major irony about American attitudes. U.S. policymakers rank promoting democracy as a top priority. Ordinary Americans do not. Pew has found that "among the foreign policy priorities of Americans, little support can be found for promoting U.S. values—including democracy."[52] In 2004, presented with nineteen potential foreign policy problems that merit top priority, Americans ranked promoting democracy abroad eighteenth.[53]

> **5.** Promote an image of honesty and sincerity.

Musharraf worked hard to project himself as honest and sincere. In suspending the Constitution with a tone that bespoke somber regret, he expressed sadness over Benazir's assassination. That was believable, given that her murder had destroyed his own political fortunes. But his credibility had dwindled to the point where little could be done.

One group of people did believe that Musharraf was honest and sincere about fighting terrorism: the violent extremists. They felt certain that he had thrown in his lot with the United States. At a minimum, he had cozied up to America more than they could countenance. Musharraf's skeptics included former ISI chief General Gul and former COAS Gen. Mirza Beg (Ret.). There was no love lost between Musharraf and such critics. In 2005 Beg, Gul, and over two dozen other flag officers—most of whom loathed the United States, opposed Musharraf's liberal reforms, and sympathized with the Taliban—publicly called for his resignation. In an ironic twist, their demand was issued in the name of restoring democracy.[54]

6. Project strength and integrity.

Musharraf believed in himself. His enemies finally knocked him out, but he went down slugging. Musharraf was savvy in asking Washington and Saudi Arabia to exert their considerable muscle to ensure his safe exit and political immunity from reprisal.[55] They obliged, and a political deal was cut. The Saudis' input was pivotal, as they had the ability to force Nawaz Sharif to acquiesce to this understanding. They knew Nawaz was still smarting from the 1999 Musharraf-led coup and an edict of exile that Nawaz likes to dismiss as "political," as if that exonerated him from nearly killing a planeload of passengers when he first tried to return in 2007. Left to his own devices, the self-righteous Nawaz would probably hang Musharraf.

How strong was Musharraf as a political leader? Journalists who covered him closely mostly give him credit for sincerely believing that he was acting in Pakistan's best interests. But they maintain Musharraf's credibility was undermined by his failure to reform the madrassas,[56] root out corruption, and get Pakistan's economy on its feet, and his ambivalent attitude about truly combating terrorism and extremism, or making good on his seven-point agenda used to justify his 1999 coup. His tough treatment of the PPP and the PML-N enabled more extreme religious parties to emerge, accentuated by his own party's coalition with the United Action Front (Muttahida Majlis-e-Amal) in Baluchistan and the North-West Frontier Province. Siding with the Islamists to bolster his credibility in an Islamic nation was dangerous. Critics fault him for fostering the crisis with those extremists he claimed to combat.

In journalist Ahmed Rashid's words, under Musharraf

the contradictions in Pakistan's counterterrorism strategy were becoming glaring. Even as the ISI helped the CIA run down al Qaeda leaders in Pakistan's cities, Pakistani Islamist militants, with quiet ISI approval, were attacking Indian troops in Kashmir or helping the Taliban regroup in Pakistan. Yet al Qaeda itself was involved in training and funding the Islamist militants ordered to kill Musharraf. The regime continued to differentiate between so-called good jihadis, who fought in Kashmir on behalf of the ISI, and bad terrorists who were largely Arabs—but such differences had long ceased to exist. In a briefing, Musharraf divided the extremists into three groups—the al Qaeda–Taliban, the Pakistani sectarian groups, and the "freedom fighters of Kashmir." The military was clearly signaling that it still considered some jihadis as acceptable and was maintaining links with them.[57]

Bahukutumbi Raman is a critic of Musharraf's policies toward militants. He contends that Musharraf personally undercut Nawaz's effort to persuade Mullah Omar to turn Osama bin Laden over to the United States. He asserts that Musharraf put together a secret ISI task force headed by ISI director general Lt. Gen. Mahmood Ahmed to break the PPP and to encourage religious extremist groups, including Qazi Hussain Ahmed's Jamaat-e-Islami, Maulana Fazlur Rahman's Jamiat Ulema-e-Islam, Sipah Sahaba Pakistan, and the especially notorious Lashkar-e-Jhangvi.[58] Raman notes, however, that tensions arose between Musharraf and Islamist generals, such as Lt. Gen. Mohammed Aziz, after Musharraf appeared amenable to coordinating action with the U.S. forces against Al Qaeda and putting the brakes on nuclear proliferation.[59]

Musharraf's views changed over time. The assassination attempts on his life in 2003 altered Musharraf's desire—if not his ability to act—to deal with violent extremists. Where Nawaz really stands on violent extremist groups is not clear. In 2009, Kayani had to force him to support the military's offensive in FATA. Musharraf has charged that the PML-N leader is a "closet Talib" who personally has held half a dozen meetings with bin Laden.

Musharraf lacked the strength to stop the ISI from maintaining strong links to extremists.[60] How he viewed this issue is murky, but the record shows that ISI has operated on both sides of the street. When U.S. surveillance made helping the Taliban more difficult, the ISI hit on a devilishly simple solution. It created a new clandestine organization that would operate outside the military and intelligence structure, in the civilian sphere. Former ISI trainers of the Taliban, retired Pashtun officers from the army and especially the Frontier Corps were rehired on contract. . . . There were no records, and logistics and expenses came not through the ISI but the less scrutinized offices of the Frontier Corps. The close-knit bond and camaraderie between former ISI and army officers who had served clandestinely in Afghanistan over the past twenty years provided just the platform needed for such an organization. Meanwhile, senior retired ISI officers in the public eye, such as former ISI chief Lt.-Gen. Hamid Gul, played an equally important role in mobilizing public support for the Taliban in the media and for political platforms.[61]

Apparently Musharraf tolerated this practice. Many ask whether Musharraf could be trusted. The issue in politics is not whether you can trust a person but with what. Too often, a politician's promise to deliver exceeds what is possible, yet limitations are rarely acknowledged. Political leaders seek to project an image of power, not weakness.

Musharraf's critics believe he could have more vigorously confronted militants. But until recently, the army showed limited inclination to take them on. In 2010, Kayani declared that the Afghan and Pakistani Taliban were the same, although many view them as distinct groups and argue that different elements have different motivations. The Haqqani network has supported the transnational aspirations of Al Qaeda. Gulbuddin Hekmatyar is identified with Al Qaeda, but his history is that of an ambitious, treacherous extremist focused on seizing power again in Afghanistan, not New York. Many Taliban appear increasingly focused on the international drug trade and money laundering, justifying these actions in the name of Islam. In Afghanistan, the Taliban have sought to posture themselves as a national force standing above any ethnic group or political faction. Still, it appears that many Afghan Taliban see their battle as an insurrection by Pashtuns to regain control of their country against a Tajik-Uzbek-Hazara government with Hamid Karzai serving as a

Pashtun facade. In Pakistan, despite the rhetoric of some Taliban who pledge allegiance to Mullah Omar and bin Laden, most politicians focus on establishing an Islamic state with sharia as the law of the land and on righting injustices of a corrupt government that denied opportunity to younger, deprived generations. Its violence against innocent civilians has undercut its credibility and potential popularity.

> **7.** Exude hope, optimism, and confidence. That message is especially relevant in Pakistan, which suffers from an insecure identity.

In dealing with militant groups, the interests of Washington and Islamabad have differed. Americans want them crushed. Pakistanis have viewed some of them as strategic assets.

Musharraf's rhetoric exemplified ebullience. He talked about a more modern Pakistan that provided security, hope, and opportunity through democracy. Pursuing strategic communication that defined the voters' choice between what he and his fellow Pakistanis stood for and what those responsible for Benazir's assassination stood for, and driving a message about the stakes, was an opportunity that he missed.

> **8.** Convince the citizens that you reflect popular values. It's smart to demonize adversaries for abusing those same values. The catch is, unless your actions uphold those values, people will lose faith in you.

Musharraf failed here. He rooted his themes in security, safety, democracy, and prosperity and defined his opponents as hooligans, terrorists, and violent extremists who sough to destabilize Pakistan. He seized power in the name of democracy. Pakistanis scorned his abuse of the judiciary and his suspension of the Constitution. He trapped himself in precisely the bog in which he hoped to cast his opponents. Musharraf showed that leaders who bend the rules too much forfeit legitimacy, credibility, and power.

> **9.** Remember that the people care about the future, not the past. Your past success is relevant primarily to prove your willingness and ability to deliver. *Exception*: Benazir faced a notable challenge for strategic communication here rooted in accusations that she and her husband had looted the national treasury of more than $1 billion. *Lesson*: Failure to exploit criticism of opponents.

Musharraf had called Benazir a thief. He blamed her and Nawaz for corruption and the country's economic problems.[62] Those charges represented a powerful argument against them. No agreement for Benazir's return was possible unless Musharraf supported the National Reconciliation Ordinance[63] that granted immunity to all public office holders against whom proceedings for acts of corruption, embezzlement, money laundering, murder, and terrorism were taken between January 1, 1986, and October 12, 1999, the period between two states of martial law in Pakistan. But that support cost him an important lever for influencing public opinion in the coming elections.

Supporting the NRO left Musharraf politically vulnerable while Benazir branded him a military dictator. In Washington, she had built an influential network of friends. She knew whom to touch and what to say. She had paid the public relations firm Burson-Marsteller $250,000—in 1987 a major fee for such services—to help her court favor with journalists, administration officials, and members of Congress. Her pitch resonated perfectly. She spoke up for democracy and described the mujahideen as brave "freedom fighters" who were battling the Soviets in Afghanistan.[64]

She had nurtured her network and, in 2007, mobilized it. She understood the political damage the allegations of corruption had inflicted. She handled the issue well, categorizing the claims as political and shifting to safer ground by talking about what she stood for. She used excellent strategic communication. Her message of idealism, hope, social justice, and democracy transcended the personal charges against her. Her personal appeal was compelling. Even top journalists who were severely critical of her record as prime minister regarded themselves as her personal friends. She was interesting, intellectual, charismatic—rare qualities in any political figure. It did not hurt that she spoke perfect English, was eloquent, and loved peppermint ice cream. Plus she had been to all the right schools and made friends with all the right people. A committed nationalist, she was also thoroughly at home in New York, Washington, Boston, and London. She would have flourished as a candidate for the U.S. Senate from New York.[65] Politically, her skills easily outclassed those of her military rival, making it difficult for him to best her in strategic communication.

Both Benazir and Musharraf viewed Washington and London as political bases. Neither liked or trusted the other, but he needed a deal and she desperately wanted one. They became locked in a game in which each could inflict real damage upon the other. For most of it, she was the one who lit up the scoreboard.[66]

> **10.** Inevitably, some people will question the official line. They may back up these questions with scientific or empirical evidence. Monitor such persons carefully. Help them see why sticking to the official narrative is a good idea. *Example*: If an opponent is assassinated and your line is that bullets missed the target, get to the attending surgeon before he tells the press that the corpse had a bullet wound. That may avoid embarrassment when surgeons sign a report to the contrary.

Dr. Mohammad Mussadiq Khan was the principal professor of surgery at Rawalpindi General Hospital (RGH) and a member of the team attending Benazir. In a twist of irony, his father had served as the attending physician when the nation's first prime minister, Liaquat Ali Khan, had been shot at the same park. Dr. Khan signed the hospital medical report, but he has told different stories about her injuries. He told one person that Benazir had two bullet wounds—one in the temporal parietal region and the other in the chest. He stated that she had initially been handed over alive to "under-training [*sic*] doctors, PG's (postgraduates) . . . while top surgeons were already present in the hospital." In this account, Dr. Khan pronounced the cause of death as excessive bleeding and vascular injuries of the brain.[67] A personal friend of Dr. Khan's who spoke to him an hour or so after she was pronounced dead, however, disclosed that Dr. Khan denied the existence of a bullet wound.[68]

Athar Minallah, at Rawalpindi General, released a medical report along with an open letter showing that the doctors wanted to distance themselves from the government's theory that Benazir had died from hitting her head on a lever of the Toyota's sunroof. He stated that Dr. Khan had told him that Benazir's cause of death was a bullet wound. Through Minallah, Khan declined to speak with the media on the grounds that he was a government employee and feared government reprisal. Minallah said the doctors had stressed to him that without an autopsy, it was not possible to determine what caused Bhutto's death.[69] The seven doctors who wrote the "treatment report" advised Athar Minallah, who is a lawyer and a member of the Board of Management of the Rawalpindi Medical College and the RGH, that they feared that their initial account would be twisted politically.[70]

The *Washington Post* described one doctor's tale:

"The government took all the medical records right after Ms. Bhutto's time of death was read out," said a visibly shaken doctor who spoke on condition of anonymity because of the sensitivity of the issue. Sweating and putting his head in his hands, he said: "Look, we have been told by the government to stop talking. And a lot of us feel this is a disgrace."[71]

Subsequent hospital statements did not refer to any bullet wounds. RGH medical superintendent Dr. Habib Ahmed Khan, Allied Hospitals chief executive Dr. Musaddiq Hussain, and Additional Superintendent Dr. Fayyaz Ahmed Khan told a press conference on the evening of Saturday, December 29, that an open head injury with depressed fracture leading to cardiopulmonary arrest caused Benazir's death. Dr. Hussain said the doctors "did not find any bullet or shrapnel." He reported no wound on her neck or body.[72] It bears noting that the United Nations Commission reviewed a great deal of evidence and heard a lot of testimony on this issue. It concluded that it had "not been provided with any credible, new information showing that Ms. Bhutto had received bullet wounds."[73]

Yet the matter is unresolved. Aside from contradicting what Minallah and Dr. Mohammad Mussadiq Khan had stated, eyewitness testimony refuted the doctors' assertion. The PPP information secretary, Sherry Rehmand, told CNN that "there were clear bullet injuries to her head. When we bathed her, we saw that."[74] Witnesses told the *Daily Times* "that five shots were fired at Liaquat Bagh in all. Three of the bullets, they said, hit Bhutto, one injured [the] People's Student Federation (PSF) city president and one missed the target."[75] Amir Mir raises the issue of whether there had been multiple sharpshooters. He cites no source for that assertion.[76] Although twenty-four people including the suicide attacker were killed by the bomb that exploded,[77] the UN Commission noted only one shooter, who fired three shots.[78]

Britain's Channel 4 Television conducted a detailed examination of the videotape of the assassination and consulted a ballistics expert. It concluded that three shots were fired and that two mortally wounded Benazir. It discounted the theory that the blast killed her, arguing that she had disappeared inside the well-armored vehicle prior to the explosion. The blast killed no one inside the vehicle.[79]

Accounts differed in how many bullets were fired and the direction from which they were fired. The shooter in the video was on her left. Scotland Yard reported that her only apparent injury was a trauma on the right side of her head. X-rays had been taken only of her head.[80] As noted earlier, that discrepancy may be explained by the trajectory of the bullet if it entered the neck and angled up through the head. The government destroyed forensic evidence by hosing down the blast scene, withheld evidence about weapons, and pressured physicians to keep their mouths shut. Why did full disclosure frighten it? Could she have been killed by sniper fire from a rifle? That seems a plausible explanation. It would obviously blow a hole in the official narrative that Al Qaeda or Baitullah Mehsud of the TTP killed her. Al Qaeda operatives have employed different tactics in attacking their targets, but outside of Iraq this style of terrorist assassination would be unexpected.

> **11.** In cases of assassination, insist on an autopsy unless there is good reason to avoid one. Otherwise, your credibility takes a hit.

No autopsy was conducted, a decision taken by Rawalpindi police chief Saud Aziz. Even for suspected murder, an autopsy was legally mandatory.[81] As Minallah pointed out, the RGH physicians had stressed that an autopsy was necessary to determine the cause of death.[82] That assertion had aggravated the challenge to the government. Matters became worse as U.S. experts in forensic pathology severely criticized the medical procedure as flawed for failing to examine thoroughly Benazir's clothing when she was killed or samples of debris in the blast zone. Strikingly, no forensic pathologist had signed the final medical report.[83] One was not conducted out of deference to her husband Asif Ali Zardari's wishes.[84]

> **12.** Credible third parties, such as Scotland Yard and the United Nations, can bolster a narrative, but limit the scope of any outside examination. Doing so can avoid undesirable reports that suggest the government was negligent or, for sinister reasons, engaged in a cover-up. Of course, for good strategic communication, it pays to look ahead. A second commission of inquiry, similar to the one convened by the United Nations, can punch holes in the conclusions of the first one. It can also produce embarrassing revelations.

Pakistan has a history of obstructing investigations in high-profile assassinations. The first inquired into the assassination of Pakistan's first prime minister, Liaquat Ali Khan.[85] For unclear reasons, the British investigator was asked to leave Pakistan only a few weeks into his investigation,[86] although ten months later a report was released that merely produced conspiracy theories. The senior police officer in charge of the case was asked to bring all his documents to the new prime minister. His plane crashed, terminating the investigation.[87]

After Gen. Zia ul-Haq was killed in 1988, COAS Gen. Mirza Beg told army colleagues that he would pursue, catch, and bring the perpetrators to justice. Nothing definitive happened. As the American ambassador had also been a casualty in the crash, by U.S. law the Federal Bureau of Investigation was required to investigate. No FBI agents were allowed into the country for seven months, and the commander of U.S. Central Command Gen. George Crist halted its investigation.[88]

In 1996 Benazir's brother—and airline hijacker—Murtaza Bhutto was killed in a shoot-out with police. Then prime minister, Benazir called in Scotland Yard to investigate. Soon after, President Farooq Leghari dismissed her as prime minister and sent Scotland Yard packing.[89]

On January 2, 2008, Musharraf summoned British investigators for the third time, stating: "We want to know what the reasons were, and who the people were behind Mohtarma Benazir Bhutto's assassination."[90] He directed Scotland Yard to make all-out efforts to get to the "bottom of the issue" into the assassination, adding that "we will do our best to know the truth about the death of the Pakistan People's Party leader."[91] Musharraf sounded resolute, but his failure to carry through further damaged his shrinking credibility.

The Pakistani Interior Ministry carefully limited the scope of Scotland Yard's investigation "to assist[ing] the local authorities in providing clarity regarding the precise cause of Ms. Bhutto's death. . . . The team will provide forensic expertise and other investigative assistance."[92] The hospital team was not allowed to conduct an autopsy. Scotland Yard was not allowed to delve into who organized the assassination. Its brief was to interview the physicians and review the evidence that the government possessed to determine the physical cause of Benazir's death.

Scotland Yard issued a report on Benazir on February 8, 2008. Acknowledging that evidence was limited, it determined there had been a single assailant.[93] Despite the absence of an autopsy, Scotland Yard felt that its examination of X-rays of her head combined with its interviews of those who washed her were sufficient to reveal that

the only tenable cause for the rapidly fatal head injury in this case is that it occurred as the result of impact due to the effects of the bomb blast. . . . Mohtarma Benazir Bhutto died as a result of a severe

Nawaz Sharif (center left) and his brother Shahbaz, leaders of PML-N.
© Rahat Dar/epa/Corbis

President Pervez Musharraf looking presidential. © Olivier Matthys/epa/Corbis

A charismatic Benazir Bhutto campaigns in 1986. © Michel Philippot/Sygma/Corbis

Pervez Musharraf and his successor as Army Chief of Staff, Lt. Gen. Ashfaq Parvez Kayani. Kayani is seen as the real power in Pakistan. © Mian Khursheed/Reuters/Corbis

Pakistanis protest the detention of nuclear scientist A. Q. Khan. © Asim Tanveer/ Reuters/Corbis

Benazir Bhutto on the campaign hustings. © T. Mughal/epa/Corbis

President Muhammad
Zia ul-Haq. © Henri
Bureau/Sygma/Corbis

Pakistan Supreme Court
Chief Justice Iftikhar
Muhammad Chaudhry
© Mian Khursheed/
Reuters/Corbis

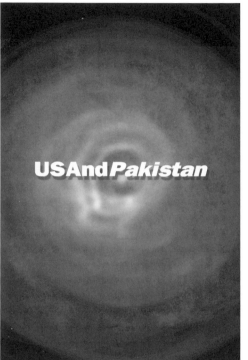

Pakistani government antiterrorist television ad series (2008–2009).

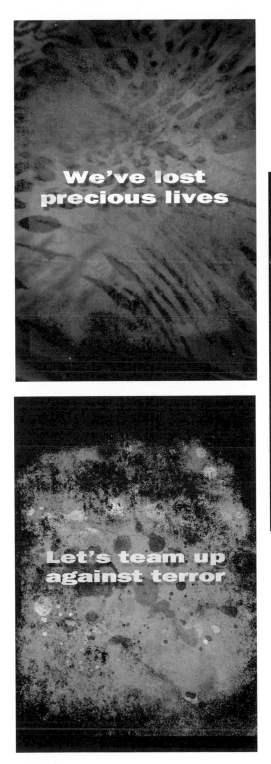

Because
when we win

the world wins

USAndUS

TEAM AGAINST TERROR

head injury sustained as a consequence of the bomb blast and due to head impact somewhere in the escape hatch of the vehicle.[94]

Scotland Yard's conclusion dismissed the government's sunroof lever theory, although Interior Ministry spokesman Brigadier Cheema by then had backed off of it as a rush to judgment.

Others have questioned both Scotland Yard's conclusions and the behavior of RGH physicians.[95] UK Home Office pathologist Dr. Nathaniel Cary was unable to exclude the possibility of a gunshot wound to the upper trunk or neck of Benazir, even though he discounted it.[96] Dr. Thomas M. Scalea, the chief physician for the University of Maryland Shock Trauma Center, found perplexing the idea that the blunt force of Bhutto's head hitting an object could have caused brain damage severe enough to kill her. "The whole thing strikes me as very unusual," he said.[97]

The United Nations examined the Scotland Yard report. It found the Scotland Yard's failure to denounce the "poor performance of the Rawalpindi police" at the crime scene as "unfortunate."[98] The police had failed to note the original location of the evidence—all twenty-three pieces of it—that had been collected. With a narrow mandate, Scotland Yard made no reference whatsoever to how the intelligence agencies collected the evidence. The United Nations concluded that much of the context of its report was "taken on good faith from the Rawalpindi police. That good faith was, in many respects, abused by officers of the Rawalpindi District Police, particularly with respect to security arrangements."[99] The commission blasted the police for providing false accounts.

13. Blessings from foreign leaders can produce mixed results.

A well-publicized vote of confidence in Musharraf from five of six Republican candidates for the U.S. presidency had a dubious impact. Senator John McCain proclaimed that "Musharraf has done most of the things we wanted him to do." As nearly 90 percent of Pakistanis opposed cooperation with the United States in fighting terrorism, and 70 percent or more not only disapproved of Musharraf's job performance but also wanted him to resign, one might wonder what effect such statements had. It's worth considering as U.S. political leaders look for allies in South Asia.

> **14.** It's good to have allies at home you can call on, but allies who behave like bullies can be a problem.

Coalitions—parties, organizations, or just collections of committed individuals—can bolster a politician's credibility. Benazir understood that concept. In 2007, she was willing to put aside bitter differences with Nawaz to forge a coalition to beat Musharraf. Musharraf should have taken note.

He preached democracy but displayed no grasp of how his allies' actions represented a form of strategic communication that could cripple him. When the lawyers marched and judges resigned to protest the suspension of Chief Justice Iftikhar Chaudhry, Musharraf's allies swung into action. All of it was misguided. Cane-wielding police beat lawyers and stamped out protests. Riot police savaged the studios of the private Geo television station. Violent clashes broke out in Karachi between the Muttahida Quami Movement—a political party allied with Musharraf that controlled Karachi—and opposition parties.

Dr. Rasul Bakhsh Rais of Lahore University described a pro-Musharraf rally: "The scenes were brutally contrasting. Young men were dying, collapsing before cameras in Karachi while people were dancing on the beat of drums in front of the national parliament."[100] Thousands of lawyers were detained.[101] The government monitored national Urdu- and English-language newspapers. Special officers scanned news, editorials, and readers' letters that criticized Musharraf or the government. Soldiers even stormed Pakistan's Human Rights Commission.[102]

Musharraf's Dutch allies responded by freezing millions of dollars in development aid, although U.S. aid remained unaffected.[103] Happily for Musharraf, his friend in the White House was still supportive. Forgotten was the Bush administration's inexpedient rhetoric about standing up for democracy. On November 11, 2007, months into the judicial crisis and weeks after the Karachi assassination attempt against Benazir, the *New York Times* reported that President Bush had offered his strongest defense yet of General Musharraf, praising his government's steps against Al Qaeda's top leaders since the 2001 terrorist attacks. Mr. Bush's remarks signaled the depth of the administration's reliance on the Pakistani leader, a position that has been widely interpreted in Pakistan as acquiescence in the general's week-old crackdown.[104]

Neither Bush nor Musharraf seemed to comprehend how badly Bush's declaration hurt efforts to mobilize Pakistani support for fighting violent extremists. Somehow, politicians forget the familiar lesson: Your enemies can hurt you, but your friends can kill you.

> **15.** When the discourse is going against you, look for side issues—for example, whether a target fell victim to a blast or to bullets. They may divert attention from awkward questions, such as who plotted the murder.

Reports vary as to what weapon was used to kill Benazir. Different accounts include a .30-caliber pistol, a 9mm gun, and a sniper rifle.[105] The police disclosed that two pistols had been recovered from the site, along with the head of the bomber, body parts, and mobile phones.[106] The government has declined to discuss who might have employed these weapons or to verify what it recovered. What did the government fear? Were the guns traceable to official sources?

After the Karachi incident, Benazir and the PPP charged that the government intentionally failed to protect Benazir and was thus complicit in the attack. Musharraf ignored repeated calls to open an investigation.[107] Some saw significance in the release from police custody of Qari Saifullah Akhtar, the former head of Harkat ul-Jihad-al-Islami (HUJI). Benazir had believed he was aiming to kill her.[108]

> **16.** Cleaning up a crime scene quickly can eliminate incriminating evidence; however, it also may lead to cries of a cover-up.

When assassins tried to kill Musharraf, the crime scene was sealed and combed for clues. Not so this time. Authorities wasted little time in cleaning up the blast site with high-pressure hoses. The police action was extremely controversial. SP Khurram Shahzad ordered the scene hosed down and cleaned after securing permission from his superior officer, Rawalpindi police chief Saud Aziz. The UN Commission reviewed this issue closely. Pakistani police practice for crime scene management is not consistent. But senior police officials it interviewed sharply criticized the decision. Sources told the Commission that Army Headquarters ordered Aziz to have the crime scene hosed down. It was an extraordinary act.[109] What was the army's motive?

Forensic evidence that may have provided clues as to the explosives utilized was obliterated.[110] An FBI special agent familiar with Pakistan commented to the *New Republic* that "hundreds of photos should have been taken. All the blood stains and bomb residue should have been swabbed, and shell casing and bomb fragments should have been mapped to 'freeze frame' the scene."[111] The UN report goes into great detail about the government's ridiculously poor performance in collecting evidence.[112] It was a whitewash.

The implications of this misstep for strategic communication are powerful. As it was, most Pakistanis believed the government was complicit in the assassination. In its arrogance, the government apparently thought it could get away with obliterating the crime scene. Instead, it complicated Musharraf's political problems and reinforced beliefs that the government was responsible and probably guilty of wrongdoing. People sensed or knew that the police were pulling a fast one. It was another reason that cut the legs out from under PML-Q and Musharraf in the 2008 election.

The U.N. Commission did a commendable job although the scope of its work was limited. But some of its analysis seems as odd as the government's inept strategic communication. For example, Khurram Shahzad appears to have said he wanted to hose down the crime scene to control the crowd at the scene. It's not clear what crowd was there or how the UN arrived at its reasoning for what he should have done about it. The Commission reported:

> One eye-witness said that there were about 100 to 200 people present at the crime scene after the blast and about 20 to 30 police

officers. One police official stated that there were about 40 police officers at the scene. The Commission finds that SP Khurram had a number of options for controlling the crowd at the crime scene short of the drastic measure of hosing it down. He could have ordered the police officers present to form a cordon around the immediate vicinity of the crime scene; he could have redeployed any of the 1,371 police officers on duty; he could have called for reinforcements. He made no attempt to do any of these things. Senior police officials told the Commission that SP Khurram could, indeed, have redeployed police officers or sought reinforcements and should have.[113]

The points made in that excerpt do not add up. The assassination occurred at 5:10 p.m.[114] It was late December. The UN time line puts Khurram Shahzad's order at about 6:40 p.m. It would have been dark at that time. The reference to a couple of hundred people and twenty to thirty police officers refers to the scene "after the blast," not at the time he ordered the scene hosed. So how many people were actually present over an hour and a half later? It's not clear. The Commission also suggests that Khurram Shahzad could have controlled the crowds at the scene by redeploying "any of the 1,371 officers on duty." Exactly what officers would that be, especially at 6:45 p.m.? The fact is, there is no evidence that the government actually deployed anything close to that number of officers at the time Benazir entered the park or during the rally. The ample video footage at the time of the attack provides no evidence of such security presence. Where did the UN get the idea that two hours later so many officers were present?

What it adds up to can be summarized in one word: cover-up. Was this to hide active government complicity or to deflect criticism from the failure to provide adequate—or promised—security at the park? Either way, the treatment of the crime scene raises grave questions about the government's behavior.

As noted in discussion of precept 1, less than twenty-four hours after the assassination the government identified a culprit, Waziristan tribal leader and Al Qaeda friend Baitullah Mehsud.[115] Known as Amir Sahab by his fol-

> **17.** Identify a plausible guilty party. You can add punch by releasing a transcript of a purported conversation in which the party named as the culprit takes credit for the killing. *Helpful hint*: Characterize the transcript as an "intelligence intercept." That makes it sound authentic. Some may also infer that the U.S. National Security Agency obtained the material, bolstering its credibility. *Warning*: Issuing transcripts that sound as if they came from a bad soap opera may provoke awkward questions.

lowers, the thirty-four-year-old Mehsud was anointed by forty senior Taliban commanders to lead Tehrik-i-Taliban-Pakistan, an umbrella organization of tribal militants.[116] Javid Cheema released English and Urdu translations of a purported intercept of a conversation between Mehsud and one of his confederates. The government did not produce an authenticated tape of the conversation in Pashto, although two days later, a recording was posted on a government website. *Dawn* newspaper said that the "recording seems unconvincing and raises doubts about its credibility and genuineness." Cheema countered that the government was in possession of the "voice signatures" of Mehsud and could thus verify its authenticity.[117] When reporters raised questions and asked how the call had been taped, a spokesman said that was a secret technical matter.[118] It is not clear if the conversation even took place.

At a press conference the day after the assassination, Cheema stuck to the official line:

> She was on the hit list of al-Qaeda. We have intelligence intercepts indicating that al-Qaeda leader Baitullah Mehsud is behind her assassination. We just have an intelligence intercept that was recorded this morning in which Baitullah Mehsud congratulated his people for carrying out this cowardly act. . . .
>
> We have irrefutable evidence that al-Qaeda, its network, and its cohorts are trying to destabilize Pakistan which is in the forefront of war against terrorism. They are systematically targeting our state institutions in order to destabilize the country.[119]

The English translation of the "transcript" follows:

Maulvi Sahib (MS): Asalaam Aleikum (Peace be with you).

Baitullah Mehsud (BM): Waaleikum Asalaam (And also with you).

MS: Chief, how are you?

BM: I am fine.

MS: Congratulations, I just got back during the night.

BM: Congratulations to you, were they our men?

MS: Yes they were ours.

BM: Who were they?

MS: There was Saeed, there was Bilal from Badar and Ikramullah.

BM: The three of them did it?

MS: Ikramullah and Bilal did it.

BM: Then congratulations.

MS: Where are you? I want to meet you.

BM: I am at Makeen (town in South Waziristan tribal region), come over, I am at Anwar Shah's house.

MS: OK, I'll come.

BM: Don't inform their house for the time being.

MS: OK.

BM: It was a tremendous effort. They were really brave boys who killed her.

MS: Mashallah (Thank God). When I come I will give you all the details.

BM: I will wait for you. Congratulations, once again congratulations.

MS: Congratulations to you.

BM: Anything I can do for you?

MS: Thank you very much.

BM: Asalaam Aleikum.

MS: Waaleikum Asalaam.[120]

This so-called transcript raised immediate questions and concerns.

- If the government was able to intercept and record a conversation with Mehsud that quickly, why could it not have pinpointed his location? Why hadn't it taken action to pursue him? Cheema's response was that Mehsud was always on the move, making it very difficult to find him.[121] This reply impressed few reporters, especially in light of reports that Mehsud had been working with the Pakistan military.[122]

- Even accepting that the English version is merely a translation, it flunks the smell test. It sounds scripted, and not like a real conversation.

- The substance is questionable. If it was an "intercept," in theory, Mehsud would not have known his conversation was being overheard. Not once, however, does he mention Bhutto's name. One might reasonably presume that Mehsud would acknowledge his own people's involvement. Yet Mehsud seems surprised to learn that Benazir's assailants were his men. He had to ask who they were; he did not know their names.[123]

- Maulvi Sahib provides Mehsud with three names. Mehsud responds as if Maulvi were referring to three people: Saeed, Bilal, and Ikramullah. Yet police later identified the shooter-bomber as a single individual, "Saeed alias Bilal."[124]

- Police also later claimed that Bilal had met with Mehsud to plan out the assassination.[125] If so, then Mehsud would have known the individuals and understood who Maulvi Sahib was talking about.

- Benazir had always said she could handle the Taliban. In criticizing violent extremists, the military, drug cartels, Al Qaeda, and other parties, she had avoided specific objections of the Pakistani Taliban but blasted militant foreigners who were now active in the Afghanistan Taliban. She had chosen her words carefully.[126] The exclusion of Pakistani Taliban from her long litany of troublemakers tends to support Mehsud's assertion that he was not her enemy and that she did not consider him one.

- On the other side of the coin, Scotland Yard and American officials who examined the transcript believed it was genuine.[127] Why they thought so is unclear. One highly experienced reporter who has examined the facts offers an interpretation of the transcript that is more supportive of the government's position. He offers the view that "the conversation suggests that while Mehsud may not have known all the details ahead of time, he was pleased with the results."

- In 2008 the Taliban apparently abducted Pakistan's ambassador to Kabul, Tariq Azizuddin. The TTP disavowed participation in the kidnapping, but the gang holding the ambassador demanded the release of eleven prisoners, including three associated with Benazir's assassination: Saeed alias Bilal, Ikramullah, and a boy named Aitazaz. Eventually, the ambassador wound up in the hands of the TTP and was released. That point, however, does not make the TTP the author of the assassination. As a *Daily Times* editorial evaluating the story points out, it was a curious incident:

> How come the ambassador was travelling without protocol and guards? How come it has taken so long for the ransom demand to be made? How come the TTP has denied it but some other unnamed group has owned it? How come the family of the ambassador has been largely silent during this time instead of wailing before the authorities and the media to do something to get their man out? How come the Taliban, jihadis and Al Qaeda are all seemingly mixed up in this kidnapping?"[128]

- The questions don't point a finger at Mehsud so much as raise questions about who the real parties of interest may be among the suspects.
- In February, *The News* reported that the government was no longer sure about Mehsud's involvement after the PPP and Mehsud completely rejected the charges against him.[129]
- Although its analysis is superficial, the UN Commission also questioned Mehsud's involvement.

> **18.** Failing to produce an authenticated recording of a conversation will cause people to wonder. *Recommendation*: Explain why everyone should believe the transcript is genuine. If third parties will do it for you, so much the better.

The discourse about politics in states like Pakistan takes place in social media such as Internet blogs, Twitter, and other forms of new media. One blogger offered a detailed analysis of the alleged Mehsud intercept to argue that Mehsud was in fact guilty. Citing the conversation between Maulvi Sahib and Mehsud, the blogger argues that "Maulvi" refers to the speaker's status as a cleric and is not part of his name. He reasons that "Sahib" is the Taliban leader Omar Khalid, who is also a member of Mehsud's TTP.[130]

While this opinion begs the question by presuming the authenticity of the transcript, it points to Musharraf's squandering an opportunity to mobilize his allies to produce and publicize similar interpretations of the transcript. He needed to campaign in each level of the vertically integrated media space to reach a broader audience. New media developed since 2004 presents innovative opportunities to rethink the possibilities for strategic communication. Today, wide ranges of individuals who engage at a distance—by cell phone, the Internet, or other means—are leveraging their combined ability, knowledge, and expertise as a collective intelligence. These media have empowered mass audiences and enable campaigns to achieve greater reach and penetration; however, they can complicate one's ability to sustain a narrative. American elections and the postelection politics offer ample illustrations of this evolution in political communication. The "Arab Spring" that toppled governments in Tunisia and Egypt, and caused unrest across the Middle East and North Africa in 2011, were spurred by social media and Al Jazeera broadcasts.

Its implications also apply to terrorist attacks. In November 2008 terrorists struck targets in Mumbai, murdering police and civilian bystanders. Trapped civilians used Twitter to report what was happening. Alas, the terrorists also read Twitter on their BlackBerrys to gather open-source intelligence on police movements, to assess the impact of their attacks, and even to pinpoint where people were hiding.[131]

New media's potential applies to Pakistan as well. Musharraf's failure to grasp it was a major missed opportunity.

> **19.** Drive your message through a multimedia campaign. Limiting the use of channels can raise doubts about how serious you are about driving it.

Musharraf drove his message about combating terrorism and extremism mainly through news media. Given his spotty record, by not mounting an intense *multimedia* campaign to discredit and marginalize violent extremists, Musharraf wasted an opportunity to rally the nation behind him. Indeed, his oversight generated more criticism. Some contend he never believed he needed such a wide-ranging campaign to hang on to power. Others point to his failure to grasp the imperative of doing so. It underscores his disconnect with the political realities.

> **20.** Promise to bring the perpetrators to justice. *Red flag*: Hopes are raised when you arrest suspects and they "confess." They are dashed when authorities fail to prosecute and convict them.

Musharraf denounced Benazir's killing as "a great national tragedy" and vowed to root out terrorists.[132] In March 2008, the police formally charged Mehsud with planning Benazir's assassination.[133] But no one tracked down and punished him. No one branded him a poster child for terror or the bad things that terrorists represent. Instead, shortly after the assassination, the government negotiated a peace deal with him, and his militants released captured members of Pakistani security.[134] In 2009, tribal militancy prompted the government again to take action against Mehsud,[135] but it was not related to Benazir's assassination.[136]

Apparently Mehsud maintained a close relationship with the Directorate for Inter-Services Intelligence. Protection by Pakistani authorities enhanced his stature. His relationship with Al Qaeda was secretive, although no one questioned the existence of a strong link.[137] In early August 2009, a Predator strike killed Mehsud. In a bizarre twist, Benazir's former security adviser and current Pakistani interior minister, Rehman Malik, reported that the Taliban then charged Mehsud's father-in-law and other family members of spying for U.S. forces in Afghanistan and executed them.[138]

> **21.** Pick up murder suspects as soon as possible, even small fry. That shows you are taking decisive action and that you care. Then forget about them. Actual trials only prompt more investigations and undesirable news stories.

Police suggested that five assailants had carried out Benazir's assassination: Saeed alias Bilal; Husnain Gul and his cousin, identified only as Rafaqat; Ikramullah; and a boy named Aitazaz. The *Daily Times* asserted that Aitazaz had first named Saeed alias Bilal and Ikramullah, and then he identified "the cleric who had first named the two in a phone conversation with Baitullah Mehsud."[139] Police said the suspects had visited the site the night before for a rehearsal and that they planned to hit her from different sides. "Saeed alias Bilal blew himself up after firing shots at her," the police said. Husnain Gul was described as out to avenge the death of friends who died when security forces attacked the Lal Masjid (Red Mosque) in July 2007.[140]

Ideologically, the mosque was anti-Shiite.[141] Although she supported the attack,[142] Musharraf—not Benazir—launched it. Benazir was living in exile at the time of that assault. That she was assassinated in revenge for the attack on the Red Mosque makes no sense. She was not involved in it. Police offered no explanation.[143] *Dawn* described the detainees as "angry over Ms. Bhutto's pro-West attitude and they were afraid of strong action against them if she came to power."[144] The police said that while Saeed alias Bilal did the killing, Ikramullah was assigned to attack if she escaped the blast.[145] A week later, police detained Abdul Rashid on suspicion of providing arms and ammunition to the assailants.[146]

Although the government had almost immediately blamed Baitullah Meshud as the mastermind behind the assassination, on February 15, 2008, Chaudhry Abdul Majid (Majeed), the additional inspector general of the Crime Investigation Department who headed the investigation into the assassination, denied that a link between the five men and Mehsud had been established.[147] Four days later, Majid fell in line and claimed that the suspects had confessed that Mehsud had approved the plan to kill Benazir. Majid said that Gul and Rafaqat had confessed to giving a suicide jacket, sunglasses, and pistol to the bomber Saeed alias Bilal.[148]

Once the hoopla died down, the investigation ground to a halt. The prosecution of the alleged killers was delayed. By the summer of 2008, the investigation was "in cold storage." Qari Saifullah Akhtar, named as a suspect in the October 18 attempt in Karachi, had been quietly released. Legal proceedings against the other detainees had gone nowhere.[149]

> **22.** Do not presume that the party you tag as guilty will own up. *Hint*: When the perpetrators are identified too quickly, examine the evidence carefully. Also remember what Benazir said about Pakistan: There is always a story behind the story.

Mehsud's guilt is doubtful. Although Mehsud seemed not to hesitate in claiming credit for other activities,[150] he went out of his way to deny complicity in the assassination. Reportedly, Benazir's assassination was the *only* incident identified with him that he denied any involvement.[151] After Karachi, Mehsud sent two separate communications to Benazir through emissaries and denied he was her enemy. "Identify your enemy. I am not your enemy. I have nothing to do with you or against you or with the assassination attempt on you on October 18," he said through intermediaries. The top PPP leadership trusted that assurance.[152]

Three days after the assassination, Mehsud rejected the accusation that he had masterminded the attack as baseless. "We are equally grieved by the tragic death of Benazir Bhutto and extend our sympathies to her family and party workers in this hour of grief," said Maulvi Omar, a spokesman for Mehsud and his TTP, a conglomerate of all the militant organizations operating in the tribal areas as well as the settled NWFP districts. Reporting on a *shura* (consultation) meeting held the night before to discuss the situation, Omar quoted Baitullah Mehsud and declared: "Why on earth would we kill her? We had no enmity with her and more importantly she had done no wrong to us."[153]

Ignoring the Taliban's habit of burning down girls' schools, stoning women, beating teenage girls, forcing women into burkas, banning them from pursuing education, denying them rights, and murdering any individual who opposed them, Omar stated that harming a woman was against the teachings of Islam and sharia as well as the centuries-old, rich traditions of their tribal people. He claimed,

By blaming us for the murder of an important political leader like Benazir Bhutto, the government is in fact misguiding the world. Planning such actions is simply beyond our imagination. We want to assure the Pakistan People's Party leaders and its workers that we can't even think of killing their leader. We are with them in this hour of grief and sorrow.[154]

Whatever its views about the Taliban, PPP leaders did not blame Mehsud for the assassination. When the tribal militant was killed in 2009, one newspaper commented: "Very strange! The diehard supporters of the former Prime Minister are not celebrating the killing of Pakistan Taliban chief Baitullah Mehsud."[155] Others shared the PPP's skepticism, which was expressed by key leaders like Safdar Abbasi.[156] They felt that Mehsud had already had his hands full supporting the Afghan Taliban and dealing with the emerging battleground in Waziristan.[157]

> **23.** Persuade big, international names to buy into your narrative. It will bolster credibility, especially if both local and international voices speak up.

The U.S. government was quick to support the Pakistani government's narrative, at least publicly. Within twenty-four hours, the FBI and the Department of Homeland Security issued a bulletin blaming Al Qaeda.[158] At the Brookings Institute, Pakistan expert and former CIA officer Bruce Riedel, currently a key adviser to President Barack Obama on the region, concurred.[159] Two weeks later, CIA director Mike Hayden advised the media that Mehsud and Al Qaeda were behind the assassination.[160] Some of Mehsud's rivals, such as Haji Turkistan Baetani, a former right-hand man of Mehsud's, also later claimed that Mehsud had plotted the attacks. It's doubtful many Pakistanis find Baetani's denunciation credible, since he also characterized Mehsud as "an American agent" who was "funded by Israel and India."[161]

> **24.** If Al Qaeda militants choose to take the credit, allow them to do so. Their bravado helps stir up hatred for a despised adversary.

Al Qaeda operatives were probably involved in Benazir's death. By one account, it stepped up immediately: "We terminated the most precious American asset which vowed to defeat [the] mujahedeen," proclaimed Mustafa Abu Al-Yazid, an Egyptian who postures himself as Al Qaeda's commander in Afghanistan, in a telephone interview.[162] Al-Yazid told journalist Syed Saleem Shahzad that a Punjabi volunteer of Lashkar-e-Jhangvi (LeJ) carried out the assassination.

Counterterrorist expert Bahukutumbi Raman identified problems with that bulletin. First, Al Qaeda has a habit of claiming credit for major events to bolster its image of effectiveness. In military jargon, it conducts "effects-based operations." Bin Laden has famously declared that his group decisively helped shoot down U.S. Blackhawk helicopters in Mogadishu during Task Force Ranger. That boast is seconded by many persuasive supporters, but others dispute it.[163] Second, Pakistani military and intelligence services have maintained close contacts with individuals and groups affiliated with Al Qaeda.[164] Al Yazid's announcement doesn't answer the underlying question about who activated the operatives.

Bahukutumbi Raman also questions the authenticity of Al-Yazid's assertion as he questions the credibility of Shahzad's journalism.[165] Raman argues that Pakistani jihadi organizations sometimes take responsibility for the terrorist strikes they carry out in India, but they rarely do for strikes within Pakistan. He also argues that while Shahzad discusses the ethnicity of Al Qaeda, organizations do not specify the ethnicity of a Muslim and that it is "very unlikely that either Al Qaeda or the LEJ would say that a Punjabi suicide bomber carried out the assassination."[166]

In making claims about their successes, Al Qaeda generally uses websites and not phone calls. It also uses letters and direct releases to the media. It may or may not take prompt credit for attacks. Al Qaeda was silent as to the May 13, 2003, attacks on residential compounds in Riyadh and a September 2006 attack on oil facilities in Yemen.[167]

In Iraq, Al Qaeda's strategy was to move rapidly. Production teams working in tandem with attackers videotaped offensives, produced video press releases, and rushed them to the media, hoping to beat the U.S. government or Iraqi government's announcements and to spin the news coverage about the attacks.[168] Al Qaeda or its groups have claimed immediate or relatively immediate responsibility for attacks on various targets: the trains in Spain in March 2004;[169] the London subway in 2005;[170] Western hotels in Amman, Jordan, on November 9, 2005;[171] a residential housing compound in Sanaa, Yemen, on April 6, 2008;[172] the U.S. Embassy in Yemen;[173] Israel with rocket launches from Lebanon in 2009;[174] an oil refinery in Abqaiq, Saudi Arabia, in 2006;[175] Algiers by the franchise Al Qaeda in the Islamic Maghreb (AQIM) on December 11, 2007;[176] the Danish Embassy in Pakistan on June 2, 2008;[177] a military convoy near Damous, Algeria, by AQIM on August 1, 2008;[178] and Saudi prince Mohammed bin Nayef in Jeddah, Saudi Arabia, in 2009.[179]

Al Qaeda has never denied responsibility for killing Benazir. It seems pleased to accept the credit. As noted, letting Al Qaeda assume responsibility was a good play for Musharraf's strategic communication. It helped deflect blame from the government. Combined with steps outlined earlier in this chapter, Musharraf might possibly have limited some of the damage to his standing. Whether that might have actually worked for him is debatable, but it is a lesson for other leaders, with greater credibility, who find themselves in a comparable strategic quandary.

> **25.** In countries like Pakistan, where devising conspiracies is a national sport, people love any theory that implicates the CIA, Blackwater, or the United States.

Pakistanis love lurid conspiracy theories, no matter how absurd.[180] In 2006, by nearly three to one, Pakistanis did not believe Arabs had carried out the 9/11 attacks.[181] Other astounding theories contend that 9/11 was a Jewish-Mossad plot and that the Pakistan Army kills innocent Muslims in Waziristan at America's direction.[182]

After Benazir's death, ISI chief Lt. Gen. Hamid Gul filled this role handsomely. With the sangfroid of a James Bond villain thumbing his nose at the media, he offered taunting interviews in which he blamed the assassination on the CIA. Gul characterized the assassination as perfectly planned and executed: "First a blast, a few pistol shots . . . they were all to create confusion but former prime minister [Bhutto] was killed by a sharp shooter from a distance."[183]

Interestingly, Punjab PPP president Shah Mehmood Qureshi reported that Benazir had informed him that she would be targeted by a long-range rifle.[184] Contradictory reports about her wounds raised questions as to whether, if all the facts are ever gathered, that theory might be vindicated.

With an air of informed objectivity, Gul criticized the government for incompetence, not criminal complicity. Gul was droll in deflecting suspicion from the military or intelligence services, as well as himself.

> **26.** Promises to combat terrorists and violent extremists are a "must do." *Bonus points*: Aside from putting you on the "right" side of the issue, making that commitment reassures those check signers who stream billions in foreign aid that you really do oppose evildoers.

Musharraf explicitly accused Baitullah Mehsud and Maulana Fazlullah, the leader of Tehrik-e-Nifaz-Shariat-e-Mohammadi (Movement for the Implementation of Sharia), for the assassination. Those hoping for swift action were rewarded. The government negotiated with them to forge new peace agreements that quickly broke down.[185] Somehow, accusations about Mehsud's complicity in Benazir's assassination were quickly forgotten.

> **27.** Trumpet the extraordinary steps taken to provide security for the target. *Red flag*: It's a good idea to make such claims sound plausible. An even better idea is to avoid making assertions that videotapes and eyewitness accounts of the event can expose as ludicrous.

Musharraf assured his citizens that Benazir had been advised of the threat to her life. He also said that more than a thousand policemen had been on duty, that police marksmen were posted on the roofs, and that mobile squads had been stationed around Benazir.[186] He even apologized for hosing down the blast site so quickly, glossing over the points that by then the damage had been done and that it had occurred on government orders.

Gretchen Peters has suggested that Musharraf may have been sincere in asserting that the park had hundreds of security people present, but she acknowledges that many of them would not have been trained or equipped to the standards Americans would expect. Videotape and eyewitness accounts open Musharraf's statements to severe criticism. As noted in chapter 15, Gen. Tauqir Zia, who was seated in a vehicle ahead of Benazir's, wondered where the security personnel were and why they allowed people to come so close to her.

Hamid Gul expressed surprise at the lax security arrangements. He asserted that the bomber could not have carried out the attack without being forewarned of Bhutto's movements via a cell phone or another device.[187] In January 2008, he joined Gen. Mirza Beg (Ret.), Lt. Gen. Faiz Ali Chishti (Ret.), and other officers of the Pakistan Ex-Servicemen Association who called on Musharraf to resign because he "does not represent the unity and symbol of the Federation as President."[188]

> **28.** When providing protection to a political leader pledged to fight international terrorists, *think twice* before assigning the job to a general who runs an intelligence agency. *Think three times* if that general has served as a liaison with Osama bin Laden. *Think a fourth time* if that general has kept such high-profile terrorists as Ahmad Omar Saeed Sheikh from punishment and if that general is close to key enemies of the person being protected. *Rethink the entire assignment* if the political leader has written the head of state to express deep suspicion that the general is actively plotting to assassinate him or her.

The Intelligence Bureau is a civilian intelligence agency and the counterpart to military intelligence and the military's Directorate for Inter-Services Intelligence. Musharraf put his personal friend (one source described him as a "drinking buddy"), colleague, and IB chief Brig. Gen. Ejaz Shah in charge of Benazir's security. That assignment raised grave questions. Shah had been accused of being the handling officer for both Osama bin Laden and Taliban leader Mullah Omar.[189] After Musharraf seized power in 1999, Shah became the home secretary in the Punjab, where Omar Sheikh helped to orchestrate the kidnapping and murder of American journalist Daniel Pearl in 2002. Omar

Sheikh surrendered to Shah after Pearl's murder. Although Omar Sheikh was tried and sentenced to death, Shah allegedly ensured that the sentence has not been carried out.[190]

After becoming president, Musharraf had inducted a large number of retired army officers into the Intelligence Bureau and into the Interior Ministry. Critics argue that Musharraf's actions further politicized the IB. Punjab, with Shah in charge, was the home to key Zia loyalists who loathed Benazir.[191] Prior to her assassination in Rawalpindi, Benazir listed Brigadier General Shah as one of several men who, she believed, wanted her dead. Appointing Shah to protect Benazir damaged Musharraf's credibility and undercut his claim to lack of reponsibility.

> **29.** An assassination may set the stage for striking a deal with the key political players. It's a good idea to make them all winners. *Red flag*: Losers complain and can become an unnecessary nuisance.

Power players waste little time grieving for the dead. Their real interest is in what happens next. After Benazir's assassination, events in Pakistan moved swiftly. Her husband, Zardari, returned from Dubai as the PPP convened to decide who would lead the party. Her son, Bilawal Bhutto Zardari, at this writing studying for the bar in London, was still a student at Oxford. At age nineteen, he was too young. Respecting the formalities, the PPP selected Bilawal to succeed Benazir as party chairman and made Zardari the cochairman, thus paving his way to aim for the presidency. The negotiations that took place among the key parties have not been detailed. Clearly, Musharraf and the military believed that the only alternative to Benazir was Nawaz Sharif. But as before, Musharraf would not do business with Nawaz.

The real issue was how the military, still the most powerful force in the nation, would respond. It seems plausible that an understanding was reached in which neither Zardari nor Nawaz would challenge the military's power, although Nawaz has pressed for trying Musharraf for treason. Charges of corruption had tainted the careers of both men, and many doubted their abilities to lead.

COAS Ashfaq Kayani kept his promise to ensure that the elections were fair and free. The February 18, 2008, election results that handed PML-Q a stinging defeat vindicated Kayani's pledge. The deal made to protect Musharraf when he resigned clearly represented an environment of accommodation at the time, although in 2011 a warrant for Musharraf's arrest was issued.

A stable succession followed Benazir's death. Whether she would have tried to ignite a popular revolution is unknown. But she had the potential to do so. Probably she had no choice but to lead one. Neither Zardari nor Nawaz had her fortitude or the ability to make that change happen. That made accommodation with the military and intelligence services possible. It seems unlikely that they would have stood by passively had either man posed a threat. As of this writing, in 2011, the military has regained and even improved its standing with the public. The military still holds the key to power in the country. There is no prospect of the International Atomic Energy Agency getting its hands on A. Q. Khan anytime soon. Nor is there talk of parliamentary hearings to subject the nuclear program to public scrutiny.

> **30.** As time passes, the media may wonder what happened to the investigation. It will be idle speculation. It lies largely in the past, except perhaps for revelations about the cause of death. Ignore media stories, unless you actually want people to know the truth.

A few years have elapsed since Benazir's assassination. In April 2010, the United Nations Commission of Inquiry issued its report amid a flurry of media stories. It came to no conclusion about who organized the assassination, leaving that task to Pakistani authorities.

Chapter 18

THE FALLOUT

Benazir's murderers got away with it. The aftershock of her murder is still felt.

No one proved that the government was criminally culpable. People sharply criticized Pervez Musharraf in failing to provide Benazir with adequate security. The government's post-assassination campaign to influence public opinion scored points by countering that Benazir also bore responsibility for disregarding warnings and failing to take basic security precautions. Musharraf had a point. Whether the police failed to show at Liaquat Bagh (the more plausible scenario) or abandoned their posts early in no way excuses the government. Still, she knew she faced a threat. She had worried about it at the planning lunch and had mentioned it on the speaker's rostrum.

At a minimum, her team violated the key precept of maintaining a distance between a potential target and the public. Her team had allowed her vehicle to leave the park and proceed without a cordon of security, the very device that had saved her life just weeks earlier in Karachi. There is no evidence that she complained to them about not having one.

Withering criticism directed at Benazir and her team obscured serious complaints about government incompetence or criminal complicity. She had popped her head out of her vehicle, exposing herself to a crowd that had been allowed to come dangerously close. The experience of Pope John Paul II and John F. Kennedy offered lessons about the risk involved. Meanwhile, Musharraf's absurd boast that a thousand police and sharpshooters had been posted to ensure Benazir's security did not excuse his ignorance—or what some call a lie—or Benazir's irresponsibility.

Her team's rationalization that politicians need to "press the flesh" doesn't wash with experienced political operatives, especially after Karachi. Politicians elsewhere manage that feat all the time without winding up as corpses. She should have insisted on better protection from her own team while still pressing the government to do its part.

Benazir had also solicited help from the U.S. Embassy. Its behavior was curious. The American response has sown bitter controversy and inspired a raft of conspiracy theories. Some media reports assert that her circle felt that the embassy stiff-armed her. The U.S. Embassy apparently did provide security advice, passed on intelligence, and urged Musharraf to make vigorous attempts to protect her. Its excuse for not doing more was that it wanted to avoid "micromanaging the security arrangements of another country."[1] Sources in Israel, to which Benazir had promised normal relations, spread the word that President Bush "might have been helpful" in getting more protection for her.[2]

Robert Novak reported that when Secretary of State Condoleezza Rice advised that she tone down her criticism of Musharraf, Benazir largely discounted the desirability of the pending alliance with Washington's favorite Pakistani. A close adviser to Benazir who was present when Secretary Rice phoned her, however, strongly defends the secretary's actions: "Emotions between Benazir and Musharraf became testy, and Condi Rice was doing her best to calm the waters and keep things on an even keel. She strongly believed that an alliance between Benazir and Musharraf was wise from all sides, and worked hard to keep things on track."

THE FATE OF KEY PLAYERS

BAITULLAH MEHSUD

The government's campaign did no harm to the chief murder suspect, Baitullah Mehsud, while blaming him provided it with a convenient whipping boy. Mehsud then received a peace treaty instead of jail time or a hangman's rope.

REHMAN MALIK

Rehman Malik's actions raised the issue of how competently and effectively he performed in doing all that he might have to ensure Benazir's safety on the day of her assassination. In his favor is the fact that Benazir's husband, Asif Ali Zardari, had every reason to punish him had he been dissatisfied. Instead, he made Malik his interior minister.

But the competency of his performance sparked criticism and questions. As noted earlier, *The News* reported that Taj had bluntly warned Benazir that an assassination attempt would be made on her life at the park and had advised that she skip the rally. As Musharraf's close colleague, he appears to have understood that Musharraf had a strong political interest in her safety. It is evident that Musharraf and his team felt frustrated by what they perceived as her refusal to cooperate or to act responsibly in taking steps to protect herself against threats of assassination in a dangerous political environment about which they felt they had provided more than ample warning. Taj's meeting was almost certainly an effort to issue a new caution. Benazir and her team were—and today remain—convinced that Musharraf had inexcusably failed to take necessary or even reasonable steps to ensure her safety. Musharraf and his team saw matters differently.

Journalist Hamid Mir filed a similar report, stating that "sources close to the then DG ISI claim that he had warned Benazir about the security threats and had expressed concern over the security of Benazir Bhutto and he even exchanged hot words with [Benazir's friend] Naheed Khan on the security issue."[3] This author and the UN Commission of Inquiry separately reached the conclusion that Taj very plausibly did warn Benazir. The UN stated: "The Commission is satisfied, that at the least, Major General Taj told Ms. Bhutto that the ISI was concerned about a possible terrorist attack against her and urged her to limit her public exposure and to keep a low profile at the campaign event at Liaquat National Bagh (Liaquat Bagh) later that day."[4]

The News goes a step further, reporting that Taj advised against attending the rally. This author's primary analysis supports that conclusion and earlier offered four reasons that would explain why he did so.

But the picture is opaque. *The News* stated that Malik argued—success-fully, as it turned out—that she reject Taj's counsel.[5] Benazir's friend Naheed Khan told reporter Hamid Mir the opposite.[6] She recalls Malik as having ad-vised Benazir *not* to attend the rally. Assuming that is accurate, how forcefully did he deliver the warning? On top of that, there is the question of what was actually said during the Taj-Benazir-Malik conversation. Malik has insisted to both *The News*[7] and Hamid Mir that Benazir "only discussed the political matters with the DG ISI and security issues were not discussed." There is no way to reconcile the stories. Pakistanis like to meet late, but does it not seem odd that Taj would appear at her home early that morning unless to warn her? The two were hardly political allies. Indeed, within a year, U.S. pressure had forced Pakistan to fire Taj on grounds that Taj had close ties to the Taliban.[8] The conflicting reports raise questions as to what actually transpired.

Benazir expressed concerns about security at the final planning lunch be-fore her departure for the park. The UN Commission agreed that while safety worried her, she felt the need to face voters and distrusted warnings from the Musharraf camp. It declared:

> While Ms. Bhutto expressed to many of her closest associates her fears about these and other threats [from extremist groups], they say that she did not fully trust the warnings on threats that Gen-eral Musharraf and his government passed on to her. According to diverse sources, she had a clear understanding of the serious risks she faced. However, Ms. Bhutto believed that General Musharraf was using the security issue to prevent her from campaigning. Ms. Bhutto's underlying distrust of General Musharraf and her fears that the elections would be rigged led her to carry out a very active campaign, with much public exposure, despite the risks she faced.[9]

Who was in charge of devising and executing plans for Benazir's security at the rally? Malik has denied having this responsibility. The UN Commission wondered about what his role and responsibilities had actually been. Malik had served as director of the Federal Investigation Agency (FIA) during Benazir's second tenure as prime minister. He was a close confidant of Zardari.[10] *The News* described Malik as "chief security officer (CSO) of Benazir Bhutto."[11] Curiously, after the assassination, as questions circulated about Malik's role after the tragedy, Malik characterized himself as her "national security adviser."[12]

The UN Commission reported that most PPP leaders "understood Mr. Malik's role as encompassing all aspects of Ms. Bhutto's security."[13] He coordinated her protection detail. He "also liaised with the federal authorities on behalf of Ms. Bhutto and participated in negotiations with General Musharraf and his aides."[14] The UN Commission found that his letters to authorities warning of security risks and "requesting specific security support reflect this involvement."[15]

Malik has asserted that the police took responsibility for Benazir's security at the park. Major Imtiaz Hussain had been selected for Benazir's "physical security and the party's volunteers also reported to him." Said Malik, "Prime responsibility of Benazir Bhutto is and was with the government because the PPP had no adequate measures."[16] If he were serving as her chief security officer, skeptics might wonder what responsibility the campaign and Benazir believed he had retained as *her* representative on security issues. The PPP had good reason to be concerned. The situation called for Malik, as her trusted adviser, to anticipate contingencies and recommend effective steps to protect Benazir. It's difficult to anticipate every contingency. Still, skeptics felt that he came up short.

The UN Commission found that the Rawalpindi police had devised a written plan to protect Benazir, but criticized it as flawed: "[The] government did not have a comprehensive security plan to protect Ms. Bhutto. It also failed to fix responsibility for her security in a specific federal official, entity, or organization."[17]

Why did that occur? Apparently, concluded the UN Commission, the police depended upon provincial authorities in the Punjab—parties who had failed to provide Benazir with security commensurate with that provided to "other ex-prime ministers" and who had failed "to strengthen Ms. Bhutto's security in December 2007."[18] Finalized on December 26,[19] the plan contemplated the establishment of a police command post at the edge of the park. It envisioned two security cordons: an inner cordon securing the park and an outer cordon covering the area surrounding it, including Liaquat and Murree Roads. It called for the deployment of 1,371 officers at the park. Three walk-through gates would stand at the entrance. Police constables bearing binoculars and automatic rifles were to be deployed on the rooftops of buildings around the park.[20] The plan also envisaged that an elite force under the command of an assistant superintendent of police would establish a box formation around Benazir's vehicle during its movement.

Flawed or not, the planning reflected that people had real concerns for Benazir's safety. And good or bad, the plan was not implemented. The "box formation" turned out to be a myth. No security "box" surrounded Benazir's vehicle as she arrived at the park, only a traffic escort. Malik commented in *Dawn* that "the presence of crowds on the Liaquat Bagh's entry and exit points was also shocking and in violation of the security drill for VIP's." He said that he pointed out the problem to SP Yasin Farooq.[21] Media reports don't make clear what other action he took.

The UN Commission found that none of the constables had binoculars or understood that they should possess them.[22] There is no evidence that authorities actually deployed 1,371 officers in the park, as the security plan had contemplated. Only 4,000 to 5,000 people attended the rally. The plan would have meant that at least a quarter of them were security personnel. The police who did show up seemed, the UN Commission found, more interested in crowd control than protection.

PPP official Farhatullah Babar and Malik had traveled to the park in the same car. Babar said that after the rally, as Benazir was leaving the park, Malik and Babar realized they were both talking on their phones. This meant "that the jammers were not working properly."[23] That was vital, as working jammers might prevent a remote cell phone from activating a bomb. That raises a question. Were they talking on their phones prior to that time? If so, did anyone become concerned and complain? The record is not clear. Babar said that Malik was "quite upset" when they realized jammers were not working and that "Ms. Bhutto should simply go home as there could be some trouble."[24] *The News* reported that Malik and Babar proceeded to Bhutto's home.

Malik's conduct at the conclusion of the rally has raised questions. Once Benazir had finished speaking, Malik jumped into a bulletproof Mercedes-Benz that sped out of the park ahead of Benazir. One might have expected him to wait until Benazir entered her vehicle before entering his own. The UN Commission did not find credible his account of where he was when the bomb blast that killed Benazir went off.[25]

Malik complained later that police at the park should have flanked Benazir's Land Cruiser on each side with two vehicles to provide better security.[26] Skeptics might ask: why he didn't ensure that the PPP itself provide the two vehicles he said were vital? How difficult was that to do? Already PPP had secured for her a privately armored Land Cruiser.[27] Could it not have secured two more vehicles?

His attitude toward ISI is curious. Before her death, the PPP had prepared a report that ran more than 150 pages detailing ISI plans to rig the 2008 parliamentary elections.[28] In April 2011, as interior minister, Malik criticized the United States for placing ISI on a list of "terrorist and terrorist support entities" alongside some seventy other groups, including Iranian intelligence and the Taliban. Malik proclaimed, "The ISI is not and has never been involved in politics."[29]

Today, the ministry that Malik heads up is conducting an ongoing investigation into the assassination. Malik remains powerful and influential inside the Pakistan government. It remains to be seen how effective he will prove at uncovering the true culprits behind the assassination.

NAWAZ SHARIF

Musharraf has called Nawaz a "closet Taliban." Former ISI officer Khalid Khwaja supported Musharraf's assertion. He says he was present when Nawaz met Osama bin Laden on six different occasions.[30] "I should know," Khwaja told the *Guardian*. "I arranged those meetings."[31] In *Seeds of Terror*, an important book that should be mandatory reading for Washington pundits and policymakers, Gretchen Peters points out that as the U.S. government cut off aid to Islamabad after the Soviet-Afghan war and Pakistan veered toward becoming a narco state, "known drug lords held seats in the national and provincial assemblies, and had access to Prime Minister Nawaz's 'inner circle.'"[32] Is there reason to believe the tiger has changed his stripes? Peters makes a powerful case that "their terrorist acts now serve to further their drug ambitions as often as their political ones." Dealing with a Taliban funded by the burgeoning drug trade requires a different war, driven by different strategies, than one against a foe whose main interest is in making sharia the law of the land or establishing a caliphate, no matter how strongly it may invoke religion to justify its crime or violence. It's a lesson, Peters rightly concludes, that Washington would do well to learn.

On corruption charges, Tariq Ali thinks the Bhuttos were and are corrupt. But he argues that compared to Nawaz Sharif, Benazir and Zardari were pikers. The latter, he alleges, accumulated a paltry $1.5 billion in assets after her two terms in office, while the more enterprising Nawaz and his brother, "with their intimate knowledge of the business cycle, probably netted double that amount."[33]

Despite consenting to a ten-year exile in 2000, Nawaz came home in 2007 to play political hardball. He did well in 2011 polling, and wanted to be prime minister. But prime ministers are elected by the Parliament. His PML-N party may or may not prove strong enough in the next election to win sufficient seats to elect him. The PPP maintains grassroots strength. PML-N must compete against PML-Q and, if he comes home, Musharraf's new party. Those three parties will compete for the same votes against PPP. Plus, Nawaz's relationship with the military is tenuous. That may well affect his political fortunes. Critics charge that he's a hypocrite on democracy. On returning to Pakistan, he stood up for an independent judiciary, conveniently forgetting that while he was prime minister he sent his own goons to bash lawyers. As of this writing, some Western policymakers, spinning their own webs of fantasy, have envisioned Nawaz as a plausible torchbearer for democracy and reform. Delusion is sweet.

ASIF ALI ZARDARI

Musharraf's campaign of influence played to Zardari only in order to show empathy for the tragedy. Until the assassination, few considered him a major political player and his critics feel he's a weak president. Evidently for religious reasons, he desired no autopsy of Benazir, although the law required one. The government obliged. It made the usual statements of sympathy. Otherwise, it ignored him. Musharraf neither asked him to join in fighting terrorism nor offered in any public way to substitute him for Benazir. Probably that overture would have been futile, as Zardari was in no way disposed—not publicly, anyway—to making deals with the president. What was worked out behind the scenes is unclear except that when Musharraf resigned, Zardari was party to a deal worked out with the United States, Saudi Arabia, and Pakistani political players meant to ensure Musharraf a safe exit from the country.

Zardari ascended to the leadership of the PPP and cobbled together a new governing coalition with Nawaz in the National Assembly. In August 2008, they forced Musharraf to resign, and Zardari got the job of president. He is convinced that he has great political instincts. Others deeply doubt that. As president, he embroiled himself in unproductive battles with former Punjab chief minister Chaudhry Pervez Elahi and his brothers.[34] He aroused hostility in opposing the reinstatement of Iftikhar Muhammad Chaudhry as Chief Justice of the Supreme Court, after Chaudhry's ouster by Musharraf in November 2007 while declaring the State of Emergency and suspending the Constitution. Many believed that Zardari feared—not unreasonably, as it turned out—that once Chaudhry was back on the Court, it would review the constitutionality of the National Reconciliation Ordinance and overturn its validity. The reinstatement was effected by Prime Minister Gilani on March 16, 2009, by executive order.[35] Zardari took heat for his refusal to do so, despite an election promise. His action hurt him badly with voters.

He is hardly the model of a populist politician. But he is not one by background. Nor was winning political office his goal in life. His inability to arouse broad popular support as Benazir had done proved to be a serious political weakness. Poll ratings consistently reflect that. On the other hand, he has survived rumor after rumor that his government was on the verge of collapsing. He has managed to get along with the military and intelligence establishment —a genuine achievement in Pakistan—while maintaining a friendly posture with the United States. For someone who could be termed an accidental president, that's not bad. The final chapter of this book discusses how he's done in addressing major challenges since assuming that role.

PERVEZ MUSHARRAF

Musharraf's strategy before and after Benazir's assassination was to undermine his opponents, reward his allies, and, for all his rhetoric about fighting violent extremists, mobilize Islamist parties—including some with ties to Al Qaeda—as political coalition partners.[36] His cheek in suspending judges on the pretext of removing obstructions to fighting violent extremism demonstrated both his chutzpah and his disconnect from political reality.

Arriving at some arrangement with Benazir was his best (and probably only) way to retain power. The proposed deal had strong U.S. backing. That support counted with the military, which was going to be a central player no matter what happened, even though most Pakistanis opposed cooperation with the U.S. in fighting terrorism. The key dynamic in coalition building is whether the parties can leverage one another's strengths to gain power. Standing alone, Benazir and Musharraf each stood on tricky ground. An alliance that consolidated their strengths might have worked, although nothing could be certain and neither desired any partnership with each other. Reaching an accommodation with Musharraf roiled her people.[37] She had presented herself as a voice against military dictatorship. Now they were standing together? She argued cogently that politics was about the art of the possible, and that coming to terms with the power players was for the good of democracy and Pakistan.

Musharraf overstayed his welcome. Despite the fact that he faces an arrest warrant in Pakistan, he has toured the United States raising campaign funds and claims that he will return to Pakistan on March 23, 2012, and run for office. It will be interesting to see if he keeps that promise.

BENAZIR BHUTTO

Sometimes forgotten in this drama was Benazir Bhutto. Benazir had been eliminated. No one was aggressively prosecuted. No one was convicted, imprisoned, or executed. Although she herself had identified key suspects, none of them was investigated. Months passed, and the story seemed to dwindle in significance as Pakistan grappled with security issues and economic turmoil. Her death prompted bitterness and anger and set off violent demonstrations in the Sindh Province. But the trauma occasioned by her murder did not approach the widespread impact that the assassinations of John F. Kennedy, Robert F. Kennedy, or Dr. Martin Luther King, Jr., had on Americans. Instead, an atmosphere of bitterness enshrouded the parliamentary elections as Zardari's emergence as head of the PPP, the curiously popular Nawaz Sharif's effort to revive his political fortunes, and Musharraf's futile struggle to keep his perch all took center stage. Ambition for the living trumped grief over the fallen.

The United Nations Commission made its report. It lambasted the Musharraf government, Pakistani police, and the PPP for their failure to ensure her security,[38] although one might reasonably conclude that no one can absolutely guarantee the safety of any political leader. We haven't done it in the United States, although the Secret Service does a tremendous job for top leaders. One reason, although it goes largely unspoken, that our country has taken a firm position against action to kill a foreign head of state is that our own elected officials, in an open democracy, are far more vulnerable than despots who operate in a police state. The UN Commission felt that the failures of police and other officials to react to the assassination were, "in most cases, deliberate."[39]

The commission declined to assign criminal responsibility, concluding that "can only be made by the competent authorities of Pakistan."[40] It did state bluntly that Rawalpindi police chief, CPO Saud Aziz, who was arrested in 2011 for dereliction of duty, "did not act independently of higher authorities, either in the decision to hose down the crime scene or to impede the post-mortem examination."[41] It expressed suspicions about various parties, including Al Qaeda, the Pakistani Taliban—a loose alliance of militant Islamist groups operating in the tribal areas—Sunni jihadi groups based largely in the Punjab, Baitullah Mehsud, elements of the military and intelligence establishments, and other militants. She had lots of supporters but also plenty of enemies.[42]

The commission noted her concerns about Musharraf without agreeing or disagreeing.[43]

THE AUTHORITIES

At best, the police and other authorities were guilty of gross negligence before, during, and after the murder. No one held them to account. As an exercise in information strategy, they made arrests, talked tough, and kicked up dust. They produced confessions that no one believed, but no one seemed to complain when the suspects walked. The authorities' attitude seemed to be "what's done is done; let's move on." There was sound and fury, nothing more. It all served the purpose, which seems to have been the intent, of interdicting a serious investigation.

THE MEDIA

Pakistan's lively media is a mixed bag. One observer who knows Pakistan has described the electronic media this way: Fox News makes no apology for its advocacy journalism. The talk shows are gladiator contests with words. Imagine a country with 50 stations like this, who will broadcast anything. At the same time, the media is willing to challenge the official line, to conduct its own investigations, and to report—depending on your point of view—the facts or aggressive interpretations of their version of the truth. It's both a bright spot and a reason why Pakistani politics are complicated, difficult, and often dysfunctional. The media's stories weakened Musharraf politically. Their diverse reports and conjectures fed Pakistan's thriving culture of conspiracy theory. All of this commotion diverted attention from fundamental questions and enabled the key players, over the course of 2008, to balance their competing interests in the emerging, new political dynamic.

THE MILITARY-INTELLIGENCE ESTABLISHMENT

Benazir had posed a potential existential threat to the military-intelligence establishment. Musharraf's campaign of influence helped ensure that no one found it criminally complicit in the assassination. After Musharraf lost the election and resigned, the Pakistan Army regained popularity. No one has challenged its dominant position in Pakistani politics today. No one on the current scene is likely to, unless you count the Taliban.

THE SHAKEOUT

After Benazir's death, Musharraf's Pakistan Muslim League–Qaid party held a majority in the national legislature, controlled Punjab, and was the main coalition partner in the provincial governments of Baluchistan and Sindh. But its domination, as the International Crisis Group observed, was fragile and "sustained more by military patronage than a social base or organizational network."[44]

Musharraf's plan was to outmaneuver Benazir, by hook or crook. Conventional wisdom dismissed his chances, which shows the peril of jumping to obvious conclusions. Actually, he might well have done it, given a break or two. In the International Republican Institute survey that September, a majority (33 percent to 19 percent) said that Benazir could best steer Pakistan out of crisis. By November 23 percent said he was the one leader who could best handle the problems facing Pakistan, and almost the same number—25 percent—felt that way about her.[45]

It's unclear which of the two leaders benefited more from the contemplated alliance. In November 2007, corps commanders expressed strong reservations about any power-sharing deal. They resented U.S. efforts to impose it as interference in a domestic matter. They especially resented Benazir's criticism of the ISI and the military.[46] Still, for Musharraf, cutting a deal was seen as a means of survival, but for her, doing so was seen as a sellout. Except for her PPP supporters, the IRI data found that most voters believed she was compromising to improve her own personal situation, not to bring democracy to Pakistan. Musharraf would have had an opportunity to exploit that impression to his advantage had she lived.

Eight months after Benazir's death, Musharraf bowed to the inevitable. The ruling coalition led by Zardari and Nawaz was preparing impeachment proceedings against him for illegally suspending the Constitution and for misconduct.[47] His voice trembling and a tear in his eye, on August 18, 2008, Musharraf went on national television and announced his resignation.[48] He had already resigned as chief of army staff on November 28, 2007.[49] Low personal popularity, a shortage of essential food items, power cuts, and skyrocketing inflation finished him. It was time. Yet one factor that did not play a role in his departure was any allegation of misconduct—negligent or criminal—in Benazir's death.

Chapter 19

WHO KILLED BENAZIR?

The question of who bears responsibility for plotting and organizing Benazir's assassination illustrates the opaque quality of politics in a nation driven by conspiracy theory and a sense of betrayal. Strategic communication takes a secondary role, but recognizing just how many forces were at play, and had a stake in her fate, tells us about the complicated, nuanced nature of Pakistani politics and the dynamics that drive it. Murder is about motive, means, and opportunity. What seems most plausible is that a combination of parties played a role. Together, they more than satisfy all three of those requirements.

It seems evident as well that from her arrival in Pakistan, a number of parties had a strong motive for attacking her. Very probably parallel efforts to assassinate her were launched by different groups. Definitive proof has not surfaced, but the perspectives and interests of key suspects give rise to serious suspicion.

BENAZIR'S IMPACT

Benazir's enemies included conservatives who distrusted the populist banner under which the Bhutto family had long stood. Her family's status as Shia disturbed some Sunnis, although despite media reports that characterize her father as Shia, Benazir's autobiography notes that only her mother was Shia.[1] Of greater significance, however, was that she was unpredictable and viewed as the only politician in Pakistan with the capacity to break its politics wide open. She was extremely eloquent. She moved people. She lit up a nation and energized it. Critics felt that she told different people different things and that one could never be certain where she really stood on certain issues.

Her campaign to win over the Washington political establishment was a model of strategic communication. In discussing the Taliban, she chose her words carefully. Although she would later distance herself from the action, as noted earlier, while prime minister she had supported the formation of the Taliban in 1996.[2] By 2007, answering a question about what should be done about tribal militancy in North Waziristan, her views were more nuanced: "In fact, we were appalled that the tribal region of our country was *handed over to foreigners*, because Afghan Taliban, Afghans, and al Qaeda are added to the Chechens and the Uzbeks. And this is Pakistani territory, and Pakistan has to protect its own territory" (emphasis added).[3]

She characterized as a "critical mistake" her prior support for the Taliban, whom she had thought would bring peace if they were allowed to function in certain parts of Pakistan. Her "us versus them" distinction went straight to identity politics, pegging foreigners—outsiders, not Pakistanis—as the true enemy. The distinction was carefully drawn and may help explain why she believed she could deal with the Pakistani Taliban. But she was discreet. Ahmed Rashid, who did a lengthy interview with Benazir a week before her assassination, remarked, "She had a very clear understanding of the Taliban and the need to take them on."[4] Rashid believes she was quite willing to do so if she became prime minister again. Still, her public policy was carefully calibrated. That lends support to those who doubt Mehsud's role as an architect of her assassination. But the widespread perception by fundamentalist and violent extremist elements from the Afghan Taliban such as the Haqqani network—with its apparent ties to the ISI—that she was untrustworthy and a deadly threat supplies an ample motive for one (or more) of those factions to assassinate her.

Gretchen Peters and Ahmed Rashid, among others, have insightfully pointed out that the Taliban is rather a different species of snake than the one pictured in the minds of many Western politicians. Rashid notes that the Pakistani Taliban consist of different elements, criminals and ideologues. A signifi cant amount of its funding, reports Peters, comes from criminal activities, in particular protecting the region's drug trade. Drug money has also corrupted elements of Pakistani intelligence.

Extremists have struggled with the issue, arguing that in Islam, the sin is in consuming hard drugs like heroin or opium and not in growing them for the consumption (and socially destructive addiction and associated criminal activity) of non-Muslims. There is big money—billions upon billions of dollars—in this business. During her last term as prime minister, Benazir's interior minister, Maj. Gen. Naseerullah Babar, had embraced the Afghan Taliban and more than once tried to take credit for creating them.[5] In 2007 she was trying to make amends for past transgressions and promising a crackdown on drug trafficking in Pakistan. This critical point raises substantial questions as to the American and NATO strategy for fighting the Taliban and whether they have mischaracterized the nature of the enemy in their attempts to defeat it. The challenge posed by drug trafficking has been ignored by many Washington insiders, despite a growing awareness in 2011 of the confluence between drug traffickers and violent extremism.

Pakistanis knew better. Benazir's close association with the United States alienated many Pakistanis and the military. Her pledge that the Americans could search for bin Laden in Pakistan certainly rankled.[6] Musharraf's handling of the A. Q. Kahn issue was skillful, but Bhutto, as noted in chapter 8, promised to turn Khan over to the International Atomic Energy Agency for questioning and to hold open parliamentary hearings that would expose the truth about Pakistani nuclear trafficking.

She promised to "normalize" relations with Israel. That was anathema to the military and intelligence communities. Israel, a nuclear state with friendly ties to India, was not seen as a potential friend of Pakistan.

Pakistan's military regards its nuclear weapons program as a foundation of the nation's defense doctrine. Would it have tolerated any chance that the unpredictable Benazir would take action that might expose the deep involvement of members of the military-intelligence establishment in nuclear trafficking? Exposure might have stopped or curtailed essential foreign assistance. It may have produced an ultimatum from the United States to slash the nuclear program or else suffer serious international sanctions.

Musharraf summed up what many of her critics believed:

The United States thought Benazir was the right person to fight terrorists. Who is the best person to fight? You need three qualities today if you want to fight the extremists and the terrorists. Number one, you must have the military with you. Well, she was very unpopular with the military. Very unpopular. Number two, you shouldn't be seen by the entire religious lobby to be alien—a non-religious person. The third element: don't be seen as an extension of the United States. Now I am branded as an extension but not to the extent she was.[7]

Her enemies despised and feared her, and with good reason. She was a powerhouse who posed a direct threat to an establishment that strongly opposed the democratic change and religious tolerance that had marked her very public—and often repeated—declarations of principles and values.

Behind the rhetoric, Benazir was a practical politician. She was goal-oriented. She believed that Pakistan needed major reforms and aimed to effect them. The politics that governed her 2007 return to Pakistan imposed constraints. She aroused enthusiasm but confronted significant political challenges. Discontent with Pakistan's government and economy was escalating. She probably would have won a landslide victory in the January 2008 elections but she had to respect what that mandate would have required: strong leadership for fundamental change to restore and vindicate democratic processes, turning back repressive practices, and putting the economy on its feet. She had to achieve these while maintaining her well-articulated views that Pakistan needed to embrace religious tolerance and democratic pluralism.

It bears stressing: Benazir had no choice but to live up to her commitment for transformation. It was an all-or-nothing effort. Although insiders report that the army was prepared to work with her, others would have worked endlessly to upend her politically. Her opposition was tough, resilient, determined. Her most plausible path to success was to lead a popular upheaval—a Pakistani-style Orange Revolution against the status quo. In her heart, that is almost certainly what she wanted to do. Ahmed Rashid agrees, arguing that "she would have banded the politicians together to stand up to the Army. Unfortunately," he adds, "she depended on the Americans to ensure free and fair elections. She was not her own master. She was dependent on too many external factors, including the military, over which she had no control."[8]

Perhaps, but political leaders like Benazir—for all of her many imperfections—are rare. She had a unique ability to bring change through her charisma, intellect, and determination. No less important, keeping her eye on the far horizon, she resolved to recruit and train a new generation of leaders in a nation.

Her enemies in Pakistan saw her as corrupt and incompetent. They saw an opportunist who identified too closely with the West. They believed she posed a clear threat to Islamic institutions. What might she have achieved? Only history could have rendered that verdict. Writing in the *New York Times* on November 28, 2009, Thomas Friedman said, "Many Arab Muslims know that what ails their societies is more than the West, and that The Narrative is just an escape from looking honestly at themselves. But none of their leaders dare or care to open that discussion."[9] Siegel says that Bhutto dared not only to start that discussion but to lead it, and to fight for a just and more democratic society. He continues:

> Her death was much more than a loss for Pakistan, it was a huge loss for the entire world. No other person could speak so clearly and eloquently of a modern, pluralistic and tolerant Islam. To the entire Muslim world she was the face of what could be. To the rest of the world she was the bridge between East and West. Her loss is immeasurable, like JFK's and Sadat's. She had intellect, vision and guts. She is entirely irreplaceable.[10]

In the closing pages of her last book, completed within days of her assassination, she worried about the "internal rift" in the Muslim world whose "destructive tension has set brother against brother" in "a deadly fratricide that has tortured intra-Islamic relations for 1,300 years." She denounced sectarian conflict that has "stifled the brilliance of the Muslim renaissance that took place during the dark Ages of Europe, when the great universities, scientists, doctors, and artists were all Muslim." She made clear that she would stand up against extremists who "have manipulated Islamic dogma to justify and rationalize a so-called Jihad against the West."[11]

Looking to the future, she declared: "Democratic nations should forge a consensus around the most powerful political idea in the world today: the right of people to freely choose their government and for governments so selected to govern democratically pursuant to the rule of law."[12] Change was imperative, she concluded, for "staying within the box has set Islam and the West on a dangerous and unnecessary collision course. . . . It is time for honesty, both among people and between people. . . . There has been enough pain. It is time for reconciliation."[13]

Benazir possessed a powerful, unique voice. No individual is indispensable for a nation, or to history. But some more than others stand apart in the courage and ability to make a difference. That is what the world lost in the tragedy of December 27, 2007.

THE PERSONS OF INTEREST

Key Militants

That tribal militants who form part of the Afghan Taliban may have been actively involved in the assassination seems highly plausible. Of these, a strong argument can be made that the Haqqani network, led by Jalaluddin Haqqani and his son Sirjuddin Haqqani, tops the list of suspects. Some characterize the Haqqanis as Pakistan Taliban, given their roots in North Waziristan, where they maintain a safe haven. It has also conducted operations in Afghanistan.[14] General Stanley McChrystal's report and others treat them as one of three key Taliban forces confronting the U.S. and NATO in Afghanistan.[15] Several confluent reasons raise suspicions about this network's potential involvement in the assassination.

One need not tarry over whether the Haqqani network should be identified with Afghanistan, Pakistan, or both. Benazir drew a careful distinction between those she viewed as part of the Pakistani Taliban and those she viewed as Afghan Taliban. She believed she could reach accommodation with fellow

Pakistanis. She pledged to defeat the Afghan Taliban, who she believed were violent extremists and represented a threat to Pakistan. But the Haqqani network was her enemy. It had aligned itself with Al Qaeda—an avowed Benazir adversary. And there seems strong evidence that Pakistan intelligence considered the network a "strategic asset."

Insiders contend that the Haqqani network enjoys strong links to ISI, and it's clear that the Pentagon believes there is a strong link. It seems plausible that those who organized, funded, and enabled the assassination included individuals with links to the Pakistani intelligence community. That community consists of diverse elements inside and outside of ISI.

How certain can one be about the Haqqani-ISI links? The *New York Times* reported that Haqqani—who has maintained a long-standing association with Osama bin Laden[16]—was a "favorite" of Pakistani intelligence agencies and considered a Pakistani asset.[17] In a transcript provided to U.S. Director of National Intelligence Mike McConnell in May 2008, the term surfaces again. In it, Army Chief of Staff Lieutenant General Kayani was overheard referring to Maulavi Jalaluddin Haqqani as a "strategic asset" of Pakistan. The intercept enabled the CIA to uncover evidence that ISI and Haqqani had cooperated to execute a bombing attack in Afghanistan.[18] During an interview with Fareed Zakaria on CNN, President Pervez Musharraf blew off the intercept, arguing that he could not "imagine that [Kayani] would have said this."[19] The denial has not proven persuasive. In 2011 U.S. Joint Chiefs of Staff Chairman Admiral Mike Mullen minced no words during a trip to Pakistan in linking the Haqqani network to ISI.[20]

All elements for a viable conspiracy for murder are present if one combines the Haqqani network, Al Qaeda, and anti-Benazir elements with Pakistan's intelligence establishment. She posed an existential threat to all of these parties, providing a clear motive. Between them, the means were readily available. The Haqqani network had access to suicide bombers, perhaps furnished by Al Qaeda. In Pakistan, finding a weapon posed no obstacle to such forces. Finally, the opportunity was self-evident. Security during her public appearances, especially her fatal one at Liaquat Bagh, was grossly inadequate. Allowing herself to become a target by appearing personally in front of very large crowds at close range provided opportunities for assassins.

The Haqqani network is only one group at whom the finger could be pointed.

Journalist Sreeram Chaulia contends that the main executor of the actual attack was Abdul Rehman Sindhi of the Al Qaeda–affiliated Lashkar-e-Jhangvi. Authorities had released him from custody just before Benazir returned to Pakistan.[21] The LeJ is considered the most violent militant organization in Pakistan. Its members include former servicemen and sharpshooters.[22] It recruits hit men for a group it calls the "armored corps of jehad." Investigative journalist Amir Mir reports that members return to their homes and jobs and live normally until summoned: "While they wait, they are under strict orders to shun beards and traditional clothes, to maintain a neat, inconspicuous appearance, to have their documents (real ones issued under fake names) in order to carry them at all times and to do nothing illegal or out of the ordinary."[23] That instruction is consistent with the appearance of the suicide-attacker who fired at Benazir and apparently blew himself up. Fiercely anti-American, the LeJ aims to force the government to declare the Shia community a non-Muslim minority. Thus her faith is another reason it would find Benazir hostile.[24] The LeJ has close links to other extremist organizations associated with Al Qaeda.

Other groups that may have played a role in the assassination include the Jaish-e-Mohammad. Its leader, Maulana Masood Azhar, lost favor with the Inter-Services Intelligence after an investigation revealed the group had been involved in the December 2003 assassination attempt against Musharraf.[25] But that was true as well of the LeJ, Lashkar-e-Taiba, Harkat ul-Mujahideen-al-Alami, and Harkat ul-Jihad-al-Islami.[26] The JeM has been hurt by division, and Amir Mir argues that some of its most dangerous members have gone underground. Bahukutumbi Raman suggests that individual Jundullah (Soldiers of Allah) may also have been involved.

The militants detained by police in January and February 2008 were described as members of the Badr Organization, which may no longer exist. It seems wholly plausible that some of the triggermen were connected to Al Qaeda or Pakistani militant groups. Still, the police ultimately detained suspects who claimed that their motive for attacking Benazir was revenge for Musharraf's attack on the Red Mosque. The most striking detail is not a single man was prosecuted, convicted, or punished. Nor is there any solid evidence that they conceived, financed, or organized the assassination.

Other suspicion has fallen on Qari Saifullah Akhtar, the amir of Harkat ul-Jihad-al-Islami. He has been associated with a shadowy network of extremist groups called the 313 Brigade. Evidently involved in the December 2003 assassination attempts against Musharraf, he fled to Dubai. In August 2006, Dubai police arrested him and turned him over to Pakistani authorities. To the surprise of many, Akhtar was detained for a short period and released. Although Benazir named him as one of the suspects following the Karachi assassination attempt, hard evidence linking him to Benazir's assassination remains lacking.

AL QAEDA

As discussed in chapter 17, Al Qaeda's top commander in Afghanistan, Mustafa Abu al-Yazid, reportedly seized credit for Benazir's assassination. The authenticity of his statement has been questioned. Still, the U.S. government was quick to accept Al Qaeda's claim, which placed the group firmly on the increasingly longer list of suspects. Scotland Yard and the British government concurred. Al Qaeda associates, notably those involved with the LeJ or the LeT, may have pulled the trigger. The real issue is not who pulled the trigger or detonated an explosive blast, but who conceived, supported, and guided the assassination.

BRIG. GEN. EJAZ SHAH

In a letter to Musharraf dated October 16, 2007, following the Karachi incident, Benazir stated that she had good reason to believe that the Intelligence Bureau chief General Shah was plotting to kill her.[27] The IB, Pakistan's main domestic intelligence and espionage agency, has responsibility for counterintelligence and internal security matters. He seems to have been a prime suspect.[28] One can understand her suspicions. He remains a prime suspect.

She did not trust him and disliked him. The feeling was mutual after she had made clear that she intended to purge Pakistan's intelligence services of hundreds of rogue agents suspected of supporting Islamic terrorism. She told the *Sunday Telegraph:* "We need a security service that is professional in its approach, which rises above ties of religious or political sentiment. I have strong reservations about some of the people still operating within the intelligence services, and we need reforms to get rid of them."[29] She made the statement just after the failed assassination attempt in Karachi, for which she blamed Shah. There didn't seem much doubt that Shah was among those who topped her list of those she intended to sack. It bears stressing: She represented an existential threat to Shah's career, the institutions he had served, and what he represented.

Some believe that Shah was Pakistani intelligence's former handler of Osama bin Laden and Mullah Omar. Reportedly, he was in regular contact with bin Laden; billionaire mobster Dawood Ibrahim, a native of India; and Ahmad Omar Saeed Sheikh.[30] Ibrahim was well connected to bin Laden and Pakistani militant groups like the LeT. Indians view Dawood in the same light that Americans view bin Laden. Although Musharraf denied his presence in Pakistan, it's clear that Musharraf gave sanctuary to Ibrahim, who has close ties to the ISI and to militants.[31]

After the Karachi attempt, leaders of the Pakistan Peoples Party accused Shah of staging the bombings. Benazir had claimed that Shah had done his best to sabotage reconciliation efforts between the PPP and Musharraf. Zardari was certain that Shah encouraged the Islamists to attack her.[32]

It was to Shah that Omar Sheikh, who was heavily involved in Daniel Pearl's 2002 kidnapping and murder, surrendered after security services detained his family.[33] Many believe he did so out of fear that if the police arrested him, he might be tortured.[34] Shah knew Omar Sheikh well. He had been in touch with Omar Sheikh regularly after India, which had arrested him in 1994 for kidnapping three Britons and an American and imprisoned him for five years, released him in a hostage swap deal.[35]

Shah is credited with protecting Omar Sheikh from execution after his conviction and death sentence. Indeed, Omar Sheikh seems able to communicate with the outside world easily enough, although he is detained in an isolated ward in Hyderabad Central Jail and guarded round the clock.[36] At the time of Pearl's killing in Punjab, Shah was the home secretary for the province, and Omar Sheik was an important player in extremist circles, an operative of JeM, and an ISI agent.[37] It's not clear exactly what Pearl was investigating, but some believe it may have been a connection between the ISI and Ummah Tameer-e-Nau (UTN), headed by Dr. Bashiruddin Mahmood, the former chief of Pakistan's nuclear power program. The UTN has been accused of leaking nuclear secrets to bin Laden.[38]

Indian counterterrorism expert Bahukutumbi Raman has reported that Shah had wanted to prevent Omar Sheikh from confessing to Karachi police that he had provided advance information of the 9/11 attack to the Peshawar corps commander, Lt. Gen. Ehsan ul-Haq, who was now the ISI chief. It appears that prior to 9/11, Omar Sheikh also had wired more than $100,000 to Mohammed Atta to fund the hijackers' flight school tuition, airfare, and living expenses.[39] Some believe that he had acted on the instruction of then-ISI chief Lt. Gen. Mahmood Ahmed.[40]

Punjab was Zia ul-Haq's political base. Its pro-Zia leaders were hostile to Benazir:[41] Shah; Hamid Gul; Chaudhry Pervez Elahi, who served as chief minister in the Punjab until December 2007; and his cousin, Chaudhry Shujaat Hussain, the leader of the Pakistan Muslim League–Qaid who controlled the Punjab government.[42] But it was Shah who received credit for creating Musharraf's political party, the PML-Q in the Punjab, and though close to Musharraf, he was viewed as closer still to the Chaudhries.[43]

Zia loyalists congregated in the IB, the Ministry of the Interior, and the Punjab administration. Benazir felt that all of them represented a threat.[44] Zardari has claimed that Shah, who had served as home secretary in the Punjab as well, encouraged radical Islamists to kill her. Almost certainly her return to power would have cost him his job. Shah had a strong motive for ensuring her elimination.

Shah did not flinch from threatening violence. Mukhtar Mai (Mukhtaran Bibi) is a courageous champion in Pakistan against rape and illiteracy and author of a respected bestselling autobiography. When she was planning a trip to New York, *New York Times* columnist Nicholas Kristof, a highly credible source, reported that Shah warned her colleague, Dr. Amna Buttar, that Pakistan might murder both of them in New York. "We can do anything," Shah allegedly said. "We can just pay a little money to some black guys in New York and get people killed there."[45] Such talk from a power player in Shah's position, at home in a culture of violence, should be taken seriously.

Shah and his confederates did not like women meddling in politics, and they hated the United States. They also loathed Benazir—her background, her career, her allies, her lifestyle, her ambition, what she stood for, and what she symbolized. She posed a direct threat to them. Shah had protected one of the most notorious terrorists that the ISI or Al Qaeda has produced. One might reasonably conclude that murder does not faze people like him. He had power. He had means. He had a motive. He is apparently a capable, effective operator, and a dangerous adversary. One can easily comprehend why Benazir believed he wanted to kill her. Apparently fearing for his life, months after the assassination, Ejaz Shah reportedly fled Pakistan for Australia.[46] Other reports said he had gone to Lahore.[47] The UN Commission of Inquiry investigating Benazir's death wanted to interview him. It did not get the opportunity.

The proof is not conclusive. But a process of deduction and examination of the evidence makes Shah a serious suspect.

HAMID GUL

Benazir rightly feared the former Inter-Services Intelligence chief Hamid Gul. He was a formidable enemy. A decorated army officer and close ally of Zia ul-Haq's, he served as the ISI director and as Zia's head of Military Intelligence.[48] Although some disagree with him, Center for Strategic and International Studies national security expert Arnaud de Borchgrave, who has long covered Pakistan, believes that Gul has remained active in the ISI's ultrasecret S section and that he will hold this job for as long as he desires. Some ISI cadres who retire on a government pension are selected for lifetime employment with this group, which conducts highly covert activities for the ISI. Gul worked closely with Washington during the Soviet-Afghan war and helped oversee mujahideen operations, providing the fighters with advice and support.[49] Interviewed by de Borchgrave, he blamed 9/11 on a plot by "Mossad and its accomplices," including the U.S. Air Force, and declared that U.S. "betrayals and broken promises and what was done to my army career," in blocking his promotion to chief of army staff, had made him virulently anti-American.[50] His opinion that the United States deserted Pakistan after the Afghans' war against the Soviets, leaving it with very difficult economic problems caused by an influx of refugees at a time when Pakistan feared India's intentions, seems to have fueled his anti-American sentiments. Gul was apparently in Afghanistan just prior to the 9/11 attack and, de Borchgrave reports, was acting as Osama bin Laden's "principal adviser before September 11, 2001." Some have questioned whether he had prior knowledge of the assault on the World Trade Center.[51]

De Borchgrave is highly respected for his expertise in intelligence matters. He believes the evidence shows the ISI knew about the 9/11 attacks beforehand.

> The fact that ISI knew about 9/11 before it happened was confirmed by a Pakistani known to me and who has worked closely with me over ten years. He has incredibly good connections and was asked by a member of the 9/11 Commission, in my presence at the Metropolitan Club in Washington, to see what he could find out. He did indeed deliver and I personally took his report to Fred Fielding at the White House. Alas, it arrived three days after the 9/11 Commission's report went to the printers. It could have been added as an addendum, but wasn't, perhaps out of fear of jeopardizing the budding relationship with President Musharraf.[52]

His statement supports Benazir's suspicions and serves as a caveat to American officials in dealing with Pakistan.

Gul is a radical Islamist. He supported trafficking nuclear arms technology to Iran. Although forced by Nawaz Sharif to retire in 1992 after blocking his ascension to COAS, Gul was a central and leading figure in the group of Pakistani generals who facilitated the rise of the Pakistan Taliban. Attending the January 2001 Darul Uloom Haqqania Islamic conference, he declared protecting the Taliban and bin Laden to be a religious duty.[53] Gul played an important role in organizing the Taliban and terror groups that fought the

Indian Army in Kashmir, in providing support to groups linked to Al Qaeda, and in mobilizing media support for it.[54] After terrorists attacked Mumbai in November 2008, the United States submitted Gul's name as an international terrorist to the UN Security Council.[55]

Some, like Pakistani military expert Shuja Nawaz, contend that by 2007, Gul's influence had significantly waned. Others doubt Gul's capacity to organize Benazir's assassination.[56] For his part, Gul remains exultantly defiant: "Nawaz Sharif and America were desperate for me not to become the army chief. . . . But they could not crush my spirit or ideology. . . . My biggest contribution was jihad. I strongly believed that jihadis were going to take over Pakistan. Everyone else, from the politicians to the army, had repeatedly disappointed the nation."[57]

Musharraf had been trained as an artillery officer and had been Gul's artillery pupil. With Gul as the ringleader, Musharraf had helped oust Benazir as prime minister. In plotting the conspiracy, Gul was a leader who got things done. He had devised a ruthless, thoroughly devious strategy to toss Benazir. She never stood a realistic chance of keeping her job. Gul and the military-intelligence establishment had all the advantages, for Gul was an old hand at manipulating elections. In 1988, he led the ISI's campaign.

That year he had helped forge nine political parties into a common front opposing the PPP.[58] In a game with no rules, no time limits, and no penalties, he had the additional director general of national security at the ISI, Brig. Gen. Imtiaz Ahmed Billa, launch a campaign to spread false rumors to discredit Bhutto as anti-Punjabi. When she won and the United States insisted that the military accept her as prime minister, Gul and COAS Mirza Aslam Beg instigated Operation Midnight Jackal to push PPP members in Parliament to back a no-confidence vote against her. He convinced the Mohajir Quami Movement (MQM)—later the Muttahida Quami Movement—to withdraw from her coalition and join the opposition.[59] The motion of no confidence, however, was defeated.

Benazir and Gul had clashed from the start. They remained bitter enemies. Each wanted the other out of the way. Every politician has priorities when it comes to his or her objectives and ambitions. Hers included reducing the power of the ISI while, perhaps naively, enhancing that of the Intelligence Bureau. She had moved to replace Gul as the ISI's chief and balance its power by appointing loyalists to the Federal Investigation Agency and to the IB. It made sense, but she lacked the political skills and the power to accomplish it. Led by COAS Mirza Aslam Beg, the army blocked her efforts to make these critical changes in the power structure.[60] Gul had been a confederate of Zia ul-Haq, who had hanged her father,[61] and Gul and the ISI had already plotted to kill her before. They had targeted her for assassination in 1989, with funding allegedly provided by Osama bin Laden.

During her second term, she again tried to diminish the ISI's power by transferring responsibility for clandestine operations to the Ministry of Interior, which was controlled by her ally Gen. Naseerullah Babar. This move did not prevent the president from removing her in 1996.

Gul despised Benazir Bhutto's pro-Western political views. He resented that she was a woman in a position of political influence and power in Pakistan. Her cosmopolitan (i.e., un-Islamic) lifestyle that could bridge diverse cultures repulsed him.[62] He regards himself as a visionary and a patriot. From a Western viewpoint, his politics are demented, but many Pakistanis view the world through a different lens. Gul asserts that Benazir was indeed the casualty of a grand conspiracy but one that was organized by the Americans, who killed her for proving too independent.

Militant groups with whom Gul has enjoyed close ties are hostile to Israel, which has also made his least-favored list. He publicly blames Israel for 9/11. The contrast with Benazir, who, as noted previously, favored normalizing relations with Israel, was stark. Indeed, as other security measures failed to pan out, Hamid Gul—not the most reliable source—claims she asked the Mossad for protection.[63] If he believed that, doubtless the idea infuriated him.

Gul is a figure who could and would make sure she no longer posed a threat to his perception of Pakistani interests, its nuclear secrets, or anyone who shared his views. Still, no proof of his criminal complicity in Benazir's death has surfaced. But one can well understand Benazir's suspicions. He had every motive to see her removed and post-assassination interviews seemed extremely well informed.

ARBAB GHULAM RAHIM AND HASSAN WASSEEM AFZAL

Arbab Ghulam Rahim was chief minister of the Sindh government from 2004 to 2007. A businessman and provincial leader during that period was Hassan Wasseem Afzal, the former deputy chairman of the National Accountability Bureau. Benazir named both in her letter of potential suspects to Musharraf. They were her political enemies. There is not, however, sufficient evidence to name them as suspects for her assassination.

PRESIDENT PERVEZ MUSHARRAF

Bhutto had charged that Musharraf was complicit in failing to provide or to allow adequate security to protect her. Her security on December 27 was grossly inadequate. However, the evidence points against Musharraf's complicity in Benazir's assassination. He planned to best her politically, not see her killed.

Moreover, it's extremely unlikely that he would have risked the potential blowback from the United States by sanctioning her murder. Musharraf grossly erred in failing to ensure her protection. Her assassination ended his own political fortunes. Musharraf had every motive *not* to see her assassinated. Why did he drop the ball? The most plausible explanation is a confluence of factors: (1) he felt his team had done everything reasonable to protect a rival whom he disliked, distrusted, and viewed as an unwelcome nuisance; (2) anger that she had disregarded warnings about threats to her life, even though as she saw it, the warnings were aimed at keeping her away from voters and not credible; (3) a sense that all Pakistani politicians tread on dangerous turf, and that one voluntarily assumes a risk in doing so; (4) the possibility that he was in fact misled as to the security provided her; and (5) above all, incredible political misjudgment. By 2007, Musharraf had grown isolated, and lacked wise advisers who could or would level with him. He did not grasp the punishing impact that her death would have on his own political fortunes, and did not do more than he mistakenly believed politically necessary.

In 2011 the political deal cut to ensure Musharraf's exit did not inhibit the Rawalpindi antiterrorism court from issuing an arrest warrant for him for being part of a "broad conspiracy" to have Benazir killed before elections.[64] The prosecutor accused him of failure to disclose knowledge of a Taliban plot to murder Benazir and failure to provide Benazir with adequate security.[65] Musharraf has strongly denied the accusations. Two police officers, Rawalpindi police chief Saud Aziz and SP Khurram Shahzad, were also arrested for dereliction of duty.

PART IV.
A NATION ON THE BRINK

Strategic communication continues to play a pivotal role in the success or failure of the key political players in Pakistan since Benazir's death. This section examines how President Zardari, Lt. Gen. Kayani, and others have addressed the crises that have beset Pakistan in the last three years, and how their use of strategic communication has made them stronger or weaker.

Chapter 20

THE AFTERMATH

On August 31, 2009, the Lahore High Court issued a summons not only to former president Pervez Musharraf, but also Interior Minister Rehman Malik, Law Minister Babar Awan, former Punjab chief minister Chaudhry Pervez Elahi, former Intelligence Bureau director Brig. Gen. Ejaz Shah, former caretaker interior minister Hamid Nawaz, Interior Secretary Syed Kamal Shah, former Interior Ministry spokesman Javed Iqbal Cheema, and eight other people. The court sought answers to questions about their knowledge or involvement in the circumstances surrounding her assassination.

Benazir's protocol officer, Chaudhry Muhammad Aslam, moved the case. The petition was assigned to Justice Chaudhry, who issued notices to the respondents. Manzoor Ahmad, counsel to Aslam, alleges that as head of state Musharraf had a responsibility, which he failed to meet, to ensure Benazir's security. He claimed Malik, who had been tasked with ensuring Benazir's safety, and Awan had fled the scene of the murder.[1]

For now, Benazir's murder remains unsolved. After her death, it felt as if a deal was struck among key political players to clamp down on any serious investigation. Perhaps too many people have too much to hide or lose should the truth come out. The shakeout, however, produced interesting results.

Zardari received a clear path to become president, although in December 2009 he willingly, consistent with Benazir's pledge to restore the 1973 constitution, yielded much of his power to Prime Minister Yousuf Raza Gilani.

The Supreme Court also overturned the National Reconciliation Ordinance, a move that may potentially expose Zardari to legal challenges once he leaves office, although the government is adamant that while in office, he enjoys immunity.[2] No one in the military or intelligence services has been prosecuted.

Today Musharraf lives in London, in fairly modest circumstances, earning income from speaking engagements.[3] In October 2010, at the age of sixty-seven, Musharraf launched his All Pakistan Muslim League political party and kicked off a new bid to run for president of Pakistan. Speaking at a club in London, he stood against a backdrop that used the white and green colors of Pakistan's flag and his party's logo, which includes the crescent and star of the national flag and a hawk's head. Musharraf pledged a "jihad against poverty, hunger, illiteracy, and backwardness" and "to make Pakistan into a progressive Islamic state for others in the Third World to emulate."[4]

Meanwhile, A. Q. Khan remains safe from interrogation by international groups like the International Atomic Energy Agency.

Chapter 21

QUO VADIS?
WHERE TO?

Pakistan is politically fragile. It lacks a strong sense of optimism, confidence, or identity. It has produced few outstanding political leaders. Mohammad Ali Jinnah and Benazir stand out as exceptions. Zulfiqar Ali Bhutto was mesmerizing, but his socialism set Pakistan back.

Divisions between rich and poor create ominous social tensions. Pakistan's brand of agrarian feudalism, rooted in wealth, kinship, connections, and leadership of families, clans, and tribes is alive and well. These leaders have real power. They resist change that erodes it. A self-propagating urban elite has its own power. Both are a barrier to economic reform and social mobility in a conservative society. They present huge obstacles to any government, whether run by civilians or the military, to effect modernization or innovation. One consequence is a sense of hopelessness. Pakistanis do not harbor the American dream that their children's lives will be better than their own. Political extremists can and do exploit the sense of injustice.

A significant demographic shift increasing the urban population will redraw the nation's politics and shift greater power in Parliament to urban constituencies. In the judgment of Pakistani expert Shuja Nawaz, "This shift is likely to increase rural-urban tensions, and these will be exacerbated by the long-term impact of the 2010 floods."[1] Half the population is younger than eighteen years old. That demographic creates daunting challenges in providing education, creating jobs, and satisfying rising expectations of a new generation.

Ethnic tensions—for example, Pashtuns and Punjabis distrust one another—define another fault line. The increased influence of Wahhabi and De-obandi Islam at the expense of the more tolerant Sufism presents a challenge to secularists and pluralism. The military is stronger than ever and its influence is growing again. Any government forced to answer to the army and Washington more than to popular sentiment is weak. At this writing, civilian and military-intelligence leaders appear to be drawing more closely together. The aim is to forge a more united front in dealing with the United States. Such close cooperation would represent a promising departure if it helps to rectify the current imbalance between the power of the military and that of civilian leadership.

In its external relations, Pakistan has played on different sides at the same time. This pattern flows from its perceptions of self-interest but creates suspicion and distrust. It has faltered in forging a stable relationship with India. Though self-defeating, India-phobia persists. Controversy has swelled over whether Inter-Services Intelligence trained and sponsored the Lashkar-e-Taiba terrorists who attacked Mumbai on November 26, 2008. It is a signal event that affects the strategic communication each nation's leaders employ at home and with one another.

India officials believe it did. India's Home Secretary G. K. Pillai declared, "It was not just a peripheral role. They [ISI] were literally controlling and co-ordinating it from beginning to end."[2] In April 2001 LeT operative Tahawwur Hussain Rana told a U.S. court about his acts of providing material support to terrorists in the Mumbai attacks, which "were done at the behest of the Pakistani government and the ISI, not the Lashkar terrorist organization."[3] LeT has also supported terrorist attacks in urban India by Harkat ul-Jihad-al-Islami.[4] U.S. views have shifted. In 2008 the *New York Times* reported that U.S. intelligence officials found "no hard evidence to link the spy service . . . ISI . . . to the Mumbai attacks. But ISI has shared intelligence with Lashkar and provided protection to it."[5] In 2010 *New York Times* reporters Mark Mazetti and Salman Masood found that "American officials believe ISI officers . . . provided support to Lashkar-e-Taiba militants who carried out the Mumbai attacks later that year."[6] In May 2011 confessed Pakistani American terrorist David Headley took the stand in Chicago and stated that ISI and LeT worked together and that he dealt with a "Major Iqbal" and ISI noncommissioned officers. Apparently they recruited him, played a central role in planning the Mumbai attacks, assured him of financial help, and trained him. He did not accuse ISI leadership of complicity. The ISI and LeT "coordinated with each other" and ISI provided Lashkar with "financial, military, and moral support," Headley testified.[7]

Pakistan has heatedly denied allegations it was involved in the Mumbai attack. Its able ambassador, Husain Haqqani, has argued vigorously that today Pakistan is moving swiftly toward strong democratic, civilian government and ending conflict with India.[8] In April 2011 he emphasized that the 26/11 strikes, as they are known in India, "were orchestrated by extremists who want India and Pakistan to go to war," dissociated the government from extremism, and pledged that Pakistan would work hard to "bring the perpetrators to justice."[9] Strongly denouncing the violent extremists who attacked Mumbai, he has emphasized elsewhere that "even our friends in India are not accusing the government,"[10] which may be officially true as a government-to-government issue. Another political insider with close ties to Pakistan's highest levels of leadership expressed a corollary sentiment as to why Pakistan continues to feel wary about its neighbor: "The Western media looks at Pakistani-India relations through pro-India eyes. There is a history of unfortunate conflict. Pakistan worried about the unresolved, potentially explosive situation in Kashmir. It is a top of mind issue for Pakistanis. That keeps tensions alive. The fact is, India has infiltrated significant numbers of agents into Pakistan and its ties to Karzai are undeniable. One needs to be fair and objective in judging whether Pakistan merits blame for what takes place between the two countries."[11]

Pakistan's concerns are evident in how it approaches the Afghanistan conflict. Many in the West portray that war as pitting the United States and the North Atlantic Treaty Organization (NATO) against global jihadis led by Al Qaeda and the Taliban. As a matter of strategic communication, that's unfortunate. Framing the conflict that way complicates the political challenges and makes it more difficult to convert hard-earned military success into sustainable political triumph. It affects Pakistani attitudes toward and weakens its desire to work more closely with the United States for a plausible solution.

Underscoring Pakistan's attitude is its sense that the United States will pull out of Afghanistan. It sees no interest in alienating parties who will become or remain players in that country after the United States departs. That immeasurably complicates American efforts to gain Pakistan's cooperation in fighting the Taliban.

The Taliban have taken pains to position themselves as a national force. They deny acting as champions for a sole ethnic group or political faction. Many Pakistanis see the war as a Taliban-led Pashtun rebellion against a Tajik-dominated government. In this scenario, Hamid Karzai serves as a token Pashtun (and pro-Indian) face. Traditionally, Pashtuns have dominated Afghan politics. Today many feel sidelined. Pakistanis see common bonds between their Pashtuns and Afghan Pashtuns.

The Pakistani military and intelligence leadership has shown little regard for Karzai, although there are signs to embrace reconciliation to resolve the fighting. Pakistani leaders do not perceive Pakistan's interests as necessarily consistent with American goals. Depending too heavily upon Pakistan to make an American strategy work is unrealistic. No matter what, do not expect Pakistan to play a positive role in a resolution unless it is accorded an active voice in the process. ISI's ties to the Taliban are historic and likely to persist. U.S. Joint Chiefs of Staff chairman Adm. Mike Mullen was sufficiently alarmed that in April 2011 he made a special trip to Islamabad to stress U.S. concerns that Pakistani intelligence was having a "longstanding relationship" with the Taliban Haqqani Network, which, he said, "is supporting, funding, training fighters that are killing Americans and killing coalition partners." Jalaluddin Haqqani and his son Sirjuddin lead one of the most formidable Taliban groups.[12] Still, the Secretary of Defense announced that the United States would provide Pakistan with eighty-five small Raven drone aircraft that can deliver real-time color or infrared imagery that gives troops on the battlefield an edge.[13]

A BITTER LEGACY FROM THE WAR AGAINST THE SOVIETS

Another complication lies in Pakistan's perception that the United States is patronizing and disdainful, and abuses Pakistan sovereignty. This sentiment is not new. Brig. Mohammad Yousaf headed the ISI's Afghan Bureau between 1983 and 1987. In his revealing memoir, written with Mark Adkin, Yousaf praised the CIA for playing "a vital role" in leading to the Soviet defeat in Afghanistan and was impressed by its "access to sophisticated technology."[14] But Yousaf denounced the Americans as disrespectful and expressed strong resentment of "the way in which the mujahideen were so often fobbed off with unsuitable weapons."[15]

A dispute ignited by Congressman Charlie Wilson, whom Tom Hanks romanticized in *Charlie Wilson's War*, a star-studded comedic film based on George Crile's colorful account, offers a telling illustration. Wilson battled on Capitol Hill to fund the mujahideen and defeat the Soviets. Crile's sources and Yousaf saw the war in different terms. The issue here is not which view is correct. The disputes help clarify what Pakistani leaders believed, the lessons they drew from their experiences with Americans, and how these experiences shaped their worldviews for today. The legacy is evident in the challenges the United States faces today in urging Pakistan to act more aggressively against violent extremists.

Yousaf's account offers insights into Pakistani hostility toward Americans. Crile reports that CIA operatives saw Yousaf as a fundamentalist Muslim who "bore considerable suspicion and even bitter resentment against the American spy agency."[16] How fair is that accusation? Yousaf's postscript does invoke the word "jihad," but merely in the context of fighting the Soviets and their Afghan allies. He favored establishing an Islamic government in Kabul. But his book is no ideological tract. It offers a coolly analytical assessment of the war between 1983 and 1987 written from the standpoint of a Pakistani military officer and nationalist.

The differences in view are cast into high relief by the two men's discussions, in their respective books, of the Swiss-designed 20mm Oerlikon anti-aircraft cannon. Wilson was its champion. Wilson argued that getting it into the hands of the mujahideen was a key to defeating the Soviets. A photo of the weapon graces the cover of Crile's book. Wilson steamrolled the opposition and obtained the weapon for the mujahideen. Crile portrays Wilson's success as a triumph of bravado over CIA bureaucrat-think. Crile and Wilson acknowledge that the Stinger antiaircraft missiles made the decisive difference in defeating the Soviets, but in their telling, forcing the agency to buy the Oerlikon was a major breakthrough toward achieving victory.[17] Yousaf judged that Wilson squandered precious resources on a fool's errand, as the Oerlikon was a poor choice of weapon for the war:

> We explained that the weapon weighed 1,200 pounds and was therefore far too heavy. It would require some twenty mules to transport a section of three guns; it would impede the Mujahideen's mobility and was more suited to positional defense of strong points. There was no way mules could use the steep mountain trails, making its deployment so restricted as to make the weapon more of a liability than an asset. We also pointed out that the long, heavy, cumbersome barrel could not be loaded lengthwise along the horse's or the mule's back. It had to be positioned across the animal, making it impossible to go through narrow defiles, where it snagged on every bush. Then we pointed out that this weapon had a high rate of fire, needed to be deployed in threes, and the Mujahideen's lack of fire control would mean excessive ammunition expenditure. With bullets costing $50 each, and a rate of fire of 1000 rounds a minute, I thought this would be a telling point for cost-conscious Americans. Finally it was explained that the Oerlikon crews would need lengthy special training.[18]

Yousaf writes that when his superior, ISI director-general Gen. Akhtar Abdur Rehman Khan, complained to the CIA,

> he was then informed that it was now a political issue, that a congressman who was a vocal supporter of the Mujahideen had insisted on the Oerlikon purchase, so to cancel it now would cause too much embarrassment all round. We eventually received between

forty and fifty guns. . . . It was popular with some Commanders as a prestige weapon, but was not particularly effective in action.[19]

The Oerlikon was no isolated example. Yousaf complains that the Americans also forced them to take obsolete Turkish weapons, unserviceable Egyptian ammunition, and an Egyptian mortar that "was of no value to us." He wrote that Pakistanis barely forestalled having to buy a Chinese antitank weapon that had worked poorly in the Pakistan-India wars.[20] He was especially bitter over what he viewed as America's desertion of an ally as the Soviets withdrew, leading to a stalemate within the country. Yousaf declared, "It was the deliberate policy of the US government that we should never achieve a military victory in Afghanistan." In the meantime, Pakistan was saddled with millions of refugees and an unstable situation that threatened Pakistani security. Yousaf argued that while the United States emerged as a winner in the Afghan conflict, it turned Pakistanis and the Afghans into losers.[21] Yousaf concluded that American talk about partnerships was hypocrisy and that when the chips were down, the United States would always leave Pakistan behind. His view persists among many in Pakistan to the present day.

THE UNITED STATES AND THE TALIBAN

Even before the heightened tensions that crystallized in 2011, Pakistanis were skeptical about working with the United States in fighting the Taliban. U.S. drone attacks in the country have angered many.[22] In 2011 COAS Lt. Gen. Ashfaq Parvez Kayani's anger had reached the point that he was privately threatening to take action against them. Publicly, he has condemned them.[23] In Washington, ISI Lt. Gen. Ahmed Shuja Pasha clashed angrily with his counterpart over the issue. A day after the meetings a new drone attack was interpreted by the ISI as a deliberate attempt to embarrass Pakistan.[24] Initially, Pakistani military and civilians leaders privately supported some attacks in North Waziristan, but the increased frequency and targeting of lower-level Taliban raised new alarms.[25]

One must consider important nuances. Polling has revealed consistent hostility to U.S. drone attacks. But poll results fail to delineate clearly between the attitudes of those Pakistanis who have witnessed or been victimized by Taliban brutality and those once or twice removed. The Aryana Institute for Regional Research and Advocacy conducted a survey in March 2009 in the Federally Administered Tribal Areas (FATA) that American drones often strike, including parts of North and South Waziristan and the Kurram Agency. By a margin of 60 percent to 40 percent, *at that time*, respondents said that drone attacks damaged militant organizations. More than half found the drones were accurate in their strikes. Less than half believed the strikes increased hostility to Americans. They wanted action taken against the Taliban, although not necessarily by Americans. Fully 70 percent said they favored strikes against militants if carried out by the Pakistan military. What emerged from interviews, also conducted by a reporter from *The News*, was strong hostility to the Taliban and Al Qaeda in those areas.[26]

Polling data are not consistent on the drones, and more recent events have shifted attitudes more strongly against the United States. A spring 2010 poll conducted by Pew Global Attitudes Research found that 90 percent of respondents believed the strikes kill too many innocent people.[27] Fewer than a third believed they were necessary. Operational assessments, however, indicate that the strikes have extracted a serious toll on militant leaders and forced them to change their operations.[28] Of some significance, the Pew poll was skewed toward urban respondents. (The sample was 55 percent urban, yet only 33 percent of the population lives in urban areas.) Nor did Pew poll Baluchistan, Pakhtunkhwa, Gilgit-Baltistan, Azad Jammu and Kashmir, or the FATA.

The New American Foundation and Terror Free Tomorrow (NAF/TFT) polling conducted in all seven tribal agencies of the FATA echoed the Pew findings.[29] NAF/TFT data revealed that more than three-quarters of FATA residents oppose American drone strikes. Only 16 percent said the strikes accurately targeted militants, 48 percent said they largely kill civilians, and 33 percent feel they kill both civilians and militants. Fully 87 percent of respondents strongly opposed allowing the U.S. military to pursue Al Qaeda and Taliban fighters in their region. Nearly 80 percent opposed the U.S.-led war on terrorism. Most hold the United States primarily responsible for violence in the region. A mere 10 percent believed the United States was motivated to defeat Al Qaeda and its allies, 75 percent considered the U.S. presence in Afghanistan a war on Islam or an effort to secure its oil and minerals, and 60 percent believe suicide attacks are often or sometimes justified against Americans, compared to only 10 percent feeling that way about such attacks against the Pakistani military and police. This information is telling. It underscores why the Pakistani military seems reluctant to pursue tribal militants with the vigor that Washington desires.

There is a bright side to NAF/TFT's data. Nearly 75 percent of the FATA respondents said they oppose Al Qaeda. More than 66 percent oppose the Pakistani Taliban while about 60 percent oppose the Afghan Taliban as led by Mullah Omar. And 70 percent support Pakistani military fighting against the militants in these areas.

Zardari took heat soon after taking office for approving a deal with the Taliban in the Swat Valley that elements of the Pakistan's military supported. Actually, he doubted that any peace agreement would hold but recognized that his was the minority view at the time. He proved subtler than his critics allowed. He acceded to the agreement, certain that it would fall apart. His strategy was simple: Once the Taliban revealed its true intent to the public, he could take action. Public polling showed deep hostility to religious extremism and the Taliban. But there was hope that a peaceful resolution could be achieved with fellow countrymen. The Taliban wasted no time in vindicating Zardari.

Moving into the Swat, they exercised their power publicly and brutally. A public whipping of a seventeen-year-old girl was caught on camera. As an example of perverse strategic communication, it proved a tour de force. It opened people's eyes. The political environment shifted against the Taliban. Zardari and his PPP team mobilized the military and went into action. Zardari rebuked those who doubted his convictions, pointing out that his wife, Benazir, and other family members had been victims of murder. No matter who devised, funded, and organized Benazir's assassination, it seemed apparent that individuals associated with the Taliban or Al Qaeda were involved in some way. He had every reason to take on violent extremism.

FIGHTING THE TALIBAN IN PAKISTAN

Washington has poured billions of dollars in aid into Pakistan and stepped up its pressure on the Pakistan military to fight the Taliban more aggressively. Although Pakistan has a civilian government, the military-intelligence establishment still holds the real power and often leaves Zardari out of the loop. Though skeptics viewed Kayani as hesitant, he proved willing to take action as Taliban violence at home increased and the United States threatened to reduce or cut financial assistance to the military. Taliban violence against civilians eased his decision. The extremists are their own worst enemy. Bombings at Sufi and Ahmadi mosques in Lahore in 2010 caused nearly eight hundred casualties, and frightened citizens. Additional attacks in 2010 and 2011 have heightened fears and added to an air of instability.

Kayani inspires different views among those who deal with him, but most see him as highly competent militarily and politically. In 2009 his leadership galvanized the political parties to support a military offensive in South Waziristan. Nuanced strategic communication played a key role. He received sound advice on themes and messages. He showed a sophisticated grasp of what might resonate. Summoning the cabinet and the main opposition, he told them, as one senior officer recounted, it's "them or us. If we don't take the battle to them, they will bring the battle to us."[30] The "us versus them" theme is familiar in U.S. politics. It also played well in Pakistan. Kayani carefully reiterated arguments that evoked Pakistani hostility toward outside forces that meddle in the country's internal affairs.

Singling out the Uzbeks, the Arabs, and the Chechens fighting alongside the Taliban,[31] he invoked the theme of patriotism. He branded the enemy as foreigners while offering a hand to fellow citizens. Baitullah Mehsud and Haikmullah Mehsud had been Taliban leaders. Yet Kayani characterized Mehsud tribal members as loyal Pakistanis. He praised all Pakistani tribes for their allegiance to, in his words, "the motherland."[32]

Kayani employed focused communication as an integral element of military operations. His message was clearly stated: Pakistan's survival required people to side with the army against terrorists. These miscreants, he said, were bent on destroying the peace and tribal traditions of the country. They aimed to hold Pakistanis hostage to their antistate agenda.[33] Kayani understood the political risks of civilian casualties, destruction of homes and property, and displacement of civilians.

The strategy worked. He garnered the needed political support to launch a controversial military offensive against militants in South Waziristan in November 2009, although at this writing, the army has resisted pressure to extend its efforts into North Waziristan, where some of the most dangerous militants are based. Still, Kayani has been aggressive on the battlefront and behind the scenes. In Arnaud de Borchgrave's words, "Those who say the Pakistanis are reluctant to fight their own nationals who are terrorists now have a different picture."[34]

Zardari merits credit for his own efforts in fighting violent extremism, although the political dynamics of Pakistan constrain flexibility. The army, not the civilian government, wields the power to decide where and how it will go into battle. Zardari and his team are guided by what they believe is politically plausible. Many journalists and political opponents believe he is weak. Actually, he's performed above expectations, doing his best to stand up to violent extremism.

His efforts broke new ground. In 2008 and 2009 the PPP government mounted a paid media campaign—on English and Urdu radio, on television, and in newspaper stories targeted toward elites and a mass audience—to influence attitudes and opinions in a nation where dozens of television stations are happy to repeat the latest conspiracy theory as regular news.

Titled "This War Is OUR War," the campaign reinforced negative opinions among Pakistanis about religious extremism, the Taliban, and Al Qaeda. The print campaign was anchored in the phrase *Humwatan–Humqadam*, which, loosely translated, means "countryman and journey partner" or "all in this together." It implored Pakistanis, "Let us fight terrorism together." It treated events around the world—such as the attacks of 9/11; the September 21, 2008, Marriott bomb blast in Islamabad; and the November 26, 2008, attack on the Taj Hotel in Mumbai—as part of the same sinister fabric of terrorism. Showing photographs of terrorist destruction, it denounced violence against civilians, declaring: "Our meaning for existence should embrace the value of life."

The print campaign (you can see some examples in the photo insert of this book) personalized its message. It aimed to win hearts and minds by using images of women, children, and families who have been affected by terrorist violence. The images were graphic and powerful: a boy, his arms turned into stumps; children with severe burns; women and children in tears; young men with disfigured legs. Posters portrayed the loss of Rajiv Gandhi and Benazir Bhutto, both important political leaders who fell victim to assassination.

Other posters called upon citizens "to prove that Pakistanis are united to not let anyone harm our country in any way," making clear that this war is to protect "our prosperity," "our future," "our hopes," "our peace." Other posters employed declarations from key leaders, including President Zardari and UN secretary-general Ban Ki-moon, extolling Pakistan's courage in standing up in the "frontlines of the international fight against terrorism" that has killed thousands and turned half a million residents of the Swat Valley into refugees. A television campaign invoked images of 9/11, the Mumbai attack, and attacks in Pakistan to drive the message that Pakistanis are not the sole targets of terrorism. Television ads portrayed the "USA and Us" as a "Team against Terror."

Airing these ads required fortitude. The campaign bolstered the efforts of the Pakistani Army. As an exercise in strategic communication with Washington and the international community, it was smart politics. Unfortunately, controversy over issues like the drone attacks, which have increased hostility toward the United States, caused the government to set aside the campaign. Events in 2011 make its revival anytime soon unlikely.

REFORMING GOVERNMENT

Zardari surprised cynics in voluntarily surrendering important executive powers. He backed constitutional reform effort to abolish the Seventeenth Amendment to the Constitution that President Musharraf had introduced.[35] That amendment had conferred sweeping powers upon the president to dissolve the national and provincial assemblies. On April 9, 2010, as PPP legislators raised slogans of "*Jeay* Bhutto," punctuated with loud desk thumping, the National

Assembly unanimously passed the Eighteenth Amendment, reversing the military's efforts to weaken the 1973 parliamentary constitution and removing the president's power to sack the prime minister and dissolve parliament.[36] The Senate later approved the amendment, and Zardari signed it into law.[37]

The amendment was historic. It changed the name of the North-West Frontier Province to Khyber-Pakhtunkhwa and gives the provinces more autonomy. It reformed the procedure for appointing certain judges; shifted the power to appoint the military service chiefs from the president to the prime minister, although the president remains supreme commander of the armed forces; and prohibited the president from dissolving Parliament. As Prime Minister Gilani put it, "The impossible has been made possible . . . and it is proved now that the parliament is not a rubber stamp."[38] In a swipe against military dictatorship, Zia's name was also removed from the Constitution.[39] Significantly, the army supported the passage of the new amendment.[40]

Poor strategic communication prevented Zardari from capitalizing on this achievement. His team has relied on the news media, which did cover the story broadly. But they did not forge a public campaign to register the narrative and message that he had lived up to his promise to carry out democratic reforms and that he's a leader who stands on principle. One gains or consolidates power by achieving success, registering the fact with the public, and building upon it to gain momentum for accomplishing other goals. Zardari and his team don't do that well. They might argue that they live in a very challenging, often hostile, media environment in which lies and half-truths can have the same currency as truth. There's much validity to this point. But it does not alter the fact. They missed key opportunities to mobilize public support. The results are manifest in consistently low public opinion ratings for Zardari.

Chapter 22

RESETTING THE TERMS
OF COOPERATION AMID
PUBLIC PARANOIA

The relationship between U.S. and Pakistani intelligence shifted in 2011. The attack on bin Laden in May worsened matters, but the year had already kicked off with a bang with the arrest of CIA contractor Raymond Davis.[1] Pakistan's military and intelligence authorities leveraged the potential prosecution of Davis by the civilian government to strategically communicate to the United States a desire to renegotiate the terms of their cooperation in fighting violent extremism within Pakistan. It was tough-minded tactics and illustrates how conspiracy theory fuels public discourse. It also showed that Zardari could marginalize competitors such as his foreign minister, Shah Mehmood Qureshi, when they challenged his handling of a sensitive public issue that generated international headlines and controversy. He had been deft in handling Naheed Khan—who had been with Benazir in the Toyota at the time of her assassination—in favor of Farahnaz Ispahani Haqqani for a slot on the PPP ticket for Parliament. He dealt with Qureshi with equal adroitness.

Davis was attached to the American consulate, based in a Lahore safe house. His mission was to conduct surveillance and reconnaissance.[2] Special Operations troops work routinely to pinpoint the location of Taliban leaders like Mullah Abdul Ghani Baradar, the deputy Taliban commander arrested in 2010. Davis was tracking militant groups in Lahore including Lashkar-e-Taiba, which has attacked targets in India, including the notorious Mumbai incident, as well as U.S. troops in Afghanistan.[3] On January 27 he was driving his Honda Civic in a market area in Lahore. Apparently two individuals on a motorbike rode alongside him, intending to commit armed robbery. Police reported that the assailants were armed.[4] The thirty-six-year-old former Special Forces veteran took no chances. He shot his assailants.

Police said he left the scene but was detained at a traffic circle a short distance away.[5] Police recovered a Glock from Davis along with a long-range wireless set, a small telescope, and a lamp.[6] Davis did not have a license to carry a gun.[7] Witnesses accused Davis of shooting at least one assailant in the back.[8] Although some media reports suggested that his assailants had a connection to ISI, Pasha has denied that. They were criminals bent on robbery. Tragedy compounded the crisis. A car responding to a call from Davis for support drove the wrong way down a one-way street and accidentally hit and killed an innocent pedestrian.[9] Public controversy intensified when a camera was found in his car that contained photographs of the Peshawar Frontier Corps headquarters and Pakistan army bunkers on the eastern border with India.[10] The paperwork on Davis's status was unclear. The legal case as to whether he was entitled to diplomatic immunity might have created severe legal problems for him in Pakistan's courts, while embarrassing the U.S. government. Amid intense negotiations between the U.S. and Pakistani government, the matter was resolved in accordance with Islamic law—which also carries the force of law in Pakistan—with the payment of financial compensation to the families of those killed. Whether the United States will reimburse Saudi Arabia seems unclear. The court in Lahore then dismissed the charges and Davis was released and flew home.[11]

The publicity rankled Pakistan civilian, military, and intelligence authorities.[12] What's relevant here is what the incident revealed about the deep-seated paranoia and suspicion of conspiracy that engulfs Pakistan as well as use of strategic communication in 2011 political decision-making.

The Davis incident provoked volatile emotions. Dubious Pakistanis were instantly ready to convict the robbery victim. After the shooting, authorities arrested Davis at a crowded traffic stop.[13] Controversy within the government broke out immediately. Foreign Minister Mehmood Qureshi complained that the Punjab police should have consulted with the Foreign Office to determine his legal status.[14] Still, that did not prevent Qureshi from rushing before news cameras to pronounce Davis guilty or to deny that Davis was a full diplomat and entitled to diplomatic immunity.[15] His behavior embarrassed President Zardari. Zardari's handling of Qureshi was subtle but extremely effective. Reshuffling the cabinet, he offered Qureshi a post at the Water and Power (WAPTA) ministry, knowing full well that Qureshi would never accept. Qureshi resigned and Zardari named Hina Rabbani Khar as the new foreign minister.[16]

In the meantime, encouraged quietly by the military-intelligence establishment, Pakistani media stoked public emotions. Conspiracy theories inflamed the public imagination. Investigative journalist Ansar Abbasi wrote that the case could further extremism and fuel terrorism.[17] Former ISI Director General Lt. Gen. Hamid Gul (Ret.) opined that letting Davis "go scot-free would be extremely serious beyond people's imagination."[18] Always happy to stir the pot, even Russia's Foreign Intelligence Service (SVR) jumped into the fray. It cautioned that open warfare could break out between Pakistan and the United States and fed a preposterous story to the *Times of India* alleging that Davis had provided nuclear fissile material and biological agents to Al Qaeda terrorists. In this apocalyptic scenario, the United States was accused of devising a scheme to ignite "all-out war" aimed at reasserting American hegemony.[19]

The assassination of a cabinet minister spawned new conspiracy theories that portrayed the murder as a diversionary tactic aimed at deflecting attention away from the Davis controversy. Assailants linked to Tehrik-i-Taliban-Punjab and Al Qaeda fired twenty-six bullets into Shahbaz Bhatti, the minister for minorities affairs and the sole Christian member of the government, as Bhatti stepped into his official black Toyota Corolla. The minister's offense was his advocacy of amendments to Pakistan's harsh blasphemy law. Suspicions deepened when it was disclosed that Bhatti had dispensed with his fifteen-member police protection.[20] Pakistanis recalled that weeks earlier, a member of Punjab governor Salmaan Taseer's security detail had shot him dead for his opposition to draconian provisions of the same law. The uproar had grown so loud that even blasphemy law supporters such as Jamiat Ulema-e-Islam chief Maulana Fazlur Rahman felt compelled to lower the political temperature, at least a little. In a tepid statement, Maulana Fazlur declared that misuse of the blasphemy law against minorities should be discussed.[21]

Commentator Zaid Hamid blamed the whole episode on the CIA as a plot to divert attention away from Davis. The son of former President Zia ul-Haq darkly warned against a "foreign plot."[22] For Americans, that may seem like lunacy. In Pakistan, it's politics as usual. The fracas upset Prime Minister Yousuf Gilani enough that he offered to resign, although cabinet colleagues dissuaded him.[23]

The high emotions handcuffed a weak civilian government. Davis was locked up at Lahore's military prison and provided special security to ensure his safety. Wild rumors floated that if Pakistanis didn't get him, Americans would have him poisoned. Drone attacks had riled Pakistanis in different parts of the nation. The Davis case united them in a national cause. Many believed the United States had infiltrated a small army of illegally armed intelligence agents inside their country. The chief of the religious party Jamaat-e-Islami claimed there are "thousands of Raymond Davises" swarming inside the borders.[24] Fakhr-e-Alam Khan, another religious party leader, declared, "They may be justifying their work as for an NGO or other U.S. agency, but their prime purpose . . . is to spy."[25]

The media blasted the government for "caving in to U.S. pressure" in allowing visas for Americans. One Pakistani commentator huffed: "What sort of 'strategic relationship' do we have with each other if America has let loose a horde of CIA operators in this country and is working towards its destabilization?"[26] Former Pakistani foreign secretary Riaz Khokhar opined to *The News* that the United States had nine hundred to a thousand security commandos roaming in different cities of Pakistan and that it was "the biggest threat to the national security of Pakistan."[27] That Pakistan depended heavily upon the United States for aid essential to its stability also went unremarked, perhaps a sign of how nervously the Zardari government viewed the ballooning crisis.[28]

As more information about the Davis case emerged, a new revelation gave conspiracy theorists more ammunition. It turned out that Davis had once worked for Blackwater, a security firm so controversial for its conduct in the early years of the Iraq War that it has rebranded itself as Xe Services LLC. In Pakistan, many view Blackwater with about the same fondness as Westerners think of James Bond's fictional nemesis, SMERSH.

The Jang Group newspaper, *The News*—which is hostile to both the United States and Zardari's Pakistan Peoples Party and has made anti-Semitic pronouncements—had published stories that talked about "Blackwater's secret war in Pakistan." Citing the Pakistani newspaper *The Nation*, it published an especially rambunctious tale that sounds like dime-store spy opera: "At a covert forward operating base run by the U.S. Joint Special Operations Command (JSOC) in Karachi, members of an elite division of Blackwater are at the centre of a secret program in which they plan targeted assassinations of suspect Taliban and al Qaeda operations . . . and other sensitive operations inside and outside Pakistan, an investigation by *The Nation* has found."[29] It sourced the story to an individual supposedly "with direct knowledge of Blackwater's involvement" who alleged that "the program is so 'compartmentalized' that senior figures within the Obama administration and the U.S. military chain of command may not be aware of its existence."[30]

Lurid stories that placed Blackwater under former vice president Cheney's supervision have sold newspapers and boosted television ratings.[31] It bears noting that many who have dealt with Blackwater view it more positively. Benazir respected the company's professionalism. Buffeted by death threats and lacking confidence in the government, she wanted Blackwater to provide for her security upon her return to Pakistan in 2007,[32] but President Pervez Musharraf denied permission for their entry.

As usual, conspiracy theorists gleefully offered up diabolical explanations for Musharraf's refusal. One put the hat on Cheney, alleging he had pressured Musharraf to say no to such security for Benazir, on the premise that she could not be trusted. The *Tehran Times* presented the converse theory. It quoted former Pakistan Chief of Army Staff Lt. Gen. Mirza Aslam Beg (Ret.), who blamed Blackwater for the assassination not only of Benazir but also Lebanon's former prime minister Rafik Hariri. Beg claimed that Blackwater had secretly placed operatives in Pakistan to protect the U.S. embassy and that Benazir was "killed in an international conspiracy because she had decided to back out of the deal through which she had returned to the country after nine years in exile."[33] This theory apparently originated with a story in *The Nation*[34] (not to be confused with the American periodical bearing the same name), which sourced it to American journalist Seymour Hersh. The scurrilous rumor spread like wildfire. It took a sharp protest by the U.S. ambassador and Hersh's debunking of the story to force its removal from the newspaper's website.

In this treacherous 2011 political environment, the military-intelligence establishment found opportunity to maneuver, while forcing the civilian government to navigate a treacherous path. Zardari's strategic communication in advancing his interests was skillful. He kept negotiations with the United States moving ahead swiftly, while reassuring Pakistanis that national sovereignty would be upheld. Dealing with a news media run amuck—routine behavior for some of its television stations—is never easy. Zardari focused on avoiding further strain on its relationship with a U.S. government increasingly angered by a perception that Pakistan wasn't tough enough on the Taliban. His strategic communication had to dovetail with what the military-intelligence establishment desired or at least did not object to. All things considered, his team managed the crisis as well as one could reasonably expect.

The military-intelligence establishment—which includes diverse elements with varying agendas—had no interest in staging a coup or taking over the burden of governing. What did it want? Clearly, it was upset by a belief that they did not know the details of, and could not control, U.S. activity inside Pakistan, including how many American assets were in play. In a fine display of savvy strategic communication, it leveraged the threat of prosecution of Davis by the civilian government to pressure the United States into disclosing all of its activity inside Pakistan.[35] According to one news story, ISI demanded that the CIA "unmask all its covert operatives" in Pakistan.[36] ISI's strategy was apparent. It sought to force the United States to rewrite the terms of cooperation within Pakistan. It faulted Musharraf for setting up a framework that gave Americans too much leeway to operate within Pakistan's borders. Musharraf has denied he did that, but the prevailing view discounts his denial.

ISI's strategy worked. Bahukutumbi Raman, former head of counterterrorism for India's Research & Analysis Wing (RAW)—that nation's equivalent to the CIA—described the outlines of the deal that was cut. Raman said that ISI and Pakistan's Foreign Office wanted the CIA and the Pentagon to avoid deploying personnel in Pakistan to collect intelligence except with ISI approval. The CIA, he said, agreed to that condition, but ensured that the United States would remain free to run its Technical Intelligence (TECHINT) network. The State Department apparently agreed to new conditions for providing diplomatic status to personnel.[37]

The option of paying blood money to resolve the Davis matter had been put on the table early on, as the controversy erupted. Islamic fundamentalist organizations pressured the victims' families not to accept it. But once the United States agreed to ISI terms, ISI "intervened and persuaded the legal heirs to accept the money and move for the withdrawal of the prosecution of Davis."[38] The money was paid by Saudi intelligence in the Lahore court before which Davis was being tried.[39] ISI did not act in isolation. Immediately prior to its action, the Army Corps commanders met and discussed the issue. Under Kayani, the corps commanders worked to reach consensus, a shift from the way things operated under Musharraf, who asserted tight control. As ISI is legally under army command, it is inconceivable that the deal would have gone through had Kayani and his corps commanders opposed it.

By mid-March, it had become clear that a wide range of military, intelligence, religious, judicial, and political players had exercised key roles that produced Davis's release. President Zardari was able to address a joint session of Parliament in which he restated Pakistan's desire for a "long-term relationship" with the United States and emphasized his intent to defeat violent extremism and defeat the mind-set behind the assassinations of Salmaan Taseer and Shahbaz Bhatti.[40] Even so, it was clear that tensions had merely been papered over. Within weeks, Pakistan publicly demanded a drastic reduction in the number of American agents working covertly in the country and a halt to drone attacks in the northwest.[41]

THE BIN LADEN ASSAULT

U.S.-Pakistani tensions over the Davis blowup paled compared to what followed. On May 2, 2011, relations between the two countries hit the rocks as U.S. Navy SEALs launched a successful assault that killed Osama bin Laden at a compound located at the end of a dirt road in Bilal Town, northeast of Abbottabad, a city of 100,000 that served as home to three military regiments.[42]

U.S. intelligence had identified a trusted bin Laden courier, known as Abu Ahmed al-Kuwaiti. His real name may have been Sheikh Abu Ahmed. Four years before, a senior Al Qaeda facilitator, Hassan Ghul, had provided the name. Additional information came from two Guantánamo inmates who identified the courier as a trusted bin Laden operative.[43] In July 2010 Pakistanis working for the CIA located al-Kuwaiti as he was driving his Suzuki in Peshawar, and recorded his license plate.[44] Intelligence phone intercepts helped trace the courier to the fortified compound guarded by two security gates and eighteen-foot walls topped by barbed wire.[45] The CIA established a surveillance post in Abbottabad, from which a team of agents monitored the suspicious complex. Local informants helped piece together a "pattern of life" inside.[46] They determined that it housed bin Laden.

On a moonless night in May 2011, two top-secret radar-evading stealth Blackhawk helicopters swooped toward the hideout. Their slower-moving rotor blades, extra blades in the tail rotor, and a hub that covered the rotor muffled their sounds, lessening chances of detection.[47] The craft were so secret that few even knew they existed. Mechanical problems forced down one helicopter, which executed a hard landing. Two MH-47 Chinooks carrying additional SEALs backed up the two Blackhawks. U.S. surveillance and reconnaissance aircraft monitored Pakistani police and military channels to ascertain how long the commanders had before Pakistani authorities might appear on the scene.[48] In the air over Afghanistan, U.S. jets were primed to fly to the aid of the SEALs or shoot down any Pakistani jets that intervened.[49] The latter was unlikely, as Pakistani F-16s generally do not fly at night.

Two twelve-member teams from the elite SEAL Team 6—nicknamed "the tip of the spear"—swung into action. They overwhelmed bin Laden's people in a one-sided, forty-minute firefight that killed al-Kuwaiti, another courier, a bin Laden son, and a woman, apparently the wife of a courier.[50] Reaching the third floor of the darkened building, two SEALs found and shot bin Laden in the head and chest with 5.56mm bullets fired from German-manufactured HK-416 rifles.[51]

Facial recognition and eventually DNA verified bin Laden's identity, but the White House wanted a height match. Unfortunately, no one thought to bring along a tape measure. A six-foot Navy SEAL laid himself down next to the corpse, which proved to be several inches taller. Minutes later, the coded message "Geronimo-E KIA" was flashed to the White House.[52] When CIA director Leon Panetta got the word at Langley, his conference room rang out with cheers and applause.[53] The SEAL teams choppered home without incident. The hunt for the world's most wanted terrorist was over.

WHO KNEW?

Many had surmised that Osama was hiding in plain sight. They were right. Google Earth showed that his compound lay within easy walking distance of the Pakistan Military Academy at Kakul. There, just over a week before, Kayani had proclaimed that "the terrorist's backbone had been broken and *inshallah* we will soon prevail."[54] The attack raised grave questions in Washington about how serious the Pakistani government had been in hunting down high-value Al Qaeda terrorists. Harsh feelings between the two nations escalated.[55] Trust was in short supply even before the bin Laden mission. As the White House made plans for the assault, President Obama himself decided to keep Pakistan in the dark. Leon Panetta made no bones about it all, declaring, "It was decided that any effort to work with the Pakistanis could jeopardize the targets. They might alert the targets."[56] Although Pakistan vehemently rejects the criticism, there is no question that American officials believe Pakistanis will tip off militants if provided information about upcoming raids.

Some Pakistanis have challenged the narrative that the United States acted alone in getting bin Laden with a competing account that places the assault into a broader context. Pakistan's ambassador to the United States, Husain Haqqani, declared that Pakistan had assisted the Americans in locating bin Laden.[57] *The Nation* insisted that "200 Pakistan Army men provided ground support," while "four helicopters of the Pakistan Army hovered over the fortress-like hideout" of the Al Qaeda chief.[58] *Dawn* quoted a "senior ISI official" who asserted that the operation had been carried out by a "joint American and Pakistani team."[59] In support of that view, a breaking story appearing in *Dawn* as the operation unfolded disclosed that an "Army helicopter crashes near Abbottabad," and that "security personnel cordoned off the area after the incident and launched relief work."[60] A media analysis of Twitter messages by chirpstory.com suggested a substantial commotion was happening in the middle of the night in a military garrison town, and counterterrorism expert tweets indicated that the army indeed cordoned off the crash area.[61]

In the United States, the respected online daily strategic analysis, *Nightwatch*, written by retired Defense Intelligence Agency expert John McCreary, suggested that denials of Pakistani involvement were "clearly a cover story for Pakistani public consumption to try and avert overwhelming anti-Pakistan and anti-U.S. demonstrations," and that the operation was part of a deal reached with the Pakistani Army to give up bin Laden "rather than sacrifice the Army's relationship with the U.S."[62] On the other hand, insiders with close ties to Pakistan's top leadership insisted that the United States acted alone and gave no prior notification.

Emotions ran high. Many Americans saw Pakistan's harboring of bin Laden as a betrayal of trust.[63] Chairman of the U.S. Senate Armed Services Committee, Senator Carl Levin, told *ABC News* he believed senior Pakistani officials had known bin Laden was there and also knew where Taliban leaders like Mullah Omar were hiding.[64] While the Defence Committee of the Pakistan Cabinet emphasized the need for a partnership approach rooted in mutual respect, Pakistanis complained angrily about breaches of sovereignty.[65] The Pakistan Parliament condemned the raid and warned that Pakistan might sever supply lines to U.S. forces in Afghanistan should another such operation take place.[66]

PML-N leader Nawaz Sharif, a leading contender for prime minister in the next elections, exploited the situation for maximum gain. He demanded that an independent judicial commission investigate the attack, "ascertain the full facts of Osama bin Laden's presence and the American operation in Pakistan," and make a report within twenty-one days. "Our secret agencies chase politicians but could not see what was happening right under their noses?" he asked incredulously. "They continue to play political chess. It has plunged the country into worldwide humiliation." Across the political divide, Prime Minister Yousuf Raza Gilani advised Parliament that a high-ranking army general would head up an internal inquiry "to get to the bottom of how, when and why" bin Laden had been hiding in the garrison town.[67]

The political firefights highlighted differences between the way Pakistanis and Americans viewed the crisis. Angry American political leaders found their patience exhausted by what they viewed as Pakistan's two-faced attitude toward violent extremists. Current and former U.S. officials acknowledged they had no evidence that top Pakistani military or civilian officials knew where bin Laden was or had authorized his presence in Pakistan and urged caution.[68] Yet suspicion abounded. In Congress, members talked about whether to limit or even terminate aid to Pakistan.[69] It didn't help that far from living in isolation in Abbottabad, bin Laden had received visits from Taliban leaders and wealthy Arab fundraisers.[70] For their part, Gilani and Sharif took the position that Pakistanis deserved to know the truth.

Conspiracy theories abounded. Some Pakistanis worried about the efficiency with which U.S. stealth technology had enabled the SEALs to penetrate deep inside the country undetected. It revealed, they felt, a serious vulnerability should U.S. forces decide to seize their nuclear armory. No fear in Pakistan resonates more deeply. Indeed, many believed that all along what the United States had been conniving to do was seize Pakistan's nuclear weapons. They viewed the bin Laden raid as a dry run for such larceny. One skeptic of Pakistan has suggested that the true goal of any internal inquiry would be to ascertain the security failure in not detecting the U.S. operation, not the intelligence failure to detect bin Laden's presence.[71]

One thing was certain. The raid knocked the military and intelligence services back on their heels and shook their image as an all-powerful force. Withering criticism of its competence challenged the military's traditional narrative that defense of Pakistan against India justified claims to a sizeable chunk of the budget.[72] A new counter-narrative demanded transparency and accountability. PML-N leader Nawaz Sharif, no friend of the army, called for a parliamentary review of military and intelligence budgets. His demand was unprecedented.[73] Needless to say, at GHQ no one rushed to open their books or summon auditors.

The military-intelligence establishment fired back. Its narrative emphasized nationalism and effective performance. Military and intelligence chiefs made an unprecedented appearance before an eleven-hour closed session of Parliament to defend their organizations.[74] ISI chief Lt. Gen. Ahmed Shuja Pasha claimed that ISI efforts had actually disrupted the Al Qaeda network even before bin Laden was killed, but, in a gesture of humility, offered to resign.[75] The offer was refused. At first, ISI sources declared that details of suspects or plots in protest against the United States would no longer be shared,[76] but by early June it appeared that joint intelligence and operations against the militants would be resumed.[77] The cooperation paid immediate dividends with a successful drone strike in South Waziristan during June that killed Ilyas Kashmiri, a top Pakistani Al Qaeda leader.[78] The Pentagon was allowed to question three bin Laden wives captured at the compound,[79] and in response to a request from Senator John Kerry, the debris of the helicopter that went down was returned.[80] *Stratfor* reported, however, that ISI allowed Chinese engineers to survey the wreckage and take samples of the stealth technology. Access was also granted to the CIA to examine the compound for clues that would help it to decipher references to names of individuals and places, and even to use special equipment to recover information that was burned or otherwise damaged.[81] Still, there's no doubt that relations between the United States and Pakistan had become badly frayed. Pakistan Army Chief of Staff Lt. Gen. Ashfaq Parvez Kayani issued a stern public warning to the United States—aimed also at India—that Pakistan would tolerate no encore to the bin Laden operation.[82]

Kayani found himself shaken by the discovery of bin Laden at Abbottabad and new violence set nerves on edge. In the weeks following the raid, the Taliban rocked Pakistan with violent attacks, including a brazen assault on a naval air base in Karachi that took elite commandos seventeen hours to quell.[83] Others worried that violent Islamists were penetrating the military.[84] The Islamist leanings of some military came as no surprise to knowledgeable experts. Shuja Nawaz has pointed out that "most cadets from the Pakistan Military Academy of the 1980s are now Colonels or Brigadiers. They were fed a restricted diet of Islam and a narrow view that presented their history from a purely Islamic perspective. India was the enemy. The West was poised against Pakistan and had deserted Pakistan at different junctures. Removing those scratches from the minds of these officers will take time and needs a Pakistani effort more than a U.S. effort."[85]

Army critics kept on voicing their disapproval. Arguing that Pakistan's honor had been trampled upon, Chaudhry Nisar, the PML-N opposition leader in the National Assembly, groused that "some heads must roll."[86] Columnists called for rebalancing the power in Pakistan and demanded that "civilian elites" put an end to compromises with a military that has for too long laid an unjustified claim to power.[87]

Pakistani opinions cut across the spectrum. Some expressed fury at the hypocrisy of their own leaders in protecting bin Laden while claiming to fight Al Qaeda.[88] Kamran Shafi pithily observed,

> Now that the Americans have done what they said they would do if they had the intelligence—go after those who they consider their enemies no matter where they are holed up—it is much more important to ask why our much-vaunted Deep State didn't know Osama bin Laden was living in Abbottabad Cantonment all these years. And to ask why everyone and Charlie's aunt in the security establishment went blue and red with anger when told that Osama and his close advisers were hiding in Pakistan.[89]

The well-respected Dr. Pervez Hoodbhoy spoke up pointedly: "Osama's killing is now a bone stuck in the throat of Pakistan's establishment that can neither be swallowed nor spat out. To appear joyful would infuriate the Islamists who are already fighting the state. On the other hand, to deprecate the killing would suggest that Pakistan had knowingly hosted the king of terrorists."[90]

In a departure, Pakistani media and opinion leaders became unusually critical of the army and ISI. *AAJ News TV* blasted Kayani for "accepting the operation" and accused ISI of being "incapable" of protecting nuclear assets.[91] *Karachi Dawn News in Urdu* broadcast criticism calling the army "clueless" and excoriating it for its own failure to take down bin Laden.[92] *Geo News TV* questioned the army's role. It also suggested that bin Laden's burial at sea created doubts as to whether he was actually dead,[93] although Al Qaeda itself released a statement on militant websites that confirmed his demise.[94] Hamid Gul, always ready to spin a theory that got tongues wagging, found suggestions of no involvement by the army "a bit amazing," noting that "the local police, the Intelligence Bureau, Military Intelligence, [and] the ISI" were all over the place and should—or did—see what was coming.[95]

The News quoted the government as expressing its "deep concern" and "reservations about the manner in which the government of the United States had carried out the operation without prior information or authorization of Pakistan."[96] Fresh from his trip to Afghanistan, where he lobbied Afghanistan president Hamid Karzai "against building a long-term strategic partnership with the U.S., urging him to look to Pakistan—and its Chinese ally—for help in striking a peace deal with the Taliban and rebuilding the economy,"[97] Prime Minister Yousuf Raza Gilani complained that "there was no need to shortcut or to bypass Pakistan."[98]

Gilani's statement was not just rhetoric. Three weeks after the raid, China agreed to provide fifty more JF-17 fighter jets to Pakistan on an "expedited" basis. Jointly developed by China and Pakistan, the jets and their acquisition were used by Gilani to portray China as an alternative to the United States as a resource for military and civilian aid.[99] Days later, Pakistan asked China to build a naval base at its southwestern port of Gwadar; plans call for China to maintain a regular presence there.[100]

Geographic proximity, a history of cooperation in building Pakistan's nuclear program, and shared concerns—although from somewhat different perspectives—offered provocative hints about where Pakistan might turn in the future for strategic alliances. Should relations between the United States and Pakistan continue to deteriorate—which seems probable—look for Pakistan to follow that yellow brick road. Pakistan's reaching out to China offered a striking example of how action can reflect internal policy and, at the same time, strategically communicate to a country as powerful as the United States that it has other friends to whom it might turn.

In a second signal underscoring Pakistan's strategic communication to the United States that it was growing weary of American behavior, Zardari paid a visit to Iran, where President Mahmoud Ahmadinejad called for a boost in bilateral relations. "Iran is ready to reinforce its cooperation with Pakistan in every field," the Iranian stated.[101]

However suspicious of one another, Pakistani and American officials both recognize that the relationship between their countries matters. In private, there have been sharp private exchanges between American and Pakistani officials. In public, both governments have chosen their words carefully. In his televised speech announcing bin Laden's death, President Obama took pains to "note that our counterterrorism cooperation with Pakistan helped lead us to bin Laden and the compound where he was hiding."[102] President Asif Ali Zardari published an op-ed in the *Washington Post* endorsing the U.S. action and expressing "satisfaction that the source of the greatest evil of the new millennium has been silenced, and his victims given justice."[103] He pointed out that terrorism had cost his people "two thousand police officers and as many as 30,000 innocent civilians and a generation of social progress."[104] It was a courageous step, given the temper of politics at home. Aligning himself with U.S. action drew criticism from some who complained that the intrusion into Pakistan to kill bin Laden abused its sovereignty and was thus a "blow to national pride."[105]

The strategic communication from all camps illuminated the political dynamics at play. The White House focused media attention on a narrative that extolled Obama for showing strength in his decision-making. It portrayed Obama as a tough, disciplined president who had focused on ensuring that intelligence leads were followed up and options thoroughly discussed. Even Obama skeptics acknowledged that the decision to green-light the helicopter assault was risky and took courage. Some White House advisers had given the operation only a 60 to 80 percent chance of success.[106] Memories of Mogadishu in 1993 and the failed rescue in 1980 of American hostages in Iran haunted the decision-making. One option had been to obliterate bin Laden's residence through air strikes. The White House argued that using SEALs proved how carefully he had thought through all implications. Bombing could vaporize the body, eliminating proof of death. Proof was needed to show that bin Laden had been captured or killed. That required putting boots on the ground.[107] There was also the issue of whether bin Laden should be killed or captured. A U.S. national security official erased any doubt about decision. "This was a kill operation," the officer said.[108]

Obama prudently refused to release photographs of the slain terrorist. "I think that given the graphic nature of these photos, it would create some national security risk," he told the CBS program *60 Minutes*.[109] He added: "It is important for us to make sure that the very graphic photos of somebody shot in the head are not floating around as an incitement to additional violence as a propaganda tool." Nor did he gloat. "That's not who we are," he said. "We don't trot out this stuff as trophies. We don't need to spike the football."

That was a key decision for White House strategic communication. Photos—a form of communication—would not have convinced doubters or conspiracy theorists. In the United States, those who believe the moon landing was a hoax were never convinced by the broadcast of images showing Neil Armstrong. People who believe in conspiracies are often deaf to dissuasion. An online YouGov/Polis survey of 1,039 educated respondents in Karachi, Lahore, and Islamabad taken a few days after the attack revealed that 66 percent of urban Pakistanis did not believe that bin Laden had been killed at the compound.[110] Al Qaeda itself set concerns to rest, confirming bin Laden's death. Reuters published photographs of three men in traditional Pakistani attire lying in pools of blood inside the house.[111] They are gory and confirmed Obama's wisdom.

Taliban who demanded proof were baiting the White House with their own strategic communication.[112] Their interest lay in pretending to doubt bin Laden's murder to pressure a photo release in hopes that the photos would inflame their followers and spur recruitment. It was a trap Obama avoided.

Two unfortunate notes marred White House strategic communication. The first lay in discrepancies that emerged in descriptions of events. The fact is, the White House should have simply announced bin Laden's demise, withheld comment on operational details, and launched its own jihad to identify and severely punish anyone who talked. Secretary of Defense Robert Gates and Chairman of the Joint Chiefs of Staff Mike Mullen expressed that view bluntly in the ensuing days.

The discrepancies included whether bin Laden had resisted capture or was gunned down; whether his wife had died in the gunfire; who had been killed; and the extent of the firefight.[113] The $25,000 stone shack that bin Laden lived in was mischaracterized as a million-dollar "mansion,"[114] although it seemed better suited to house feed and livestock than people. The operation aimed to kill bin Laden. They should have stated that without apology. Bin Laden was a criminal. He led a death cult. He had caused the murder of tens of thousands of innocent people. He celebrated his gory slaughter by composing poetry.

Even if you get past the imprudence of talking operational details, the White House should have tread cautiously. A fast-paced, unpredictable military operation often produces unclear details and inaccurate first reports.[115] It was a lesson in the need to get the facts straight. Contradictions inevitably raise questions as to whether the truth is being told, even if they emanate from innocent errors or incomplete information. Still, Obama's action sent a clear message. Those who attack U.S. citizens will be tracked down, however long it may take.

For Pakistan's government, the impact at the time of this writing was still uncertain. Many found it implausible that bin Laden could hide out in Abbottabad without the knowledge of certain elements of the intelligence services. Many believe that Ayman Zawahiri and Taliban leader Mullah Omar are holed up in the country. The United States is demanding an investigation into the ISI, especially its *S* Section, in an effort to discover links to Al Qaeda and the Taliban.[116] Questions were raised about what light Lt. Gen. Nadeem Taj (Ret.), who successively led Pakistan Military Intelligence, the Pakistan Military Academy, and ISI during the period that bin Laden may have resided in Pakistan, could shed on their whereabouts. Others wondered what information Brig. Ejaz Shah, the head of the Intelligence Bureau during that period, might have known. *Pajhwok Afghan News* reported on May 17 that "Pakistan's former Inter-Services Intelligence (ISI) Chief [Hamid Gul] has asked the Taliban leader, Mullah Mohammad Omar, to leave Pakistan."[117] If that story is true, one wonders what the Pakistan government is doing to press Gul for more information. As interior minister, Rehman Malik needs to explain what he knows.

The Zardari team's strategic communication in this tough situation was measured. Zardari had to balance his government's interest in satisfying Washington—on whom it depended for vital aid—that it had not protected the terrorist while reassuring Pakistanis that he was not kowtowing to the Americans. As noted, Zardari published an op-ed in the *Washington Post* supporting Obama's actions. His own wife a victim of political murder. Zardari personally supports the U.S. fight against violent extremists. In their pronouncements, Prime Minister Gilani and many other Pakistani politicians took a more nationalistic tack. Gilani advised *Time* magazine that the claim that bin Laden had been hiding in Abbottabad was "not authentic," as "terrorists don't normally stay in one place for more than 15 days. He was not confined to Pakistan alone. He was everywhere," including Yemen.[118]

In a speech written for him by the military, Gilani appeared before Parliament where he blasted Al Qaeda for terrorism and the United States for breach of Pakistani sovereignty. Angrily dismissing suggestions that Pakistan was ignoring the threat, the prime minister praised the ISI for enabling the United States to employ its technology to find bin Laden.[119] Upping the losses that Zardari had quantified, he stated that in battling terrorism, Pakistan had lost "some 30,000 men, women and children, and more 5,000 armed forces personnel" as well as billions of dollars in economic losses. The discrepancy in the number of armed forces casualties between what Zardari wrote and Gilani invoked was a matter of how you count. Zardari was talking about the military. Gilani's figure included 3,000 police and paramilitary constables. Either way, the losses appall and anger Pakistanis.

Gilani's point bears highlighting. Many Pakistanis feel harshly about the United States and its criticisms of their nation. Many Americans fault Pakistan for poor governance, military-intelligence domination of its politics, timidity in fighting violent extremism or recognizing its threat to its own citizens, being too accepting of religious intolerance, possessing a weak self-identity, and paranoia over India. The criticisms irritate many Pakistanis, who see the United States as an unreliable ally that has visited slight after slight upon

Pakistani dignity and pride. Many feel that the United States favors India over Pakistan. No idea riles Pakistanis more. The sentiment is compounded by conspiracy theorists always ready to argue that the United States and India are in cahoots to steal Pakistan's nuclear inventory and leave it defenseless. Many Pakistanis blame America for Pakistan's losses to the economy and the stiff price it has paid in blood. They view the current violence and instability as a direct result of U.S. intervention in Afghanistan in 2001. Lingering anger persists over what they see as America's desertion of its ally in 1989 once the Soviets were defeated there, leaving Pakistan with an enormous refugee problem on its hands. Pakistanis believe that they, not Americans, have paid the steepest price for American policies and actions. In their view, Americans abandoned Pakistan before and will do so again, so why trust America? They resent a perceived American failure to recognize that Pakistan has suffered. Relations between the United States and Pakistan will experience rough sledding as long as this perception persists. It seems likely to persist for a long time.

Sharply divergent responses to the attack on bin Laden underscore the differences in perspective. America had made clear that it would track down the terrorist and mete out justice, no matter how long it took. For Americans, two words well summarize his ignominious demise: mission accomplished. For Pakistan, bin Laden's death represented one more telling blow and was perceived as a clear abuse of their increasingly precarious sovereignty.

The attack has complicated our already complex relationship with Pakistan. Pakistanis have long blamed the United States for their country's instability. Though Americans enjoin Pakistan to seize responsibility for its future, many Pakistanis feel they are victims of external influences they cannot control, an attitude that shifts the blame away from them. They believe that the attack placed them in an untenable position: either they did not know bin Laden was there, rendering them ignorant or incompetent; or else they were willing conspirators. The emotionally charged response is an outgrowth of a long-standing political culture that has bred conspiracy theories and a sense of betrayal. Americans and the West may find such thinking absurd. Still, Pakistan is a nuclear power with 180 million people. It plays a key role in the region. We have to engage with it effectively. Doing so requires a clear-sighted grasp of Pakistani politics and attitudes, and their effects on our nation.

Chapter 23

LOOKING AHEAD

Pakistanis are proud and patriotic. Billions of dollars in foreign assistance will not alter their fundamental attitudes toward the United States. Indeed, in mid-May, Pakistan's most politically important province, Punjab, announced it would cancel four aid agreements worth $232 million for education, health care, and waste management in protest over the bin Laden raid.[1] The United States needs to encourage good governance and support Pakistan's ability to provide it, while working for regional solutions that stabilize Pakistan and its neighbors, including Afghanistan. The solutions to the challenges posed by violent extremists require that broader approach.

Today many Westerners lump the Taliban beneath one umbrella. Pakistanis tend to view the Taliban as comprising different tribal factions that pursue individual agendas. Jalaluddin Haqqani's network and the Quetta Shura—identified with Mullah Omar—engage actively with the Pakistani government.[2] Gulbuddin Hekmatyar's Hizb-e-Islami has proven transactional in its alliances, but as of this writing it appears to favor reconciliation with the Afghan and Pakistani governments. His true intention is never clear. The Lal Masjid (Red Mosque) faction remains bitter over the government's assault on the mosque and challenges the authority of Pakistan's government. A coalition of anti-Pakistani government groups that oppose the United States and NATO have organized as Tehrik-i-Taliban-Pakistan. The TTP is aligned with Al Qaeda,[3] which opposes the governments of Pakistan and Afghanistan as well as the United States and NATO.[4] Most Taliban groups oppose the United States and India and would expel foreigners from Afghanistan. Others oppose all three and support the defeat of Karzai's government. Still others include criminals who masquerade as jihadists.[5] The lesson is to avoid overgeneralizing. In politics, people friendly to one another are not necessarily friends. Friends, as Pakistan expert Brian Fishman pithily notes, may not be allies.[6]

Many in the West misread Pakistani attitudes toward violent extremism. Pakistanis dislike religious extremists who wish to overthrow the government in order to impose their very strict interpretation of Islam. They dislike the Taliban and there's no evidence that they could soon take over the country. Still, violence sows fear. It destabilizes. And it provides one of the most enduring challenges to Pakistani leaders when it comes to employing strategic communication.

Militant violence has alienated most Pakistanis and created important opportunities to discredit the Islamist extremists. Yet the civilian government has held back, concerned that it lacks the power to properly fight back. That has proven especially true when it comes to Pakistan's draconian blasphemy law, which Benazir wanted to repeal. This attitude was evident in the wake of Punjabi governor Salmaan Taseer's assassination in January 2011 for his defense of a Christian woman, Asia Bibi, who was on trial for violating the law.[7] Though Taseer's close friend, Zardari avoided the funeral partly for fear that his government could collapse should he so visibly align himself with the slain minister.

As usual in Pakistan, the politics beneath the surface proved more subtle and nuanced. Prime Minister Gilani did attend. Zardari's motive was rooted partly in altruism. He felt that attending Taseer's funeral could lead to Asia Bibi's extrajudicial murder. His strategy had Pakistan Peoples Party leaders go to the funeral while the next generation spoke out for the family and the PPP. An Oxford graduate now studying in London to become a barrister, Bilawal Bhutto Zardari is the chairman of the PPP. Speaking at the Pakistan High Commission in London, Benazir's son issued a commanding, eloquent statement that powerfully denounced Governor Taseer's murder and, with the same intensity that epitomized his mother's speeches, embraced religious tolerance and democratic values.

His words are worth quoting. Bilawal declared,

At a time when evil masquerades as people of faith terrorizing all those who oppose or disagree with them, Shaheed Salmaan Taseer fought back. He spoke without fear. . . . His murder is more than a political assassination. Like the assassination of Shaheed Benazir Bhutto, it is a message. It is a message to all of us who believe in the peaceful teachings of our beloved Prophet. . . . The only way to rid our country of all its ills is to ensure that democracy prevails. Thus I still stand by the slogan I raised after my mother's assassination: Democracy is and always will be the best revenge. Anyone can hold rallies in support of Islam in a Muslim-dominated country and people will turn up. Those who preach hatred in the name of Islam have never and will never have the electoral support of the people of Pakistan. . . . The assassination of Shaheed Salmaan Taseer is not about liberals versus conservatives or moderate Islam versus radical Islam. It is about right and wrong. It is about the real Islam and a fictional Islam funded from abroad and espoused by violent extremists.[8]

Obviously, to make a difference in the long term, Bilawal must return to Pakistan.

Zardari's strategy helped strengthen Bilawal's position. Zardari's concern for Asia Bibi was humanitarian. Alas, politics does not necessarily respect virtue. As strategic communication, Zardari's approach made him look weak. The blasphemy issue points up a challenge that confronts any Pakistani leader. As the Quilliam Foundation founder and codirector Maajid Nawaz observes, one must distinguish between violent Islamists who would impose their own interpretation of Islam upon Pakistan, and extremists who sanction the use of violence against anyone they consider blasphemous.[9] Zardari and his prime minister, Yousuf Gilani, can fight violent Islamists. But they possess limited power or ability to alter Pakistani attitudes on the blasphemy law.

Behind the scenes, Zardari lacks retail political appeal for many Pakistanis, but outsiders make a mistake in selling short his political savvy for inside plays. Despite very low—and sinking—poll ratings, he understands Pakistani politics and the PPP remains formidable. Still, he has failed to rally the public in fighting violent Islamists and it has weakened his government. Using their bully pulpits as president and prime minister, respectively, he and Gilani could do far more to achieve that goal. Cooperation of the military is vital in this task. Defeating violent extremism requires civilian information and political strategy as well as military action. Is this plausible? Others have stood up to resist violent Islamists. Benazir was committed to clamping down on their violence. Bilawal has picked up her standard. Kayani has also spoken out forcefully against them. The government would serve itself and Pakistan well by showing equal fortitude on this issue.

THE THREATS TO PAKISTAN'S FUTURE

The real threat to Pakistan is that absent social transformation, violent extremists may capture the mantle of nationalism and discredit their enemies as secularists who have sought to forge a peaceful coexistence with India at the expense of maintaining a strong line against a hated enemy. Some in Washington seem more concerned with keeping Pakistan's nuclear arsenal away from control by violent extremists hostile to the United States. Actually, there seems little danger that the arsenal would fall into such hands.

Good governance is arguably the best antidote to Pakistani political extremism. The 2010 floods showcased Pakistani strategic communication at its best and worst. Actions as well as words defined it. Extremist organizations such as Jamaatud Dawa, Jamaat-e-Islami, and the LeT gained credibility by funneling aid through Islamic charities.[10] Criticizing civilian government incompetence, author Amil Khan stated that "not only are extremist groups easy to find, they stand in for the state in times of crisis."[11]

The army's strategic communication bolstered its standing. Soldiers donated a day's salary to aid victims. Airwaves conveyed images of soldiers plunging into high waters to rescue people. Kayani made a personal visit to affected areas.[12] For their part, the political parties drew scathing fire for getting bogged down in partisan wrangling instead of providing flood relief. Zardari's strategic communication was a debacle. He had embarked on a trip to Europe in early August. Instead of returning to oversee relief efforts, he was seen "floating across northern France in a private helicopter to visit his family's chateau in Normandy." He made few references to the tragedy at home.[13] Belatedly, he choppered to his native province, the Sindh; handed out checks; stroked the heads of suffering children; then went back to Islamabad.[14] It was political leadership at its worst. The crisis eroded the standing of the government, the political parties, and the ruling elite of Pakistan.

In the meantime, fears among foreign donors that corrupt leaders would squander aid chilled international willingness to provide greater support. U.S. Marines moved in to help. Yet, highlighting the fear that drives Pakistan's political dynamic, some Pakistanis worried whether such efforts were covert forays to carry on war effort rather than to help citizens. The full political impact of this disastrous flood was still unfolding as of this writing. It depleted further the already shaky confidence in the PPP government. Some believe its consequences even set the stage for a new military coup, but it's doubtful the Pakistan Army wants responsibility today for running the government. The situation underscores the central role that strategic communication plays in shaping attitudes and opinions.

WHO WILL LEAD PAKISTAN?

Politics changes with the wind. Inevitably there will be a new government. Nawaz Sharif's PML-N political party is thought to hold an inside edge for the next election to gain the post of prime minister and perhaps a plurality in Parliament, but the adage that nothing is certain until the votes are counted applies to Pakistan as much as to other democracies. Nawaz faces a very specific problem in that it's not at all clear the military would accept him as prime minister. They can probably block his ascendancy. The National Assembly elections are scheduled for 2013. The PPP has fared well recently in parliamentary by-elections and PML-N faces problems with the army, Washington, and in three of the four provinces. The presidential election will be held in 2013.

As many of the president's powers have shifted back to the office of prime minister, Nawaz seems more likely to try to gain that job rather than the presidency. If he can get past his problems with the military-intelligence establishment, Nawaz could wind up as prime minister while Zardari and the PPP retain the presidency. That could set up a competitive dynamic in which an Army-supported Zardari has to work with a prime minister whom people view as closely aligned with Chief Justice Chaudhry, who has credibility and actively intrudes in politics.

Nawaz has his own agenda. Musharraf once branded Nawaz a "closet Taliban." How true that label proves remains to be seen. It bears noting that in his last outing as prime minister, Nawaz proved intolerant of dissent. Many assume Nawaz Sharif will become the new prime minister but Nawaz has a tenuous relationship with the military. He is not certain to succeed Zardari. The PML-N leader engenders plenty of opposition, inside and outside the military.

Cricket Star Imran Khan would like to lead Pakistan but lacks the political organization needed to secure the post of prime minister or president. Parliament elects the prime minister. An electoral college consisting of Parliament, the Senate, and the Provincial Assemblies elects the president. Khan is a powerful voice for the view that the Afghan conflict could cause Pakistan to implode. Musharraf also wants to lead Pakistan again. Lack of political appeal, organization, and legal problems render his candidacy implausible.

General Kayani's extension as chief of army staff was welcomed in Washington, with whose leaders he has forged a good working relationship. Reportedly, his potential successors range widely in their views.[15] It bears stressing: No matter who serves as head of state in Pakistan, the real power continues to reside in the chief of army staff. After sinking in public esteem during the latter years of Musharraf's presidency, the military has rebounded and is reasserting its dominance. Public polling shows that it enjoys the highest favorable rating of any organization in the country. While battlefield success may be achieved, as Quilliam Foundation's Maajid Nawaz has pointed out, Pakistan has yet to forge an effective strategy to counter extremist ideologies that spur militancy. Having awakened to the threat that violent extremism poses, the nation and its political leaders, one hopes, will come to terms with that necessity and deal with it. Pakistan's security and a prosperous future depend on their doing so.

Notes

FOREWORD

1. Discussion sponsored by the Brookings Institution featuring Richard C. Holbrooke, "The Obama Administration's Challenges in Afghanistan and Pakistan," Washington, DC, January 7, 2010.
2. Deepak Chopra and Salman Ahmad, "How to Win Pakistan's Culture War," *Huffington Post*, March 2, 2009.

INTRODUCTION

1. Benazir Bhutto's close friend and counselor Mark Siegel helpfully recommended that using her first name would be the appropriate way to refer to her.
2. "Art of Design, Student Text, Version 2.0," School of Advanced Military Studies, http://www.cgsc.edu/events/sams/ArtofDesign_v2.pdf, 96.
3. Id., 10.
4. Col. Stefan Banach, "Why Design?," *Combined Arms Center Blog*, March 6, 2009, http://usacac.army.mil/blog/blogs/sams/archive/2009/03/06/why-design.aspx.

CHAPTER 1. THE CURIOUS CASE OF A. Q. KHAN

1. See Gordon Corera, *Shopping for Bombs: Nuclear Proliferation, Global Insecurity, and the Rise and Fall of the A. Q. Khan Network* (Oxford: Oxford University Press, 2006); Douglas Frantz and Catherine Collins, *The Nuclear Jihadist: The True Story of the Man Who Sold the World's Most Dangerous Secrets—and How We Could Have Stopped Him* (New York: Twelve, 2007); Adrian Levy and Catherine Scott-Clark, *Deception: Pakistan, the United States and the Global Nuclear Weapons Conspiracy* (London: Atlantic Books, 2007); Owen Bennett Jones, *Pakistan: Eye of the Storm* (New Haven: Yale University Press, 2002; 3rd ed., 2009); Steve Weissman and Herbert Krosney, *The Islamic Bomb: The Nuclear Threat to Israel and the Middle East* (New York: Times Books, 1981); William Langewiesche, "The Wrath of Khan," *Atlantic Monthly*, November 2005; William Langewiesche, "The Point of No Return," *Atlantic Monthly*, January/February, 2006, http://www.theatlantic.com/doc/200601/aq-khan; and International Institute

for Strategic Studies, "Nuclear Black Markets: Pakistan, A. Q. Khan, and the Rise of Proliferation Networks: A Net Assessment," June 2008, http://www.iiss.org/publications/strategic-dossiers/nbm/; Michael Laufer, "A. Q. Khan Nuclear Chronology," *Carnegie Endowment for International Peace Proliferation Brief* 8, no. 8, http://carnegieendowment.org/publications/index.cfm?fa=view&id=17420; Thomas C. Reed and Danny B. Stillman, *The Nuclear Express: A Political History of the Bomb and its Proliferation* (Minneapolis: Zenith Press, 2009).

2. Ayesha Jalal, *The Sole Spokesman: Jinnah, the Muslim League, and the Demand for Pakistan* (Cambridge: Cambridge University Press, 1985).
3. "Who Has the Bomb?," *Time*, June 3, 2005.
4. The statement is in Hamid Jalal and Khalid Hasan, eds., *Awakening the People: Speeches of Zulfikar Ali Bhutto, 1966–1969* (Rawalpindi: Pakistan Publications, 1970). It has been quoted widely. See also: Ashok Kapur, *Pakistan's Nuclear Development* (London: Routledge Kegan & Paul, 1987), 107; Weissman and Krosney, *The Islamic Bomb*, 44–45; and in "Project 706: The Muslim Bomb," *Panorama*," BBC TV, June 16, 1980. Weissman and "Project 706" are in turn cited by Corera, *Shopping for Bombs*, 10.
5. See Kapur, *Pakistan's Nuclear Development*, 99–113.
6. Corera, *Shopping for Bombs*, 20. He offers a clear description of what is required to create a nuclear weapon.
7. Frantz and Collins, *The Nuclear Jihadist*, 110.
8. A U.S. government report dated May 20, 1983, confirmed that Pakistan was developing a nuclear capability. Id., 126, 133; and Corera, *Shopping for Bombs*, 41. The agency understood that Pakistan was on track to develop a weapon but considered that it would take several years before it would be operational. The CIA's penetration of Pakistan's program was so complete that by 1984, it showed a scale model of the Pakistani bomb to Foreign Minister Sahabzada Yaqub Khan (see Frantz and Collins, *The Nuclear Jihadist*, 133). The United States repeatedly pressed Zia to honor his promise. He said he would do so with a straight face right until the day that a hot test was conducted.
9. Ambassador Peter Galbraith explains the background: "Pressler offered his version in 1984 as a substitute for my Cranston-Glenn Amendment to the 1984 Foreign Aid bill. Pressler's language was identical to Cranson-Glenn but with two fewer things to be certified. The Foreign Aid bill failed that year, and I got Senator [Charles "Mac"] Mathias to offer the same amendment in 1985 to the Foreign Aid bill that became law." Peter Galbraith, in interview with author.
10. Corera, *Shopping for Bombs*, 48.
11. Levy and Scott-Clark, *Deception*, 124–25.
12. William E. Burrows and Robert Windrem, *Critical Mass: The Dangerous Race for Superweapons in a Fragmenting World* (New York: Simon & Schuster, 1994), 65.
13. International Institute for Strategic Studies, "Nuclear Black Markets,"" 80. A detailed description of the key individuals who ran the network appears in Frantz and Collins, *The Nuclear Jihadist*, chapter 22.
14. Id., 119.
15. International Institute for Strategic Studies, "Nuclear Black Markets," 80; and Frantz and Collins, *The Nuclear Jihadist*, chapter 22

16. R. Jeffrey Smith and Joby Warrick, "Pakistani Scientist Khan Describes Iranian Efforts to Buy Nuclear Bombs," *Washington Post*, March 14, 2010. The story discusses various dealings Khan and his network, as well as Pakistani officials, pursued with Iran.

17. Id.

18. Arnaud de Borchgrave, "Pakistani-Saudi Trade Nuke Tech for Oil," *UPI*, October 20 2003; Uri Dan, "Saudis Trying to Buy Nukes," *New York Post*, October 22, 2003; David R. Sands, "Israeli General Says Saudis Seek to Buy Pakistani Nukes," *Washington Times*, October 23, 2003; and Ze'ev Schiff, "Iran: Pakistan Helping Saudis Develop Nukes," *Haaretz*, December 8, 2004.

19. A. J. Venter, *Allah's Bomb: The Islamic Quest for Nuclear Weapons* (Guilford, CT: Lyons Press, 2007), 150.

20. Michael Scheuer, *Marching Toward Hell: American Islam after Iraq* (New York: Free Press, 2008), 130: "Sunni Pakistan has the bomb and only a fool would be confident that the Saudis do not have nuclear warheads nestled on the top of their China-provided CSS-2 ICBMS."

21. Corera, *Shopping for Bombs*, 86–102, which deals extensively with this engagement; Pervez Musharraf, *In the Line of Fire: A Memoir* (New York: Free Press, 2006); and International Institute for Strategic Studies, "Nuclear Black Markets," 72; David E. Sanger and Steven R. Weisman, "Pakistan Leader Confirms Nuclear Exports," *New York Times*, September 13, 2005; Dr. Rajesh Kumar Mishra, "Pakistan as a Proliferator State: Blame It on Dr. A. Q. Khan," South Asia Analysis Group, Paper no. 567, December 20, 2002; and Bruno Tertrais, "Pakistan's Nuclear Exports: Was There a State Strategy?," *Nonproliferation Policy Education Center*, October 20, 2006, http://www.npolicy.org /article_file/20061023-Tertrais-Pakistan_310111_0722.pdf.

22. See International Institute for Strategic Studies, "Nuclear Black Markets," 76–80.

23. Catherine Collins and Douglas Frantz, *Fallout: The True Story of the CIA's Secret War on Nuclear Trafficking* (New York: Free Press, 2011), 99.

24. Corera, *Shopping for Bombs*, 95–96.

25. Levy and Scott-Clark, *Deception*, 268.

26. It's unclear precisely when the United States concluded that Pakistan had a working weapon, although experts such as Bob Galluci had developed a clear picture of the progress being made. Pakistan conducted its earliest cold test in 1983. It's possible that the Chinese may have conducted one earlier and turned over the test data. Frantz and Collins report that in the early 1980s, British intelligence discovered that Khan had Chinese plans for a warhead. The CIA dispatched Gen. Vernon Walters to warn Zia ul-Haq not to build a bomb. Again, keeping a straight face, Zia made the commitment. He lied. See: Frantz and Collins, *The Nuclear Jihadist*, 113. A 1983 CIA report confirmed that Pakistan was on course to develop a weapon (id., 126). In 1987, Khan himself gave an interview to Indian journalist Kuldip Nayar in which he boasted that Pakistan had the bomb (id., 148). On March 1, 1987, *The Observer* (London) published the story. See also Kuldip Nayar, "A Day with A. Q. Khan," *Indian Express.com*, February 16, 2004, http://www.indianexpress.com/oldStory/41165/. Nayar recalls Khan blurting out that Pakistan had the bomb and saying, "America knows it. What the CIA has been saying about our possessing the bomb is correct."

27. Levy and Scott-Clark, *Deception*, 270.
28. Id., 273–74.
29. Langewiesche, "The Point of No Return"; and Tertrais, "Pakistan's Nuclear Exports," 14, citing David Sanger, "The Khan Network," Conference on South Asia and the Nuclear Future, Stanford University, June 4–5, 2004.
30. "1999 Kargil Conflict," *GlobalSecurity.org*, http://www.globalsecurity.org/military/world/war/kargil-99.htm.
31. Dr. Subhash Kapila, "Pakistan's Lessons from Its Kargil War (1999): An Analysis," South Asia Analysis Group, Paper no. 1231, January 25, 2005.
32. Levy and Scott-Clark, *Deception*, 291.
33. Corera, *Shopping for Bombs*, 212. In fairness, however, the evidence does not support the conclusion that Khan was driven by greed. He had access to a large budget, which he used to take good care of his team, and lavished charities with donations of money that bolstered his standing. Doubtless his expense account was unlimited. He lives in a nice section of Islamabad, but his residence is a one-story bungalow that one might find in a middle-class American suburb. Khan appears to have been strongly motivated by nationalism and, as he grew older, a sense of Islamic identity.
34. George W. Bush in a joint press conference with President Jacques Chirac. "You Are Either With Us or Against Us," CNN, November 6, 2001.
35. Corera, *Shopping for Bombs*, 213.
36. Paul Eckert, "U.S. Senate Approves Bill to Triple Aid to Pakistan," Reuters, June 24, 2009. In theory, the aid is for schools, the judicial system, parliament, law enforcement agencies, and the military.
37. See Tertrais, "Pakistan's Nuclear Exports," 15–17. Tertrais excellently summarizes the extensive participation, knowledge, or complicity of key military and political figures in the nation's nuclear program.
38. See "Inter-Services Intelligence," *New York Times*, March 26, 2009. See also Mark Mazetti and Eric Schmitt, "Afghan Strikes by Taliban Get Pakistan Help, U.S. Aides Say," *New York Times*, March 26, 2009. Ahmed Rashid also describes these relationships in *Descent into Chaos: The U.S. and the Failure of Nation Building in Pakistan, Afghanistan, and Central Asia* (New York: Viking, 2008).
39. Amir Mir, "foreword," in *A to Z of Jehadi Organizations in Pakistan*, ed. Muhammad Amir Rana, trans. Saba Ansari (Lahore: Mashal Books, 2006), 11.

CHAPTER 2. REMOVING KHAN FROM PLAY

1. Langewiesche, "The Point of No Return"; and Corera, *Shopping for Bombs*, 207.
2. Id. Still, Khan's contacts with the DPRK apparently continued for at least another year.
3. Douglas Frantz and Catherine Collins argue that the CIA found out about Khan while he was still in Holland, followed his activity in Pakistan, and through the Tinner family, penetrated his inner circle and had detailed knowledge of his activities early on. See *The Nuclear Jihadist*, 246–50. Others argue that in 2000, the picture was only just then becoming clear. There is a consensus that by 2002 a definitive picture of Khan's operation had emerged. See Corera, *Shopping for Bombs*, 157, 168.

4. Levy and Scott-Clark, *Deception*, 334. Some have questioned whether this story might have been a ploy orchestrated by the United States. There is no publicly available evidence, however, to support that conclusion. Urs Tinners, who supplied the CIA with information about Khan's network and operation, was recruited much later.
5. Collins and Frantz, *Fallout*, 105.
6. Id. See also David E. Sanger, "Pakistan, North Korea Set Up Nuclear Swap," *New York Times,* November 22, 2002. The United States sanctioned Khan Research Laboratories but not the Pakistan government for this activity.
7. For example, U.S. intelligence had tracked a C-130 cargo plane that Washington had provided Pakistan to fight Al Qaeda, as it flew to North Korea, where it picked up missile parts, and returned. See "Pakistan–North Korean Weapons Trade Continued through 2002," *Pakistan Defence Forum,* August 14, 2005, http://www.defence.pk/forums/wmd-missiles/10699-pakistan-north-korea-weapons-trade-continued-through-2002-a.html.
8. Seymour M. Hersh, "Annals of National Security: 'The Cold Test,'" *New Yorker,* January 27, 2003, 42. Hersh is a controversial journalist, but Douglas Frantz, Catherine Collins, Adrian Levy, and Catherine Scott-Clark all concluded from their own investigations that the United States was well aware of Pakistan's nuclear arms program but elected to look the other way, because it wanted the Pakistanis' help in fighting the Soviets in Afghanistan in the 1980s and then Al Qaeda after 9/11. Gordon Corera is more sympathetic to the difficulty that U.S. intelligence encountered in reaching definitive conclusions about what Khan was doing, but he concurs in *Shopping for Bombs,* 46–47, that "the U.S. had multiple sources of intelligence—derived from human spies and technical devices—which gave it an incredibly detailed picture." CIA director George Tenet was to brag about the penetration of Khan's network.
9. "Pakistan–North Korean Weapons Trade."
10. Urs Tinner, a key Khan employee, had passed on regular reports to the U.S. government about what Khan was doing. See Frantz and Collins, *The Nuclear Jihadist,* chapter 12. British intelligence had also been tracking the Libyan transaction. By 2003, as the United States invaded Iraq, Muammar Qaddafi had decided to normalize relations with the West. His foreign minister at the time, Musa Kusa, opened what proved to be painstaking negotiations with Libya. In December 2003, Libya accepted International Atomic Energy Agency (IAEA) inspectors and answered questions. In January 2004, Libya handed over plans for a Chinese-designed implosion bomb that replicated Pakistan's bomb. They contained handwritten notes in English that criticized PAEC chief Munir Ahmed Khan.
11. Musharraf has claimed that the meeting with Tenet was the most embarrassing moment of his life. Whether it was because of what Pakistan had done or because the CIA had discovered his deception is less clear.
12. Levy and Scott-Clark, *Deception,* 354–55; and Frantz and Collins, *The Nuclear Jihadist,* 308–9.
13. Mir, "foreword," in Rana, *A to Z of Jehadi Organizations,* 14.
14. Levy and Scott-Clark, *Deception,* 379.

15. Id., 380. In the foreword to Rana, *A to Z of Jehadi Organizations*, Amir Mir reports that while attributed to Al Qaeda, the attacks also involved members of Musharraf's inner circle, that the attacks in the heavily secure military zone in which Musharraf was traveling would have been impossible without help from those with regular access to top-secret information about the presidents' movements, and that the two suicide bombers "had links with the intelligence agencies."

16. Launching the attempts on Musharraf in the army's cantonment was similar to planning a suicide attack against a U.S. president at Ft. Bragg. They illuminated the explosive, deeply treacherous political environment in which Musharraf had to operate. Although an in-depth analysis lies beyond the scope of this book, the challenges Musharraf faced are also illustrated by Benazir Bhutto's assassination in December 2007. The quick spin after Benazir's death—put out by Pakistani intelligence and endorsed by the United States—fingered Al Qaeda, which gleefully took credit for the deed, and militant tribal leader Baitullah Mehsud, whom media reports suggest may have been killed during the week of August 7, 2009. See Joshua Partlow, Joby Warrick, and Haq Nawaz Khan, "Pakistan Taliban Leader Mehsud Dead, Officials and Aide Say," *Washington Post*, August 7, 2009. A closer examination of the facts strongly suggests that while the triggerman and bomber(s) may well have been linked to Al Qaeda, those people who initiated her murder and guided the operation—for that is the real issue—were elements of Pakistani intelligence. Musharraf was probably not directly involved, although he may possibly have played the role of Pontius Pilate.

17. Levy and Scott-Clark, *Deception*, 379–80.

18. Frantz and Collins, *The Nuclear Jihadist*, 342–43. One friend of Khan's maintains that what he had given his daughter included a hundred-page document that detailed his proliferation activities and the military's involvement in his program.

19. Simon Henderson, "Investigation: Nuclear Scandal—Dr. Abdul Qadeer Khan," *Sunday Times* (London), September 20, 2009.

20. Levy and Scott-Clark, *Deception*, 381.

21. Id., 386.

22. Id., 341–42. Some have wondered whether the ISI might have provided the U.S. government with a full debriefing about what Khan knew, thus making the need to interview Khan unnecessary. As Ahmad Rashid details in *Descent into Chaos*, a full disclosure to the United States about its program was not going to happen. There is no reason to believe ISI made Khan shut down his network, as clear evidence shows that Pakistan continued to proliferate. See also B. Raman, "Nuclear Wal-Mart: US as Guilty of Cover-up as Pakistan," *South Asia Study Group*, Paper no. 2759, July 5, 2009, and accompanying annexes.

23. Id., 388.

24. Levy and Scott-Clark, *Deception*, 384–85.

25. Id., 387.

26. Id., 397.

27. Christiane Amanpour, "Musharraf Interview," CNN, January 23, 2004, http://www.cnn.com/2004/WORLD/asiapcf/01/23/musharraf.transcript.cnna/index.html.

28. Levy and Scott-Clark, *Deception*, 389.

29. John Lancaster and Kamran Khan, "Musharraf Named in Nuclear Probe," *Washington Post*, February 3, 2004.

30. Id.

31. Levy and Scott-Clark, *Deception*, 390.

32. Abdul Khadeer Khan, "Speech of Dr Abdul Qadeer Khan on Pakistan Television," Millat, February 4, 2004, http://millat.com/qadeer%20images/speech .htm.

33. See "President Announces New Measures to Counter the Threat of WMD," National Defense University, Fort Lesley J. McNair, Washington, DC, February 16, 2004, http://www.nti.org/e_research/official_docs/pres/whitehouse20040211_ wmd.pdf.

34. Levy and Scott-Clark, *Deception*, 392. See also "AQ Khan Seen as National Hero in Pakistan, Says Powell," *Pakistan Times*, February 27, 2004.

35. Levy and Scott-Clark, *Deception*, 393.

36. "U.S. Supports A.Q. Khan Pardon," Rediff India Abroad, February 6, 2004, http://www.indiaabroad.com/news/2004/feb/06khan.htm, quoting U.S. State Department spokesperson Rich Boucher.

37. Levy and Scott-Clark, *Deception*, 392–93.

38. Id., 393.

39. In December 2008, Urs was released from prison after more than four years of investigative detention. "Swiss Release Man Held in Smuggling Case," *New York Times*, December 28, 2008.

40. Hansjurg Mark Wiedmer (spokesperson for the Swiss attorney general), along with David Albright and Zia Mian, was interviewed by *Democracy Now!* See "Why Is the U.S. Hampering a Swiss Investigation into A.Q. Khan's International Nuclear Arms Smuggling Ring?," June 2, 2006, http://www.democracynow .org/2006/6/2/why_is_the_u_s_hampering.

41. David Albright is the president and founder of the Institute for Science and International Security and a former U.S. weapons inspector in Iraq.

42. "Why Is the U.S. Hampering?" Some have asked why the U.S. government failed to interdict Khan's efforts before he dealt with Iran, Libya, and others. There are different theories about that failure. Some, like Douglas Frantz and Catherine Collins, are aghast at what they believe was a conscious decision not to act. Others, like Gordon Corera, believe that only in 2002 did the picture of what Khan was doing become really clear.

43. Collins and Frantz in *Fallout* were highly critical of the agency's actions and question whether its efforts to retard Iran's nuclear program worked.

44. Id.

45. Kate Pickert, "2-Minute Bio: A.Q. Khan," *Time*, February 9, 2009.

46. John Wilson, "A.Q. Khan Network: Alive & Still Working," Institute of Peace and Conflict Studies, January 25, 2006, http://www.ipcs.org/article/nuclear /aq-khan-network-alive-still-working-1934.htm. British MI5 compiled a list of 360 companies in different countries involved in the covert nuclear trade. Pakistan's High Commission in London is high on the list.

47. "Pakistani Revelations Just the 'Tip of the Iceberg': IAEA," *Pakistan Times*, February 6, 2004.

48. Babar Dogar, "Pakistan Court Maintains Curbs on AQ Khan," *Washington Post*, March 29, 2010.

CHAPTER 3. CONSPIRACY LAND

1. "Book Claims Mossad Could Target AQ Khan," *domain-b.com*, February 9, 2009, http://www.domain-b.com/defence/general/20090209_aq_khan.html.
2. "Taliban May Kidnap AQ Khan for Hefty Ransom: Pak Editorial," *thaiindiannews.com*, September 4, 2009; and "Editorial: Dr AQ Khan, National Politics, and the National Interest," *Daily Times*, September 3, 2009, http://www.dailytimes.com.pk/default.asp?page=2008%5C07%5C06%5Cstory_6-7-2008_pg3_1.
3. "LHC Lifts Restrictions on Dr. Qadeer," *The News*, August 29, 2009.
4. "AQ Khan Again under Restrictions," *Daily Times*, September 3, 2009.
5. Rauf Klasra, "Dr. Khan's Daughter Challenges Kidwai's Claim," *The News*, February 8, 2008.
6. "Mystery Remains Behind A. Q. Khan's Security Restrictions Removal," *New Kerala.com*, August 30, 2009.
7. Salman Masood and David E. Sanger, "Pakistan Frees Nuclear Dealer in Snub to U.S.," *New York Times*, February 6, 2009, quoting Talat Masood, a retired Pakistani lieutenant general. "This has taken pressure away from the government," Mr. Masood said. According to Masood and Sanger, *Daily Times* columnist Rafia Zakaria concurred that it was "essential if Pakistanis are to believe that the war on terror is not just being fought at America's behest and is something in their own interest."
8. Langewiesche, "Point of No Return."
9. See Masood and Sanger, "Pakistan Frees Nuclear Dealer.""
10. For the text of these, see Peter Bergen, *The Osama Bin Laden I Know: An Oral History of al Qaeda's Leader* (New York: Free Press, 2006), 165, 195.
11. R. Jeffrey Smith, "Pakistan's Nuclear-Bomb Maker Says North Korea Paid Bribes for Know-How," *Washington Post*, July 6, 2011.
12. Kaushik Kapisthalam, "U.S. Tied over Nuclear Kingpin," *Asia Times*, December 10, 2004.
13. See David Rohde and Amy Walman, "Pakistani Leader Suspected Moves by Atomic Expert," *New York Times*, February 10, 2004. "If they knew it earlier, they should have told us," General Musharraf said. "Maybe a lot of things would not have happened." Musharraf acknowledged that investigating a "national hero" could have provoked a political backlash. "It was extremely sensitive," he said. "One couldn't outright start investigating as if he's any common criminal." Washington officials admitted that Musharraf was provided highly specific information about Khan only in late 2003. Keeping a straight face, Musharraf insisted by removing Khan that "we nipped the proliferation in the bud, we stopped the proliferation. . . . That is the important part." Exactly what he meant by "nipping it in the bud" after Khan had already spent sixteen years of trafficking with at least North Korea, China, Libya, Syria, Iraq, and Iran was not explained. As usual, Musharraf stuck to his strategy of separating Khan from official government complicity or engagement.

14. Corera, *Shopping for Bombs*, 198.

15. David Sanger, "In North Korea and Pakistan, Deep Roots of Nuclear Barter," *New York Times*, November 24, 2002.

16. David E. Sanger, "U.S. Rebukes Pakistanis for Lab's Aid to Pyongyang," *New York Times*, August 1, 2003. Most sanctions against Pakistan were lifted after 9/11 in exchange for Pakistan's commitment to fight Al Qaeda. Condoleezza Rice and others went out of their way to praise Musharraf's efforts in fighting Al Qaeda, in reaching out to India and Israel, and in discouraging militancy by working to improve education and the economy. See Sanger and Weisman, "Pakistan Leader Confirms Nuclear Exports."

17. Carla Anne Robbins, "Mr. Bush Gets Another Look into Mr. Putin's Eyes," *New York Times*, June 30, 2007. By contrast, Senator John McCain stated: "I looked into Mr. Putin's eyes and I saw three things—a K and a G and a B." (The footage of McCain making this statement is posted on YouTube, at http://www.youtube.com/watch?v=lAVlaIJWP-Q.)

18. Christopher Baruchli, "Bush, Musharraf Are Disturbingly Similar," *Boulder Daily Camera*, September 7, 2002. The administration stood by silently as Musharraf persecuted Pakistan's judges and bloodily opposed legal protests to a self-interested suspension of the chief justice. Only in 2007 did Bush exhort Musharraf to hold elections and relinquish his army post. See Matthew Lee, "Bush Exhorts Musharraf to 'Restore Democracy,'" Associated Press, November 5, 2007.

19. See Douglas Waller, "Bush and Musharraf: Friends Again," *Time*, September 22, 2006.

20. Saeed Shah, "Bush Backs Musharraf as Pakistani Leader's Support Wanes," *McClatchy*, May 30, 2008.

21. Id.

22. Corera, *Shopping for Bombs*, 198.

23. Levy and Scott-Clark, *Deception*, 443.

24. Ian Traynor and Ian Cobain, "Intelligence Report Claims Nuclear Market Thriving," *Guardian*, January 4, 2006.

25. Traynor and Cobain, "Intelligence Report Claims Nuclear Market Thriving."

26. Levy and Scott-Clark, *Deception*, 443.

27. See Tariq Ali, *The Duel: Pakistan on the Flight Path of American Power* (New York: Scribner, 2008); and Rashid, *Descent into Chaos*, 90–92. A distinguished journalist, Rashid eviscerates Pakistan for double-dealing the United States. Musharraf and the ISI did cooperate in rounding up Arabs who were helping Al Qaeda, but they did the opposite regarding both the Afghan and Pakistan Taliban. They went so far as persuading the United States to allow it to airlift key Taliban and ISI operatives out of Afghanistan at critical points. Rashid is no less critical of U.S. leaders whose instructions aroused the anger and horror of U.S. soldiers on the ground who were forced to stand by and watch as the evacuation took place.

28. See "Military Confirms Mullah Baradar's Arrest," *Dawn.com*, February 17, 2010; and "Taliban Leader's Arrest a New Blow to Insurgents," *The News*, February 17, 2010. The Taliban in Afghanistan have been directed by a fifteen person council.

In a joint U.S.-Pakistan operation, Mullah Abdul Ghani Baradar, second in command behind Taliban founder Mullah Mohammad Omar, was arrested. In February 2010, seven of the fifteen members of the Afghan Taliban's senior leadership council were also arrested. See Anand Gopal, "Half of Afghanistan Taliban Leadership Arrested in Pakistan," *Christian Science Monitor*, February 24, 2010. Recognizing the threat that the Taliban posed to his nation, Pakistan COAS Ashfaq Kayani also told the then–U.S. CENTCOM commander Gen. David Petraeus that Pakistan would pursue the extremists in every part of Afghanistan. Not everyone believed him.

29. Raman, "Nuclear Wal-Mart.'"

30. See Gordon G. Chang, *Nuclear Showdown: North Korea Takes on the World* (New York: Random House, 2006), 126–28. Chang argues that Pakistan has also served as a strategic proxy for China's proliferation activities as China channeled aid to North Korea through Pakistan. Ostensibly, China ceased dealing with Pakistan in the late 1990s, but Chang challenges that perception. See also: Selig S. Harrison, *Korean Endgame: A Strategy for Reunification and U.S. Disengagement* (Princeton, NJ: Princeton University Press, 2002), on U.S.-DPRK relationships; and Don Oberdorfer, *The Two Koreas: A Contemporary History* (New York: Basic Books, 2001).

31. Levy and Scott-Clark, *Deception*, 444.

32. Collins and Frantz, *Fallout*, 24.

33. See: Frantz and Collins, *The Nuclear Jihadist*, 246–48, describing what transpired; "Spy Thriller with Swiss Role," *NZZ OnLine*, December 15, 2007 (Google translation); and William J. Broad and David E. Sanger, "In Nuclear Net's Undoing, a Web of Shadowy Deals," *New York Times*, August 25, 2008.

CHAPTER 4. THE MYSTERIOUS ENCOUNTER

1. Shakeel Anjum, "One Year on, Benazir's Murder Is Still a Mystery, but Not So Much," *The News,* December 27, 2008; and Hamid Mir, "Musharraf Let off the Hook in Benazir's Murder Probe," *Canada Free Press*, December 27, 2009.

2. "Report of the United Nations Commission of Inquiry into the facts and circumstances of the assassination of former Pakistani Prime Minister Mohtarma Benazir Bhutto" (April 15, 2010), 14, http://www.un.org/News/dh/infocus /Pakistan/UN_Bhutto_Report_15April2010.pdf. This book had separately examined this issue prior to release of the U.N. report and concluded that Taj had come to warn her that danger awaited her in the park. The author requested an interview with a senior person involved in the United Nations' investigation as to its findings. The request was refused.

3. Shakeel Anjum, "One Year on, Benazir's Murder."

4. Levy and Scott-Clark, *Deception*, 193–94.

5. See Benazir Bhutto, *Daughter of Destiny: An Autobiography* (New York: Simon & Schuster, 1989), chapter 1.

6. Tony Clifton, in phone interviews with the author. A distinguished reporter, during several interviews, he was extremely generous in providing the author with many vital insights based on his own experience and knowledge.

7. "Benazir Bhutto Arrives in Pakistan," *Independent*, October 18, 2007.

8. Naveed Mughal, "The Making of a Martyr," *PPP.org.pk*, February 7, 2008, http://www.ppp.org.pk/party/issues/p_articles150.html.
9. "Benazir Bhutto Arrives in Pakistan."
10. "Lawyers Observe Black Day in Memory of Karachi Martyrs; ANP Asks Chief Justice to Probe May 12 Massacre," *Pakistan Times*, May 13, 2009.
11. Benazir Bhutto, *Reconciliation: Islam, Democracy, and the West* (New York: Harper, 2008), 6–7.
12. Id.
13. Id. In December 2007, the PPP assembled a 147-page document titled "Another Stain on the Face of Democracy," detailing allegations of vote rigging by the PPP Election Monitoring Cell. It is damning. In any event, Bhutto's assassination changed the equation. When elections were held on February 18, 2008, Musharraf's Pakistan Muslim League–Qaid (PML-Q) Party was crushed, garnering only 23 percent of the vote, against 30.6 percent for Benazir Bhutto's PPP and 19.6 percent for Nawaz Sharif's PML-N.
14. See also A. K. Verma, "Benazir's Death Won't Have Long-term Impact," *Rediff India Abroad*, December 28, 2007. Verma is a former secretary of India's Research and Analysis Wing (RAW), which handles that country's external intelligence.
15. National Reconciliation Ordinance (NRO-2007), October 5, 2007, http://www.pakistani.org/pakistan/legislation/2007/NationalReconciliation Ordinance.html. The concern was well justified. In December 2009, the Pakistani Supreme Court nullified the law. See Griff Witte, "Pakistan's Top Court Nullifies Amnesty for Zardari, Other Officials," *Washington Post*, December 17, 2009; and Nahal Toosi, "Pakistani Ruling Party Grapples with Amnesty's End," Associated Press/*Washington Post*, December 19, 2005.
16. Hamid Mir, "How Benazir Played into Musharraf's Hands," *Canada Free Press*, October 7, 2007.
17. Id. Mir quotes PPP legal expert Chaudhry Aitzaz Ahsan, who questioned the constitutionality of the National Reconciliation Ordinance.
18. "Government Retreats on NRO Spat," *Dawn*, November 3, 2009; and Mayed Ali, "NRO Irrelevant for President for the Time Being," *The News*, October 26, 2009. The Supreme Court is requiring Parliament to approve the NRO. Under political pressure, Zardari's government was forced to table the bill doing so, potentially exposing Zardari again to criminal prosecution once he leaves office.
19. "The NRO Is Dead," *The News*, November 13, 2009.
20. Mark Siegel, in interview with author.

CHAPTER 5. A LIFE ROOTED IN BLOOD AND TURMOIL

1. Benazir Bhutto, *Daughter of the East: An Autobiography* (London: Simon & Schuster, 2008), xi. Her earlier edition was published in the United States as *Daughter of Destiny*.
2. Mary Anne Weaver, "Bhutto's Fateful Moment," *New Yorker*, October 4, 1993.
3. Zulfiqar Ali Bhutto, *My Dearest Daughter: A Letter from the Death Cell*, 81–82, (http://www.bhutto.org, reproduced in PDF format by Sani H. Panhwar, Sindh Council, PPP), on Scribd.com, http://www.scribd.com/doc/4908163/My-Dearest-Daughter-A-letter-from-the-death-cell.

4. Benazir Bhutto, interview in London with Academy of Achievement, October 27, 2000, http://www.achievement.org/autodoc/printmember/bhu0int-1.
5. A cliché holds that history is larger than any individual. Still, the fate of key political figures can radically affect a nation. In the United States, the assassinations of three leading figures—John F. Kennedy, Robert Kennedy, and Dr. Martin Luther King, Jr—clearly altered America's political environment. Had Nelson Rockefeller contested the Republican nomination in 1960, he probably would have secured it and become president. Given his philosophy, Republicans, not Democrats, would have led the civil rights revolution in the White House and in Congress, perhaps reshaping the structure and dynamics of U.S. political parties in the second half of the twentieth century. World War I was touched off by an assassination. Abraham Lincoln's death radically redirected Reconstruction and the post–Civil War political environment. Bhutto was a mercurial, unpredictable figure, but she made no bones about her intention to lead an "orange" revolution in Pakistan and to crack down on the military-intelligence establishment. What that action might have solved is a separate issue. That she would have brought change seems highly plausible.
6. "Obituary: Benazir Bhutto," *BBC News*, December 27, 2007.
7. She started with wealth but vastly increased it amid controversy. She vigorously denied wrongdoing. Still, an investigation charged that she and her husband, Asif Ali Zardari, amassed a $1.5 billion fortune through corrupt practices. See: Mary Anne Weaver, *Pakistan: In the Shadow of Jihad and Afghanistan* (New York: Farrar, Straus and Giroux, 2002), 211–12; and Ali, *The Duel*, 5. In Ali's words (also from *The Duel*): "Corruption envelops Pakistan like a sheet of water." At the time of her death, she and her husband had been under criminal investigation by Swiss investigators. The Swiss apparently believed that she was complicit in payoffs, drug dealing, and money laundering. See "Former Pakistani PM Benazir Bhutto Appears before Swiss Court in Money-laundering Probe," Associated Press, September 20, 2005. That investigation was open at the time of her death. In 1999, the Lahore High Court had sentenced Benazir to imprisonment for corruption, disqualified her from holding federal office, and leveled a fine of $8.6 million against her. She was in London at the time and avoided prison. She denied all wrongdoing. Her husband was locked away in 1996 on allegations of corruption and for his alleged role in the murder of his brother-in-law, Mir Murtaza. Some have praised Murtaza's integrity, but he was no saint. He was implicated as a mastermind in the 1981 hijacking of a Pakistan International Airlines flight from Peshawar to Kabul. Two good friends of this book's author were passengers. After releasing one in New Delhi, the plane flew on. A Pakistani diplomat who had been seated next to the other was executed.
8. Bhutto, *Daughter of Destiny*, 45.
9. Weaver, "Bhutto's Fateful Moment."
10. Bhutto, *Daughter of Destiny*, 46.
11. Bhutto, interview with Academy of Achievement.
12. Bhutto, *Daughter of Destiny*, 46–53; and Siegel, in interview with author.
13. Weaver, "Bhutto's Fateful Moment."
14. Bhutto, interview with Academy of Achievement.
15. Id.

16. Id.
17. Weaver, "Bhutto's Fateful Moment"; Levy and Scott-Clark, *Deception*, 201.
18. Walter Isaacson, in interview with author.
19. Id.
20. Bhutto, *Daughter of Destiny*, 81.
21. Id., 81–82.
22. William Dalrymple, "Pakistan's Flawed and Feudal Princess," *Observer*, December 30, 2007.
23. Id.

CHAPTER 6. THE POPULIST ARISTOCRAT

1. Husain Haqqani, *Pakistan: Between Mosque and Military* (Washington, DC: Carnegie Endowment for International Peace, 2005), 58.
2. Id., 58–59.
3. Musharraf, *In the Line of Fire*, 53, 158. Musharraf's autobiography has the feel of a ghostwritten book aimed for Western audiences. Part of it tries to vindicate his tenure as president. There's no reason to doubt the sincerity of his criticisms of Zulfiqar Ali Bhutto or Zia ul-Haq.
4. Hassan Abbas, *Pakistan's Drift into Extremism: Allah, the Army, and America's War on Terror* (London: M. E. Sharpe, 2004), 60–61; and Haqqani, *Pakistan*, 66.
5. Ali, *The Duel*, 77. Husain Haqqani translates it as "you over there, we over here." He says that Bhutto never actually spoke the words and described them as the headline in a pro-PPP newspaper that reflected a headline writer's summary of Bhutto's formula for power sharing. Haqqani, *Pakistan*, 101.
6. Laila Ebadi, "ZAB Never Said Idhar Hum Udhar Tum: These Words Were Concocted by Abbas Ather—Contributed by Eqbal Alavi," *criticalapp.com*, http://criticalppp.com/archives/26168.
7. Haqqani, *Pakistan*, 62.
8. Id., 63.
9. Id., 84.
10. "The Bloody Birth of Bangladesh," *Time*, December 20, 1971.
11. "Pakistan's Lt. Gen. A. A. K. Niazi Signs the Instrument of Surrender," *War1971. com*, http://www.war1971.com/page.php?id=7. Watch a video of the surrender at http://www.youtube.com/watch?v=Q8MO52QQ6_o.
12. Musharraf, *In the Line of Fire*, 55.
13. Haqqani, *Pakistan*, 91.
14. Id., 67.
15. Musharraf, *In the Line of Fire*, 60, 159.
16. Haqqani, *Pakistan*, 100–101.
17. Ali, *The Duel*, 93.
18. Bhutto, *Daughter of the East*, 78–83.
19. Stephen Philip Cohen, *The Idea of Pakistan* (Washington, DC: Brookings Institution Press, 2004), 83. Benazir recalled matters differently. In *Daughter of Destiny*, 87–88, she makes the case for her father as a courageous agent for populist reform: fixing a minimum wage; bringing electricity to rural areas; building roads, parks, and gardens; encouraging unions; and nationalizing industries owned by Pakistan's "Twenty-Two Families" to channel profits back into the country.

20. Cohen, *The Idea of Pakistan*, 95.
21. Bhutto, *Daughter of Destiny*, 86–87.
22. Haqqani, *Pakistan*, 111.
23. Id., 113.
24. Mullick and Yusuf, *Pakistan*, 16.
25. Amir Mir, *The True Face of Jehadis: Inside Pakistan's Network of Terror* (New Delhi: Roli Books, 2006), p. 1.
26. Cohen, *The Idea of Pakistan*, 35–37.
27. Mullick and Yusuf, *Pakistan*, 16.
28. Tony Clifton, in interview with author.
29. Cohen, *The Idea of Pakistan*, 78.
30. Ali, *The Duel*, 101.
31. Id., 78.
32. Id., 116.
33. Id., 120–22.
34. Id., 124–25.
35. The chief of army staff has been generally considered the most powerful position in Pakistan's government. Until Musharraf seized power in a 1999 coup, power was exercised by a troika consisting of the COAS, the president, and the prime minister. Under that system, the president held great power, including the authority to dismiss the prime minister, and it was assertively exercised to oust Benazir twice and Nawaz Sharif twice. Pervez Musharraf changed the system and retained the post of COAS while installing himself as a chief executive with the title of president.
36. Haqqani, *Pakistan*, 126.
37. Bhutto, *Daughter of Destiny*, 107.
38. Brig. Syed A. I. Tirmazi, *Profiles of Intelligence* (Lahore: Fiction House, 1995); Levy and Scott-Clark, *Deception*, 48; and Corera, *Shopping for Bombs*, 27. In a widely quoted statement, Henry Kissinger apparently told Bhutto he would "make a horrible example of him" unless the nuclear program was shut down.
39. Tariq Ali states: "Military coups in Pakistan are rarely, if ever, organized without the tacit or explicit approval of the U.S. embassy. Bhutto's 'treachery' was the principal reason why the United States gave the green light for his removal." Ali, *The Duel*, 113.
40. Mir, *The True Face of Jehadis*, 2.
41. Dr. Ayesha Jalal, in interview with author.
42. Ali, *The Duel*, 114.
43. This information comes from a very reliable source who knows Kasuri and has spoken with him about the charges.
44. Zulfiqar Ali Bhutto, *My Pakistan* (http://www.bhutto.org, reproduced in PDF format by Sani H. Panhar, Sindh Council), on Scribd.com, http://www.scribd.com/doc/2022007/My-Pakistan-by-Zulfikar-Ali-Bhutto.
45. Bhutto, *Daughter of Destiny*, 128.
46. Ali, *The Duel*, 115. The close verdict came on the heels of strong army pressure applied to the court. One judge, who was considered unreliable, was forced into retirement. A second had to withdraw from the bench after being denied sick

leave and a request to delay the trial. Zia conferred with Chief Justice Anwarul Haq every day.

47. Tirmazi, *Profiles in Intelligence* (Lahore: Combined Printers, 1995), 32–40.

48. Id., 240.

49. Weaver, "Bhutto's Fateful Moment."

50. Arnaud de Borchgrave, "Ex-Prime Minister Benazir Bhutto Targeted," *Newsmax.com*, October 28, 2007. A renowned senior expert on diplomatic affairs and the director for transnational threats at the Center for Strategic and International Studies (CSIS), de Borchgrave writes a hard-nosed, no-nonsense, twice-weekly column for the *Washington Times* and UPI. He is known for his excellent international sources within the intelligence community.

CHAPTER 7. THE YEARS HARDEN HOSTILITIES

1. Weaver, *Pakistan*, 208–9.

2. Musharraf, *In the Line of Fire*, 63.

3. Id., 67.

4. Mullick and Yusuf, *Pakistan*, 14.

5. Libby Hughes, *Benazir Bhutto: From Prison to Prime Minister* (Lincoln, NE: iUniverse, 2000), chapter 5.

6. Id.; and see also Mary Anne Weaver's chapter "Daughter of Pakistan" in *Pakistan*, which incorporates material from the earlier article in the *New Yorker*. Benazir described to Weaver, from whose accounts the biographical material from 1979 until 1985 is drawn, that in prison, one experiences vast mood swings. Benazir also discusses her imprisonment at length in her autobiography.

7. Hughes, *Benazir Bhutto*, 76–79; and Tariq Ali, "Daughter of the West," *London Review of Books*, December 13, 2007. Once again, Benazir saw the power of U.S. influence on Pakistan's military.

8. Hughes, *Benazir Bhutto*, 65.

9. Id., 68.

10. Id.

11. Weaver, "Bhutto's Fateful Moment."

12. Id.

13. Id.

14. Bhutto, *Daughter of Destiny*, 350.

15. Id., 352.

16. John F. Burns, "Bhutto Clan Leaves Trail of Corruption in Pakistan," *New York Times*, January 9, 1998.

17. Hughes, *Benazir Bhutto*, 102–3. See also Bhutto, *Daughter of Destiny*, chapter 14, in which she talks at length about entering an arranged marriage and about Zardari.

CHAPTER 8. PRIME MINISTER AT THIRTY-FIVE

1. Mohammad Yousaf and Mark Adkin, *Afghanistan: The Bear Trap—The Defeat of a Superpower* (Haverton, PA: Casemate, 2001), 18–19.

2. His dismissal of other culprits revolves around their inability to stop the autopsies or gain access to the crashed plane.

3. Christina Lamb, in interview with author; and see her article, "My Life with Benazir," *Sunday Times*, December 30, 2007.
4. Haqqani, *Pakistan*, 201.
5. Id., 201.
6. Id.; and Levy and Scott, *Deception*, 185.
7. Haqqani, *Pakistan*, 201.
8. Id., 202.
9. Siegel, in interview with author.
10. Id.
11. Husain Haqqani also references it in *Pakistan*, 185.
12. Galbraith, in interview with author.
13. Id.
14. Siegel, in interview with author.
15. Haqqani, *Pakistan*, 189, citing an interview with Robert Oakley.
16. Lamb, in interview with author. Also, Husain Haqqani references the point in *Pakistan*, 204, citing Christina Lamb, *Waiting for Allah: Pakistan's Struggle for Democracy* (New Delhi: Viking, 1991), 39.
17. Haqqani, *Pakistan*, 206.
18. Id., 206–7.
19. Id., 208.
20. Lamb, "My Life with Benazir"; and affirmed in an interview with Lamb.
21. Weaver, in "Bhutto's Fateful Moment," cites a top bureaucrat who believed that in Khan, "she could have found a friend, a philosopher, a guide." One could easily dispute that conclusion.
22. Siegel, in interview with author.
23. See Amnesty International, "Women in Pakistan: Disadvantaged and Denied Their Rights," December 6, 1995, http://www.amnesty.org/en/library/asset/ASA33/023/1995/en/6bdb1cf3-eb22-11dd-98d3-79fb64d46c94/asa330231995en.html.
24. Massoud Ansari, "Pakistan Ends Zina," *Hindu Business Line*, February 23, 2007, http://www.thehindubusinessline.in/life/2007/02/23/stories/2007022300150400.htm/. Enacted by Zia ul-Haq in 1979, the Zina ordinance silenced rape victims and punished them instead of their rapists. It produced gross abuse as well in adultery, kidnapping, and abduction cases.
25. Haqqani, *Pakistan*, 201–2.
26. Ali, *The Duel*, 5. Ali also is critical of Benazir's and Zardari's financial dealings.
27. Haqqani, *Pakistan*, 205. Relations between the Bhutto and the Sharif families resembled a blood feud.
28. Id.
29. Siegel, in interview with author; and Levy and Scott-Clark, *Deception*, 191–92.
30. Levy and Scott-Clark, *Deception*, 193–94.
31. Frantz and Collins, *The Nuclear Jihadist*, 144.
32. Levy and Scott-Clark, *Deception*, 202–3.
33. Galbraith, in interview with author. Galbraith believed the amendment in both the original and the passed form was a sensible, actionable step from the U.S. perspective and had hoped, in his heart, that it would provide leverage at the time to force Zia ul-Haq to release Benazir Bhutto from her torturous imprisonment.

34. Siegel, in interview with author.
35. Siegel and Galbraith, in interviews with author. It also appears that the ISI secretly recorded this conversation, which took place in a garden. Siegel says he was taken aback when Robert Windrem called him up to ask about the conversation and read from what sounded like a transcript.
36. Burrows and Windrem, *Critical Mass*, 61.
37. K. Subrahmanyam, "How ISI Engineers Pakistan Elections," *Boloji.com*, January 7, 2008.
38. Haqqani, *Pakistan*, 220.
39. Siegel, in interview with author. Husain Haqqani recounts that the IJI identified Siegel as a "well-known Zionist" (*Pakistan*, 220).
40. Id.
41. The JI enjoys the support of a diverse cross section of Pakistani society, including students, unions, and professional organizations. However, its strongest ties are to the political elite, and it remains a focal point in the debate over Islam's role in Pakistan's politics and national identity. When Gen. Zia ul-Haq made Islamism an official state policy after seizing power in 1977, the JI benefited as the regime's ideological arm. It is linked to militancy and is close to the ISI. More recently, in line with Musharraf's "moderated jihad strategy," it has wanted to distance itself publicly from militancy and has established separate groups dedicated solely to jihad, of which the most prominent is Hazb-ul-Mujahideen (HM, Organization of the Mujahideen). See "The Jihadi Terrain in Pakistan: An Introduction to the Sunni Jihadi Groups in Pakistan and Kashmir," *Indian Security & Intelligence*, January 7, 2009.
42. See Rana, *A to Z of Jehadi Organizations*, 328. The Lashkar-e-Taiba (LeT) is one of the primary groups suspected of attacking the Indian Parliament in 2001, along with Jaish-e-Mohammad (Army of Mohammed). The Pakistani government froze the LeT's assets in 2002.
43. Mir, *The True Face to Jehadis*, 67.
44. Truth was fungible to Benazir. For instance, despite solid evidence, she insisted that in acquiring North Korea's No Dong missile, Pakistan paid cash and did not barter or engage in nuclear trafficking. See Corera, *Shopping for Bombs*, 86–102.
45. Ahmed Rashid, *Taliban: Islam, Oil, and the New Great Game in Asia* (London: I. B. Tauris, 2000), 90.
46. General Stanley A. McChrystal, "COMISAF'S Initial Assessment," August 30, 2009, 2–6 (UNCLASSIFIED), published in a slightly redacted form in the *Washington Post*, http://media.washingtonpost.com/wp-srv/politics/documents/Assessment_Redacted_092109.pdf.
47. Tony Clifton, "Pakistan: A New Leader All Over Again?," *New Matilda*, August 15, 2007.
48. Permission to quote but not attribute was given. This high-ranking adviser enjoyed Bhutto's confidence and greatly admired her, although the person felt that she had misjudged how to handle this situation.
49. Burns, "Bhutto Clan Leaves Trail of Corruption."
50. Id.
51. Clifton, "Pakistan: A New Leader."
52. See, e.g., Bhutto, *Daughter of the East*, 408.

53. Haqqani, *Pakistan*, 219.
54. Tim McGirk, "Fall from Grace Marks the Last Hurrah of the Bhutto Dynasty," *Independent*, November 6, 1996.
55. Ali, "Daughter of the West."
56. John F. Burns, "Pakistan's Premier Bhutto Is Put under House Arrest," *New York Times*, November 5, 1996. Zardari was arrested as he dined in the governor's old colonial palace in Lahore. See McGirk, "Fall from Grace."
57. Jones, *Pakistan: Eye of the Storm*, 1st ed., 232. In the third edition, he uses the name Rockwood Palace. See *Pakistan: Eye of the Storm*, 3rd ed., 301. See also "'Surrey Palace' Saga for Benazir," *BBC News*, December 19, 1999. The BBC pointed out that while adept at acquiring property, Zardari failed to pay his bills. Zardari and Benazir, however, denied owning it until Britain threatened to liquidate the property and turn over the proceeds to the Pakistan government.
58. Jones, *Pakistan: Eye of the Storm*, 3rd ed., 301.
59. Michael Peel and Farhan Bokhari, "Doubts Cast on Zardari's Mental Health," *Financial Times*, August 25, 2008; and Jones, *Pakistan: Eye of the Storm*, 3rd ed., 301.
60. Peel and Bokhari, "Doubts Cast on Zardari's Mental Health." According to court documents examined by the *Financial Times*, New York–based psychologist Stephen Reich said Zardari was unable to remember the birthdays of his wife and children and had thought about suicide. New York City–based psychiatrist Philip Saltiel diagnosed Zardari as suffering from "emotional instability." It was partly blamed on his imprisonment.
61. Burns, "Bhutto Clan Leaves Trail of Corruption."
62. Id.
63. Jones, *Pakistan: Eye of the Storm*, 3rd ed., 301.
64. Lamb, "My Life with Benazir."
65. "Husband of Benazir Bhutto May Be Freed from Pakistan Prison," VOANews.com, November 22, 2004.
66. Id. There is controversy as to who was complicit in this murder. Benazir was not implicated formally, but Tariq Ali's account of the killing—"Daughter of the West," *London Review of Books*—raises grave questions. Ali suggests that the decision to kill Murtaza, who had quarreled with Zardari, was taken at a high level. Zardari was jailed over suspicion of his involvement. Eleven years later, Murtaza's daughter, at age twenty-five, publicly accused Zardari of complicity. All witnesses to the murder were arrested or killed. In an interview at an independent television station, Benazir was asked how, while she was prime minister, Murtaza was allowed to bleed to death outside his home. She walked out of the studio. She always staunchly maintained the accusation that she was in any way responsible for Murtaza's death was outrageous and without basis. As president, Musharraf would grant amnesty to both Benazir and Zardari, but only in April 2008 was Zardari acquitted, through a ruling in the Sindh High Court. See Ishaq Tanoli, "SHC Acquits Zardari in Murtaza Murder Case," *Dawn.com*, April 8, 2008. The eminent counterterrorism expert B. Raman contends that Murtaza was murdered by the ISI, which mounted a disinformation campaign against Zardari as part of an effort to discredit Benazir and to pave the way for

her ouster as prime minister. He also contends that in 1985, the ISI poisoned and killed Benazir's brother Shah Nawaz Bhutto in an attempt to intimidate her against returning to Pakistan and leading a movement against Zia ul-Haq. See B. Raman, "Pakistan's Inter-Services Intelligence (ISI)," South Asia Analysis Group, Paper no. 287, August 1, 2001.

67. Information revealed without attribution during an interview with Tony Clifton. I reconfirmed this information with him twice. Although he requested that the sources not be identified here, they are entirely credible.

68. Siegel, in interview with author.

69. Burns, "Pakistan's Premier Bhutto." See also Levy and Scott-Clark, *Deception*, 253–63.

70. McGirk, "Fall from Grace." The police said that Murtaza started the fight, but not a single police officer was injured. Then it was said he committed suicide, but the lethal shots were fired from five feet away. Finally, the security services were fingered.

71. Musharraf, *In the Line of Fire*, 71.

72. Id., 65.

CHAPTER 9. MUSHARRAF BATTLES TO SURVIVE

1. Ali, *The Duel*, 5. As one measure of the Bhuttos' wealth—some of which was inherited and much of it, he says, was amassed through public office—Ali writes that both Bhutto and Nawaz had private zoos at their opulent estates.

2. Maseeh Rahman, "The Zardari Behind the Bhutto," *India Express*, January 6, 2008, http://www.indianexpress.com/news/the-zardari-behind-the-bhutto/258033/0. Benazir's niece, Fatima, calls Zardari Mr. Ten Percent. See the documentary *Bhutto*, directed by Duane Baughman and Johnny O'Hara; and Fatima Bhutto, *Songs of Blood and Sword: A Daughter's Memoir* (London: Nation Books, 2010).

3. Christina Lamb, "Whoever Killed Benazir Wants to Kill Me," *Spectator*, September 6, 2008.

4. Musharraf, *In the Line of Fire*, 98.

5. Zahid Hussain, *Frontline Pakistan: The Struggle with Militant Islam* (New York: Columbia University Press, 2007), 4.

6. Musharraf, *In the Line of Fire*, 137.

7. Jones, *Pakistan: Eye of the Storm*, 1st ed., 39. After seizing power, Musharraf dumped the plan. It probably didn't matter. Michael Scheuer, a U.S. government official involved in tracking down bin Laden, reported that President Bill Clinton passed on two chances to kill and eight chances to capture bin Laden. See Scheuer, *Marching Toward Hell*, 61.

8. "How the 1999 Pakistan Coup Unfolded," *BBC News*, August 23, 2007.

9. Musharraf, *In the Line of Fire*, chapter 14.

10. Hussain, *Frontline Pakistan*, 5–6.

11. Caroline Frost, "Pervez Musharraf: Profile," *BBC Four Documentary*, August 12, 2003, http://www.bbc.co.uk/bbcfour/documentaries/profile/pervez-musharraf.shtml.

12. Jones, *Pakistan: Eye of the Storm*, 1st ed., 34–55; Musharraf, *In the Line of Fire*, 143.

13. Richard Wike, "Musharraf's Support Shrinks, Even as More Pakistanis Reject Terrorism . . . and the U.S.," Pew Research Center Publications, November 7, 2007, http://pewresearch.org/pubs/561/pakistan-terrorism. Polling data prior to 2002 was not discovered.

14. Declan Walsh, "Bhutto Close to Deal with Musharraf," *Guardian*, August 30, 2007. On July 17, 2009, a Pakistani court overturned the conviction. See Rasool Dawar, "Former PM Cleared of Hijacking Musharraf in Alleged Coup," news.scotsman.com, July 19, 2009.

15. Musharraf, *In the Line of Fire*, 143–44.

16. Id., 144.

17. Id., 152.

18. Daniel Schorn, "Pakistan's President Tells Steve Kroft U.S. Threatened His Country," *CBS News*, September 24, 2006, http://www.cbsnews.com/stories/2006/09/21/60minutes/main2030165.shtml.

19. Walsh, "Bhutto Close to Deal with Musharraf"; Levy and Scott-Clark, *Deception*, 318.

20. International Republican Institute polls, for example, did not poll the Federally Administered Tribal Areas (FATA), Chitral and Kohistan. Pew Global Attitudes surveys tended to poll all four provinces in Pakistan but excluded FATA, Azad Jammu and Kashmir (AJK), and areas of instability in the North-West Frontier Province (NWFP) and Baluchistan.

21. Shuja Nawaz, in interview with author.

22. Ahmed Rashid, in interview with author; Rashid, *Descent into Chaos*, 380; and Jones, *Pakistan: Eye of the Storm*, 3rd ed., 240.

23. David Rohde, "Musharraf Redraws Constitution," *New York Times*, August 21, 2002. Critics challenged the referendum as fixed. Opinion polls showed most Pakistanis opposed his action.

24. Encarta.MSN.com, s.v. "Pervez Musharraf," http://encarta.msn.com/encyclopedia_701667135/musharraf_pervez.html (no longer available).

25. Ron Moreau, in interview with author. Moreau is *Newsweek*'s correspondent in Islamabad, and has lived there for the last eight years.

26. Zahid Hussain, in interview with author.

27. Shuja Nawaz, *Crossed Swords: Pakistan, Its Army, and the Wars Within* (Karachi: Oxford University Press, 2008), 507.

CHAPTER 10. CUTTING THE CARDS

1. "Musharraf Political Foes Plan Strategy," *USA Today*, September 16, 2007.

2. See Pervez Musharraf, "A Plea for Enlightened Moderation," *Washington Post*, June 1, 2004.

3. See Robbins, "Mr. Bush Gets Another Look into Mr. Putin's Eyes." Bush said that he had looked Vladimir Putin in the eye and "was able to get a sense of his soul." He did make those sorts of remarks frequently as president.

4. See Musharraf, *In the Line of Fire*, chapter 24, which describes in detail the December 2003 plots against his life.

5. Nawaz, *Crossed Swords*, 506.

6. Nawaz, in interview with author.

7. Shaheen Sehbai, "Role of Pakistan Army under Musharraf Just Stinks," *chowk.com*, June 13, 2004.
8. Rashid, *Descent into Chaos*. Rashid reports that while Pakistani intelligence helped fight Al Qaeda and rounded up Arabs, it duplicitously provided support to the Afghan and Pakistani Taliban. Musharraf's links to militant groups did not escape notice, although his attitude changed after the December 2003 assassination attempts on his own life. Although distinct, many of these militant groups had links to one another.
9. Vali Nasr, "Musharraf Fears Democracy, Not Extremism," Op-Ed, *Christian Science Monitor*, November 5, 2007. Many feel the situation hasn't changed much. See Sushant Sareen, "The More Pakistan Changes the More It Stays the Same," Rediff.com, July 27, 2009: "Right from day one of the so-called War on Terror, the Pakistani policy was 'don't touch the Taliban, don't spare the Al Qaeda's.' As a result, while Pakistan flaunted the arrest of quite a few high-profile Al Qaeda operatives, not a single Taliban commander of any significance was ever apprehended by the Pakistani authorities."
10. Bhutto, *Reconciliation*, 215.
11. Mir, *The True Face of Jehadis*, 24. Mir seemed to feel at the time that Musharraf was more prone to fighting extremists after the 2003 assassination attempts. In *Descent into Chaos*, Ahmed Rashid offers a skeptical view of Musharraf more in line with the views of Benazir and Nasr. His book is a scathing indictment of the duplicity of Musharraf and the Pakistan Army, as well as of the Bush administration's policies in the region.
12. Mir, *The True Face of Jehadis*, chapter 2.
13. International Republican Institute (IRI), "IRI Index: Pakistan Public Opinion Survey, July 15–August 7, 2009," released October 1, 2009, http://www.iri.org/news-events-press-center/news/iri-releases-survey-pakistan-public-opinion. Bear in mind the sample frame used, noted above.
14. Sami Abraham, "Pak Anti-terror Role Not Recognized Properly: Haqqani," *The News*, November 13, 2009.
15. Nawaz, in interview with author.
16. Rashid, in interview with author. See also his *Descent into Chaos*, 72–73.
17. Id., 273. Rashid notes that Donald Rumsfeld and U.S. CENTCOM commander Gen. Tommy Franks, among others, declined to criticize Musharraf for failing to crack down on the militants, despite his commitment to do so in a national speech on January 12, 2002. Franks "made no bones about how much he trusted Musharraf as one soldier to another"(id., 118).
18. Id., 274.
19. Id., 221.
20. Abraham, "Pak Anti-terror Role."
21. Scheuer, *Marching Toward Hell*, 166.
22. Nawaz, in interview with author.
23. "Report of the United Nations Commission of Inquiry," 10, http://www.un.org/News/dh/infocus/Pakistan/UN_Bhutto_Report_15April2010.pdf.
24. Id.
25. Siegel, in interview with author.

26. "Report of the United Nations Commission of Inquiry," 10. The commission says that the United Kingdom played an early role in 2004 and 2005 in urging Benazir and Musharraf to engage in discussion and encouraging the United States to see her as a potential partner.
27. Bhutto, *Reconciliation*, 227–28.
28. The United Nations Commission reports that issues she laid out included: "(i) her return to Pakistan to participate in politics; (ii) free and fair elections in 2007; (iii) Musharraf's resignation from the Army; (iv) amnesty in the criminal cases against her and her husband, Asif Ali Zardari; and (v) the elimination of the ban on third terms for former prime ministers, which would impede her from holding that office again. The same sources indicated that General Musharraf's chief goals were to accommodate international interests in having Ms Bhutto return and to ensure his continuity in power." See "Report of the United Nations Commission of Inquiry," 10.
29. Siegel, in interview with author.
30. The United Nations Commission twice—on pages 10 and 12 of its report—refers to a November 2007 election schedule, but they were scheduled for January 2008. After the assassination, they were delayed until February 2008.
31. Bhutto, *Reconciliation*, 227.
32. Id.
33. Robin Wright and Glenn Kessler, "U.S. Brokered Bhutto's Return to Pakistan," *Washington Post*, December 28, 2007. See also Rashid, *Descent into Chaos*, 376. The idea that the United States would accept a facade in place of real democracy is why many Pakistanis remain skeptical of America.
34. Wright and Kessler, "U.S. Brokered Bhutto's Return."

CHAPTER 11. THE RED MOSQUE

1. "Lawyers Protest against Musharraf," *BBC News*, March 12, 2007; and Rajan Menon, "Strange Bedfellows," *Newsweek*, August 6, 2007.
2. Aryn Baker, "Storming the Red Mosque," *Time*, July 10, 2007; and "Red Mosque Offensive 'Nears End,'" *BBC News*, July 11, 2007. The standoff took a week, culminating with troops storming the mosque on July 10 after talks failed.
3. Syed Shoaib Hasan, "Profile: Islamabad's Red Mosque," *BBC News*, July 27, 2007.
4. Syed Irfan Raza and Munawar Azeem, "Fierce Gunbattles Rock Capital," *Dawn*, July 4, 2007.
5. See Nicholas Schmidle, *To Live or to Perish Forever: Two Tumultuous Years in Pakistan* (New York: Henry Holt, 2009), 143. Schmidle's book provides a detailed and excellent account of the siege and information about Ghazi.
6. "Red Mosque Offensive 'Nears End.'"
7. Raza and Azeem, "Fierce Gunbattles Rock Capital."
8. Schmidle, *To Live or to Perish Forever*, 145–46.
9. Declan Walsh, "Army Ready to Storm Mosque as Conflict Grows," *Guardian*, July 4, 2007.
10. Raza and Azeem, "Fierce Gunbattles Rock Capital."
11. Id.
12. Syed Shoaib Hasan, "Anguish of Pakistan Mosque Parents," *BBC News*, July 4, 2007.
13. Walsh, "Army Ready to Storm Mosque."

14. "Forces on Alert as Deadline to Lal Masjid Passes," *The News*, July 5, 2007.
15. Schmidle, *To Live or to Perish Forever*, 148.
16. "Pakistan Cleric Offers Surrender," *BBC News*, July 5, 2007.
17. Id.
18. "Fresh Fighting at Pakistan Mosque," *BBC News*, July 6, 2007.
19. Raza and Azeem, "Fierce Gunbattles Rock Capital."
20. "Islamabad Red Mosque Cleric Ghazi Killed," *Pakistan Times*, July 11, 2007; and "Red Mosque Offensive 'Nears End.'"
21. Dean Nelson and Ghulam Hasnain, "Bin Laden's Deputy behind the Red Mosque Bloodbath," *Sunday Times*, July 15, 2007.
22. Isambard Wilkinson, "Red Mosque Suicide Attack Kills 13 in Pakistan," *Telegraph*, July 27, 2007.
23. "Musharraf Vows War on Militants," *BBC News*, July 12, 2007.
24. Dr. Marvin Weinbaum, in interview with author.
25. Jalal, in interview with author.
26. See the International Republican Institute (http://www.iri.org); and Richard Wike, "View from Pakistan: Before Bhutto's Assassination, Public Opinion Was Increasingly Opposed to Terrorism," Pew Global Attitudes Project, December 28, 2007, http://pewresearch.org/pubs/674/view-from-pakistan-before-bhuttos -assassination-public-opinion-was-increasingly-opposed-to-terrorism. The two polls used slightly different wording but looked at the same sentiment. The Pew polls from August–September 2002 and April–May 2007 asked whether Musharraf had a good or bad influence in Pakistan. The February–March, June–July, August–September, and November 2007 IRI polls asked whether respondents approved or disapproved of the job Musharraf was doing. An August–September 2007 poll found that only 21 percent approved of Musharraf's job, compared to 62 percent who disapproved (http://www.scribd.com/doc/7166465/IRI-Pakistan-Public-Opinion-Survey-2007). Results were compared to polls conducted over the prior twelve months. The comparison showed that Musharraf had suffered a sharp decline from a June 2007 IRI survey, in which his job approval was 34 percent compared to only 49 percent disapproval, indicating a slight recover from a February 2007 IRI poll, in which approval was 26 percent and disapproval was 54 percent. All of these numbers showed a precipitous reversal from the prior fall.
27. "Police Probe Attack at Red Mosque," *BBC News*, July 28, 2007.
28. "Survivors Recount Narrow Escape from Deadly Peshawar Market Bombing," CNN, October 29, 2008.
29. "Terror Spate Continues: Bomb Blasts Kill 38 in Lahore Market, 9 in Peshawar," *Daily Times*, December 8, 2009.
30. "Islamists Deny Peshawar Blast; Conspiracy Theories Proliferate," *World War 4 Report*, October 30, 2009, http://ww4report.com/node/7876.
31. "JI Blames Blackwater for Lahore Bombings," *Geo Television Network*, March 13, 2010, www.geo.tv/3-12-2010/60944.htm.
32. See Matt Deller, "The Enemy Is Using Your Mistakes against You," *Coin Common Sense*, from International Security Assistance Force–Afghanistan 1, no. 1 (February 2010), http://www.isaf.nato.int/COIN-publication/feb10.pdf.

CHAPTER 12. BHUTTO AND MUSHARRAF REACH AN AGREEMENT

1. Musharraf, *In the Line of Fire*, 164–65.
2. "Report of the United Nations Commission of Inquiry," 12.
3. Id.
4. Musharraf, *In the Line of Fire*, 166.
5. Rashid, *Descent into Chaos*, 376; and Wright and Kessler, "U.S. Brokered Bhutto's Return."
6. Siegel, in interview with author.
7. Wright and Kessler, "U.S. Brokered Bhutto's Return."
8. "Bhutto, Musharraf Reach Agreement," Agence France-Presse, October 5, 2007.
9. It was called the National Reconciliation Ordinance (NRO-2007). See "National Reconciliation Ordinance Promulgated," *The News*, August 14, 2009.
10. "Bhutto, Musharraf Agree on Powering Sharing Agreement," Agence France-Presse, October 5, 2007. The text is different from the Agence France-Presse story cited in note 8.
11. In 2009, Farooq Ahmad Khan Leghari blasted it in stark terms: "When corrupt rulers of a country illegitimately acquire not millions but billions of wealth in U.S. dollars, when they hide their ill-begotten wealth with the help of international money-laundering consultants in one shell company after another in foreign countries, when they obfuscate their criminal past by massive bribery through a corrupt judicial system, then they are easy prey to any foreign power that wishes to exploit them for their own purposes." See Leghari, "The Existentialist Threat to Pakistan," *The News*, October 12, 2009.
12. International Republican Institute, "IRI Index: Pakistan Public Opinion Survey, August 29–September 13, 2007," released October 11, 2007, http://www.iri.org/sites/default/files/2007-10-11-pakistan-SR.pdf.
13. Id.; and IRI, "IRI Index: Pakistan Public Opinion Survey, November 19–28, 2007," released December 13, 2007, http://www.iri.org/sites/default/files/2007-12-12-pakistan-poll.pdf.
14. Rauf Klasra, "Benazir Defends Deal with Musharraf," *The News*, April 26, 2007; and Bhutto, *Reconciliation*, 225.
15. Benazir Bhutto, "Democracy for Pakistan," *Wall Street Journal*, June 8, 2007.
16. Richard N. Haass, moderator, "A Conversation with Benazir Bhutto," Council on Foreign Relations, New York, August 15, 2007, http://www.cfr.org/pakistan/conversation-benazir-bhutto/p14041. The transcript leaves no doubt that she intended to crack down hard on the army and its intelligence services.
17. Id.
18. Id.
19. Syed Saleem Shahzad, "Benazir Bhutto's Answer to al-Qaeda," *Asia Times*, November 3, 2004.
20. Moreau, in interview with author.
21. "Pakistan Extends Army Chief Kayani's Term Amid Taliban Fight," *Bloomberg*, July 23, 2010. On that date, Prime Minister Syed Yousef Raza Gilani announced Kayani would receive a three-year extension. See also "Kayani Term Extended by 3 Yrs," *Telegraphindia.com*, July 22, 2010.
22. "Benazir Bhutto's Answer to al-Qaeda."

23. K. Alan Kronstadt, *Pakistan-U.S. Relations* (Washington, DC: Congressional Research Service Report for Congress, February 22, 2008), 16.

CHAPTER 13. KARACHI

1. Bhutto, *Reconciliation*, 2–12.
2. Id., 9.
3. Id., 219.
4. B. Raman, "Bin Laden's Former Handling Officer Was in Charge of Benazir's Security," *International Terrorism Monitor*, Paper no. 288, South Asia Analysis Group, October 19, 2007. Mr. Raman was an additional secretary, in the Cabinet Secretariat, for India's government and also a former chief of counterterrorism for the Research and Analysis Wing of the nation's external intelligence agency. His insights are extremely penetrating.
5. "Police Detain 3 in Deadly Karachi Bombing," Associated Press, October 21, 2007.
6. Carlotta Gall and Salman Masood, "Shaken Bhutto Says Islamists Were behind Karachi Blasts," *New York Times*, October 19, 2007.
7. "Defiant Bhutto Says Blasts Were 'Attack on Democracy,'" Agence France-Presse, October 18, 2007.
8. "Scores Dead in Pakistan Bomb Blasts," AlJazeera.net, October 22, 2007.
9. Id.
10. Id.
11. Gall and Masood, "Shaken Bhutto."
12. "Mehsud Was Not Benazir's Enemy," *The Hindu*, December 30, 2007.
13. "Death Toll Rises in Bhutto Attack," CNN, October 18, 2007.
14. Colin Freeman, "Benazir Bhutto Takes on a Powerful Enemy (ISI)," *Telegraph*, October 20, 2007. Freeman cites C4.
15. Raman cites RDX as the explosive used. B. Raman, "Pakistan: Attempt to Kill Benazir Bhutto—an Update," *Global Analyst OnLine*, October 21, 2007. Military experts say that what matters is the quality of the explosive. Was it military grade? The evidence is not clear.
16. Id.
17. The United Nations' inquiry notes that the Sindh police investigation of the attack "never advanced," while an ISI investigation discounted the involvement of various suspects she named as possibly involved in the attack. "Report of the United Nations Commission of Inquiry," 13.
18. Carlotta Gall and Salman Masood, "After Bombing, Bhutto Assails Officials' Ties," *New York Times*, October 19, 2007.
19. "New Tribunal to Probe Bombing of Bhutto's Karachi Rally," *Hindustan Times*, April 7, 2008. For reasons that the research conducted did not uncover, apparently, Rahim was later cleared of suspicion.
20. Ron Suskind, *The Way of the World: A Story of Truth and Hope in an Age of Extremism* (New York: Harper, 2008), 281.
21. In 2009, the alleged presence of Blackwater in Pakistan, for which there is no evidence, became a hot topic of conspiracy theorists and central to the Taliban's messaging against the United States and the Pakistani government.

22. Siegel, in interview with author.
23. Galbraith, in interview with author.
24. Lamb, "My Life with Benazir."
25. Id.
26. Lamb, in interview with author.
27. Bronwen Maddox, "Benazir Was Fragile Best of Bad Bunch," *The Australian*, December 31, 2007.
28. Clifton, in interview with author.

CHAPTER 14. THE STATE OF EMERGENCY

1. "Musharraf Suspends Pakistan's Constitution," *CBS News*, November 4, 2007.
2. "October 12 Coup, Bugti's Murder and Nov 3 Steps, Musharraf Passes the Buck to Army," *The News*, September 14, 2009.
3. Umar Cheema, "Musharraf's Comrades Feeling Embarrassed, Shy," *The News*, September 16, 2009.
4. Gretchen Peters, in interview with author.
5. Mohammed Hanif, "The Case of Musharraf and the Drunk Uncle," Rediff India Abroad, November 6, 2007.
6. Id.
7. Bill Roggio, "Pakistan: Musharraf Suspends Constitution, Declares State of Emergency," *The Long War Journal*, November 3, 2007.
8. "Musharraf Imposes Emergency Rule," *BBC News*, November 3, 2007.
9. See Pervez Musharraf, "Letter to the American Bar Association," December 26, 2007, http://teeth.com.pk/blog/2008/02/01/musharrafs-letter-to-aba-accusing-cjp-iftikhar-chaudhry. The letter summarizes the charges that Musharraf consistently raised against his judicial adversary. He accused Chaudhry of exercising undue pressure on the prime minister and government functionaries to get his two sons jobs in the Federal Investigation Agency and Punjab's Health Department; misusing and abusing power to influence other courts and for self-gain; as part of judicial excess, releasing "more than 60 hardcore terrorists" who "have become instruments in the hands of terrorist networks and could be fully involved in the recent spate of terrorist attacks in the country"; demoralizing law enforcement agencies and thus causing an upsurge of terrorist activity in FATA and other parts of Pakistan; "making effective action impossible" against terrorists; and paralyzing the government. See also Azhar Masood, "Musharraf Suspends SC Chief Justice," *Arab News*, March 10, 2007.
10. "General Musharraf's Second Coup," *Dawn*, November 4, 2007. Musharraf's emergency order accused some judges of "working at cross purposes with the executive" and "weakening the government's resolve" to fight terrorism.
11. Jane Perlez and David Rohde, "Pakistan Attempts to Crush Protests by Lawyers," *New York Times*, November 6, 2007.
12. Matthew Pennington, "Opposition Leaders Rounded Up in Pakistan," Associated Press, November 4, 2007.
13. Jane Perlez and David Rohde, "Pakistan Rounds Up Musharraf's Political Foes," *New York Times*, November 5, 2007.
14. "Musharraf Suspends Pakistan's Constitution."

15. Perlez and Rohde, "Pakistan Rounds Up Musharraf's Political Foes."
16. Robin McDowell, "Pakistan TV Fights Back," AP News, November 8, 2007.
17. Hussain, in interview with author.
18. Ron Moreau and Fasih Ahmed, "Bhutto Fights Back," *Newsweek*, November 7, 2007.
19. Ron Moreau, "Redrawing the Lines," *Newsweek*, November 13, 2007.
20. Id.
21. Gary Thomas, "Pakistan Opposition Leader Bhutto Leaves Door Open to Compromise," VOANews.com, December 14, 2007.
22. "Musharraf Says Emergency Rule Saved Pakistan," Agence France-Presse, December 14, 2007; and "Musharraf Restores Constitution in Pakistan," *ABC News*, December 15, 2007.

CHAPTER 15. LIAQUAT BAGH
1. "Benazir Photographer Surprised by Her Waving to Supporters," *Daily Times*, December 30, 2007.
2. Saeed Shah, "Attendee at Bhutto Rally: 'There Was Pandemonium,'" *McClatchy Newspapers*, December 27, 2007.
3. Fareed Zakaria, interview with Pervez Musharraf, "Pakistanis Know I Can Be Tough," *Newsweek*, January 12, 2008.
4. Apparently the warning came from the United Arab Emirates.
5. Fareed Zakaria interviews Pervez Musharraf, CNN, May 17, 2009, transcript at http://www.riazhaq.com/2009/05/musharraf-on-cnn-gps-with-fareed.html.
6. Peters, in interview with author.
7. Anjum, "One Year on, Benazir's Murder"; and Mir, "Musharraf Let off the Hook." Mir is the executive editor of Geo TV in Islamabad. Anjum and Mir offer contradictory reports as to Malik's response, except to say that Malik claimed afterward that the discussion was about politics, not security. Anjum reports that Malik was dismissive about the threats and said that Benazir had to meet her public, but Mir says that Malik opposed her going to the rally.
8. Hamid Mir, "Asif Zardari Tipped as New PPP Chief," *The News*, December 29, 2007. Malik's behavior has raised numerous questions.
9. Id.
10. Irshad, "Who Assassinated Benazir Bhutto?," Allvoices.com, http://www.allvoices.com/contributed-news/2077084-who-assassinated-benazir-bhutto. It provides a report of the Geo News TV show *Capital Talk* and Hamid Mir's investigation into what happened.
11. "Report of the United Nations Commission of Inquiry," 14–15.
12. Id., 15. The author had reached the same conclusion earlier and found it striking that UN sources confirmed this interpretation of Taj's action.
13. Id., 16.
14. Id.
15. Id., 18.
16. Id., 19–20.
17. Id., 22.
18. Id. Mir cites Benazir's security officer Chaudhry Aslam, who also told Mir that the behavior of the police that day was "weird."
19. "Report of the United Nations Commission of Inquiry," 22.

20. Shah, "Attendee at Bhutto Rally."
21. Irshad, "Who Assassinated Benazir Bhutto?"
22. Anjum, "One Year on, Benazir's Murder"; Augustine Anthony, "Pakistan's Bhutto Assassinated in Gun, Bomb Attack," *National Post*, December 27, 2007; and "Benazir Bhutto Killed in Attack," *BBC News*, December 27, 2007.
23. Irshad, "Who Assassinated Benazir Bhutto?" In the report, Hamid Mir quotes Ibn-e-Rizvi, the organizer of the procession. Chaudhry confirms Rizvi's recollection. A report in *The News* on December 27, 2008, concurs that the vehicle departed from its planned route but describes its movement in these terms: "For unknown reasons, the vehicle took a U-turn on the College Road to head back towards the Muree Road instead of playing the route chosen for her return to Islamabad. According to the security plan already finalized, Benazir's convoy was scheduled to return from the other way—first heading to the Raja Bazaar and then taking the alternative route." The point is the vehicle was diverted from its intended route.
24. "Here's What Happened," *Daily Times*, December 28, 2008.
25. Anjum, "One Year on, Benazir's Murder."
26. Channel 4's report uses video and expert opinion to describe what transpired and persuasively contradicts both the Pakistani government's and Scotland Yard's version of what happened. See "Benazir Assassination Channel 4 Video," http://www.youtube.com/watch?v=pwB8rFmDr6k.
27. Salman Masood and Carlotta Gall, "Bhutto Assassination Ignites Disarray," *New York Times*, December 28, 2007.
28. Terence J. Sigamony, "Benazir Was Gunned Down, Say Injured PPP Workers," *Daily Times*, December 30, 2007.
29. "Scotland Yard Statement on Bhutto Report," *Wall Street Journal*, February 8, 2008. The report notes: "It is also important to comment upon the construction of the vehicle. It was fitted with B6 grade armour and designed to withstand gunfire and bomb-blast. It is an unfortunate and misleading aspect of this case that the roof escape hatch has frequently been referred to as a sunroof. It is not. It is designed and intended to be used solely as a means of escape. It has a solid lip with a depth of 9cm."
30. Anjum, "One Year on, Benazir's Murder."
31. Irshad, "Who Assassinated Benazir Bhutto?," citing Amin Fahim.
32. Azaz Syed, "Suicide Bomber Was a Clean-shaven Youth," *Daily Times*, December 30, 2007. Syed states: "The appearance is different from that of popularly known suicide bombers who wear long hair and thick beard."
33. Jane Perlez, "New Questions Arise in Killing of Ex-Premier," *New York Times*, December 31, 2007.
34. Sigamony, "Benazir Was Gunned Down," citing eyewitness Nawaz Ali, who was standing right next to the gunman.
35. Najam Sethi, "News Analysis: Who Killed Benazir Bhutto?," *The News*, December 31, 2007. Witnesses told the *Daily Times* five shots were fired. See Terence J. Sigamony, "No Shrapnel or Bullet Found in Benazir's Wound," *Daily Times*, December 29, 2007. Only three shots are audible on the video footage broadcast by Channel 4.

36. "New Angle of Benazir Assassination," http://www.youtube.com/watch?v=efB_ wCK2biQ.
37. Syed, "Suicide Bomber Was a Clean-shaven Youth."
38. "Pakistan: Bhutto's Assassin Belonged to al-Qaida Group," *WorldNetDaily.com*, December 28, 2007, http://www.wnd.com/news/article.asp?ARTICLE_ID= 59418. There was initial confusion as to whether the shooter was accompanied by a bomber. Scotland Yard insisted there was only one assailant.
39. Mir, "Musharraf Let off the Hook."

CHAPTER 16. "BUSHARRAF" OF PAKISTAN

1. Paul Wiseman, "Musharraf Gambles by Giving up Leadership of Army," *USA Today*, November 28, 2007.
2. Id.
3. Id.; and Rashid, in interview with author.
4. September 5, 2002: http://www.investors.com/NewsAndAnalysis/Article/3314 26/200902200212/Some-Question-Pakistani-Role-In-US-War-On-Global-Terror.aspx Quoted by Peter Benesh, "Some Question Pakistani Role in U.S. War on Global Terror," *Investor's Business Daily*, http://membres.multimania.fr/ tthreat/article15.htm.
5. Hussain, *Frontline Pakistan*, 3.
6. "Musharraf's Biography," *Alaiwah!*, August 12, 2009, http://alaiwah.wordpress .com/2009/08/12/musharrafs-biography/.
7. Frost, "Pervez Musharraf: Profile"; and "General Pervez Musharraf," *The Story of Pakistan*, http://www.storyofpakistan.com/person.asp?perid=P029.
8. "Musharraf's Biography."
9. Frost, "Pervez Musharraf: Profile."
10. Musharraf, *In the Line of Fire*.
11. "Musharraf's Biography."
12. Pierre Tristam, "Profile: Pakistan's Gen. Pervez Musharraf," Middle East Issues, About.com, http://middleeast.about.com/od/pakistan/p/me07110507.htm.
13. Jones, *Pakistan: Eye of the Storm*, 3rd ed., 297.
14. Hussain, *Frontline Pakistan*, 7. See also Jones, *Pakistan: Eye of the Storm*, 1st ed., 19.
15. Lamb, in interview with author. She discusses her experience as well in "My Life with Benazir."
16. Frédéric Grare, "Reforming the Intelligence Agencies in Pakistan's Transitional Democracy," *Carnegie Endowment for International Peace* (2009), 24, http://www .carnegieendowment.org/files/pakistan_intelligence_transitional_democracy .pdf.
17. "October 12 Coup, Bugti's murder."
18. Claude Arpi, "Busharraf of Pakistan," Rediff India Abroad, November 15, 2007; and Ali, *The Duel*, 148.
19. Robert Spencer, "Musharraf, You're No Churchill," *FrontPageMagazine.com*, July 7, 2004.
20. James C. Humes, *The Wit & Wisdom of Winston Churchill* (New York: Harper-Collins, 2004, 2005), 16.
21. In this category, career military officers do not include guerrilla leaders who led popular revolutions, politicians with a service record, intelligence agents like

Vladimir Putin, or military personnel who managed to impose a repressive dictatorship by maintaining in power through armed might, even if first elected. In the United States, Senator John McCain merits note. He qualifies as a highly successful political leader and had a valiant record over the course of two decades in the U.S. Navy. Since 1983, his career has been in politics, as a congressman and then as a senator. Israelis would probably argue that Ariel Sharon makes the list. Israel has produced great leaders. He wasn't one of them.

22. Jones, *Pakistan: Eye of the Storm*, 1st ed., 119–23.
23. Mir, *The True Face of Jehadis*, 239–40.

CHAPTER 17. THE CAMPAIGN OF INFLUENCE

1. See Kamran Haider, "Pakistani Vote Authorities Face Wave of Complaints," Reuters, December 24, 2007; Raja Asghar, "Level Playing Far Afield," *Dawn,* December 24, 2007; Mohammad Waseem, "January 8 Elections Will Be a Meaningless Exercise in Voting," *Dawn,* December 25, 2007; "PML-Q Candidates Harassing Opponents," *Daily Times,* December 25, 2007; "HRCP Doesn't See Polls Leading to Democracy," *Worldnews.com,* December 25, 2007; "PPP Accuses Punjab Government of Forming Body to Rig Elections," *Daily Times,* December 25, 2007; "Modus Operandi of Rigging in Pakistan," *ANI,* December 24, 2007; Amnesty International, press release, "Amnesty USA Letter to Secretary Rice, on Pakistan," December 25, 2007; "US Warned over Pakistan Elections," *BBC News,* December 14, 2007; "Pakistan's Bhutto Accuses Spy Agency of Pressuring Election Candidates," VOANews.com, December 20, 2007; and "Pakistan Elections: PPP Says Candidates Threatened, Abused," *Merinews,* December 17, 2007.
2. Abbas, *Pakistan's Drift into Extremism,* 199–200.
3. "Musharraf Agrees to Scotland Yard Help in Probe," *Dawn,* January 3, 2008.
4. "Three Days' Mourning Declared," *The News,* December 28, 2007. The PPP declared a mourning period of forty days: "PPP Announces 40-Day Mourning," *The News,* December 28, 2007.
5. She did so on numerous occasions. In a book that in good measure restates the "Report of the United Nations Inquiry into the Facts and Circumstances of the Assassination of Former Pakistani Prime Minister Mohtarma Benazir Bhutto," Amir Mir recounts a long interview with Benazir that is heavily devoted to pointing a finger at him. See Amir Mir, *The Bhutto Murder Trail: From Waziristan to GHQ* (Chennai, India: Tranquebar Press, 2010), 23. She had raised suspicions about many different individuals. She had plenty of enemies along with her legions of friends. Significantly, she ignored apparent counsel from Musharraf's trusted confidant and ISI chief Lt. Gen. Nadeem Taj to stay away from Liaquat Bagh on the day of her assassination. Why would Musharraf or Taj warn her if they intended foul play? And if she believed Musharraf wanted to kill her, why did she go to the rally? The circle is hard to square. Could she have been using the journalist to do what most journalists would do—go ask Musharraf or his close colleagues if her suspicions were well founded as a way of strategically communicating that people were watching him and he needed to avoid engaging in any foul play?

6. International Republican Institute, "IRI Index: Pakistan Public Opinion Survey, January 19–29, 2008," released February 11, 2008, http://www.iri.org/sites/default/files/2008-February-11-Survey-of-Pakistan-Public-Opinion-January-19-29-2008.pdf. The poll includes the four major provinces but did not include FATA, Chitral, or Kohistan. That sample biases the anti-Taliban and Al Qaeda responses slightly but does not alter the overall national picture.

7. Iftikhar A. Khan, "President Orders Crackdown on Rioters, Arsonists," *Dawn*, December 29, 2007.

8. Mobarik A. Virk, "Govt Ready to Exhume Benazir's Body: Cheema," *The News*, December 30, 2009.

9. Shakil Shaikh, "No Decision on Poll Postponement Yet, Says Soomro," *The News,* December 29, 2007.

10. A U.S. Predator strike killed Mehsud in August 2009.

11. Adrian Levy, "On the Trail of Pakistan's Taliban," *Guardian*, January 10, 2009.

12. See, e.g., Sami Yousafzai, "Al Qaeda's Newest Triggerman," *Newsweek*, January 5, 2008.

13. See, e.g., Nic Robertson, "Pakistan: Taliban Buying Children for Suicide Attacks," CNN, July 7, 2009. While this story is from 2009, recruiting children from madrassas for suicide attacks took place in 2007.

14. Anwar Iqbal, "CJ's Sacking Was Mistake, Admits Musharraf," *Dawn.com*, October 10, 2009.

15. Jeremy Page, "The Benazir Bhutto Dossier: 'Secret Service Was Diverting US Aid for Fighting Militants to Rig the Elections,'" *Times*, January 1, 2008.

16. The PPP provided the report to both officials. Congressman Kennedy's office provided it to this author.

17. Page, "The Benazir Bhutto Dossier."

18. Hussain, in interview with author.

19. "Agencies Didn't Order Cover-up: President," *Dawn*, January 4, 2008; and "Musharraf Seems in Control, for Now," *Dawn*, January 7, 2008.

20. See Wolf Blitzer, "Bhutto from the Grave: Blame Musharraf," *The Situation Room,* December 27, 2007, http://www.youtube.com/watch?v=kOko7DgBI_c.

21. Ashraf Mumtaz, "Presidency Dismisses BB's Email," *Dawn*, December 30, 2007.

22. Khaleeq Kiani, "Musharraf Assures Rice on Democracy," *Dawn*, January 24, 2008.

23. "President, PM Discuss Law & Order Situation," *Dawn*, January 2, 2008.

24. "President, PM Call for Promoting Spirit of Unity," *Dawn*, January 11, 2008.

25. Pervez Musharraf, interview with Fareed Zakaria on CNN, January 8, 2008, http://ourleadermusharraf.wordpress.com/2008/01/08/musharraf-with-fareed-zakaria-cnn/.

26. The interview was off the record, or not for attribution, because the employer's rules prohibit on-the-record interviews without going through a complicated process of approval.

27. "Inquiry into Benazir Bhutto's Assassination Ordered," *Dawn*, December 28, 2007.

28. Shaikh, "No Decision on Poll Postponement Yet."

29. Syed Irfan Raza, "Suspects in BB's Letter May Come under Probe," *Dawn*, January 9, 2008.

30. Rauf Klasra, "Democracy Is the Best Revenge," *The News*, December 31, 2007.

31. "PPP Rejects Move to Seek Scotland Yard Help, Demands UN Probe," Rediff India Abroad, January 4, 2008.

32. Klasra, "Democracy Is the Best Revenge."

33. "PPP Rejects Scotland Yard Report," *The News,* February 9, 2008; Nksagar, "PPP Unsatisfied with Scotland Yard Report," *Thaindian.com*, February 9, 2008; and Kalsoom, "Disputes from Scotland Yard Investigation Released; PPP Disputes Findings," *ChangingUpPakistan*, February 8, 2008, http://changinguppakistan .wordpress.com/2008/02/08/results-from-scotland-yard-investigation-released-ppp-disputes-findings/.

34. The secretary-general appointed Ambassador Heraldo Muñoz, the permanent representative of Chile to the United Nations, to head the commission with Marzuki Darusman, former attorney general of Indonesia, and Peter FitzGerald, a former deputy commissioner of the Irish Police (Garda Siochana). The commission commenced its investigation on July 1, 2009, and provided its report to the secretary-general on March 30, 2010. It was released on April 15, 2010.

35. "Hillary Demands International Probe into Benazir's Murder," *The News*, December 29, 2007.

36. Id.

37. "Pakistan Bar Council Wants Ex-CJ to Probe Bhutto's Murder," *Indiaexpress .com*, January 2, 2009.

38. Nawaz, *Crossed Swords,* 532.

39. Nawaz, in interview with author.

40. "Punjab Govt Offers Rs5m Reward," *Dawn*, January 1, 2008.

41. Irshad, "Who Assassinated Benazir Bhutto?"

42. Larisa Alexandrovna, "US Intelligence Suggests Coverup in Bhutto Assassination," *The RawStory.com*, January 7, 2008.

43. Mobarik A. Virk, "Mehsud Behind Benazir's Assassination: Spokesman," *The News* December 29, 2007.

44. The government used the word "sunroof," but Scotland Yard characterized the opening in the roof as an escape hatch and not a sunroof.

45. Alexandrovna, "US Intelligence Suggests Coverup."

46. Id.

47. Shaheen Sehbai, "Caretaker Govt Apologizes for Interior Ministry's Blunder," *The News,* January 1, 2008.

48. Pew Research Center, "The Great Divide."

49. International Republican Institute, "IRI Index: Pakistan Public Opinion Survey, March 7–30, 2009," released May 11, 2009, http://www.iri.org/sites/default/ files/2009-News-Release-Files/2009%20May%2011%20Survey%20of%20 Pakistan%20Public%20Opinion,%20March%207-30,%202009.pdf.

50. Pew Research Center, "Global Unease with Major World Powers: A 47-Nation Pew Global Attitudes Survey," Pew Global Attitudes Project, released June 27, 2007.

51. International Republican Institute, "IRI Index: Pakistan Public Opinion Survey, July 15–August 7, 2009," released October 1, 2009, http://www.iri.org/

sites/default/files/2009%20October%201%20Survey%20of%20Pakistan%20
Public%20Opinion,%20July%2015-August%207,%202009.pdf.

52. Andrew Kohut and Bruce Stokes, *America Against the World* (New York: Times Books, 2006), 47. Protecting against terrorist attacks ranked first. Kohut is the director of the Pew Research Center for the People and the Press, and the book assimilates findings in surveys conducted between 2002 and 2005.

53. Id.

54. "Retired Generals, Officers of Other Ranks Urge Musharraf to Step Down," *Dawn*, January 23, 2008. Not all of the officers whose names appeared on the resolution for Musharraf to resign actually attended the meeting, and their support for it was questionable. That list included former ISI chief Lt. Gen. Javed Ashraf Qazi, who had been a key aide of Musharraf's and a minister in his government.

55. Syed Irfan Raza, "Musharraf's 'Safe Exit' Deal Confirmed by Zardari," *Dawn*, September 15, 2009. In October 2009, the Pakistan Supreme Court held that Musharraf was guilty of treason, and it's not clear that he can safely return.

56. The United States bears some responsibility for what was taught in madrassas. Jihadi groups were favored in the 1980s to defeat the "godless communists." For example, manuals taught the mujahideen to place bombs under dining tables at Kabul University. Many manuals, written by Americans, were written and produced at the University of Nebraska in Omaha. See Ali, *The Duel*, 130. Later, an effort was made to rewrite the manuals, but the damage was done.

57. Rashid, *Descent into Chaos*, 155.

58. Raman, "Pakistan's Inter-Services Intelligence."

59. B. Raman, "Musharraf vs. Lt. Gen. Mohammed Aziz," South Asia Analysis Group, Paper no. 298, August 20, 2001.

60. See, e.g., Rashid, *Descent into Chaos*, which analyses Musharraf's posture on fighting militants at length; Mir, *The True Face of Jehadis*, chapters 1, 17, and 20; Afzal Khan, "Pakistan: Uncertain Ally in the War on Terror," Jamestown Foundation, *Terrorism Monitor* 2, no. 17 (March 10, 2005); Irfan Husain, "Pervez Musharraf, the Commando Who Couldn't," *Open Democracy*, August 19, 2008; and Tony Karon, "Why Musharraf Failed," *Time*, August 19, 2008.

61. Rashid, *Descent into Chaos*, 221–22.

62. See, e.g., Isambard Wilkinson, "Benazir Bhutto Charges 'to Be Dropped,'" *Telegraph*, August 30, 2007.

63. National Reconciliation Ordinance (NRO-2007), promulgated by the President of Pakistan exercising his powers conferred by clause (1) of Article 89 of the Constitution, and amending the Criminal Procedure Code (CrPC-1898), the Representation of the People Act of 1976, and the National Accountability Bureau Ordinance (NAB-1999).

64. Elisabeth Bumiller, "How Bhutto Won Washington," *New York Times*, December 2007.

65. Obviously one has to be a U.S. citizen to run for the Senate, but with Benazir's style and charisma, she would have been a formidable candidate for the office.

66. The *New York Times* had done a brutal exposé that offered plenty of ammunition. See Burns, "Bhutto Clan Leaves Trail of Corruption."

67. Shakeel Anjum, "Bullet Wounds Confirmed," *The News*, January 4, 2007.
68. Privately provided information by a well-placed source.
69. Perlez, "New Questions Arise in Killing."
70. Ansar Abbasi, "Pindi Police Chief Did Not Agree to Benazir's Autopsy," *The News*, December 30, 2007.
71. Emily Wax and Griff Witte, "Doctors Cite Pressure to Keep Silent on Bhutto," *Washington Post*, January 1, 2008. See also Laura King, "Little Done in Bhutto Investigation," *Los Angeles Times*, July 4, 2008. King points out that even though Benazir's husband, Asif Ali Zardari, was now president, "doctors who attended to Bhutto on the night she was killed also have been ordered to remain silent— restrictions put in place by the previous government loyal to President Pervez Musharraf."
72. Sigamony, "No Shrapnel or Bullet Found."
73. "Report of the United Nations Commission of Inquiry," 37.
74. "Bhutto Examination OK, Pakistan Official Says," *CNN*, December 29, 2007, http://articles.cnn.com/2007-12-29/world/bhutto.death_1_pakistan-peoples-party-benazir-bhutto-bullet-wounds?_s=PM:WORLD.
75. Sigamony, "No Shrapnel or Bullet Found."
76. Mir, *The Bhutto Murder Trail*, 72–74.
77. "Bhutto Examination OK, Pakistan Official Says," *CNN*; Mir, *The Bhutto Murder Trail*, 75.
78. "Report of the United Nations Commission of Inquiry," 28.
79. Channel 4, "Benazir Assassination Channel 4 Video." See also "New Controversy over Circumstances of Benazir's Death," *The News*, January 1, 2008.
80. "Scotland Yard Report into Assassination of Benazir Bhutto Released: Press Release IP-455," CNN, February 8, 2008, http://www.cnn.com/2008/WORLD/asiapcf/02/08/bhutto.report/index.html. The report excluded the possibility of a wound to her mid or lower trunk, as that part of her body was inside the vehicle. The report did not exclude the possibility of a gunshot wound to the upper trunk or neck, although it discounts that possibility.
81. Perlez, "New Questions Arise in Killing." The reporter quotes Wajahat Latif, a former senior Pakistani police official who headed the Federal Investigative Agency in the early 1990s about the legal requirement. In fairness to the government, Asif Ali Zardari told a news conference that he had declined a request for a postmortem examination.
82. Id.
83. Lawrence K. Altman, "U.S. Experts Criticize Bhutto Post-Mortem," *New York Times*, December 31, 2007. New York City chief medical examiner Dr. Michael M. Baden pointed out that "with [John F.] Kennedy, the treating doctors were wrong about the entrance and exit wounds" of the bullet-damaged skull. Baden chaired the forensic pathology panel of the U.S. House of Representatives Select Committees on the assassinations of Kennedy and the Reverend Dr. Martin Luther King, Jr.
84. "Report of the United Nations Commission of Inquiry," 36.
85. Omar Waraich, "Scotland Yard's History of Assisting Pakistan in Times of National Crisis," *Independent*, January 3, 2008.

86. Mazhar Zaidi, "Scotland Yard's Pakistan Casebook," *BBC Urdu Service*, January 3, 2008.

87. Shuja Nawaz, "Will We Ever Know Who Killed Benazir Bhutto?," *Huffington Post*, January 4, 2008.

88. Nawaz, "Will We Ever Know?"

89. Zaidi, "Scotland Yard's Pakistan Casebook."

90. Shakil Shaikh, "Scotland Yard to Probe Benazir's Murder: Musharraf," *The News*, January 3, 2008.

91. Ihtasham ul Haque, "Musharraf Asks UK Team to Get to 'Bottom': BB's Assassination," *Dawn*, January 9, 2008.

92. British High Commission, press release, "Benazir Bhutto Investigation: Working Arrangements between Scotland Yard Team and Pakistani Authorities," January 11, 2008.

93. That finding did not mean the assailant acted unaided.

94. Arthur Bright, "Scotland Yard: Bhutto Killed by Bomb, Not Bullet," *Guardian*, February 8, 2008, quoting UK Home Office pathologist Nathaniel Cary; and the *Wall Street Journal*'s reprint of "Scotland Yard Statement on Bhutto Report."

95. Syed Irfan Raza and Muhammad Asghar, "Questions Raised over Scotland Yard Report: 'Benazir Killed by Bomb, Not Bullet,'" *Dawn*, February 9, 2008. Regarding the physicians, see, e.g., Baqir Sajjad Syed, "Medical Report Fraught with Lacunae: Experts," *Dawn*, January 6, 2008. A senior medical-legal expert, Dr. Zaman Niazi opined that the hospital's medical report contained "alarming technical lapses" and was "prima facie a case of foul play."

96. Raza and Asghar, "Questions over Scotland Yard Report."

97. Wax and Witte, "Doctors Cite Pressure to Keep Silent."

98. "Report of the United Nations Commission of Inquiry," 45.

99. Id., 46.

100. Salman Masood, "Police Officials Suspended in Pakistan over Battle with Lawyers," *New York Times*, October 2, 2007; Salman Masood, "Violence Puts More Pressure on Musharraf," *New York Times*, May 14, 2007; and Somini Sengupta, "Musharraf Finds Himself Weakened after Firing of Judge Stirs Anger in Pakistan," *New York Times*, March 25, 2007.

101. "Violent Crackdown on Pakistan Protests," Associated Press/MSNBC.com, November 5, 2007.

102. "Judge Chaudhry Calls for a Popular 'Uprising,'" *AsiaNews.it*, November 6, 2007.

103. "Violent Crackdown on Pakistan Protests."

104. David Rohde, "Closely Watched, Bhutto Is Allowed to Move," *New York Times*, November 11, 2007.

105. Sethi, "News Analysis: Who Killed Benazir Bhutto?" Sethi describes the gun as "30-bore," probably meaning .30-caliber. An earlier report identified the gun as a Kalashnikov. A second report stated that the gun was a 9mm and suggested that someone who could land so many shots from thirty feet away had to have been trained by the military or intelligence agencies. See M. A. U., "Who Killed Benazir?," *Guardian*, December 29, 2007. Former ISI chief Lt. Gen. Hamid Gul (Ret.) admired the planning and offered a third theory, which made him sound like a man who knew too much. He described the shots, defined their effect,

and attributed Benazir's death to a sharpshooter. See Azhar Masood, "Benazir Bhutto Was Assassinated by a Professional Sharp Shooter: Hamid Gul," *Pakistan Times*, April 16, 2008. In a separate interview, Gul—fiercely anti-American—predictably accused the United States of killing Benazir, out of fear that she was too independent and was going to violate her agreement to form a coalition government with Musharraf. "Alex Jones Interviews Lt. Gen. Hamid Gul—Full Transcript," PrisonPlanet, December 12, 2008.

106. "Agencies Didn't Order Cover-up."
107. The Sindh government did a report on what happened on October 18 but did not include who was involved. See "Benazir Was Target of Suicide Bombers: Pak Report," *Indian News*, November 30, 2007.
108. Bhutto, *Reconciliation*, 221–22; and B. Raman, "Benazir Bhutto's Assassination Case in Cold Storage," *International Terrorism Monitor*, Paper no. 403, South Asia Analysis Group, June 23, 2008.
109. "Report of the United Nations Commission of Inquiry," 32–33.
110. Wax and Witte, "Doctors Cite Pressure to Keep Silent."
111. Schmidle, *To Live or to Perish Forever*, 211, quoting the *New Republic*.
112. "Report of the United Nations Commission of Inquiry," 30–35.
113. "Report of the United Nations Commission of Inquiry," 32.
114. Id., 25.
115. As previously mentioned, Mehsud was killed in 2009 by a Predator strike.
116. Rahimullah Yusufzai, "A Who's Who of the Insurgency in Pakistan's North-West Frontier Province: Part One—North and South Waziristan," Jamestown Foundation, *Terrorism Monitor*, September 22, 2008. See also Hassan Abbas, "A Profile of Tehrik-i-Taliban," *CTC Sentinel*, January, 2008.
117. Virk, "Govt Ready to Exhume Benazir's Body."
118. Syed Irfan Raza, "Govt Uploads Recording of Suspect's Call," *Dawn*, December 31, 2007.
119. Virk, "Mehsud Behind Benazir's Assassination."
120. "Text of Alleged al-Qa'eda Phone Call," *Daily Telegraph*, December 28, 2007, http://www.telegraph.co.uk/news/worldnews/1573885/Text-of-alleged-al-Qaeda-phone-call.html.
121. Syed Irfan Raza, "Govt Gives New Twist to Probe: Al Qaeda Blamed for Killing," *Dawn*, December 29, 2007.
122. "Al Qaeda Assassinated Benazir: Report," *Dawn*, January 14, 2008.
123. See also Delawar Jan, "Intercepting the Taliban," *The News*, July 18, 2009.
124. Mohammad Asghar, "Five Involved in Assassination," *Dawn*, February 14, 2008.
125. "'Solid Proof' Mehsud behind Benazir's Murder: Police," *PakTribune*, February 18, 2008.
126. See, e.g., Haass, "A Conversation with Benazir Bhutto." She deplored her prior support for the Afghan Taliban, whose formation she had strongly supported while prime minister.
127. "Al Qaeda Assassinated Benazir."
128. "Editorial: Baitullah, Ambassador Azizuddin and BB's Assassins," *Daily Times*, April 22, 2008. Right after Benazir's assassination, this publication took the position that Mehsud was involved.

129. Ansar Abbasi, "Are Our Agencies Far Better than Scotland Yard?," *The News*, February 9, 2008.
130. "Terrorism and Pakistan, Part 2," Dumb Looks Still Free, http://ajacksonian .blogspot.com/2007/12/terrorism-and-pakistan-part-2.html.
131. "Mumbai Attacks," *twitter.com*, November 27, 2008.
132. Masood and Gall, "Bhutto Assassination Ignites Disarray."
133. Rezaul H. Laskar, "Pak Police Charge Baitullah Mehsud with Bhutto's Assassination," *Press Trust of India*, March 2, 2008.
134. Ismail Khan and Carlotta Gall, "Pakistan Asserts It Is near Deal with Militants," *New York Times*, April 23, 2008. They did make a deal, which Mehsud promptly broke.
135. Pamela Constable, "Pakistan to Pursue Taliban Leader," *Washington Post*, June 15, 2009.
136. See King, "Little Done in Bhutto Investigation." She cited police sources who stated that they were ordered not to speak publicly about the case and that "those who financed the operation and recruited the assailants" remained at large.
137. Jane Perlez, "Taliban Leader Flaunts Power inside Pakistan," *New York Times*, June 2, 2008.
138. "Meshud's Father-in-law Killed by Taliban: Malik," *The News*, August 24, 2009.
139. Editorial, "Baitullah, Ambassador Azizuddin and BB's Assassins," *Daily Times*, April 22, 2008. The *Daily Times* is among those news outlets that accepted that Baitullah Mehsud was behind the assassination and rejected Meshud's denial, although the PPP leadership accepted it.
140. Asghar, "Five Involved in Assassination"; and Shakeel Anjum, "Gang of Five Killed Benazir: AIG Police," *The News*, February 14, 2008.
141. See: Ali, *The Duel*, 12; and Schmidle, *To Live or to Perish Forever*, chapter 8. One of the mosque's leaders, Abdul Rashid Ghazi, was close to Qari Saifullah Akhtar, and Benazir had fingered the latter for his role in the Karachi bombing. Id., 140.
142. "Benazir Bhutto Backs Decision to Storm Mosque," *Financial Express*, July 14, 2007; and Syed Manzar Abbas Zaidi, "A Profile of Baitullah Mehsud," *Long War Journal*, September 2008, 11, http://www.scribd.com/doc/6344793/Baitullah-Profile.
143. "Men Arrested in Bhutto Assassination Confessed to Helping Bomber: Police," *CBC News*, February 13, 2008.
144. Asghar, "Five Involved in Assassination."
145. "'Solid Proof' Mehsud behind Benazir's Murder."
146. "Pakistan Police Arrest Another Suspect in Bhutto Case," Reuters, February 15, 2008.
147. Asghar, "Five Involved in Assassination."
148. "Men Arrested in Bhutto Assassination Confessed." Gul was also accused of being involved in three other suicide bombings in Rawalpindi.
149. Raman, "Benazir Bhutto's Assassination in Cold Storage."
150. Omer Farooq Khan, "Baitullah Mehsud, the 'Bhutto Killer,'" *Times of India*, August 11, 2009. Khan notes that Mehsud took credit even for acts the FBI was satisfied he did not do, including the attack on a U.S. immigration assistance center in New York in April 2009.
151. Id.

152. "Mehsud Was Not Benazir's Enemy," *The Hindu*, December 30, 2007.
153. Mushtag Yusufzai and Javed Afridi, "Baitullah Denies Hand in Benazir's Assassination," *The News*, December 30, 2007.
154. Id.
155. Khan, "Baitullah Mehsud, the 'Bhutto Killer.'"
156. Interview with Safdar Abbasi, "Mehsud Did Not Kill Benazir Bhutto: Safdar Abbasi," *In Session* (TV talk show), August 12, 2009.
157. Afzal Khan, "Baitullah Mehsud: Scapegoat or Perpetrator in Benazir Bhutto's Assassination?," *Terrorism Monitor* 6, no. 5 (March 7, 2008).
158. "Officials: Al Qaeda Claims Responsibility for Bhutto Killing," CNN, December 28, 2007.
159. Bruce O. Riedel, interviewed by Bernard Gwertzman, "Riedel: Bhutto's Assassination 'Almost Certainly' Work of Al-Qaeda," *Council on Foreign Relations*, December 27, 2007, http://www.cfr.org/pakistan/riedel-bhuttos-assassination-almost-certainly-work-al-qaeda/p15133.
160. Joby Warrick, "CIA Places Blame for Bhutto Assassination," *Washington Post*, January 18, 2008.
161. "Mehsud Masterminded Benazir's Murder, Says Former Aide," *Taragana.com*, June 19, 2009, http://blog.taragana.com/n/mehsud-masterminded-benazirs-murder-says-former-aide-86540/.
162. Bill Roggio, "Al Qaeda Takes Credit for Bhutto Assassination," *Long War Journal*, December 27, 2007.
163. See, e.g., "Ambush in Mogadishu: Tapes & Transcripts," *Frontline*, directed by William Cran, November 1, 2001, http://www.pbs.org/wgbh/pages/frontline/shows/ambush/etc/script.html.
164. See, e.g., Mir, foreword, in Rana, *A to Z of Jehadi Organizations*; Ali, *The Duel*; Rashid, *Descent into Chaos*, which describes the relationship between the ISI and the Taliban extensively; and Mir, *The True Face of Jehadis*.
165. The source was the Italian independent news agency Adnkronos International, which said that Mustafa Abu Al-Yazid had called the agency to make the claim. See "Al Qaeda Claims Responsibility for Killing Bhutto," *Novinite.com*, December 28, 2007.
166. B. Raman, "Who Killed Benazir Bhutto?," *International Terrorism Monitor*, Paper no. 336, South Asia Analysis Group, December 31, 2007. He suspects the call was made to exacerbate tensions between Punajabis and Sindhis.
167. See "Powell: Saudi Terror Attack Has 'Earmarks of Al Qaeda,'" *Fox News*, May 13, 2003; and "Authorities Foil Two Attempts to Blow up Oil Facilities in Yemen," *USA Today*, September 15, 2006.
168. See, e.g., "Al Qaeda Claims Responsibility for Baghdad Carnage," Agence France-Presse, August 25, 2009.
169. "Breaking: Al Qaeda Claims Responsibility," Reuters, March 11, 2004. The claim of responsibility came in the form of a letter faxed to the London-based *Al-Quds al-Arabi* newspaper.
170. "Al Qaeda Claims Responsibility for Subway Attacks in Videotape Where London Bomber Issued Call to Arms," *Militant Islam Monitor.org*, September 2, 2005. This claim came on September 2 for a July 7 bombing. On July 22, a phantom Al Qaeda group calling itself the Abu Hafs al Masri Brigade also claimed

responsibility. See Paul Joseph Watson, "Another Phony al Qaeda Group Claims Responsibility for Latest London Bombings," *Sky News*, July 22, 2005.

171. "Review of Significant Terrorist Activity and Events—November 2005," *Insite Advanced Security Management* (newsletter), November 2005.

172. "Al-Qaeda Confirms Responsibility for Yemen Compound Attack—Summary," *Earthtimes.com*, April 8, 2008.

173. Hussein al Jirbani, "Al Qaeda Claims Responsibility for Failed Attack on US Embassy," *Asharq Alawsat*, March 25, 2008.

174. "Al Qaeda Claims Responsibility for Rocket Launches into Israel from Lebanon," *Menassat*, July 28, 2009.

175. Bill Roggio, "Al Qaeda Offensive on the Arabian Peninsula," *Long War Journal*, February 25, 2006.

176. Nick Grace, "Al Qaeda Claims Responsibility for Algiers Attacks," *Threats Watch*, December 11, 2007.

177. "Al Qaeda Claims Responsibility for Attack on Danish Embassy in Pakistan," *Middle East Media Research Institute*, June 5, 2008. It took credit on June 4.

178. "Al-Qaeda Claims Responsibility for Latest Attack on Algerian Army," *Magharebia*, August 2, 2008.

179. Caroline Faraj and Raja Razek, "Al Qaeda Claims Responsibility for Attempt on Saudi Prince," CNN, August 30, 2009.

180. Mullick and Yusuf, *Pakistan*, 38. They observe on page 39 that Pakistan's lack of transparency has helped spawn the culture of conspiracy and "fed into a culture of denial about the internality and actuality of the problems that Pakistan faces. In this vein, there has been a tendency to dismiss Jihadist terrorism and Islamist extremism as an import from the United States."

181. Pew Research Center, "The Great Divide." As noted in chapter 3, the margin was 41 percent to 15 percent. That was about the same number for British Muslims, who include many Pakistanis. Fully 56 percent of that group said Arabs hadn't carried out 9/11, compared to 17 percent who said Arabs had done so.

182. Obaid-Chinoy, "Pakistan," quoted by Mullick and Yusuf, *Pakistan*, 40.

183. Masood, "Benazir Bhutto Was Assassinated by a Professional."

184. "Benazir Anticipated Long-range Rifle Shot: Qureshi," *Dawn*, January 4, 2008.

185. Syed Irfan Raza, "Jirgo Formed to Negotiate with Militants," *Dawn*, February 7, 2008; Rahimullah Yusufzai, "A Formidable Enemy," *Newsline*, July 6, 2009; and Mazhar Tufail, "Swat Taliban Getting Active Help from Baitullah," *The News*, May 1, 2009.

186. "Benazir's Assassination," *The News*, January 4, 2008.

187. "Who Killed Benazir Bhutto?," Associated Press, December 28, 2007.

188. "Retired Generals, Officers of Other Ranks."

189. Raman, "Bin Laden's Former Handling Officer."

190. Id.

191. B. Raman, "Benazir's Death: Army, ISI Keep Low Profile," *International Terrorism Monitor*, Paper no. 341, South Asia Analysis Group, January 1, 2008.

CHAPTER 18. THE FALLOUT

1. Paul Richter, "Questions Are Raised about Whether Islamabad—and Washington—Did Enough to Try to Protect Her," *Los Angles Times*, December 29, 2007.

2. Id.
3. Hamid Mir, "Musharraf Let Off the Hook in Benazir's Murder Probe," *Canada Free Press*, December 27, 2008, http://www.canadafreepress.com/index.php /article/7177.
4. "Report of the United Nations Commission of Inquiry," 15.
5. Anjum, "One Year On, Benazir's Murder."
6. Mir, "Musharraf Let Off the Hook in Benazir's Murder Probe."
7. Anjum, "One Year On, Benazir's Murder."
8. "Pakistan Sacks Chief of Powerful Spy Agency," *Radio Free Europe*, September 30, 2008; Bruce Loudon, "ISI Chief Urged to Quit as Battle Rages at Border," *The Australian*, September 29, 2008; and Karen DeYoung, "Pakistan Has New Head of Intelligence," *Washington Post*, October 1, 2008.
9. "Report of the United Nations Commission of Inquiry," 12.
10. B. Raman, "Benazir Bhutto's Assassination Case in Cold Storage," *International Terrorism Monitor, Paper No. 403, South Asia Analysis Group*, June 23, 2008.
11. Rauf Klasra, "PPP Asking Many Questions About Rehman Malik," *The News*, January 2, 2008.
12. "Report of the United Nations Commission of Inquiry," 12.
13. Id. See also Anjum, "One Year On, Benazir's Murder," which described Malik as the "security adviser to the former premier."
14. "Report of the United Nations Commission of Inquiry," 12.
15. Id.
16. Shamim-ur-Rahman, "Jammers Were Not Provided, Says Malik," *Dawn*, January 6, 2008.
17. "Report of the United Nations Commission of Inquiry," 18.
18. Id.
19. Id., 22.
20. Id.
21. Shamim-ur-Rahman, "Jammers Were Not Provided, Says Malik."
22. Id.
23. Klasra, "PPP Asking Many Questions About Rehman Malik."
24. Id.
25. "Report of the United Nations Commission of Inquiry," 25–26.
26. Shamim-ur-Rahman, "Jammers Were Not Provided, Says Malik."
27. "Report of the United Nations Commission of Inquiry," 20.
28. Saeed Shah, "Bhutto Report: Musharraf Planned To Fix Elections," *McClatchy*, December 31, 2007.
29. "ISI Is Being Wrongfully Defamed Internationally: Malik," *Dawn*, April 26, 2011.
30. "Nawaz Tried to Stop 2008 President Poll: Ex-ISI Official," *The News*, September 17, 2009.
31. Declan Walsh, "Pakistan's Ex-leader in Exile: Pervez Musharraf's Quiet New Life in London," *Guardian*, September 9, 2009.
32. Gretchen Peters, *Seeds of Terror: How Heroin is Bankrolling the Taliban and al Qaeda* (New York: St Martin's press, 2009), 64–65.
33. Ali, *The Duel*, 5.
34. See Hasnaat Malik, "Accusations against Chaudhries," *Daily Times*, March 5,

2011; "FIA Issues Arrest Warrants of Moonis Elahi," *Pakistan Observer*, January 29, 2011.

35. See, e.g., Press Release, "Pakistan–ICJ welcomes reinstatement of Chief Justice Chaudhry," *International National Commission of Jurists (ICJ)*, March 20, 2009, http://www.icj.org/IMG/Pakistan_PR_20_Mar_09_revised_3_.pdf; Nick Schifrin, "Pakistani Chief Justice Iftikhar Chaudhry Reinstated," *ABC News*, March 16, 2009;"Justice Iftikhar Chaudry to Be Restored as Chief Justice of Pakistan," *Geo TV,* March 16, 2009.

36. "Elections, Democracy and Stability in Pakistan," International Crisis Group, Asia Report no. 137, July 31, 2007, 9.

37. Klasra, "Benazir Defends Deal with Musharraf."

38. "Report of the United Nations Commission of Inquiry," 54–56.

39. Id., 63.

40. Id., 47.

41. Id., 62.

42. Id., 47–53.

43. Id., 53.

44. "Elections, Democracy and Stability in Pakistan," 14.

45. International Republican Institute, "IRI Index: Pakistan Public Opinion Survey," August 29–September 13, 2007"; and "IRI Index: Pakistan Public Opinion Survey, November 19–28, 2007. The wording of the questions differed, but the political implications of each were similar. The November survey showed significant geographical disparities. Musharraf fared better than Bhutto did only in Punjab, though he did worse than Nawaz Sharif. By November, Benazir enjoyed hugely higher positives on the question as to who could best handle the problems facing Pakistan in the Sindh and Baluchistan, though she trailed Nawaz in the NWFP.

46. B. Raman, "Pakistan Corps Commanders Oppose Deal with Benazir," South Asia Analysis Group, Paper no. 2454, November 13, 2007.

47. Reza Sayah and Saeed Ahmed, "Musharraf's Resignation Accepted," CNN, August 18, 2008.

48. Saeed Shah, "Pervez Musharraf Resigns as President of Pakistan," *Guardian*, August 18, 2008.

49. "President Pervez Musharraf Resigns: Timeline," *Daily Telegraph*, August 18, 2008.

CHAPTER 19. WHO KILLED BENAZIR?

1. Bhutto, *Daughter of Destiny*, 45.

2. Rashid, *Taliban*, 26, 184. Her interior minister during her second term, Naseerullah Babar, promoted the Taliban. Rashid reports that he wanted to free Afghan policy from the ISI, of whose power and resources he and Benazir were "deeply suspicious" (id., 184). Eventually the ISI, which been supporting the warlord Gulbuddin Hekmatyar, threw its weight behind the Taliban.

3. Haass, "A Conversation with Benazir Bhutto."

4. Rashid, in interview with author.

5. Peters, *Seeds of Terror*, 78.

6. See Zaidi, "A Profile of Baitullah Mehsud." Pakistani resentment over this issue was especially bitter in discussions over proposed U.S. aid restrictions. See Karen DeYoung and Scott Wilson, "Pakistanis Balk at U.S. Aid Package," *Washington Post*, October 8, 2009.

7. Zakaria, "I Know I Can Be Tough."

8. Rashid, in interview with author.

9. Thomas L. Friedman, "America vs. the Narrative," *New York Times*, November 28, 2009.

10. Siegel, in interview with author.

11. Bhutto, *Reconciliation*, 2.

12. Id., 307–8.

13. Id., 515.

14. See Jeffrey A. Dressler, "The Haqqani Network," *Institute for the Study of War*, October 2010, updated April 2011, http://www.understandingwar.org/files/ Haqqani_Network_Compressed.pdf. Dressler offers a comprehensive analysis of the network.

15. General Stanley A. McChrystal, "COMISAF's Initial Assessment," August 30, 2009, 2–5, http://media.washingtonpost.com/wp-srv/politics/documents/ Assessment_Redacted_092109.pdf; see also Anand Gopal, Mansur Khan Mahsud, and Brian Fishman, "The Haqqanis and al-Qaeda," *The Af-Pak Chiannel/ Foreign Policy/New America Foundation*, June 30, 2010.

16. Id. Al Qaeda's main role in the Haqqani network is to facilitate attacks and to provide suicide bombers. There is also some strain because while Al Qaeda has pledged to overthrow Pakistan's government, the Haqqanis maintain friendly ties to it.

17. Carlotta Gall, "Old-Line Taliban Commander Is Face of Rising Afghan Threat," *New York Times*, June 17, 2008.

18. Catherine Philip, "Pervez Musharraf Was Playing 'Double Game' With US," *London Sunday Times*, February 17, 2009.

19. Zakaria, interview with Pervez Musharraf.

20. Ben Arnoldy, "Why Admiral Mullen Is Talking Tough With Pakistan Over Haqqani Militants," *Christian Science Monitor*, April 21, 2011; Bill Roggio, "Pakistan's ISI Has a 'Relationship' With the Haqqani Network," *Long War Journal*, April 20, 2011.

21. Sreeram Chaulia, "Benazir's Assassination: A Tragedy Foretold," *BoloJI.com*, December 28, 2007. The Lashkar-e-Jhangvi (LeJ) has strong links to the ISI.

22. B. Raman, "Benazir's Assassination: Q&A," *International Terrorism Monitor*, Paper no. 343, South Asia Analysis Group, January 2, 2008. Raman puts LeJ first among possibilities.

23. Mir, *The True Face of Jehadis,* 129.

24. Hussain, *Frontline Pakistan*, 94.

25. Mir, *The True Face of Jehadis,* 45.

26. Mir, "foreword," in Rana, *A to Z of Jehadi Organizations*, 21, 24.

27. She discussed this suspicion in an Al Jazeera television interview with David Frost, *Frost Over the World*, November 2, 2007, http://www.youtube.com/ watch?v=UnychOXj9Tg. Here, she asserted that Osama bin Laden had been killed by Ahmad Omar Saeed Sheikh. She may have misspoken and meant

that he was involved in Daniel Pearl's death. See also: Mir, "Baitullah Made a Scapegoat?" The piece was based on his book, *The Fluttering Flag of Jehad*. Mir questions as well the involvement of Qari Saifullah Akhtar, the amir of the ISI-linked Harkat ul-Jihad-al-Islami (HUJI). Mir had also interviewed Benazir in November 2007. She named Shah as a principal suspect in the failed attempt to kill her in Karachi on October 18, 2007, a few hours after her return home from exile. Although any link between the release of Qari Saifullah Akhtar and the murder of Bhutto remains uncertain, Mir says, some PPP officials have asked how and why, shortly before Benazir's homecoming, intelligence agencies had set free an Al Qaeda–linked, dreaded terrorist. Associated with the Taliban militia, he had been deported from the United Arab Emirates on charges of masterminding the December 2003 suicide attacks on Musharraf in the garrison town of Rawalpindi, after keeping him behind bars for three years. See also Amir Mir, "Who Killed Benazir Bhutto?," *The News*, December 27, 2007, http://jang .com.pk/thenews/dec2008-weekly/nos-28-12-2008/spr.htm#2. Mir's comments are excerpted from *The Fluttering Flag of Jihad*, in which he also quotes Bhutto as saying that Musharraf was secretly in league with HUJI as well as Abdul Rehman Otho of LeJ. Mir told *OutlookIndia:* "Benazir told me, 'I have come to know after investigations by my own sources that the October 18 bombing was masterminded by some highly-placed officials in the Pakistani security and intelligence establishments who had hired an Al Qaeda-linked militant—Maulvi Abdul Rehman Otho alias Abdul Rehman Sindhi—to execute the attack.' She said three local militants were hired to carry out the attack under the supervision of Abdul Rehman Sindhi, an Al Qaeda-linked Lashkar-e-Jhangvi (LeJ) militant from the Dadu district of Sindh." Quoted by the Pakistani blog *Watandost* on *StrategyTalk.org, December 30, 2007*, http://www.strategytalk.org/phpBB2/ viewtopic.php?p=60186&sid=f31354f12936f9f61c3b444f54285588.

28. See Bhutto's interview with David Frost, http://www.youtube.com/watch?v =oIO8B6fpFSQ.

29. Freeman, "Benazir Bhutto Takes on a Powerful Enemy." Freeman was focused on the ISI, but his reporting also applied to the IB.

30. Ahmar Mustikhan, "Bhutto Blamed Ejaz Shah for Plots to Kill Her," *Newsvine*, June 29, 2009. Bin Laden was Benazir's sworn enemy, primarily for ideological reasons. He did not believe that a woman should lead a Muslim nation. He apparently offered huge sums of money to oust Bhutto during her 1988–1990 tenure as prime minister.

31. Mir, *The True Face of Jehadis*, chapter 12. Mir details Ibrahim's past and connections within Pakistan.

32. Hamid Mir, "Why Benazir Points Finger at IB Chief," *The News*, October 20, 2007.

33. Hussain, *Frontline Pakistan*, 125.

34. Mir, *The True Face of Jehadis*, 236; Hussain, *Frontline Pakistan*, 125–26.

35. Ilyas Mehraj, "Threatened," *Weekly Independent*, March 10, 2003.

36. Amir Mir, "Daniel Pearl Killer Dodging Death for Six Years," *Middle East Transparent*, November 11, 2008, http://www.middleeasttransparent.com/spip .php?article4820.

37. Mir, *The True Face of Jehadis*, 36.

38. Robert Sam Anson, "The Journalist and the Terrorist," *Vanity Fair*, August 2002.
39. Id.; and Paul Sperry, "Did Ally Pakistan Play Role in 9-11?," *WorldNetDaily*, January 30, 2002.
40. "ISI Chief Asked to Quit: Had Links with IA Plane Hijacker," *Press Trust of India*, October 8, 2001.
41. B. Raman, "Osama's Handling Officer Was in Charge of Benazir's Security," Rediff India Abroad, October 19, 2007.
42. Id.
43. Mir, "Why Benazir Points Finger at IB Chief"; and Shaan Akbar, "Investigatory Findings into the Bhutto Shootings," *Insider Brief*, October 21, 2007, http://www.pakintel.com/2007/10/21/investigatory-findings-into-the-bhutto-bombings/.
44. Raman, "Benazir's Death."
45. Nicholas D. Kristof, "A Heroine Walking in the Shadow of Death," *New York Times*, April 4, 2006.
46. "Former IB Chief Leaves for Australia," *Daily Times*, April 29, 2008. See also Zubair Kasuri, "Brig Ejaz Shah Moves to Australia," *The News*, May 19, 2008.
47. "Ex-ISI Chief Hamid Gul Says Benazir Implicated Him in Karachi Blasts on US' Direction," ANI, October 18, 2008, available at *NewstrackIndia.com*, http://www.newstrackindia.com/newsdetails/29161.
48. "Undercover Chaos—Role of Pakistani Armed Forces Intelligence Agencies in Domestic Arena," *Defence Journal*, December, 2005.
49. Mir, *The True Face of Jehadis*, 2.
50. "Interview with Hamid Gul," by Arnaud de Borchgrave, *Newsweek Web Exclusive*, September 14, 2001, http://www.twf.org/News/Y2001/0914-Gul911.html.
51. Arnaud de Borchgrave, "Report: Pakistan's ISI 'Fully Involved' in 9/11," *Newsmax.com*, August 3, 2004; and Arnaud de Borchgrave, in interview with author.
52. De Borchgrave, in interview with author.
53. Hussain, *Frontline Pakistan*, 21–24, 80.
54. Rashid, *Descent into Chaos*, 222; and Simon Robinson, "Bhutto Conspiracy Theories Fill the Air," *Time*, December 28, 2007. See also Mir, *The True Face of Jehadis*, chapter 1. Mir's research details connections between extremists and Pakistani intelligence.
55. "Hamid Gul & LeT's Chachu May Get Official Terrorist Tag," *Economic Times*, December 6, 2008, http://www1.economictimes.indiatimes.com/PoliticsNation/Hamid_Gul__LeTs_Chachu_may_get_official_terrorist_tag/articleshow/3799024.cms.
56. A highly placed Pakistani source, in interview with author.
57. Levy and Scott Clark, *Deception*, 227, in their interview with Gul. Gul had been the choice of another Islamist, former COAS Gen. Mirza Aslam, to succeed him. Critics consider Nawaz mediocre and corrupt, but he was savvy enough to find a way to keep that from happening.
58. Tirmazi, *Profiles of Intelligence*, 358. Tirmazi was critical of what Gul had done in politicizing the ISI.
59. See Frédéric Grare, Reforming the Intelligence Agencies in Pakistan's Transitional Democracy (Washington, DC: Carnegie Endowment for International Peace, 2009), 24.

60. Id., 37.
61. Her first autobiography, *Daughter of Destiny*, opens with her bitter, emotional memory of her father's execution and Zia's brutal treatment of Benazir and her mother. No human being subjected to that experience would forgive the behavior of Zia or his close allies.
62. De Borchgrave, "Ex-Prime Minister Benazir Bhutto Targeted."
63. "Alex Jones Interviews Lt. Gen. Hamid Gul." It is apparent that Gul also thinks that 9/11 was an American fabrication.
64. "ATC Issues Arrest Warrant for Musharraf," *Dawn.com*, February 12, 2011.
65. Declan Walsh, "Pakistan Court Issues Arrest Warrant Against Musharraf," *Guardian*, February 12, 2011.

CHAPTER 20. THE AFTERMATH

1. "LHC Moved for Case against Musharraf on Benazir's Murder," *Pak Tribune*, August 29, 2009, http://www.paktribune.com/news/index.shtml?218644.
2. See, e.g., Syed Irfan Raza, "NRO Case: Govt Ready to Defend President's Position, in SC," *Dawn*, April 6, 2012, http://www.dawn.com/2011/04/06/nro-case-govt-ready-to-defend-presidents-position-in-sc.html; "Pakistan Throws Out NRO Corruption Amnesty Putting Zardari Allies in Firing Line," *Telegraph*, December 16, 2009, http://www.telegraph.co.uk/news/worldnews/asia/pakistan/6828254/Pakistan-throws-out-NRO-corruption-amnesty-putting-Zardari-allies-in-firing-line.html; and "Pak SC Indicates It Could Summon PM in NRO Case," *IBNlive*, April 19, 2011, http://ibnlive.in.com/generalnewsfeed/news/pak-sc-indicates-it-could-summon-pm-in-nro-case/653480.html.
3. Walsh, "Pakistan's Ex-leader in Exile." The article points out that his flat is worth about $1.6 million. In London, that amount of money doesn't buy much.
4. "Musharraf Apologises for Mistakes, Launches Party," *Dawn.com*, October 2, 2010.

CHAPTER 21. QUO VADIS? WHERE TO?

1. Shuja Nawaz, in interview with author.
2. "Pakistan ISI Behind Mumbai Attacks: India Official," Reuters, July 14, 2010, http://www.reuters.com/article/2010/07/14/us-india-pakistan-idUSTRE66D11720100714.
3. "Mumbai Terror Attack: LeT's Tahawwur Rana Confirms Pakistan Government, ISI's 26/11 Role," *Economic Times*, April 13, 2011, http://articles.economictimes.indiatimes.com/2011-04-13/news/29413739_1_rana-and-headley-tahawwur-hussain-rana-isi.
4. See Rajeev Sharma, "Pakistan's Terror Wheel Comes to Full Circle in Karachi," South Asia Analysis Group, Paper no. 4080, October 6, 2010, http://www.southasiaanalysis.org/papers41/paper4080.html.
5. Eric Schmitt, Mark Mazzetti, and Jane Perlez, "Pakistan's Spies Aided Group Tied to Mumbai Siege," *New York Times*, December 7, 2008; see also "Pakistan 'Role' in Mumbai Attacks," *BBC News*, September 30, 2006, http://news.bbc.co.uk/2/hi/5394686.stm.
6. Mark Mazetti and Salman Masood, "Pakistani Role Is Suspected in Revealing U.S. Spy's Name," *New York Times*, December 17, 2010.

7. Sebastian Rotella, "David Headley, Witness in Terror Trial, Ties Pakistani Spy Agency to Militant Group," *Washington Post*, May 23, 2011; Ginger Thompson and David Rhode, "Chicago Trial May Unmask Pakistan's Links to Militants," *New York Times*, May 14, 2011; "Mumbai Attacks Witness Recounted Many Mundane Details, but Testimony May Fray US-Pakistan Ties," Associated Press, June 2, 2011; and Ginger Thompson, "Mumbai Plotter Testifies About Training," *New York Times*, May 25, 2011.

8. "Pakistan Democracy: An Interview with Husain Haqqani," *YaleGlobal OnLine*, October 15, 2008, http://yaleglobal.yale.edu/content/pakistan-democracy-interview-husain-haqqani.

9. "Terrorists not in Favour of Good Indo-Pak Ties: Haqqani," *The Nation*, April 10, 2011, http://www.nation.com.pk/pakistan-news-newspaper-daily-english-online/Politics/10-Apr-2011/Terrorists-not-in-favour-of-good-IndoPak-ties-Haqqani.

10. "Pakistani Envoy Details Government's Response to Mumbai Investigation," *PBS.org*, December 4, 2008, http://www.pbs.org/newshour/bb/asia/july-dec08/haqqani_12-04.html.

11. Off-the-record interview with the author.

12. Ben Arnoldy, "Why Admiral Mullen Is Talking Tough with Pakistan over Haqqani militants," *Christian Science Monitor*, April 22, 2011.

13. "U.S. to Send 85 Drones to Pakistan," Reuters/*Huffington Post*, April 21, 2011.

14. Yousaf and Adkin, *Afghanistan: The Bear Trap*, 96. One of the most striking points in Yousaf's account (see page 55) relevant to comparing the current Afghan conflict with the Soviet-Afghan war is his assessment of effective Soviet fighting strength. The Soviet Fortieth Army had more than 100,000 troops in or close to Afghanistan. On the surface, the numbers seem somewhat comparable to what the United States has poured into Afghanistan. Yousaf's analysis of the poorly provisioned and trained, mostly conscript Soviet army led him to conclude that no more than 10,000–12,000 Soviet troops inside the country could be committed to active operations at any one time.

15. Id., 86.

16. George Crile, *Charlie Wilson's War: The Extraordinary Story of How the Wildest Man in Congress and a Rogue CIA Agent Changed the History of Our Times* (New York: Grove Press, 2004), 351–52, 459.

17. Id., 218, 229, 230, 246, 419.

18. Yousaf and Adkin, *Afghanistan: The Bear Trap*, 86–87.

19. Id., 87.

20. Id., 89.

21. Id., 233.

22. See, e.g., Eric Schmitt, "New CIA Drone Attack Draws Rebuke from Pakistan," *New York Times*, April 13, 2011; "Drones Kill 19 on the First Day of 2011," *The Nation*, January 2, 2011, http://www.nation.com.pk/pakistan-news-newspaper-daily-english-online/Politics/02-Jan-2011/Drones-kill-19-on-first-day-of-2011; and Keith Jones, "Drone Attacks Trigger Fresh Crisis in US-Pakistani Relations," *World Socialist Web Site*, April 15, 2011, http://www.wsws.org/articles/2011/apr2011/dron-a15.shtml.

23. See, e.g., Salman Masood and Pir Zubair Shah, "CIA Drones Kill Civilians in Pakistan," *New York Times*, March 17, 2011; and "U.S. Military Chief Arrives in Pakistan for Talks," *RTT News*, April 20, 2011, http://www.rttnews.com /Content/GeneralNews.aspx?Node=B1&Id=1602064.

24. Schmitt, "New CIA Drone Attack Draws Rebuke from Pakistan."

25. Id.

26. Fahat Taj, "Drone Attacks—a Survey," *The News*, March 5, 2009.

27. Pew Research Center, "Concern about Extremist Threat Slips in Pakistan," Pew Global Attitudes Project, July 29, 2010, http://pewglobal.org/2010/07/29 /concern-about-extremist-threat-slips-in-pakistan/2/. Pew claims that the poll covered 84 percent of the adult population and claimed a 95 percent confidence that the error attributable to sampling and other random effects is plus or minus the margin of error, but one might challenge some of the poll's conclusions as skewed by its frame, despite weighting of data.

28. See Fishman, "The Battle for Pakistan."

29. Peter Bergen and Patrick C. Doherty of New American Foundation, and Ken Ballen of Terror Free Tomorrow, "Public Opinion in Pakistan's Tribal Regions," September 28, 2010, http://counterterrorism.newamerica.net/publications /policy/public_opinion_in_pakistan_s_tribal_regions.

30. Asim Yasin, "Politicians Assure Full Support to Army," *The News*, October 17, 2009; Comment, *The Nation*, October 18, 2009; and Rahimullah Yusufzai, "Waziristan—the Mother of All Battles," *The News*, October 20, 2009.

31. Irfan Burki and Daud Khattak, "Tough Fight on for Hakimullah Hometown," *The News*, October 22, 2009.

32. Muhammad Anis, Irfan Burki, and Daud Khattak, "COAS Urges Mehsuds to Stand Up against Militants," *The News*, October 20, 2009.

33. "Operation against Only a Handful of Terrorists: COAS," *The News*, October 26, 2009.

34. Arnaud de Borchgrave, "Army Back on Top," *Washington Times*, March 30, 2010.

35. "Zardari Says 17th Amendment to Go in December," *Dawn*, November 27, 2009.

36. "NA Passes 18th Amendment," *The News*, April 9, 2010.

37. "President Zardari Signs 18th Amendment Bill," *Dawn*, April 19, 2010.

38. "Parliament Is Sovereign Now: PM Gilani Vows to Take Opposition along to Resolve Problems; Praises Nawaz," *The News*, April 9, 2010.

39. Sabir Shah, "They Did It Yesterday, They Undid It Today," *The News*, April 9, 2010.

40. Asim Yasin, "Gilani Lauds Army for Not Impeding 18th Amendment," *The News*, April 10, 2010.

CHAPTER 22. RESETTING THE TERMS OF COOPERATION AMID PUBLIC PARANOIA

1. Mark Mazzetti, Ashley Parker, Jane Perez, and Eric Schmitt, "American Held in Pakistan Worked with CIA," *New York Times*, February 21, 2011. The *Times* and other American media had initially withheld identifying Davis as working for the CIA on a temporary basis. Later, the story reports, CIA officials "lifted the request to withhold publication."

2. Mazzetti, Parker, Perlez, and Schmitt, "American Held in Pakistan Worked with CIA"; Waqar Gillani and Jane Perlez, "American Charged in Pakistan Killing," *New York Times*, January 28, 2011.
3. Id.
4. Waqar Gillani and Jane Perlez, "American Charged in Pakistan Killing," *New York Times*, January 28, 2011.
5. Mazzetti, Parker, Perlez, and Schmitt, "American Held in Pakistan Worked with CIA."
6. Id.
7. Gillani and Perlez, "American Charged in Pakistan Killing."
8. Mazzetti, Parker, Perlez, and Schmitt, "American Held in Pakistan Worked with CIA."
9. Id. See also "Timeline: The Raymond Davis Case," *Dawn*, February 4, 2011; Rob Crilly, "Raymond Davis Incident: What Sort of Diplomat Carries a Loaded Gun?" *Telegraph*, February 1, 2011; and "U.S. Official Raymond Davis on Lahore Murder Charges," *BBC News*, January 28, 2011.
10. "Pics of Pak Defence Sites Found in Davis' Camera," *Times of India*, February 10, 2011, http://articles.timesofindia.indiatimes.com/2011-02-10/pakistan/28540867_1_digital-camera-defence-installations.
11. Declan Walsh, "Pakistan Frees CIA Spy Charged with Murder," *Guardian*, March 16, 2011; and Greg Miller and Shaiq Hussain, "CIA Contractor Raymond Davis Freed after 'Blood Money' Payment," *Washington Post*, March 16, 2011.
12. Mazzetti, Parker, Perlez, and Schmitt, "American Held in Pakistan Worked with CIA."
13. Id.
14. "Punjab Govt Mishandles Raymond Issue: Qureshi," *Online International News Network*, http://www.onlinenews.com.pk/details.php?id=175782.
15. Mohammad Malick, "It's not a Rumor, Americans did Get Qureshi's Scalp," *The News*, February 12, 2010, http://www.thenews.com.pk/TodaysPrintDetail.aspx?ID=3939&Cat=13&dt=2/12/2011. *The News*, whose tone is anti-American, alleged that the U.S. pressured Zardari to drop his foreign minister and that he did so after a meeting that included Gilani and Pasha.
16. Safar Hilaly, "The Rise and Fall of Shah Mahmood Qureshi," *Express Tribune*, February 19, 2011; Anwar Syed, "Analysis: The Case of Shah Mehmood Qureshi," *Daily Times*, March 1, 2011; and "Hina Rabbani Khar Appointed as Pakistan's Foreign Minister," *One India News*, June 24, 2011.
17. Ansar Abbasi, "Raymond Davis Case: The Lal Masjid of Present Govt," *The News*, February 9, 2011.
18. Id.
19. "CIA Spy Captured Giving Nuclear Bomb to Terrorists," *EU Times*, February 11, 2011.
20. Pervez Shaukat, "Jang Had Warned of Plot against Bhatti Twice," *The News*, March 3, 2011.
21. Raja Asghar, "Fazl [sic] Says Misuse of Blasphemy Law Can Be Discussed," *Dawn*, March 5, 2011.
22. Shakeel Anjum, "Shabaz Bhatti Silenced Forever," *The News*, March 3, 2011; Munawwer Zeem and Khawar Ghumman, "Terrorists Silence Another Voice of

Interfaith Harmony," *Dawn*, March 3, 2011; and Declan Walsh, "Shabaz Bhatti: Another Voice against Pakistan's Extremists Dies," *Guardian*, March 2, 2011.

23. Muhammed Saleh Zaafir, "PM Offers to Quit but Stopped by Colleagues," *The News*, March 3, 2011.

24. Karin Bruillard, "In Aftermath of Shooting, Rising Skepticism about American Presence in Pakistan," *Washington Post*, February 22, 2011.

25. Id.

26. Taj M. Khattak, "Beyond the Davis Affair," *The News*, February 26, 2011.

27. Abbasi, "Raymond Davis Case."

28. Sadiq Salim, "Last Visa of Raymond Davis Issued in Islamabad, not Washington," *The News*, February 3, 2011.

29. "Blackwater's Secret War in Pakistan?" *The News*, November 25, 2009; see also Jeremy Scahill, "The Secret U.S. War in Pakistan," *The Nation*, November 23, 2009, http://www.thenation.com/doc/20091207/scahill, reprinted in part by *The News*.

30. "Blackwater's Secret War in Pakistan?"

31. Id. See also Scott Horton, "Blackwater's Pakistan Capers," *Harper's Magazine*, November 24, 2009.

32. The author lives in New Orleans, which in 2005 was struck and nearly destroyed by Hurricane Katrina and the flooding that took place in its aftermath. Blackwater was hired by various residents to protect their property after they evacuated. The company drew strong praise from clients for its excellence in carrying out its tasks.

33. "Blackwater Involved in Bhutto and Hariri Hits: Former Pakistani Army Chief," *Tehran Times*, September 14, 2009.

34. "US Special Squad Killed Benazir," *The Nation*, May 18, 2009.

35. "Gilani Government Blamed for Davis' Secret Entry in Pakistan," *The News*, February 26, 2011.

36. "ISI Asks CIA to Unmask Covert Operatives in Pak," *The News*, February 26, 2011.

37. Bahukutumbi Raman, "Davis Deal: US to Limit Humint Ops in Pak Territory," South Asia Analysis Group, Paper no. 4383, March 17, 2001, http://www.southasiaanalysis.org/papers44/paper4383.html.

38. Id.

39. Id.

40. "President Zardari addresses Parliament's joint session," *Dawn*, March 22, 2011; and Pamela Constable, "Pakistan president, opponents mend fences over CIA contractor case," *Washington Post*, March 23, 2011.

41. Jane Perlez and Ismail Khan, "Pakistan Tells U.S. It Must Sharply Cut CIA Activities," *New York Times*, April 11, 2011; and Ariel Zirulnick, "Pakistan Demands Drawdown of US Drones, CIA Agents," *Christian Science Monitor*, April 12, 2011.

42. *Stratfor* reported that "the very same property was raided in 2003 by Pakistani intelligence with American cooperation." "Who Was Hiding Bin Laden in Abbottabad?," *Stratfor*, May 5, 2011.

43. Tom Ross and Conrad Quilty-Harper, "Wikileaks: Bin Laden's Courier Trained 9/11 Hijack Team,'" *Telegraph*, May 3, 2011.

44. Mark Mazzetti, Helene Cooper, and Peter Baker, "Behind the Hunt for Bin Laden," *New York Times*, May 2, 2011.
45. Bob Woodward, "Death of Osama bin Laden: Phone Call Pointed U.S. to Compound—and to 'the Pacer,'" *Washington Post*, May 6, 2011.
46. "CIA Monitored bin Laden Compound from Surveillance Post: Report," *The Express Tribune*, May 6, 2011.
47. Christopher Drew, "Attack on bin Laden Used a Stealthy Helicopter That Had Been a Secret," *New York Times*, May 5, 2011; and "Stealth Choppers Played a Key Role in bin Laden Raid, but Some Secrets May Have Been Exposed," Associated Press, May 6, 2011.
48. Declan Walsh and Sam Jones, "Osama bin Laden Raid Team was Prepared to Fight Pakistani Forces," *Guardian*, May 10, 2011.
49. David Martin, "Bin Laden Intel Revealing New Leads Every Hour," *CBS News*, May 10, 2011.
50. "Official: Woman Killed in bin Laden Raid not Wife," *MSNBC*, May 2, 2011. Apparently authorities took two wives and four bin Laden children into custody afterward.
51. Mark Landler and Mark Mazzetti, "Account Tells of One-Sided Battle in Bin Laden Raid," *New York Times*, May 4, 2011; and Paul Bedard, "The Gun That Killed Osama bin Laden Revealed," *U.S.News*, May 11, 2011.
52. Jack Tapper, Huma Khan, Martha Raddatz, and Lauren Effron, "Osama Bin Laden Operation Ended With Coded Message 'Geronimo-E KIA,'" *ABC News*, May 2, 2011.
53. "Osama Bin Laden Dead: Inside The Raid That Killed Him," *Huffington Post*, May 5, 2011.
54. Pervez Hoodbhoy, "The Curious Case of Osama Bin Laden," *Express Tribune*, May 3, 2011.
55. See, e.g., Karin Brulliard and Debbi Wilgoren, "Pakistan's Critics Ask How bin Laden's Refuge Went Unnoticed," *Washington Post*, May 2, 2011.
56. "US Had Concerns Pakistan Might Jeopardize bin Laden Operation," Reuters, May 3, 2011, http://tribune.com.pk/story/161013/us-had-concerns-about-pakistan-cia-chief/; and Mark Mazetti and Helene Cooper, "Detective Work on Courier Led to Breakthrough on Bin Laden," *New York Times*, May 2, 2011.
57. "Pakistan Assists US in Locating Bin Laden: Haqqani," *The Nation*, May 2, 2011.
58. Sikander Shaheen, "American Troops Kill Osama," *The Nation*, May 3, 2011, http://nation.com.pk/pakistan-news-newspaper-daily-english-online/Politics/03-May-2011/Americantroops-kill-Osama.
59. "Senior ISI Official Confirms bin Laden Killed," *Dawn*, May 2, 2011.
60. "Army Helicopter Crashes near Abbottabad," *Dawn*, May 1, 2011.
61. See http://chirpstory.com/li/1294. One tweet put the helicopter crash near the intersection of Kakul and Awami Roads, away from bin Laden's house. See also Bahukutumbi Raman, "Abbottabad Raid: A Reconstruction through Tweets," *International Terrorism Monitor Page No. 715*, South Asia Analysis Group, Paper no. 4471, May 5, 2011, http://www.southasiaanalysis.org/papers45/paper4471.html.
62. *Nightwatch* for the night of May 1, 2011. *Nightwatch* is a publication of KGS, http://www.kforcegov.com/AboutUs/Leadership/John_McCreary.aspx/

63. Anwar Iqbal, "US Lawmakers Threaten to Suspend Aid," *Dawn*, May 3, 2011.

64. "Pakistan Government Knew Where Osama Was: Carl Levin," *Express Tribune*, May 6, 2011.

65. "Some Clarity at Last," *The Nation*, May 14, 2011; Karin Brulliard, "Pakistan Defends Role, Questions 'Unilateral' U.S. Action," *Washington Post*, May 3, 2011; Karin Brulliard, "Pakistan Questions Legality of U.S. Operation That Killed Bin Laden," *Washington Post*, May 5, 2011; and Jane Perlez, "Pakistan Pushes Back Against U.S. Criticism on bin Laden," *New York Times*, May 3, 2011.

66. Zeeshan Haider, "Pakistan's Parliament Warns U.S. over bin Laden Raid," Reuters, May 14, 2011.

67. Jane Perlez, "Pakistani Is Seeking Inquiry on U.S. Raid," *New York Times*, May 11, 2011; Sajjad Tarakzai, "Pakistan Opposition Demands bin Laden Probe," http://www.asiaworks.com/news/2011/05/11/pakistan-opposition-demands-bin-laden-probe-afp/.

68. Devonia Smith, "Rumsfeld: 'No evidence' Pakistanis knew Osama bin Laden was under Their Noses," *Examiner*, May 20, 2011; and "No Sign Pakistan Knew bin Laden Whereabouts: U.S.," Reuters, May 18, 2011.

69. Karen deYoung and Karin Brulliard, "Obama Administration Is Divided over Future of U.S.-Pakistan Relationship," *Washington Post*, May 14, 2011.

70. "Osama bin Laden Hiding Place Visited by Taliban," *Telegraph*, May 14, 2011.

71. Bahukutumbi Raman, "Pakistan—Talk, Talk, Hit, Hit," South Asia Analysis Group, Paper no. 4491, May 15, 2011, http://www.southasiaanalysis.org/papers 45/paper4491.html.

72. Officially, the army receives about 22 percent of the budget. Some analysts estimate higher figures. See Issam Ahmed, "Pakistan's Military Faces Calls for Major Shakeup after bin Laden Failure," *Christian Science Monitor*, May 5, 2011. Other sources report that the army's percentage of the budget is now in the teens.

73. "Army, Agencies' Budget Be Presented in Assembly: Nawaz," *The News*, May 14, 2011.

74. "U.S. Operations in Pakistan Upset Domestic Balance of Power," *Stratfor*, May 18, 2011.

75. Zeeshan Haider, "Pakistan's Parliament Warns U.S. over bin Laden Raid," Reuters, May 14, 2011; and "Pakistan: ISI Paralyzed al Qaeda, Should Not Be Criticized—Agency Head," *Stratfor*, May 13, 2011.

76. "Osama bin Laden hiding place visited by Taliban," *Telegraph*.

77. "Pakistan, U.S.: Joint Intelligence Operations to Resume," *Statfor*/Reuters, June 3, 2011.

78. "Top Pakistani al Qaeda Leader Reportedly Killed," *Stratfor*, June 4, 2011. Kashmiri was the leader of Harkat ul-Jihad-al-Islami, the 313 Brigade, and Al Qaeda's elite unit Lashkar al-Zil. His death represented a significant success.

79. "Pentagon: U.S. Has Questioned bin Laden's Widows," Associated Press, May 13, 2011.

80. "Pakistan Returns Stealth Helicopter Debris to US," *CBS News*, May 24, 2011.

81. Greg Miller and Karen DeYoung, "CIA to Search bin Laden Compound," *Washington Post*, May 26, 2011.

82. "More Abbottabad-like Raids not to Be Tolerated: COAS," *The News*, May 10,

2011; and Jane Perlez, "Pakistani Army Chief Warns U.S. on Another Raid," *New York Times*, May 5, 2011.

83. Karin Brulliard, "Pakistani Military Quashes Taliban Attack on Karachi Naval Base," *Washington Post*, May 23, 2011.

84. Karin Brulliard, "Pakistan's Top Military Officials Are Worried about Militant Collaborators in Their Ranks," *Washington Post*, May 27, 2011.

85. Nawaz, in interview with author. See also Nawaz, *Crossed Swords*, 571.

86. "Abbottabad Operation: 'Heads Must Roll,' Says Chaudhry Nisar," *Express Tribune*, May 6, 2011.

87. S. Akbar Zaidi, "The National Insecurity State," *Dawn*, May 14, 2011.

88. Kamran Shafi, "Truth Will Out," *Dawn*, May 3, 2011.

89. Id.

90. Hoodbhoy, "The Curious Case of Osama Bin Laden."

91. "TV Show on Bin Laden Killing, Deal with US for Abbottabad Operation," *Karachi AAJ News Television in Urdu*, May 3, 2011.

92. "Analysts Argue That bin Laden Raid Puts Pakistan Air Defense Under Question," *Karachi Dawn News in Urdu*, May 3, 2011.

93. "TV Show Calls on Army to Declare Involvement in Abbottabad Operation," *Karachi Geo News TV*, May 2, 2011; and "Burial of Bin Laden's Body in Sea, Post-Killing Scenario," *Karachi Geo News TV*, May 2, 2011.

94. Elizabeth A. Harris, "Al Qaeda Confirms Bin Laden's Death," *New York Times*, May 6, 2011, citing SITE Intelligence Group.

95. Hoodbhoy, "The Curious Case of Osama Bin Laden."

96. See Mariana Baabar, "Govt Expresses 'Deep Concern' over Osama Operation," *The News*, May 4, 2011.

97. Matthew Rosenberg, "Karzai Told to Dump U.S.," *Wall Street Journal*, April 27, 2011.

98. "There Was No Need to Bypass Pakistan," *Dawn*, May 7, 2011.

99. Jeremy Page, "China to Fast-Track Jets for Pakistan," *Wall Street Journal*, May 20, 2011.

100. Farhan Bokhari and Kathrin Hille, "Pakistan Turns to China for Naval Base," *Financial Times*, May 22, 1011. China has provided economic aid as well, although it exports Chinese workers to perform the work and exploits the aid for every ounce of propaganda value possible.

101. "Iran, Pakistan Urge Stronger Ties," *Channel NewsAsia*, July 17, 2011.

102. The full text of President Barack Obama's speech, televised at 11:35 p.m. EDT on May 1, 2011, was made available online by the *New York Times* (May 2, 2011). See http://www.nytimes.com/2011/05/02/us/politics/02text .html?scp=4&sq=%22Obama%22%20%22speech%22%20%22bin%20 laden%22&st=cse.

103. Asif Ali Zardari, "Pakistan Did Its Part," *Washington Post*, May 2, 2011.

104. Id.

105. Farooq Hameed Khan, "Abbottabad Debacle and After!" *The Nation*, May 13, 2011.

106. Leon Panetta, interview with *Time* magazine, May 3, 2011.

107. See Mark Mazetti, Helene Cooper, and Peter Baker, "Behind the Hunt for Bin

Laden," *New York Times*, May 2, 2011; Mazzetti and Cooper, "Detective Work on Courier Led to Breakthrough on Bin Laden."

108. Mark Hosenball and Matt Spetainick, "U.S. Team's Mission Was to Kill bin Laden, not Capture," Reuters, May 2, 2011; and "Bin Laden Was Unarmed, Fueling Questions Whether US Ever Planned to Capture Him Alive," Associated Press, May 3, 2011.

109. Jeremy Pelofsky and Kamran Haider, "Obama Decides not to Release bin Laden Photos," Reuters, May 4, 2011.

110. Dr. Joel Faullkner Rogers, "Pakistan Poll: 66% Say US Forces didn't Kill bin Laden," *YouGov@Cambridge*, Cambridge University, http://www.yougov.polis .cam.ac.uk/pakistan-poll-66-say-us-forces-didnt-kill-bin-laden. The survey was "broadly representative of the online population in Pakistan," which meant its most educated group.

111. Chris Albritton, "Photos Show Three Dead Men at bin Laden Raid House," Reuters, May 4, 2011, http://www.reuters.com/subjects/bin-laden-compound.

112. "Taliban React to Report of bin Laden's Death with Suspicion, Demand Proof," Associated Press, May 3, 2011.

113. Michael D. Shear, "White House Corrects Bin Laden Narrative," *New York Times*, May 3, 2011; and "Contradictions, Misstatements from White House in Telling Story of bin Laden Raid," *Washington Post*, May 3, 2011.

114. Anne E. Kornbult and Felicia Sonmez, "White House Goes Silent on bin Laden Raid," *Washington Post*, May 4, 2011.

115. "Contradictions, Misstatements from White House in Telling Story of Bin Laden Raid," *Washington Post*, May 3, 2011.

116. Helene Cooper and Ismail Khan, "U.S. Seeks Details of ISI's S Directorate," *The Hindu*, May 8, 2011.

117. See "Ex-ISI Chief Hamid Gul Asks Mullah Omar to Leave Pakistan: Official," *Afghanistan Matters*, May 17, 2011, http://www.pajhwok.com/en/2011/05/17/ ex-isi-chief-asks-omar-leave-pakistan-official.

118. Omar Waraich, "Pakistan PM Gilani: Osama bin Laden Hid in Yemen Too," *Time/Yahoo News*, May 12, 2011.

119. "PM Yousaf Raza Gilani Says Osama Bin Laden Raid Violated Pakistan Sovereignty," speech, http://www.youtube.com/watch?v=7WDlnbZaots.

CHAPTER 23. LOOKING AHEAD

1. "Pakistan Province Cancels US Aid Deals: Official," Agence France-Presse, May 20, 2011.

2. Anand Gopal, Mansur Khan Mahsud, and Brian Fishman, "The Haqqanis and Al-Qaeda," *The AfPak Channel*, June 30, 2010, http://afpak.foreignpolicy.com/ posts/2010/06/30/the_haqqanis_and_al_qaeda.

3. Kathy Gannon, "The Ghazi Force: Vengeful New Militant Group Emerges in Pakistan," *Huffington Post*, July 1, 2010.

4. See, e.g., B. Raman, "Action against Haqqani & Ilyas Networks: CIA Chief's Agenda," *International Terrorism Monitor*, Paper no. 681, South Asia Analysis Group, October 1, 2010, http://www.southasiaanalysis.org/papers41/paper4073.html. U.S. frustration with Pakistani inaction has spurred the U.S. forces to take matters

into their own hands with cross-border raids under the doctrine of hot pursuit as well as stepped-up drone strikes in North Waziristan.

5. See Brian Fishman, "The Battle for Pakistan: Militancy and Conflict across the FATA and NWFP," New America Foundation's Counterterrorism Strategy Initiative, April 2010, http://counterterrorism.newamerica.net/publications/policy /the_battle_for_pakistan_fata_and_nwfp. Fishman's incisive analysis of this complex milieu supports the conclusions embraced by Pakistani military leaders. Pakistanis might disagree, but Fishman argues strongly that distinguishing between a "Pakistani" and an "Afghan" Taliban is a canard. But he concurs that these groups differ, hold distinct agendas, and need to be assessed individually in terms of social geography, religious and political outlook, and strategy.

6. Id.

7. Salman Masood and Carlotta Gall, "Killing of Governor Deepens Crisis in Pakistan," *New York Times*, January 4, 2011.

8. The statement "Bilawal Bhutto Zardari Condemns Salmaan Taseer's Assassination" (TV786.net) can be seen at http://www.youtube.com/watch?v=iYflGu1nmW0.

9. Maajid Nawaz, in interview with author.

10. See "Militant Charities versus US Aid," *Express Tribune*, August 12, 2010; and B. Raman, "US Marines in Swat for Flood Relief: Misgivings in Pakistan," South Asia Analysis Group, Paper no. 3980, August 15, 2010, http://www.southasia analysis.org/papers40/paper3980.html. In Egypt, the Muslim Brotherhood had powerfully strengthened its credibility among ordinary citizens by providing relief to earthquake victims. Its efforts stood in stark contrast to the government's ineptitude.

11. Amil Khan, "Beyond a Military Solution for Pakistan," *The AfPak Channel*, August 6, 2010, http://afpak.foreignpolicy.com/posts/2010/08/06/beyond_a_ military_solution_for_pakistan.

12. "Program Summary: Pakistan's Radio Swat FM 96," August 10, 2010 (OSC).

13. Raman, "US Marines in Swat for Flood Relief"; and Dr. Hasan-Askari Rizvi, "Is There a Way Out?," *Daily Times*, August 15, 2010.

14. Omar Waraich, "Will Pakistan's Floods Take Down the Economy and the President?," *Time/Press Pakistan*, August 17, 2010, http://groups.google.com/group/ PressPakistan/browse_thread/thread/1790f5fe4b00c954/2f4538d1a07b5fab?sh ow_docid=2f4538d1a07b5fab.

15. Praveen Swami, "Pakistan Army: The Struggle Within," *The Hindu*, March 6, 2010.

Selected Reading

The politics is fascinating. These books were either cited or provide relevant insights into Pakistani politics. Also important is understanding what's going on in Afghanistan and its relations with India, so some of these references deal with or touch on those nations.

Abbas, Hassan. *Pakistan's Drift into Extremism: Allah, the Army, and America's War on Terror*. London: M. E. Sharpe, 2005.

Ahmed, Akbar S. *Jinnah, Pakistan and Islamic Identity: The Search for Saladin*. New York: Routledge, 2007.

Ali, Tariq. *The Duel: Pakistan on the Flight Path of American Power*. New York: Scribner, 2008.

Benjamin, Daniel, and Steven Simon. *The Age of Sacred Terror*. New York: Random House, 2002.

Bhutto, Benazir. *Daughter of Destiny: An Autobiography*. New York: Simon & Schuster, 1989.

———. *Daughter of the East: An Autobiography*. New York: Simon & Schuster, 2008.

———. *Reconciliation: Islam, Democracy, and the West*. New York: Harper, 2008.

Burrows, William E., and Robert Windrem. *Critical Mass: The Dangerous Race for Superweapons in a Fragmenting World*. New York: Simon & Schuster, 1994.

Cohen, Stephen Philip. *The Idea of Pakistan*. Washington, DC: Brookings Institution Press, 2004.

Coll, Steve. *Ghost Wars: The Secret History of the CIA, Afghanistan, and Bin Laden from the Soviet Invasion to September 10, 2001*. New York: Penguin Press, 2004.

Collins, Catherine, and Douglas Frantz. *Fallout: The True Story of the CIA's Secret War on Nuclear Trafficking*. New York: Free Press, 2011.

Corera, Gordon. *Shopping for Bombs: Nuclear Proliferation, Global Insecurity, and the Rise and Fall of the A. Q. Khan Network*. Oxford: Oxford University Press, 2006.

Crew, Robert D., and Amin Tarzi, eds. *The Taliban and the Crisis of Afghanistan.* Cambridge: Harvard University Press, 2008.

Dorronsoro, Gilles: *Pakistan and the Taliban: State Policy, Religious Networks and Political Connection,* Paris: CERI. http://www.ceri-sciencespo.com/archive/octo00/artgd.pdf.

———. "Think Again: The Afghan Surge." *Foreign Policy,* October 7, 2010. http://www.foreignpolicy.com/articles/2010/10/07/think_again_the_afghan_surge.

Frantz, Douglas, and Catherine Collins. *The Nuclear Jihadist: The True Story of the Man Who Sold the World's Most Dangerous Secrets—and How We Could Have Stopped Him.* New York: Twelve, 2007.

Giustozzi, Antonio. *Koran, Kalashnikov, and Laptop: The Neo-Taliban Insurgency in Afghanistan,* New York: Columbia University Press, 2008.

———. *War, Politics, and Society in Afghanistan, 1978–1992.* Washington, DC: Georgetown University Press, 1999.

Gul, Imtiaz. *The Most Dangerous Place: Pakistan's Lawless Frontier.* New York: Viking Press, 2010.

Haqqani, Husain. *Pakistan: Between Mosque and Military.* Washington, DC: Carnegie Endowment for International Peace, 2005.

Hughes, Libby. *Benazir Bhutto: From Prison to Prime Minister.* Lincoln, NE: iUniverse, 1990.

Hussain, Zahid. *Frontline Pakistan: The Struggle with Militant Islam.* New York: Columbia University Press, 2007.

International Institute for Strategic Studies. "Nuclear Black Markets: Pakistan, A. Q. Khan, and the Rise of Proliferation Networks: A Net Assessment." June 2008. http://www.iiss.org/publications/strategic-dossiers/nbm/.

Jaffrelot, Christophe, ed. *Pakistan: Nationalism without a Nation?* New York: Zed Books, 2002.

Jalal, Ayesha. *The Sole Spokesman: Jinnah, the Muslim League, and the Demand for Pakistan.* Cambridge: Cambridge University Press, 1985.

Jones, Owen Bennett. *Pakistan: Eye of the Storm.* New Haven, CT: Yale University Press, 2002. 3rd ed., 2009.

Kavalski, Emilian. *India and Central Asia: The Mythmaking and International Relations of a Rising Power.* London: I. B. Taurus, 2010.

Lamb, Christina. *The Sewing Circles of Herat: A Personal Voyage through Afghanistan.* London: HarperCollins, 2002.

Langewiesche, William. "The Point of No Return." *Atlantic Monthly,* January/February 2006.

———. "The Wrath of Khan." *Atlantic Monthly,* November 2005.

Laufer, Michael. "A. Q. Khan Nuclear Chronology." *Carnegie Endowment for International Peace Proliferation Brief* 8, no. 8. http://carnegieendowment.org/publications/index.cfm?fa=view&id=17420.

Levy, Adrian, and Catherine Scott-Clark. *Deception: Pakistan, the United States and the Global Nuclear Weapons Conspiracy.* London: Atlantic Books, 2007.

Luce, Edward. *In Spite of the Gods: The Strange Rise of Modern India*. New York: Doubleday, 2007.

Mir, Amir. *The Bhutto Murder Trail: From Waziristan to GHQ*. New Delhi, India: Tranquebar Press, 2011.

———. *The True Face of Jehadis: Inside Pakistan's Network of Terror*. New Delhi: Roli Books, 2006.

Mullick, Fatima, and Mehrunnisa Yusuf. *Pakistan: Identity, Ideology and Beyond*. London: Quilliam Foundation, August 2009. http://www.quilliamfoundation.org/acatalog/Books.html.

Musharraf, Pervez. *In the Line of Fire: A Memoir*. New York: Free Press, 2006.

Nawaz, Shuja. *Crossed Swords: Pakistan, Its Army, and the Wars Within*. Karachi: Oxford University Press, 2008.

Peters, Gretchen. *Seeds of Terror: How Heroin is Bankrolling the Taliban and al Qaeda*. New York: St. Martin's Press, 2009.

Rana, Muhammad Amir, ed. *A to Z of Jehadi Organizations in Pakistan*. Translated by Saba Ansari. Lahore, Pakistan: Mashal Books, 2004.

Rashid, Ahmed. *Descent into Chaos: The U.S. and the Failure of Nation Building in Pakistan, Afghanistan, and Central Asia*. New York: Viking, 2008.

———. *Taliban: Islam, Oil and the New Great Game in Central Asia*. New York: I. B. Tauris, 2000.

Reed, Thomas C., and Danny B. Stillman. *The Nuclear Express: A Political History of the Bomb and its Proliferation*. Minneapolis: Zenith Press, 2009.

Rehman, Shahid-ur. *Pakistan: Sovereignty Lost*. Islamabad: Mr. Books, 2006.

Riedel, Bruce. *Deadly Embrace: Pakistan, America, and the Future of Global Jihad*. Washington, DC: Brookings Institution Press, 2011.

———. *The Search for al Qaeda: Its Leadership, Ideology, and Future*. Washington, DC: Brookings Institution Press, 2008.

Sattar, Abdul. *Pakistan's Foreign Policy, 1947–2005: A Concise History*. New York: Oxford University Press, 2007.

Schmidle, Nicholas. *To Live or to Perish Forever: Two Tumultuous Years in Pakistan*. New York: Henry Holt, 2009.

Tenet, George. *At the Center of the Storm: My Years at the CIA*. With Bill Harlow. New York: HarperCollins, 2007.

Tirmazi, Brig. Syed A. I. *Profiles of Intelligence*. Lahore, Pakistan: Combined Printers, 1995.

Venter, Al J. *Allah's Bomb: The Islamic Quest for Nuclear Weapons*. Guilford, CT: Lyons Press, 2007.

Weaver, Mary Anne. "Bhutto's Fateful Moment." *New Yorker*, October 4, 1993.

———. *Pakistan: In the Shadow of Jihad and Afghanistan*. New York: Farrar, Straus and Giroux, 2002.

Weissman, Steve, and Herbert Krosney. *The Islamic Bomb: The Nuclear Threat to Israel and the Middle East*. New York: Times Books, 1981.

Woodward, Bob. *Obama's Wars*. New York: Simon & Schuster, 2010.

Yousaf, Mohammad, and Mark Adkin. *Afghanistan: The Bear Trap—The Defeat of a Superpower.* Havertown, PA: Casemate, 2001.

Zahab, Mariam Abu, and Olivier Roy. *Islamist Network: The Afghan-Pakistan Connection.* London: Hurst, 2004.

Zaheer, Hasan. *The Separation of East Pakistan: The Rise and Realization of Bengali Muslim Nationalism.* New York: Oxford University Press, 1994.

Zaidi, Syed Manzar Abbas. *The New Taliban: Emergence and Ideological Sanctions.* New York: Nova Science Publishers, 2009.

Index

Beg, Mirza Aslam, 104, 162–63
  assassination of Benazir and, 171–
    72, 190, 219, 220, 244
  Benazir as prime minister and, 80–81
  elections after Zia's death and, 73–77
Bhatti, Shahbaz, 242, 246
Bhutto, Benazir, xv, xvi, 37, 60, 64, 67,
  91, 105
  allegations of corruption and investi-
    gation of, 87–90, 93, 119, 167, 200
  background and education of, 51–53
  character of, 49–50, 53, 71
  Ejaz Shah and, 214–15
  elections and, 74–78, 83–84, 154, 199
  Gul and, 219–20
  impact of, 206–11
  imprisoned by Zia ul-Haq, 69–71
  marriage of, 71–72
  Musharraf and, 37, 41–43, 46–47,
    105–8, 117–21, 133–34, 136
  on Musharraf and Taliban, 100
  Pakistan's nuclear program and, 13
  as prime minister, 13, 78–83, 85–87,
    90–92, 172, 207–8
  strategic communication of, 47,
    85–86, 167–68, 207
Bhutto, Benazir, assassination of, 37,
  47–48, 138–41, 202–3
  changing information about cause of
    death, 159–60, 168–70
  investigation of, 50–51, 171–73,
    175–82, 192
  key players' fates, 194–205
  lack of autopsy, 171, 200
  security concerns and, 135–38,
    189–90, 193–94, 244–45
  strategic communication about,
    136–37, 143–46, 149–92, 225–26
  Taj's warning of and motives, 39,
    43–46, 135, 137
  unsuccessful attempts, 81, 123–30, 133
Bhutto, Mir Murtaza, 67, 68, 69, 88,
  90, 91, 172
Bhutto, Nusrat, 67, 68, 75, 89, 206
Bhutto, Shah Nawaz, 68

Bhutto, Zulfiqar Ali, 49–50, 227
  framing, arrest, and execution of, 40,
    65–67
  Pakistan's nuclear program and,
    4–5, 11
  political career of, 54–59
  as prime minister, 59–65, 68–69
  strategic communication of, 58–59
Bibi, Asia, 260–61
Biden, Joe, 107
Billa, Imtiaz Ahmed, 75, 219
bin Laden, Osama, 27, 81, 94, 109,
  164, 187, 191, 199, 212, 215
  strategic communication about death
    of, 246–58
  U.S.-Pakistani relations and killing
    of, 246–58
bin Nayef, Prince Mohammed, 188
Blackwater Security, 116, 126, 155,
  242–43
blasphemy law, 143, 260–62
Boucher, Richard, 105
Burns, John, 71, 86, 89
Burrows, William, 7
Bush, George H. W., 52, 82–83
Bush, George W.
  Musharraf and, 96, 99–107, 143, 174
  Pakistan's nuclear program and, 10,
    13, 14, 23, 29, 30–31
Butler, Rab, 63, 209
Buttar, Amna, 216–17
Butt, Ziauddin, 94–95

Carter, Jimmy, 66
Cary, Dr. Nathaniel, 173
Central Intelligence Agency (CIA), U.S.,
  24, 35
  bin Laden's death and, 247–48, 251
  Davis incident and, 240–45
Chaudhry, Iftikhar Muhammad, 96–97,
  109, 158, 174, 201, 264
Chaulia, Sreeram, 213
Cheema, Javed Iqbal, 116, 124, 150,
  152, 159, 160, 173, 178, 180, 225
Cheney, Dick, 81, 99, 106–7, 244

About the Author

James P. Farwell is an attorney and a political consultant who has advised the U.S. Department of Defense—the U.S. Special Operations Command, Office of Under Secretary of Defense for Policy, the Office of Under Secretary of Defense for Intelligence, the Office of the Assistant Secretary of Defense for Special Operations and Low Intensity Conflict, and the U.S. Strategic Command—on information strategy, information operations, strategic communication, and cyberwar strategy. In particular, he has advised the Department of Defense and the U.S. Strategic Command on Pakistan. Farwell has written articles for the International Institute for Strategic Studies, the Middle East Institute, Defence IQ, and the *IO Journal.* His second book, *The Sword of Truth: Communication & Influence*, is to be published in 2012. He lives in New Orleans.